THE EMOTIONAL REVOLUTION

THE
EMOTIONAL REVOLUTION

*How the New Science of Feelings
Can Transform Your Life*

NORMAN E. ROSENTHAL, M.D.

CITADEL PRESS
Kensington Publishing Corp.
www.kensingtonbooks.com

CITADEL PRESS BOOKS are published by

Kensington Publishing Corp.
850 Third Avenue
New York, NY 10022

For Thomas Wehr

Contents

PART THREE: CHANGE

Acknowledgments

THIS BOOK WOULD NOT have been possible without the help of many people. First, thanks to the patients whose stories appear throughout the book, anonymously, as I have removed all identifying information for the sake of confidentiality. You have taught me much of what I know about the emotions.

I wish to thank my agent, Jenny Bent, and Paul Dinas, the editor-in-chief at Kensington Books, for believing in the project. Thanks also to my editors at Kensington, Tracy Bernstein and Elaine Will Sparber, and to Elise Hancock for following her Tao, and for her invaluable creative input.

Parts or all of this manuscript were read by many people who made helpful suggestions: Jenny Bent, Larry Blossom, Halcy Bohen, Jean Carper, Michelle Etlin, Richard A. Friedman, Jay Giedd, Kay Redfield Jamison, Brian Knudson, Michael Liebowitz, Wilfred Lieberthal, Leora Rosen, Esta Rosenthal, Jerilyn Ross, Richard Ross, Peter Sacks, Cadi Simon, Chip Tafrate, Jeremy Waletzky, Helen Wall, and Tom Wehr. Thank you all.

Many experts were kind enough to grant me interviews or engage in extensive e-mail exchanges. I hope I have done justice to your excellent work. Thanks to all of you who answered my many questions (and follow-ups): John Barefoot, Duke University; David Barlow, Boston University; John Cacioppa, University of Chicago; Jerry Cott; Richard Davidson, University of Wisconsin; Michael Davis, Emory University; Ed Diener, University of Illinois in Champaign; Jerry Deffenbacher, Colorado State University; Eva Feindler, Long Island University; Helen Fisher, Rutgers University; Edna Foa, University of Pennsylvania; Nathan Fox, University of Maryland; Viktor Frankl; Richard C. Friedman, Cornell University; Jay Giedd, National Institute of Mental Health; Ron Glaser and Janice Kiecolt-Glaser,

Ohio State University; Robert Glick, Columbia University; Dean Hamer, National Cancer Institute; Janet Halperin, University of Maryland; Joseph Hibbeln, National Institute of Alcoholism and Alcohol Abuse; Siegfried Kasper, University of Vienna; Donald Klein, Columbia University; Bessel van der Kolk, Boston University; Gary Lavergne; Joseph LeDoux, New York University; Mark Lawrence; Michael Liebowitz, Columbia University; Ellen Leibenluft, National Institute of Mental Health; Ian Livingstone; David Myers, Hope College; Ken Paller, Northwestern University; Lisa Parr, Emory University; James Pennebaker, University of Texas; Steve Porges, University of Maryland; Jerilyn Ross, Ross Center, Washington, D.C.; Richard Ross, University of Pennsylvania; Peter Salovey, Yale University; Francine Shapiro, Mental Health Research Institute, Palo Alto; Peter Schmidt, National Institute of Mental Health; David Spiegel, Stanford University; Stephen Suomi, National Institutes of Child Health and Human Development; Sue Swedo, National Institute of Mental Health; Chip Tafrate, University of Connecticut; Martin Teicher, Harvard University; Dorothy Tennov; Robert Thayer, University of California, Long Beach; Stephen Vasquez; Frans de Waal, Emory University; David Watson, University of Iowa; Thomas Wehr, National Institute of Mental Health; Paul Whalen, University of Wisconsin; Rachel Yehuda, Mount Sinai Medical Center; Isaiah Zimmerman.

Special thanks are due to Larry Blossom for his help with the artwork and computers; to Tom Insel for his thoughtful comments, for his tour of the Yerkes Primate Center, and, particularly, for his friendship over the years; and to Debbie Insel for her friendship, hospitality, and candor. Also to Jay Giedd and Brian Knudson of the NIH, for subjecting me to rewards and punishments while my head was in a functional magnetic resonance machine.

Thanks to Michelle Etlin, Catherine Tuggle, and Josh Rosenthal for their research assistance.

Finally, I owe a huge debt of gratitude to my wife, Leora Rosen, for her love and encouragement throughout; and to my wonderful friends for their emotional support through the ups and downs of *The Emotional Revolution*.

Preface

It was a Saturday night in Johannesburg, April Fools' Day to be precise. I was a medical intern in my mid-twenties, and my date and I had gone out to a Chinese restaurant with friends. I ordered sweet and sour shrimp—the juicy giant prawns imported from Mozambique that were greatly prized in South Africa. After dinner as we drove toward her home, we decided to park for a while in a shaded lane in her neighborhood. The night was warm and dry, and the car was filled with the fragrance of my girlfriend's perfume—Impulse, it was called. We chatted about other times when we had parked in cars with lovers late at night. I still remember our conversation as though it happened yesterday.

In those days, Johannesburg was not the violent city that it has since become. A hand tapping on the window of a parked car was more likely to belong to a patrolling policeman than anyone else. Perhaps that was why I was in no way concerned when a man peered into my girlfriend's window and said "yes." I should have been. His word must have signaled to a second man that we were a good target.

The details of what happened next are rather blurred in my mind. A rock hurtled toward the windshield, shattering it; the window on the driver's side was smashed open; and a sharp object was thrust into my side repeatedly, by the second man, who was obscured by the surrounding darkness. The smell of dust and pine trees combined with the sensation of powdered glass in my nostrils.

What I do remember, quite distinctly, is my terror and a galvanizing sense of purpose, which drove me to grab the hand of my assailant and grind it against the broken shards of my window while leaning hard on the horn. My girlfriend started to scream as well, and the din aroused the neighborhood. I could hear doors and windows slamming open. Porch lights flicked on and the men vanished into the woods.

I threw the car into reverse, spun it around, gunned the engine, and drove the half mile to my girlfriend's home. As she helped me up the stairs, the same question occurred to each of us: "Are you hurt?" She said she was fine; I was less sure. The warm liquid running down my side felt suspiciously like blood, yet I felt no pain, just a vague faintness and wobbliness on my feet. This was accompanied by a strong resolve to get where I needed to go, which let up only when we reached her living room, where my legs gave way and I collapsed on the carpet in a pool of blood.

That is the only time I ever experienced terror. I discovered that night that it is different from fear. Terror is a sense of every resource in your body being mobilized, everything you know at every level of your mind being brought into laser focus. It is a sense of now or never, life or death. Certainly I didn't stop to think about what to do. I acted reflexively.

Some called me a hero. But I take no credit for fending off the assailant or for having presence of mind. As a physician, I know that what happened arose from a magnificently complex set of reflexes that we all possess as a result of millions of years of evolution; it has been called the fight-or-flight response. When confronted by a serious threat, we have two choices—to fight or to flee. Actually, there is a third choice—to freeze in place and do nothing. I was trapped in my car. I could not flee. I was being stabbed. I was not about to freeze. So I did the only thing I could. I fought back.

I am grateful for the terror that saved my life that day, for those millions of years of evolution that engineered the choreography of responses necessary to survive the ordeal. For it was terror that brought to bear the part of my nervous system specifically designed to deal with emergencies, driving blood into the muscles of my forearm to counter my assailant's attack. It was terror that caused the lifesaving cascade of chemicals to course through my bloodstream—adrenaline, a galvanizing hormone; endorphins, potent painkillers; and steroids, hormones to help me recover. Those powerful substances, products of my own body, kept my brain alert and my blood pressure steady despite the bleeding, which continued on the way to the hospital and into the operating room.

There the surgeon found six stab wounds, which had punctured several of my internal organs. These he stitched up and five weeks later I was back in the ward, continuing my internship. We heal fast when we are young.

The police found the men responsible for the attack, literally red-handed, as well as the eighteen-inch sharpened screwdriver they had used as the weapon.

All of this occurred half a lifetime ago. But though the physical wounds healed quickly, the emotional impact stayed with me. For months afterward, the fragrance of Impulse would send shivers through me, and I have never regained my taste for sweet and sour shrimp. To this day, if I park in a darkened place, the hairs on the back of my neck begin to bristle and I look around to make sure I can escape if I have to.

I have thought many times how curious it was that in the immediate aftermath of the stabbing, I should feel no pain and a numbing of my emotions. Yet, the emotional power of the experience etched every detail of the event into my memory and left me with visceral reactions to the small environmental triggers that remind me of that night almost three decades ago. I came to realize I owed my life to my emotional responses that night, and that recognition fortified my desire to study emotions in one form or another.

Since that day, I have spent a large part of my personal and professional life thinking about feelings, my own and those of others. As a practicing psychiatrist, I have learned the value of getting in touch with the emotions in yourself and in others and the damage caused by emotions that run out of control. As a researcher, I have explored the subtle ways in which our environment can influence the way we feel, often without our being aware of it. As an avid reader of professional literature, I have observed with great excitement the breakthroughs in neuroscience in general and in the science of emotion in particular.

In recent years, we have learned a great deal about how to help people feel better by using medications to modify their brain chemistry. Now research is revealing many other ways to alter brain functioning, thereby alleviating emotional suffering and promoting well-being. New research points out that specific emotional benefits can be obtained from exercise, friendship, relaxation, acupuncture, religious faith, and nutritional supplements. These are just a few of the many strategies for enhancing well-being that I will discuss in this book.

Because all brain processes utilize similar neurons, circuits, and chemicals, discoveries about one brain function, such as language development or movement, may directly apply to the way we process emotions. Now more than ever there is reason for those who suffer emotionally to hope for relief from their pain and access to positive emotions, such as love and happiness.

Each week brings us news of some novel scientific finding about the way we experience our feelings—a newly discovered gene, a brain image of some experienced passion, or a new herb or technique for overcoming some painful emotion. Though each snippet of new information about the emotions is intriguing in itself, like a piece of a jigsaw puzzle or a square of colored glass, these discoveries are most revealing when seen in context. In this book I will put these new findings in their place in the great mosaic that is emerging.

Taken together, these developments represent more than simple steps in the accumulation of knowledge. Rather, they constitute an ongoing revolution in how the emotions can and should be viewed. It is the exhilarating goal of this book to share this new vision and to show how we can already use the discoveries of the Emotional Revolution to lead richer, happier, and more meaningful lives.

PART ONE

REVOLUTION

Chapter 1

Welcome to the Emotional Revolution

Most scientists believe that the brain will be to the twenty-first century what the genome was to the twentieth century.
—Eric Kandel, winner of the Nobel Prize for Medicine, 2000[1]

W HEN Joseph LeDoux, a prominent emotions researcher, first applied to the National Institutes of Health (NIH) a few decades ago for a grant to study fear in rats, his application was rejected outright. In those days cognition was king. The burning question for neuroscientists was "How do we think?" not "How do we feel?" The research climate has changed dramatically since then. A recent computer search revealed more than 5,000 citations involving emotion published during the preceding five-year period.[2]

But a scientific revolution requires more than merely large numbers of scientists at work in an area. Instead, according to Thomas Kuhn, author of *The Structure of Scientific Revolutions*, it requires a shift in paradigm.[3]

In the first part of this book, "Revolution," I devote a chapter to each of the radically new ways that scientists are thinking about emotions, which collectively compose the Emotional Revolution:

1. *Emotions are critical survival mechanisms that have evolved over millennia.*
   No longer content to regard feelings as soft and mushy con-

cepts, scientists are beginning to view emotions in evolutionary terms, as Darwin did. Those animals with properly functioning emotions are more likely to survive and succeed in passing on their genes. Fear protects us from danger. A rat will not play in the vicinity of cat hairs, but is unaffected by hairs from a dog, which is not one of it's natural predators. Anger helps protect our turf. A dog that barks at a stranger who ventures into his yard will be indifferent to the stranger's interest in a yard three houses farther down the road. Love helps us bond and procreate. A male prairie vole, a type of small ground-dwelling rodent found in the United States, spends a great deal of his time alongside his mate and makes aggressive moves toward other males who venture too close to her. Sadness is a natural response to loss, helping us conserve our resources as we adjust to new realities. And happiness signals that we are in an environment where it is safe to play and explore opportunities. Emotions provide us with a special kind of intelligence and are important for proper decision making. This point of view contrasts sharply with traditional Western philosophy, which generally favors reason above emotion.

2. *Emotions are processed in the brain by specialized circuits that are geared to anticipate, evaluate, and respond to reward and punishment—but the rest of the body is very much involved too.*
When we impulsively hug someone, jump for joy, or stiffen in offense, we are experiencing emotions in our bodies, with which our brains are in intimate and continual connection. In the early part of the twentieth century, emotions were thought by many to be experienced in the body only, whereas later in the century they were thought to take place mostly in the brain. Today's new and far more detailed understanding of the balance and interplay between body and brain in the experience of emotions represents a major scientific shift. In their exploration of the basis of emotions, scientists are looking at everything from the genes and single nerve cells to the whole organism.

3. *The relationship between emotions and memory is now understood in considerable detail.*
Separate types of memory, mediated by different parts of the

brain, have been discovered. One memory system seems to record facts and events, while another records emotional experiences. Given this separation, it is no wonder that emotional reactions to situations may arise without being clearly linked to any conscious memories. For example, a person may feel queasy and scared at the smell of a surgical disinfectant without remembering that it was the disinfectant used to treat a wound he sustained as a child many years before. We now have a scientific basis for understanding unconscious emotions.

4. *While intelligence has traditionally been considered a purely intellectual function, the concept of emotional intelligence is gaining ground.* In both personal and professional life, we now know, success depends to some extent on understanding your own emotions and those of others, coupled with the ability to communicate, modulate, and channel these emotions.

5. *Emotions profoundly affect physical health, even making the difference between life and death.*
The so-called psychosomatic effect has mainly been regarded as a problem. Only recently have scientists really attempted to understand this powerful influence and understand what feelings can and cannot do to make us healthier or less healthy, to promote recovery or induce death.

Taken together, these new approaches constitute nothing less than a radical revision, not only of the role emotions are believed to play in our lives, but of the role it is believed they *ought* to play.

Many of these new insights would not have been possible without the discoveries of neuroscientists such as those awarded the Nobel Prize in Medicine in 2000.[4] One of the winners, Arvid Carlsson, discovered years ago that the substance dopamine is a chemical messenger that helps to pass nerve signals from one neuron to another. Dopamine helps regulate many brain functions, including the experience of pleasure. A second winner, Paul Greengard, helped figure out how nerve signals are passed along at synapses. A third, Eric Kandel, helped work out how nerve cells learn and record memories. (For a more detailed discussion of how the brain works, see chapter 3.)

Groundbreaking research has also been done by many other scientists whose work I discuss in this book. New discoveries and advances can be expected to proliferate at a dizzying pace, given the marvels of modern technology. Thanks to machinery of ever-increasing power and sophistication, it is now possible to see the regions of the brain that light up when people feel happy or sad, loving or hateful. The human genome, the basic human set of chromosomes, can now be unspooled to reveal which coding variations make people vulnerable to the painful experiences of anxiety and depression. Just as the Renaissance sea voyages of discovery would have been impossible without the sextant, the mariner's compass, and the clock, so the Emotional Revolution depends on magnetic resonance imaging (MRI), gene technology, and other technological discoveries. But it is the fundamental shift in perception among scientists, the view that emotions are vitally important and worth studying, that is driving the revolution as much as any technological breakthrough.

Another insight that has been key is the general recognition that animals other than humans also experience emotions. There are millions of pet lovers in the United States who can readily tell when their cat or dog is happy or sad. When a dog wants to play with his master, he may lean forward, tail wagging, ears pricked up, eyes shining with hopeful anticipation. When feeling affectionate, he may roll on his back, asking to be scratched. When angry, he may spread his ears, bare his teeth, and crouch, ready to attack.[5]

Evidence of emotions can be found in every mammal studied. After her calf died, one mother elephant stood beside its lifeless body for days before moving on. Over a year later, when she passed the same spot, photographers filmed her fondling the bones of her deceased calf with her trunk. For a long period she probed the contours and crevices of the skull, like a human mother might gaze at photographs, trying to recapture every memory of her lost baby. A continent away, off the coast of Argentina, two right whales were observed mating and, afterward, lingering and caressing each other with their flippers before they swam off.

While elephants and whales do not lend themselves to being studied in the laboratory, other animals do. Scientists have learned a good deal by studying fear in rats, rage in cats, monogamy in voles, and separation anxiety in monkeys. It is never possible to know exactly what an animal is feeling, since animals cannot talk, yet scientists increasingly accept that the emotional states of animals bear an important resemblance to those of humans. Scientists are careful, however, to distinguish between *emotions*, states that can be observed by outsiders, and *feelings*, internal states known only to the individual experiencing them. Emotions can therefore be studied in animals, whereas feelings can be studied only in humans. Of course, in most cases these two concepts overlap. A happy person will generally look happy. In this book I use the terms "feeling" and "emotion" interchangeably.

Although the emotions have evolved to protect us and advance our interests, like all brain functions they do not always work as they should. Animals (humans included) whose emotions do not work properly are at a distinct disadvantage, for the world harbors threat and menace side by side with opportunity and challenge. The inability to fear can result in death; the inability to love, in failure to pass on your genes.

Problems of a different type occur when emotions are experienced to excess, resulting in some of the worst suffering imaginable. Acute anxiety can leave a person unable to sleep or act, and depression can be so unendurable that it may lead to suicide. Unfortunately, millions of Americans suffer from such emotional difficulties. For them in particular, it is good news that the emotions have entered the research spotlight.

In the second part of this book, "Feelings," I discuss the five sets of emotions that have been studied most extensively. The first pair of emotions, fear and anxiety, as well as the second pair, anger and rage, typically arise in response to threats. The next two sets relate to the bonds between people. Love and lust arise when bonds occur, whereas sadness and depression accompany their dissolution. I close this section with an emotion that is universally desired—happiness. In each of these chapters I discuss the emotion as it has evolved to promote survival—the healthy form. I also describe the problems that result when the emotion goes awry.

One prevailing myth about emotions is that there is nothing we can do about them. While we may take some responsibility for our thoughts and ideas, we tend to consider emotions as states of mind that arise willy-nilly. According to this view, we are like tiny boats on a vast and rocky sea of emotions, buffeted helplessly about. Fortunately this is far from the truth. The more we learn about emotions, the more we see how much we can do to treat troublesome emotions and develop healthy ones.

Throughout this book I will point out how you can already use the discoveries from the new science of feelings to improve your life. In each chapter on specific emotions, I discuss ways to lessen painful feelings and enhance pleasurable ones. Given the pain of depression and the many ways in which it can be alleviated, I devote an entire chapter to strategies for treating it.

In the last section, "Change," I discuss general principles for changing the way we feel, and outline scientifically and clinically validated strategies for leading a more fulfilling life.

Without further ado, welcome to *The Emotional Revolution*.

Chapter 2

The Intelligence of Emotions

The heart has a reason that reason cannot know.
—Blaise Pascal, *Pensées*[1]

When we feel deeply, we reason profoundly.
—Mary Wollstonecraft[2]

ALTHOUGH they came from different cultures and different eras, French mathematician Blaise Pascal and pioneering British feminist Mary Wollstonecraft both recognized that feelings are intelligent. For Wollstonecraft, deep feeling constituted a profound type of reasoning. For Pascal, feelings were reasons of the heart that could not be fathomed by the force of intellect. In this regard, he was only partly correct.

Science has now shown that certain parts of our brain specialize in processing emotional information; these parts are somewhat distinct from those responsible for intellect. Further, the different regions may not always work in concert; we may experience feelings and not understand why. Even feelings that drive our actions may never surface into awareness. Pascal anticipated both Freud and those modern neuroscientists who have demonstrated the existence of unconscious feelings. But Pascal underestimated the power of the human intellect to comprehend mysterious and elusive things, feelings included. Now that thousands of scientists are focusing their intellect on the mysteries of emotion, reason is finally starting to comprehend the reasons of the heart.

Some feelings are instinctive, so obviously important to survival that their selection in the course of evolution is easy to fathom. When a creature is threatened by a deadly foe, fear-driven actions occur by reflex. We act without input from the intellect, even when we know intellectually that we are safe. Charles Darwin provided the following example of a reflex emotion during a trip to the zoo:

> I put my face close to the thick glass-plate in front of a puff-adder in the Zoological Gardens with the firm deter-mination of not starting back if the snake struck at me; but, as soon as the blow was struck, my resolution went for nothing, and I jumped a yard or two backwards with as-tonishing rapidity. My will and reason were powerless against the imagination of a danger that had never been experienced.[3]

Fearing snakes appears to be hardwired in humans and other ani-mals, existing independent of prior exposure.[4] Even though such reflex emotional responses are obviously critically important to survival, one would be hard put to elevate them to the level of profound rea-soning. Neuroscientist Joseph LeDoux has shown that reflex fearful responses can occur without involvement of the cerebral cortex, where higher reasoning occurs.[5]

In contrast to these reflex emotions are other, more complicated feelings that can probably be experienced only by complex organisms such as humans, who have highly developed reasoning centers. Such feelings include love, vengeance, and anger channeled into political activism. Let us consider one historical example of how deeply held feelings, operating like a profound process of reasoning, can lead to political action, in this case changing the face of race relations in the United States—the case of Rosa Parks.[6]

Rosa Parks: A Historic Act of Feeling

One December day in Montgomery, Alabama, Rosa Parks was riding the bus home from work. She was sitting in a seat at the back of the bus in the section reserved for blacks when some whites got on. All the seats in the white section were taken, so the white bus driver looked back and said, "Let me have those front seats [in the black section]." Rosa Parks remained seated, as did the other blacks. "Y'all better make it light on yourselves and let me have those seats," the driver continued. Three of her fellow commuters stood up, but Ms. Parks remained seated. The rest, as they say, is history. Rosa Parks's one-woman stand against discrimination eventually led to a U.S. Supreme Court ruling that desegrated buses across the nation.

What was Rosa Parks thinking and feeling as she sat there on that bus in Alabama? According to her own recollections, she was not tired, as people often imagine, at least not physically. Rather, she was tired of being pushed around.

It would be fair to say that Ms. Parks was angry and that her anger resulted in her breaking the law. She was probably also afraid. She recalled that while riding on the bus, she thought back to a time when she would sit up all night, unable to sleep. Her grandfather would keep a gun by the fireplace, and when traveling by wagon, he would always keep his gun in the back.

Fear and anger often go together, and which one gains the upper hand is to some degree a matter of choice. On this occasion, it was defiance rather than submission that won out. What drove her choice? Was Ms. Parks's decision to remain seated on the bus the result of careful thought and analysis or was it driven primarily by her feelings?

In a memoir, she answers that question. While sitting on the bus, she tried not to think of what might happen—arrest or, worse still, physical violence. She gave no thought to the possibility that her defiance might provide the National Association for the Advancement of Colored People (NAACP) with a test case to challenge the segregation laws. Had she thought too deeply about what might befall her, she acknowledges, she might have disembarked.

Parks's recollections suggest that her decision to remain on the bus was driven primarily by her feelings—of outrage and of weariness at being mistreated and determination to resist it—rather than by a careful analytic process. She did not consciously ask herself: "What is the likelihood of my being arrested, hurt, and abused further, and how do I weigh that against the possibility that this will become a test case that will change the course of race relations in this country?" She felt, and she acted accordingly.

Now, any thug can break the law and get arrested. What distinguishes such a person from Rosa Parks? Daniel Goleman, in his excellent book *Emotional Intelligence*, quotes the philosopher Aristotle: "Anyone can become angry—that is easy. But to be angry with the right person, to the right degree, at the right time, for the right purpose, and in the right way—that is not easy."[7] And that is what Rosa Parks did.

She chose the right target for her anger—the Alabama Transit Authority, which had discriminated unfairly against blacks for decades. In fact, prior to 1900, blacks were not allowed to sit in any seat on the bus.

Parks expressed her anger in the right way—a way that met her objective without resulting in any bodily harm to her. Had she cursed at the bus driver, been physically violent, or made a scene, the result of her anger might have been very different. She might have been assaulted and would certainly have given her adversaries ammunition to portray her as a hoodlum. Instead, when the bus driver asked her to stand up, she simply said no. When he threatened to have her arrested, she replied, "You may do that." When two policemen arrived and asked why she had not stood up, she replied simply, "Why do you all push us around?" She accompanied them without protest as they led her to City Hall.

She expressed her anger to the right degree. In the car on the way to City Hall, one of the policemen asked her, "Why didn't you stand up when the driver spoke to you?" She remained silent. As she entered City Hall, she asked if she could have a drink of water. One policeman said yes, but before she could take a sip from the water fountain next to her, another said, "No, you can't drink no water. You have to wait until you get to jail." She acknowledges, "That made me angry, but I did not respond." Initially she was denied her right to make a phone call. Again she chose not to respond. Responding to those provocations would have done her no good.

The timing of her anger could not have been better. The civil rights movement was under way in the South, and there was a political structure in place to take advantage of her act of civil disobedience. From a political point of view, the time was right for a person of unimpeachable respectability to serve as a test case to fight discrimination on buses. Rosa Parks fit the bill. As to the validity of her anger, few people would argue that point.

So Rosa Parks's act of defiance met every one of Aristotle's conditions, and that is what distinguishes her action from that of a common lawbreaker. In his writings, Aristotle does not set out rules for what is the right way, the right degree, or the right object of anger. He leaves room for an individual to judge this, recognizing that the proper way to express feelings depends upon context and history, which will vary from person to person and from situation to situation.[8]

The capacity to feel profoundly and act on those feelings in a measured way generally does not come easily. Rather, it requires patience, contemplation, and reflection. Although Rosa Parks is best known for keeping her seat on that December day in 1955, she had previously defied the Alabama Transit Authority in small ways. As she put it, "You didn't have to wait for a lynching. You died a little each time you found yourself face to face with this kind of discrimination." By the time she arrived at that fateful day, she was prepared for her act of defiance. She had thought and felt deeply about the discrimination she had experienced and observed, and she had learned about the strategic use of passive resistance. That was how she was in a position to do what is not easy—to express her anger effectively in exactly the right way and at the right time.

It is by recognizing our feelings and thinking deeply about them that we are able to reach the most important decisions of our lives.

I Feel, Therefore I Am

I do, therefore I be—Descartes
I be, therefore I do—Sartre
Doo-bee, doo-bee, doo—Sinatra
—Graffiti seen on a bathroom wall

The story of Rosa Parks bears out recent research that has helped scientists come to see the central importance of feelings in the decision-making process.[9] This new insight comes largely from research on patients with certain types of brain injuries, which has been described most comprehensively by Antonio R. Damasio, professor of neurology at Iowa University, whose book *Descartes' Error* is recommended to the interested reader. Damasio's studies are fascinating not only because they reveal to us the importance of feelings to normal functioning, but also because they introduce us to a group of people whose lives have been radically transformed by their brain injuries. His work shows that when brain centers that coordinate feelings are damaged, people are unable to make even the simple decisions of everyday life.

An early clue to this line of thought came about 150 years ago from the curious case of Phineas Gage.

The Phineas Gage Syndrome

In the mid-1800s, Phineas Gage was a construction foreman in New England, supervising a gang responsible for laying railroad tracks across Vermont.[10] To lay these tracks, it was necessary to blast through rock. One hot afternoon Gage was distracted while putting gunpowder into a hole in the rock. Inadvertently he tamped the gunpowder directly with a narrow iron bar. The charge blew up in his face, and the iron bar blasted upward through his left cheek, the base of his skull, the front of his brain, and clean through the top of his head.

After his head wounds had healed, Gage appeared to be normal. He spoke rationally and his reasoning powers appeared to be intact. But it was soon apparent that some profound change had overcome the man. Before the accident, Gage had been known as a temperate, energetic, shrewd businessman with a "well-balanced mind." Afterward, he appeared to lose some essential aspects of his character. He became rude and disrespectful, capricious and temperamental, and though he initiated many plans, he was unable to follow through on them. According to those who knew him, "Gage was no longer Gage."

Before his injury, at age 25, Gage had been able to supervise a large group of men. After his injury, he was unable to hold a regular job, drifted around the country without making any solid personal attachments, and died in obscurity at age 38 after a prolonged bout of seizures (no doubt the result of the accident). His skull, however, was preserved.

In recent years, using modern brain-scanning techniques, Gage's skull, and computerized maps of brains of different shapes and sizes, Damasio and his research team modeled by computer the likely region of Gage's injury. These researchers concluded that the man had suffered damage specifically to the prefrontal cortex on both the left and the right sides of the brain, the portion of the brain just behind the forehead, which caused Gage's behavioral trouble. Later, Damasio studied dozens of other patients with damage in this area, all of whom experienced the same type of personality transformation as Phineas Gage did.

People with damage to the prefrontal cortex often become rude, insensitive, and boastful, which causes trouble in their personal relationships. There is a certain lack of emotional depth in the way they relate to others. And although they may score normally on many standardized tests of intellectual functioning, planning—especially over the long range—is extremely difficult, if not impossible. They may, in fact, have trouble making even trivial decisions. For example, one of Damasio's patients, though an intelligent man, was unable to decide on the time and date of his next medical appointment.

The inability to experience a full range of emotions is associated with extreme difficulty in planning, confirming the importance of feelings in decision making.

Notwithstanding the gross problems that people with the Phineas Gage syndrome encounter in their day-to-day lives, the exact nature of their incapacity has been impossible to nail down using conventional psychological tests. Damasio and colleagues are now making inroads into understanding the problem by combining an old technique, the galvanic skin response (GSR), with an ingenious new test, a gambling experiment. The GSR is a sensitive measure of emotions such as anxiety or excitement, which increase sweating as part of an overall increase in arousal.

Damasio and colleagues measured GSR while showing a variety of slides to people with the Phineas Gage syndrome as well as to a group with no brain damage. Some of these slides showed disturbing images, such as a vicious dog baring its fangs or a person with a bloody wound, while the others were bland. What were the GSR results? As predicted, the people in the control group were aroused by the disturbing images, but not by the bland ones. In contrast, the subjects with prefrontal cortex damage showed no GSR response to either type of image. Their GSR tracings were flat, as were their emotions. Their minds and bodies were unable to mount a normal response to pictures that disturb normal people.[11]

To simulate the type of decision making that causes people with prefrontal cortex damage to run into trouble in real life, Antoine Bechara, a scientist in Damasio's laboratory, devised a gambling experiment. In the experiment, subjects are asked to turn over cards from four decks, A, B, C, and D. Everyone is given a certain amount of play money to start, and told they will either win or lose money with each card they turn over. The goal of the game is to accumulate as much money as possible. If the players run out, they can "borrow" more from the experimenter.[12]

What the subjects are not told is that the decks are stacked: Turning over cards from Decks A and B will often produce a large sum of money—but will occasionally also cause the loss of an even larger sum! Turning over cards from Decks C and D, however, will produce smaller rewards, but also smaller penalties. The odds are biased in such a way that people who play consistently from Decks C and D will win, while those who turn over cards from Decks A and B will lose.

The results are intriguing. People without brain damage will begin by sampling all four packs to discover any patterns that may be associated with the different decks. Initially they tend to prefer A and B, the losing decks, because the rewards can be so great. Over a whole game, however, even individuals who call themselves "risk takers" will shift to the winning decks once they realize the losing decks' heavy penalties.

People with prefrontal cortex damage, however, never quite scope out the game. They tend to sample all four decks in the normal way, but then go for the big rewards, preferring cards from A and B despite the big penalties. Often they go "bankrupt" before the game is over, needing to "borrow" from the experimenter. Just as in real life, they seem unable to learn from their mistakes and form a long-term strategy.[13]

This game is the first laboratory test that successfully elicits the specific abnormality in making decisions that occurs in people with Phineas Gage syndrome, perhaps because it simulates those aspects of life that bring them up short. As with the gambling experiment, real life requires decisions, and it rewards and punishes according to the choices we make. If our choices are consistently good, we will generally come out ahead; if they are consistently bad, we will generally lose, one way or another.

In teasing out explanations for these results, Damasio suggests that people with prefrontal cortex damage suffer a "myopia for the future." Although they enjoy rewards and dislike punishments, they seem unable to remember reward and punishment as do their normal counterparts. By crippling their ability to make appropriate choices, this deficit causes them to fail in many aspects of their lives.

Damasio and colleagues also measured GSR in subjects who took part in the gambling experiment. The normal individuals displayed a consistent pattern: After sampling a few cards from the different decks, they began to show galvanic skin responses just before turning over a card from one of the losing decks. At some level, their bodies registered danger. As the experiment progressed, their GSR spiked higher in anticipation of turning a card from a losing deck, even before they changed their card-turning strategy.

In sharp contrast, the subjects with prefrontal lobe damage showed no anticipatory response whatsoever prior to turning a card from a bad deck. At a very visceral level, it seems, they were unable to *feel* the danger associated with the losing decks and thus were unable to learn from their failures. These same deficits in experiencing emotion probably impair their ability to make good decisions in real life as well. Patients with damage to many other parts of the brain do not show this particular learning deficit, which suggests the specific importance of the prefrontal cortex in the experience of feeling and in the translation of this experience into making good decisions.

Damasio's experiments illustrate a very important point about emotions: Often we experience emotions physically before we become aware of them and well before we decide to act on them. For example, if a friend ceases to show the degree of emotional connection you have come to expect from him or her, you may realize this change by degrees. First you might notice little shocks of dismay, unpleasant physical sensations such as muscle tension or hand tremors after telephone conversations with your friend. Only later might you become aware that feelings of emptiness or dissatisfaction have replaced the feelings of pleasure you formerly experienced in your friend's company. Finally, you might decide to take some action in relation to your friend. For example, you might choose to discuss your observations about the changes to see whether you can repair your friendship. This sequence of events appears to be orchestrated in large measure by the prefrontal cortex.

As in the gambling game, *the first experience of an emotion may be registered in the body before it is experienced by the mind and before it influences behavior. For this reason you will find it helpful to tune in to what your body is telling you if you want to understand what is going on in your emotional world.*

In Damasio's studies, we see a stark contrast between people with intact brains and those with blatant injuries to their prefrontal cortex. In real life, as with most aspects of brain functioning, such as intelligence, coordination skills, or musical ability, there is probably a wide range in prefrontal cortical functioning. At one end of the scale are people like Rosa Parks, who have an outstanding capacity to convert feelings into actions. At the other end stand people like Phineas Gage, whose prefrontal skills are seriously impaired.

What is less clear at this time is how differences in prefrontal cortical functioning play out in the middle zone. It may be that such differences account, at least to some degree, for the differences in what has been called *emotional intelligence* or *emotional competence*, which is the subject of chapter 5. The good news is that emotional skills, like all other skills, can be learned. I will discuss ways to improve your ability to recognize and manage your emotions so as to function more effectively and lead a happier and more satisfying life.

Before we leave the prefrontal cortex, let us consider another group of people in whom this fascinating part of the brain may not be functioning properly—individuals diagnosed as having antisocial personality disorder, also known as psychopaths.

The Mask of Sanity

The Mask of Sanity is the apt title of a classic work on the antisocial personality by psychiatrist Harvey Cleckley.[14] People with antisocial personality may appear normal but do not conform to social norms and are often in trouble with the law. They tend to be deceitful, and they delight in lying to and conning others. Impulsive in their actions, they tend to plan poorly for the future. As a group they are irritable and aggressive, get into frequent fights, and may show reckless disregard for the safety of others. They are frequently unable or unwilling to work consistently or to honor their financial obligations. In the wake of the damage they cause others, they show little remorse and will often lay the blame on others for the consequences of their behavior.[15]

Certain elements of the antisocial personality, such as deficient planning and difficulty with relationships, resemble the behavior seen in Phineas Gage and his modern counterparts. Yet most people with Phineas Gage syndrome show a sense of morality and an ability to conform to social norms lacking in psychopaths.

A recent paper by Damasio and colleagues sheds light on this difference.[16] The researchers report on two people, a woman and a man, whose prefrontal lobes were damaged before 16 months of age. Both were later diagnosed as having antisocial personality disorder. Both had the typical problems associated with prefrontal lobe damage, including a failure to perform normally on the gambling experiment. The researchers speculate that, in contrast to prefrontal injuries in adulthood, *early* damage to this crucial brain area may result in a failure to learn social norms. This theory would suggest that once these values are acquired, they are stored elsewhere in the brain, so that even if the prefrontal cortex is damaged in adulthood, some of these values and mores are retained.

Many people currently languishing in our prisons may have suffered damage to their prefrontal cortex or to some other part of the brain. In addition, many people not as yet safely sequestered from society may have similar problems and may be at risk for committing crimes.

In a recent case in Maryland, for example, a young man in a middle-class neighborhood killed an acquaintance, then dismembered and burned the body. His parents said they had sought help for their son when he was 12 because, although he was quiet and obedient, he showed very little emotion and almost never laughed or cried. Even during the two years of court hearings, according to a newspaper report, "he sat stone-faced, never cracking a smile or shedding a tear, barely blinking when the dozens of cameras flashed in his face."[17] There may be many other such individuals whose inability to experience emotions may predispose them to criminal actions.

Adrian Raine, professor of psychology at the University of Southern California in Los Angeles, and his colleagues recently compared twenty-one men with antisocial personality disorder with both healthy controls and patients with other psychiatric disorders.[18] To explore whether the antisocial group had a deficit in the body's ability to experience feelings, the scientists had them take two minutes to prepare a speech about their faults, then give the speech in a two-minute period while being videotaped. Compared with the other groups, those with antisocial personality disorder showed less bodily disturbance while giving the speech, as indicated by smaller changes in their heart rate and skin conductance. MRI studies showed that the antisocial group also had significantly less gray matter in their prefrontal cortex than the others. The authors conclude that:

- People with deficits in their prefrontal cortex and in their ability to mount bodily responses to stressful social situations have a hard time learning appropriate behavior, which may result in the development of antisocial personality disorder.

- The inability to mount appropriate bodily responses to risk or threat may result in unwise life decisions even in people who know intellectually that what they are doing is dangerous or self-destructive.

Normal individuals instinctively mistrust people who show little emotion. Two compelling fictional examples of this occur in the novel *The Stranger* by Albert Camus[19] and the horror movie *Invasion of the Body Snatchers*.

In *The Stranger*, Camus writes about a man who experiences and expresses very little feeling, as revealed by the novel's famous first sentence, "Mother died today, or was it yesterday?" This antihero goes on to commit a casual murder on a beach in Algeria, which he subsequently attributes to the effect of the heat on his mind. When he goes on trial, he is unable or unwilling to show any remorse for the crime and, as a consequence, is sentenced to death.

In *Invasion of the Body Snatchers*, humans are taken over by "pod people" while they sleep. These aliens look for all the world like normal human beings, with one huge exception—they lack emotion. Much of the horror of the movie comes from the idea of aliens who look human but lack an essential part of humanity—the capacity to feel.

We instinctively mistrust people who show no feeling, and the new scientific findings mentioned above suggest that we may be on solid ground in doing so. If someone seems eerily lacking in feeling, listen to your gut. Proceed with caution in dealing with that person.

It is also important to recognize that deficiencies in the ability to feel normally exist to greater and lesser degrees. For example, some people may express feelings, but do so in a way that suggests their feelings are not strongly felt or sincerely meant.

The Prefrontal Cortices: Seat of the Soul?

René Descartes thought that he had localized the seat of the soul. It was, he claimed, the pineal gland, a small pea-sized structure located at the center of the brain, which we now know is responsible for secreting the hormone melatonin. Perhaps it was this central location that made the pineal seem so important, as well as the fact that it is the only unpaired structure in the brain. In this opinion Descartes was once again in error, and there have been reports of individuals who led apparently normal lives after their pineal was removed for medical reasons.

Neuroscientists now recognize that there is no single area that is responsible for what makes us human—no single seat of the soul. Many areas of the brain must operate properly for us to feel and behave as human beings. The prefrontal cortex is only one of them, but a very important one.

The prefrontal cortex is well placed to act as a decision-making center. It is a hub, receiving information from other parts of the brain, as well as from all that we feel, hear, see, touch, smell, and taste. It assembles and coordinates all this information. It is also important for working memory, the process whereby we hold several different thoughts in mind at the same time for long enough to use them together. Finally, the prefrontal cortex is wired into those parts of the brain responsible for movement, arousal, and hormonal secretion. Small wonder then that a person whose prefrontal cortex is damaged should be so severely impaired.

Why Robots Should Have Feelings

We live in an era of smart machines: computers that keep getting smaller and more powerful, bombs that seek out their targets with surgical accuracy, and robots that can produce other robots. Is it possible or desirable to build emotions into machines such as robots? In the *Star Wars* trilogy viewers came to develop a special affection for the droids R2D2 and C3PO largely because of their endearing, almost human qualities. These loyal machines work on behalf of their masters with unswerving fidelity. R2D2 carries the critical message from Princess Leia to Obi-Wan Kenobi asking for help, while the articulate C3PO worries and fusses about the fate of the rebels.

Is this only science fiction, or is there a role for emotions in robots? Indeed there is, says Janet Halperin, research associate in the Department of Animal Sciences at the University of Maryland. Halperin notes that engineers working in robotics and artificial intelligence are increasingly imitating brain functioning when designing the most efficient and intelligent machines possible. In doing so, they are taking advantage of the millions of years of trial and error in brain evolution. Borrowing ideas from nature is turning out to be easier than building intelligent robots from scratch.

In a lecture entitled "Why Should Robots Have Emotions?" Halperin points out the advantages that emotions could confer on robots.[20] Being emotionally aroused could shorten reaction time and improve learning, which would be especially valuable in certain situations, such as when faced with danger. Emotions such as fear and aggression are modes of being that correspond to specific motivations, such as defense and attack. Like a human being, a robot has finite resources at its disposal—only so much energy, memory, and time. Emotions could help a robot choose the most important task to do at any given time. Emotions have a valence, prompting us to approach or avoid certain objects. Robots need to make similar critical decisions.

Imagine that you have a robot as a domestic servant. You have left for work and the robot is busy doing household chores. It is in "relaxation mode" as it makes the bed, dusts the furniture, takes the frozen chicken out of the freezer, and puts it in the microwave. Then the robot detects footsteps coming down the garden path and a knock on the door. It has been programmed not to open the door for anybody. If it is the mailman, he can just leave the parcel on the front step, the robot reasons. Then something unusual happens. The interloper moves across the yard to a window and smashes it. Suddenly the robot moves into "fear" mode. Now it must shift all its attention to the stranger, activate an alarm system, and hide in the closet to avoid being detected while videotaping the interloper's activities and relaying the information to a computer at the security station.

In a happier scenario, the footsteps on the path are yours as you arrive home after a long and bruising day at the office. The robot shifts into "love mode." It asks you how your day went and tunes in to the tone of your voice to respond appropriately.

The inclusion of emotions in robots will certainly make them more user-friendly and commercially appealing. More important for our present discussion, however, is the interest in emotions on the part of the artificial intelligence community—yet another indication of the growing appreciation that the emotions are an enormously important part of intelligence and necessary for proper decision making.

The Power of Unconscious Emotions

The idea that many of our emotions are unconscious was not new even a hundred years ago, when Freud set about making a life study out of the subject. Nowadays it is generally assumed that many emotional processes are unconscious. What can science tell us about the existence of the emotional unconscious? How does it influence our behavior?

To illustrate the different ways in which the unconscious may play a role in the emotional life, consider this simple example: You go to a restaurant with a friend, and halfway through a pleasant dinner, you begin to feel vaguely uneasy. Suddenly you lose interest in the meal. Even though you usually enjoy your friend's company, you become distracted. You have difficulty following the conversation, and haven't much to say when it's your turn to keep the flow going.

Your attention is mostly diverted inward, wondering what might be causing the knot that has developed in your stomach. Perhaps the seafood is off, you speculate, which would account for your queasiness. Then in a flash you realize what triggered you. The man or woman sitting at the table in the corner, just at the edge of your field of vision, is the spitting image of an ex-lover who caused you considerable heartache. As you become aware of this association, you begin to analyze the resemblance, the same contemptuous curl of the lip and smug, self-satisfied smirk.

You become angry as you remember how despicably he or she behaved when you were breaking up. Then, as you look at the person further, you focus on the stranger's features, which are quite different from those of your ex-lover—a longer chin and nose, hair of a different color. Of course they look different, you tell yourself. They are different people! Now your upset seems funny. You think of what an ass your ex-lover was. Good riddance, you tell yourself.

You point out to your friend the resemblance between the stranger and your ex. "That loser," your friend says. "You are well out of it!" You gossip for a while about relationships and what makes them good or bad. Now you are feeling much better. The knot in your stomach has vanished. The food tastes good again and you are fully engaged in the conversation.

What can the science of emotion tell us about the types of unconscious processes that occurred here? First, scientists have shown that it is possible to respond emotionally to subliminal stimuli—that is, stimuli that are unconsciously perceived. You were queasy before you were aware of that familiar curling lip in the corner. Second, the brain responds differently to consciously and unconsciously perceived stimuli. Once you were aware of what triggered you, you could dissect it and feel better. Third, we may misattribute the cues responsible for the emotions that we experience. At first you thought the seafood was bothering you. Finally, we may act on emotions without being aware that we are doing so. Had you not realized what was upsetting you, you might have become angry and sent the food back to the kitchen.

Let us consider the science behind each of these four processes. A few decades ago, pioneering research psychologist Robert Zajonc first showed that it is possible for people to respond emotionally to cues without being aware what was causing their responses.[21] In a series of studies, Zajonc and colleagues flashed images at people too briefly for them to be aware of the stimulus (that is, subliminally). Even though the study subjects were unaware that they had seen these images before, they tended to prefer those images they had seen subliminally over unfamiliar ones. Familiarity apparently may not breed contempt, but rather comfort. This observation, called the *mere exposure effect*, has been replicated many times over.

A meta-analysis of such studies reveals that the mere exposure effect is much stronger when the images are presented subliminally than when they are shown long enough to be recognized consciously.[22] One important function of the emotions is to act as a rapid early warning system. Subliminally perceived emotions may have evolved as potent response triggers because immediate action in response to fleeting impressions may be necessary for survival.

Literature on the subliminal response is consistent with the observations of many clinicians, myself included, that unconscious emotions often exert a more powerful influence on our preferences and actions than conscious emotions. For example, a woman may repeatedly seek out relationships with abusive men. She recognizes that these men are bad for her, but tells herself that they are more exciting and interesting than men who might treat her well. After some time in therapy, however, she realizes that her choices are being driven by the unconscious desire to repeat the type of abusive relationship that her father had with both her and her mother.

More recently, scientists have taken advantage of new technology to further explore conscious and unconscious emotional responses to cues. In one study, researchers presented pictures to subjects subliminally. When the researchers paired these subliminally presented pictures with electric shocks, they observed certain specific changes in the brain's electrical activity that would be expected to occur in response to painful stimuli. Later, when the subjects were once again shown the pictures subliminally—though without the electric shocks—the same changes in brain electric pattern were seen. In other words, the subjects responded to the pictures as if they feared an electric shock, even though they were not aware of seeing the pictures.[23]

In another study using phobic individuals, the same group of researchers measured brain electrical responses to words presented either too briefly or just long enough to be perceived consciously. Certain emotionally laden words were more effective at evoking emotional responses in brain wave patterns when presented subliminally than when presented in a way that made the subjects aware of them.[24]

Researchers are beginning to discover which parts of the brain register unconscious emotions. Paul Whalen, assistant professor of psychiatry and psychology at the University of Wisconsin, and colleagues presented fearful or happy faces subliminally to subjects and measured their brain responses by MRI.[25] The researchers detected signals in the left and right amygdalae, parts of the brain responsible for registering fear, when the subjects were exposed to the fearful faces, but not when they were exposed to the happy faces. In other words, the amygdalae registered the angry faces even though the subjects were not conscious of having seen them.

In another study that employed similar technology, subjects were initially exposed to two angry faces, one of which (the aversive stimulus) was paired with an unpleasant stimulus (a loud blast of white noise).[26] Later the subjects were exposed to these same two faces either subliminally or in such a way that they were conscious of the stimuli. In this study, the right amygdala showed more activity than the left when the aversive stimuli were subliminal, whereas the opposite was true when the subjects were aware of the stimuli. This showed that emotionally evocative stimuli are processed differently depending on whether they are unconsciously or consciously perceived.

There is considerable evidence that emotional experiences, especially negative ones, are processed on the right side of the brain, whereas logical analysis and reasoning occur on the left side. Conscious emotional processes are more amenable to being analyzed than unconscious ones. The results of this study provide some support for the psychoanalytic position that there is value in making unconscious processes conscious to allow them to be properly analyzed by the powerful forces of reason. Many unconscious emotional processes may proceed smoothly without such conscious analysis. When there are emotional difficulties that cannot be solved by the unconscious mind alone, however, active efforts are warranted to bring the troubling feelings into consciousness. There is value in having the left hemisphere know what the right hemisphere is doing.

Experiments such as the imaging studies of subliminal responses help us understand situations like the hypothetical experience in the restaurant that I just described. You perceived the stranger subliminally and that perception triggered a sense of uneasiness because of the association with your ex-lover. That subliminal impression was registered perhaps by your right amygdala, which signaled to the rest of your brain and your body that there was a threat in the environment; hence your feelings of unease. At a gut level you sensed danger and lost your appetite. From an evolutionary point of view, it makes sense that an animal cannot relax to a meal in the presence of danger.

Once you became aware of the source of your discomfort, you were able to subject your emotional response to a process of reasoning. The left side of your brain, including your left amygdala, took over and reassured you that the fearful response to the stranger was in fact a false alarm. At that point you could settle down and enjoy your meal.

But before you realized the source of your unease, you misattributed your unpleasant feelings to your food. What evidence do we have that this type of misattribution occurs? In psychiatric practice, we see it all the time. Depressed people, for example, will find many good reasons for their depression—a bad job, a poor marriage, financial circumstances, the state of the environment. But after taking an antidepressant for a while and feeling better, these same people often find that life looks different. All of a sudden, the same old job is not so bad, the poor marriage has redeeming features, and the finances are manageable.

How this misattribution occurs becomes much clearer when we look at patients with specific neurological problems, such as the split-brain patients observed by Joseph LeDoux. In these unfortunate people, the right and left cerebral hemispheres cannot communicate with each other; each must process information independently. It is therefore possible, for example, to present information to one hemisphere without the other hemisphere being aware of the content of the presented information.

When LeDoux and his colleague, Michael Gazzaniga, would attempt to get a split-brain patient to laugh by presenting funny information verbally to the person's right hemisphere, the person would proceed to laugh.[27] When the researchers asked the person via his left hemisphere why he was laughing, the left hemisphere, which is responsible for talking in most people, unaware of the earlier instruction, would make up reasons to explain the laughter. In another experiment, researchers made a young girl laugh by stimulating a certain region in her cerebral cortex.[28] When they asked her why she was laughing, she, too, made up reasons. In fact, both this young girl and LeDoux's subjects reported that they were laughing because the researchers just looked funny.

Researchers Richard Nisbett and Timothy Wilson performed several studies in which they showed that people often make up demonstrably incorrect reasons for why they feel a certain way or prefer certain things.[29] For example, in one study, they gave women an assortment of mesh stockings and asked them which ones they preferred. After making their selections, the subjects provided various reasons for their preferences. In fact, the stockings were identical.

All of these studies point out our need to make sense of our universe. If we cannot readily explain our preferences or actions, our brains are designed to come up with explanations rather than admit that we really don't have a clue. One goal of psychotherapy is to help people question their reasons and motivations for doing things so they can develop a better understanding of what drives their behavior. Once they better understand these influences, it becomes easier for them to consider alternative ways to act.

A good example of how unconsciously perceived feelings can drive actions comes from the addiction literature. Researchers Fischman and Foltin brought people addicted to cocaine into their laboratory and installed intravenous lines, one in each arm, that were connected to bottles containing various solutions.[30] The subjects were informed that the drip lines might contain cocaine at different dosages or just plain saltwater, but were not told what was in any particular bottle. They were then allowed to press a button that delivered a bolus of the solution into their veins.

At moderate or high levels of cocaine, the subjects easily distinguished the drug solution from the saltwater solution, recognizing the typical pleasant emotions that they associated with the drug. At the lowest dosage of cocaine, however, something interesting happened. The people reported that they were receiving only a placebo, and their heart rate and other bodily responses showed no changes. Yet when the researchers counted the number of times the button had been pushed, they found that the subjects had pressed it far more often to obtain the low cocaine solution than the saline, even though they themselves were unaware of it.

In summary, the latest scientific findings endorse the existence of unconscious emotional processes and their powerful influence on preferences and actions. We are beginning to understand how unconscious and conscious emotional events are processed differently in the brain. These findings lend some support to Pascal's insight that the heart has its reasons that reason cannot understand. They also support Freud's idea that there is some value in making unconscious processes conscious. By bringing new brain areas—for example, the left cerebral hemisphere—into play in the processing of emotional events, we are more likely to see our world in a different and novel way and thereby improve our chances of reaching fresh solutions to problems.

Also, these studies suggest that *if you want to understand your unconscious feelings, look at your behavior.* Ask, "If other people were behaving this way, what would I conclude they were feeling?" The answer will often provide a clue to your own hidden fears and desires.

Passions Unchecked by Reason

Although I have argued in favor of the emotions as intelligent and necessary for proper decision making, as with any biological function, the emotions do not always work as they should. Major problems can occur when emotions are experienced to excess or are unchecked by reason, morals, or common sense.

To find examples of emotion run amok, you need look no further than your daily newspaper. There you can find stories of suicide bombers, teenagers shooting their classmates, children battered by their own parents, an African-American man chained to the back of a pickup and dragged to his death, and a gay youth beaten, tied up, and left to die against a country fence. Those responsible for these blood-chilling events were apparently ordinary people who might have lived out their years in obscurity were it not for the horrors with which they are now indelibly associated.

Emotional excesses and poor judgment in the exercise of emotion occur at every level of society, in every time and every place. The bloody Trojan War was fought over the beautiful Helen. Anthony dawdled in Egypt with Cleopatra. In our own times a president's poorly controlled lust almost cost him his office. A football hero, jealous that his ex-wife was beginning a new life, was later found to be responsible for her death. The examples are endless.

Just as each emotion has a value, each can be experienced or expressed to excess, resulting in pain to oneself or others. Just as it is important to give weight to the emotions when they offer us useful information, so must we be able to know when our feelings are inappropriate in direction or excessive in degree. In recent decades clinical science has made enormous headway in helping individuals feel less anxious and depressed, less enraged, and more able to love and be happy. I deal with each of these areas in the chapters on the individual feelings.

Reconciling Reason and Passion

It is clear now that the two great domains, reason and passion, are both critical to our ability to make proper decisions. Emotion unchecked by reason can lead to disaster, but without emotion, a person is unable to plan properly or form and sustain social bonds, even in the presence of adequate reasoning ability.

In the next chapter we will see that emotion and reason are mediated to some degree by different nerve pathways in the brain. There has been considerable debate as to which area of experience, emotion or cognition, takes precedence in the stream of consciousness. According to Dr. John Cacioppo, professor of psychology at the University of Chicago, "We should not concern ourselves with which comes first. Both emotion and cognition are critical to our emotional life, and they work reciprocally with each other."

When passion and reason work well together, like the partners in a successful marriage, the outcome is a happy one. When they are at war, like hostile spouses, the result is no end of grief. One of the central goals of many different forms of psychotherapy is to help bring emotion and reason in line with each other.

Chapter 3

The Anatomy of Feeling

> *Heavenly Hurt it Gives us;*
> *We can find no Scar,*
> *But Internal Difference*
> *Where the Meanings are.*
> —Emily Dickinson[1]

> *Then felt I like some watcher of the skies*
> *When a new planet swims into his ken*
> —John Keats[2]

WHERE do we experience the emotions that we feel? When we grieve for a loved one or mourn the loss of a relationship, are we brokenhearted, as our language suggests? When our lives are threatened, do we experience terror in the pit of our stomach, where the hairs stand up on the nape of our neck or in our trembling hand? To understand the nature of emotions, it is important to pinpoint where they happen, where the meanings are.

Matter Over Mind

"What is Mind? No Matter. What is Matter? Never Mind." With this flippant epigram, the grandmother of the famous philosopher Bertrand Russell dismissed the field of philosophy.[3] But in its funny way, the putdown does encapsulate one of the issues that has preoccupied Western thinkers for centuries. How do we reconcile the very physical mass of our brain with the concept of mind, an entity that operates in the realm of words and symbols?

This question was alive at least a century ago when two giants in the field of brain and mind, Ivan Pavlov and Sigmund Freud respectively, staked out their opposite points of view. As you probably know, Pavlov discovered that if he gave a dog food at the same time that he rang a bell, the dog would soon begin to salivate at the sound of the bell alone. The food he called an unconditioned stimulus: the dog salivated instinctively when seeing the food. The bell he called a conditioned stimulus: the dog learned to salivate when hearing the bell because of its connection with the food. Pavlov also showed that dogs could learn to be afraid as a conditioned response. This process of learning is now known as classical conditioning. Conditioning is central to the way we adapt as life goes on. This was an immensely important discovery, which Pavlov made by applying the methodical, physical, step-by-step kind of science he used in his studies of digestion.

Freud, by contrast, was a model builder, spinning a concept of the mind—ego, id, and superego—that bore no direct relation to the brain, then or now. Freud began his work as a neurologist, and he would have liked more physical, brain-type explanations for emotion. But given the science of the time, he saw no alternative to writing in terms of the mind.

Modern researchers, in their approach to understanding emotional life, are more the intellectual descendants of Pavlov than of Freud. For example, neuroscientist Joseph LeDoux relied upon Pavlovian fear conditioning to elucidate the brain architecture responsible for fear.[4] By setting aside questions of mind and consciousness, researchers have been able to analyze emotions in animals at a microscopic level. That information carries over to clarify how emotions work in humans. Pavlovian plodding has created tremendous advances.

Nevertheless, the concept of mind still has value, not only as a shorthand for describing brain function, but also in understanding and communicating what we feel to others. For example, if you tell a friend that you are feeling guilty, embarrassed, or ashamed about something you did or said, she will understand what you mean. You would hardly want to sit down and confess the details of your neural circuitry. In psychotherapy, likewise, emotional problems are expressed in terms of "mind," not "brain." This dichotomy is paradoxical, for the Emotional Revolution has been largely powered by training the wonders of neuroscience upon the brain. Yet its mind-based approaches, such as cognitive therapy, have also produced many therapeutic breakthroughs.

The bottom line is that modern psychiatrists find it useful to think of emotions as both brain processes and mental experiences, just as physicists find it useful to view photons of light as both waves and particles. In contrast to previous generations, however, modern researchers and clinicians recognize that all mental processes are based on brain functions. When we discuss an emotion in terms of the brain and the mind, we are simply using two languages to talk about one event.

The Bear in the Woods: Body Versus the Brain

What happens when you are walking in the woods and all of a sudden you see a bear? This question was posed more than a hundred years ago by the famous psychologist William James in his classic paper "What Is an Emotion?"[5] Your heart beats, your hands tremble; perhaps unwisely, you run. And of course you are afraid. But which comes first, the fear or your bodily responses? According to James, first your body responds, then your brain interprets the body's response and becomes afraid. This line of thinking became the basis of the influential James-Lange hypothesis of emotions, which holds that feelings are the mind's interpretation of the bodily changes that accompany emotions.[6]

By the 1950s, however, based on the way brain injuries could cripple a person's emotions, researchers began to view the brain as a central processing unit for the emotions. Investigating the emotional brain has brought breakthrough after breakthrough. In the last few years alone, from the realms of imaging and brain surgery, we have learned which parts of the brain are responsible for humor, dreaming, and sexual urges. Working with animals, scientists have gained insight into the microscopic, finely crafted neural circuits that mediate our feelings of fear and love, of memory and desire. By the subtle art of genetic analysis, researchers have unspooled and decoded the deoxyribonucleic acid (DNA) of humans and animals to reveal the molecular underpinnings of anxiety and fidelity.

In this way, step by step, scientists are discovering those brain centers in which the emotions of humans and other animals are perceived, stored, and expressed. We are finally proving what we have only surmised—that there are specific places deep within the brain that register the emotional impact of experience. It is these centers that imbue our lives with a sense of meaning and drama.

Curiously, however, the body is making a comeback.[7] More and more, it turns out that input from our limbs, skin, eyes, and other senses is important to emotional experience. The body secretes many chemicals that influence the brain, not only hormones, but also chemicals from the immune system. It is these latter substances that cause the fatigue and lethargy we so commonly experience during infections. The fatigue may be adaptive, putting an infected person to bed so the body can conserve its resources and defend itself better against the viral or bacterial attack.

More and more, it's clear that what we do with our body can modify our emotions profoundly. Exercise is a potent mood elevator. Rest is restorative. Bright light can enhance energy, while deep abdominal breathing may reduce anxiety. Shiatsu massage and acupuncture, which stimulate particular points in the periphery of the body, may counteract depression, as may the novel process of stimulating the vagus nerve in the neck. All these techniques have drawn attention to the body as an important player in emotional states.

If the experience of emotions can be compared to a symphony, then the brain must surely be considered both the conductor and many of the major instruments. But the body has its music too, and we need to recognize that if we are to have a comprehensive understanding of where feelings are experienced.

Our latest understanding of where the emotions are experienced involves a balance between the brain and the body.

The Wonder of the Human Brain

It is a small organ, the brain. It would sit easily in your cupped hands. Yet this three-pound mass of mortal coils contains 100 billion neurons, each connected to a thousand other neurons at trillions of junctions known as synapses. At any instant, billions of infinitesimal electrical sparks and trillions of molecules pass signals from neuron to neuron, transmitting the myriad messages that create the consciousness and mood of a single moment. Think of the fireflies that flicker on a summer evening or the fireworks that fill the darkened sky with whirls of color and form on Independence Day and you will have but the palest vision of the miraculous complexity of this moist gray structure no larger than a cantaloupe.

How can we begin to understand the brain, this soft, soggy organ small enough to fit into your hands, yet wide enough to encompass a vision of the universe? Not by its outward appearance. It is shaped like a giant walnut, its spongy gray lobes folded over a white core as tough and fibrous as a heart of palm. The brain of Albert Einstein, which now sits in preservatives in a bottle, looks much like yours or mine. Obviously the secrets of the brain's power lie not in its gross appearance but rather in its microscopic features and the roiling mass of chemical and electrical signals.

Consider first the numbers. Each brain has about 100 billion neurons, arranged in ever-changing, overlapping circuits that store and transmit and create all our thoughts and feelings. But before we examine the particulars, consider for a moment what the figure "100 billion" means. If 100,000 words are needed to write an average-size book, 100 billion words would fill a library of a million books.

To take this comparison a step further, consider how the meaning of a word depends upon its relationship to the other words in the sentence or paragraph. Take "the," for example. What is "the"? By itself, nothing. In the same way, the information that a neuron communicates depends upon the other neurons with which it is connected. But while a word is given additional meaning by a mere handful of surrounding words, each single neuron is arrayed in relation to hundreds or even thousands of other neurons. No wonder, then, that two identical-looking, soft, soggy masses of brain may produce individuals of vastly different skills and temperaments.

But that is only the beginning of what makes each brain unique. The brain, more than any other organ in the body, is shaped by experience. In response to every event or stimulus, the brain undergoes chemical and anatomical changes. New synaptic connections are continuously formed and altered, formed and altered, formed and reformed in a process of wiring and rewiring that occurs all day every day—and to some extent at night too—throughout a person's lifetime.[8] So each one of us is unique not only by virtue of the genetic programming that causes our brains to grow and develop in highly particular ways, but also because each of us is exposed to different life experiences.

Not only that, we keep growing new neurons, a fact discovered only in the last few years. Scientists used to think each brain had a kind of quota, some number of neurons that was established by adulthood, after which it was all downhill as nerve cells died. Very recent research using our close relatives the macaque monkeys reveals to the contrary: Fresh neurons are created in the cortex, the outer, "rational" layers of the brain, on a daily basis.[9] In humans, we find that the hippocampus, the part of the brain that is critical for memory, keeps generating new cells well into old age.[10]

With this perspective in mind, let us consider the brain's neurons, star-shaped cells that send fibers through the base of the skull to affect all the aspects of bodily function. Brain neurons also order the release of hormones, powerful chemicals that influence the behavior of every cell in our body. In short, they are responsible for our every sensation, emotion, thought, and deed.

The Neuron: An Amazing Unit of Feeling

All neurons have certain basic features, regardless of their function. The neurons responsible for enabling you to comb your hair or order a pizza share critical features with those that tell you that you have fallen in love or hate your job. Each neuron contains four elements: a cell body, a tree of shortish, threadlike structures called dendrites, which branches out from the cell body, a long, tubular structure called an axon, which also sprouts from the cell body but then travels some distance (from the backbone to the foot, for instance); and a number of fine branching terminals that sprout from the axon.[11]

Just as no man is an island, no neuron stands by itself in the nervous system. To have any effect, neurons must collaborate. To do this, they "talk" to each other via their membranes, which are rather like thin skins that carry an electric charge. The membrane is like an electric fence around a piece of private property, surrounded by billions of other pieces of private property, each one snapping and crackling in readiness as electricity sweeps over their surfaces from their neighbors. And every now and then, when a neuron is sufficiently stimulated, the cell will fire off an electrical signal of its own. Neuronal activity takes place in the brain circuits that involve emotion, just as for any other brain function. A failure of proper neural functioning can lead to emotional problems, such as those encountered in Phineas Gage.

Neuroscientists now understand these electrochemical events in exquisite detail.

The Synapse: Where Two Neurons Meet

Each neuron is connected to about a thousand other neurons, which means that there are about a trillion synapses in the human brain. Discovering how neurons talk to each other was a great scientific accomplishment. Neurons do not actually touch, and it is impossible for electrical signals to jump the space between them. Instead, at the synapse, an electrical signal converts into a chemical, makes the jump, and is reconverted to electrical form by the receiving neuron.

The all-important chemicals involved in this synaptic transmission are called *neurotransmitters*. They are stored in packages called vesicles in the axon terminals, then downloaded into the synapse when an electrical discharge travels down the axon. Neurotransmitters are highly specialized. Once released into the synaptic cleft, they attach to special receptors on the membrane of the adjacent neuron. So precise is the match between neurotransmitter and receptor that we often think of them as keys and locks. Only the right key can open a lock. Once a neurotransmitter has attached to a matching receptor, it triggers chemical processes that in turn alter the electrical charge on the surface of the receiving neuron, which sends a signal down its axon, and so on. In this way, nerve signals are passed from neuron to neuron to neuron.

After the neurotransmitters have passed on the signal, it is clean-up time at the synapse. The neurotransmitters are reabsorbed into the releasing neuron, broken down in the axon terminal, and repackaged for future use. There is a balance between neurotransmitters and receptors. If there is not enough neurotransmitter, the receptors become more sensitive, perhaps oversensitive. If there is too much neurotransmitter, the receptors shut down. That is one way in which the emotional brain maintains equilibrium, which differs from person to person. Gung-ho, timid, placid, or excitable are just a few gross ways of looking at where a particular person's balance tends to settle.

Neurotransmitters: Molecules of Emotion

Different neurons use different neurotransmitters, of which some forty have so far been discovered. Five that we know to be important to emotion (there are probably many more) are serotonin, norepinephrine, dopamine, gamma-aminobutyric acid (GABA), and the endorphins. Some neurotransmitters stimulate neurons, while others relax neurons. As life changes around us, we change in response, and different chemicals will predominate. There is an ever-changing balance between the neurotransmitters to help us meet the demands of every changing moment.

Serotonin and norepinephrine are central to regulating mood. We know that because so many effective antidepressants zero in on the nerve pathways that use these neurotransmitters (see Table 12.1 on page 323). Although a neurotransmitter may serve different functions in different parts of the brain, certain general principles apply. Serotonin, for example, influences a person's ability to refrain from aggression and impulsive behavior, as well as enhances mood and relieves anxiety.[12] Drugs that modify serotonin transmission, such as Prozac and Zoloft, can lift the spirits and reduce anxiety, but can also help people who struggle with impulse control, eating binges, rage attacks, and sexual compulsions.

Norepinephrine, like its close chemical relative epinephrine (also known as adrenaline), has to do with arousal and alertness. Enhancing it helps people who feel lethargic and slowed down.

Dopamine is a versatile neurotransmitter that has different functions in different parts of the brain. It helps regulate movement, for example. (Parkinson's disease, primarily a disorder of movement, results from a lack of dopamine in certain parts of the brain.) Dopamine also plays a vital role in what you might call the pleasure pathways, the neural circuitry that registers enjoyment. Without dopamine, even sex and chocolate would be blah. As you might expect, many addictive drugs tickle the dopamine pathways, as do love and lust. So antidepressants that boost dopamine can help a depressed person once again feel joy. One of them, bupropion (Wellbutrin), has helped people quit smoking.

The neurotransmitter GABA inhibits neural activity. The alprazolam (Xanax) family of drugs calm and sedate by enhancing GABA activity.

Herbs used to treat depression and anxiety affect the same neurotransmitters as synthetic drugs. The herbal antidepressant St. John's wort works on several neurotransmitters, including serotonin, norepinephrine, and dopamine, while the sleep remedy valerian and the anti-anxiety herb kava-kava both act on GABA, the soother.

The endorphins, the brain's own naturally occurring opiates, help us experience diverse pleasures, from the warm, fuzzy feeling that an infant feels when snuggling up to Mom to the elation that follows exercise to sexual ecstasy.

The Importance of Networking

If nerve cells are so much alike, what determines whether they do one thing or another? The answer appears to depend not only on the neurotransmitters they release, but also on how they are arranged in relation to one another. By analogy, every piece of writing is composed of the same twenty-six letters of the alphabet. It is the precise sequence of letters that determines whether you have a Shakespeare sonnet or a shopping list.

Individual nerve cells can be responsible for a single function. For example, in the visual system, a particular nerve cell will be responsible for registering a single dot in a single spot in the visual field. But when neural functions become complex, a large number of interconnected neurons must work in harmony.[13] To decipher a silhouette, for example, many neurons must pool together their separate dots to register the scene. Those neurons constitute a neural network—a functionally linked group of neurons involved in executing a particular action.

Experience shapes the way your neural networks develop. Say, for example, you are walking along a narrow lane just as the sun is setting when you are mugged by a tall man. The relevant neurons will register the time of day, the long shadows cast by the buildings along the lane, the sounds of the birds that may be singing, the tall man walking toward you, and your physical and emotional feelings of fear. The experience will be almost literally etched in your brain: afterward, all the various neurons from all their separate positions will stay linked by synapses more strongly than before. They will form a neural network.

As neuroscientists often say, "Neurons that fire together wire together," and a single experience can do it. Years later, when you walk along a similar narrow lane at dusk and a man approaches you, the neural network may well fire once more, making you afraid all over again. When you feel afraid but don't know why, it may be that some neural network representing some buried memory has been triggered. The formation of neural networks is the basis of conditioning and can apply to any type of emotion.

Ultimately, researchers expect to understand precisely how this intricate web of sensation, memory, and emotion forms. Already we have some ability to watch neural networks fire. In a recent study, for example, researchers monitored the brains of dreaming rats and saw patterns of electrical activity like those seen when the rats ran through mazes. Presumably the rats were dreaming about the mazes.[14] By the same method, birds have been "seen" rehearsing their songs in sleep, with small variations.

The Emotional Brain

The quest to localize the specific regions of the brain responsible for feelings goes back to the nineteenth century, when a group of so-called phrenologists tried to determine the emotional makeup of individuals from the shapes and patterns of the bumps on their skulls. They constructed maps of the cranium on which they sketched the areas responsible for various personality attributes.[15] One such illustration, for example, shows "destructiveness" (represented by a predator chasing its prey) just above the right ear, "erotic love" (discreetly depicted by a cupid with his bow) at the base of the skull, and "conjugal love" (a couple being united in holy matrimony) directly above the cupid.[16]

Although phrenology has long since been disproved, its fundamental concept that certain parts of the brain are responsible for certain emotional experiences was legitimate. We now know that brain tissue is highly specialized. Just as specific areas of the brain are responsible for movement, reasoning, eating, and sleeping, so other parts handle particular emotional experiences. Do not imagine single centers for love, happiness, fear, and loathing. That would be just as simple-minded as the phrenologists' "Bump of Amativeness." Instead, think of neural networks connecting several brain centers. Jaak Panksepp, professor of psychobiology at Bowling Green State University, gave names to these various neural circuits, actually the same names as the emotions they mediate, for example, *rage, seeking, fear, panic, play,* and *lust*.[17] The sum of the regions that mediate emotional experiences is referred to as the *emotional brain,* or the *limbic system*.

To date, it appears that cognitive and emotional information is processed along separate (albeit connected) pathways in the brain, and it is useful at times to consider these circuits separately. If you are walking in the woods and see an unusual tree or flower, you may stop to consider its species or wonder how it came to be there. On the other hand, if you see a bear, such intellectual speculation would be ill-advised. Your nervous system will scream "Danger!" and take it from there. These two very different experiences are regulated by different parts of the brain, respectively the rational neocortex and the limbic system.[18]

In my clinical work with patients, I often talk to them about their limbic news, those all-important flashes of information from the ancient, survival-savvy regions of the brain. Emotions act as news flashes that something important is going on, and it pays to heed them. When you feel creepy on meeting a new coworker, your limbic system is telling you, "Watch out! This one's trouble." Or when an attractive neighbor moves in across the hall, your limbic system may alert you, "Hmmm, what have we got here? Romance, perhaps?"

Of course, the limbic system does not always function as it should. A person may fail to identify a danger or overlook a possible romance. At other times, the limbic system overdoes it, and the newswires are abuzz with emotional hype. You may feel frantic about matters that in fact pose no threat, depressed about things you really can manage, or so overcome with lust that you ignore other, more urgent matters. I once knew a graduate student who invited his advisor over to dinner. But halfway through the meal, the student and his wife vanished into the bedroom and had still not emerged an hour later when the advisor left. Avoiding that degree of stupidity is one reason why the separate yet connected nerve pathways responsible for emotion and reason must work in concert.

A (Very) Brief Tour of the Emotional Brain

If you look at the brain from the outside, it has the appearance of a shelled walnut. The fleshy folds of the surface are the neocortex, the crowning glory of millennia of human evolution. It is this most recently evolved part of the brain, six layers of neurons deep, that accounts for the highest achievements of the human mind, such as Einstein's theory of relativity, Bach's Brandenburg Concertos, and the discovery of the double helix.

Now let's go beneath the surface and take the walnut image a step further. Imagine breaking the nut in half and looking at its folded flesh from the inner aspect. That is the vantage point shown in Figure 3.1 on the next page, which displays the brain structures common to all mammals, including humans.[19] The cingulate cortex, for example, lights up in imaging studies when mothers hear a baby's cry.[20] The ability to hear and interpret a cry for "Mamma," and to respond by feeding the infant with milk from the mammary glands, represents the essence of what it means to be a mammal.

Around the middle of the last century, neuroscientist Paul MacLean used the term "limbic system" to encompass an interconnected group of structures.[21] According to MacLean, the limbic system evolved before the neocortex but after the very primitive parts of the brain, which are found even in reptiles. Reptiles are literally cold-blooded, unemotional creatures that lay their eggs in the sand and crawl or slither away, leaving their hatchlings to fend for themselves. According to MacLean's model, which is still regarded as a useful simplification, the limbic system (derived from the Latin word *limbus*, meaning "ring" or "margin") represents a transitional zone between the oldest and the newest parts of the brain.

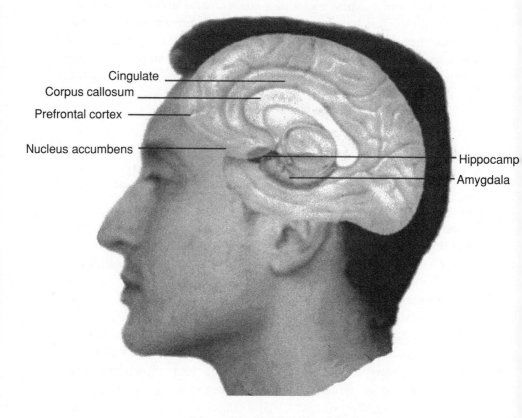

Figure 3.1. The Emotional Brain.
Photo and graphic by Larry Blossom.
Source: *Neuroanatomy: Text and Atlas,* Appleton & Lange, 1989.
Used with permission.

Limbic Music: Members of the Emotional Orchestra

Experiencing an emotion is like listening to a symphony. Whereas the one involves the carefully orchestrated sounds of many different musical instruments, the other involves the coordination of many different brain centers. Let us consider some of the more important members of the emotional orchestra, that are responsible for creating your limbic music.

The Amygdala: An Almond-Shaped Alarm System

One morning in late autumn I was walking with a friend along a canal that overlooks the Potomac River. It was still dark, and the cool wind blowing off the river suggested that winter was not far away. Suddenly I noticed a skinny, black cylinder on the path ahead. I froze; my heart skipped a beat and then started to pound. A snake! My friend and I both jumped back several paces. Was it a snake? we asked each other. The black shape did not move, but neither of us dared to approach it. We threw stones at it. We shouted. It gave no response. Finally, we decided to wait till the early rays of dawn would show us what it was.

It was a stick. We stepped over it, feeling foolish, and continued on our way.

Joseph LeDoux has used this very snake-versus-stick scenario to explain how animals process fearful stimuli.[22] He and his colleagues have shown that fear responses travel from the eyes along two separate neural pathways. One passes directly to the amygdala, quicker than thought. The other reaches the amygdala more slowly, taking a roundabout route through the cerebral cortex. The quick route allows an animal to respond almost instantaneously to potential danger—a brisk response that favors survival. That is why this route remains a powerful influence on behavior, despite its many "false alarms." On that morning by the canal, my first response to the cylindrical object was pure amygdala; only later did the cortex process all the complicated signals that confirmed the object was merely a stick and allow us to walk forward. Feeling foolish is unimportant. From an evolutionary point of view, as LeDoux points out, "It's better to mistake a stick for a snake than the other way round."[23]

Now imagine that while walking along the path, you were to see a tall, well-groomed white poodle. Most people would pass the dog without much fear, but had you been savagely attacked by just such a poodle previously, you might experience bodily and emotional fear responses similar to those triggered by a snake. This is an example of conditioned fear, triggered by stimuli that are not hardwired into the nervous system (such as with snakes), but are a product of learning. By using classical fear conditioning in rats, LeDoux and colleagues have shown that the amygdala is critically important for acquiring fearful responses. If both their amygdalae (left and right) are destroyed, rats are not able to develop normal conditioning to fearful stimuli. Neither are humans who have suffered damage to both amygdalae.

People unworthy of trust are an important form of danger. How do we recognize them? Again, the amygdala is central. Antonio Damasio and colleagues showed pictures of faces to normal individuals, then to people with various kinds of brain damage. Almost everyone agreed which faces were "untrustworthy." The only ones who didn't were the people with the damage to both of their amygdalae.[24]

Interestingly, if they hear stories about the people in the pictures, individuals with damage to both amygdalae can recognize which stories justify mistrust. They still recognize danger. The problem is that they cannot read the faces. For this ability to be intact, at least one amygdala needs to be in working order.

FEAR AND LOATHING IN THE AMYGDALA
The normal emotional responses to threat include both fear and anger, and the amygdala helps mediate both. In animals, electrically stimulating the amygdala produces fear, anger, or both. With repeated stimulation, anger escalates into rage until the animal will finally attack any moving object—a state resembling a human rage attack.[25] Quite possibly rage attacks are caused by a hyperirritable amygdala.

If their amygdalae on both sides are destroyed, animals show less aggression and violent behavior.[26] For example, monkeys that are normally hostile to strangers will approach them willingly and even allow themselves to be groomed. People with this damage, likewise, are not good at sensing threats, but have a Pollyanna attitude—that is, they are hopeful and trusting beyond belief.[27] Pollyanna, you may recall, was the little girl who was so grateful to receive crutches from the poor box at Christmas because the gift reminded her to be glad she did not need them.

Since the amygdala constitutes the body's warning bell, it is fortunate that bilateral damage is rare. However, many people who were abused as children are more susceptible to dangers in later life. They may choose violent partners, be unwisely trusting, allow people to take advantage of them, or put themselves in harm's way. I have often wondered whether these people might have subtle abnormalities in the amygdala that scientists have yet to discover. Perhaps their traumatic youth conditioned the amygdala to sound off only in the face of life-threatening danger.

THE WIRING OF THE AMYGDALA

Viewed under the microscope, this almond-shaped structure resembles a cluster of grapes, with each "grape" representing a nucleus or group of neurons that share a function. One nucleus receives incoming stimuli from the organs of sensation—the eyes, ears, and nostrils. Other nuclei integrate this information within the amygdala, while yet another communicates it to various other parts of the brain and body. Under certain circumstances, these amygdala signals trigger the fear response: increased blood pressure, startle, and a flood of stress hormones.[28] But when the threat has passed, nerve fibers using the chemical transmitters serotonin and GABA quiet the amygdala.[29]

It makes sense, then, that drugs such as Zoloft and Xanax, which boost the supplies of serotonin and GABA respectively, can help people who are overanxious. Zoloft can also tame rage attacks.[30] The more we know about how the amygdala is regulated, the more we can help individuals for whom the world is too scary or menacing a place.

The Hypothalamus: An Ancient Center for Reward and Punishment

The hypothalamus, which evolved very early on, sits at the base of the brain. This structure is critically important for regulating hormonal balance, temperature, and many bodily functions, such as appetite and the timing of sleeping and wakefulness. When a person is depressed, all these functions are disturbed, which suggests that depression may result from neural or chemical disturbances in the hypothalamus. Other emotional areas feed into the hypothalamus, which is important for general feelings of reward and punishment. Stimulating one part of the hypothalamus in waking patients may lead to comments such as "I feel good" or "I feel excited," while stimulating another part may lead to feelings of displeasure.[31]

Anything that presses on the hypothalamus can disturb emotion. One man, for example, had a fit of uncontrollable laughter at his mother's funeral, to his tremendous embarrassment. After he died, he was found to have arterial swelling that compressed his hypothalamus. Another woman literally died laughing after a blood vessel in her brain burst, which pressed the hypothalamus. This type of sham laughter is unrelated to enjoyment or humor. Humor, as you might expect, is complicated and involves the cerebral cortex.

The Thalamus: A Newly Suggested Function for an Ancient Structure

Another very ancient brain structure, the thalamus is an important way station for information passing to the brain from the senses. Most researchers did not think it important to the emotions, however, until a 1999 plenary presentation to thousands of members of the Society for Neuroscience by Dr. Rodolfo Llinas, professor of neuroscience at New York University Medical School. Llinas has found that the cells of the thalamus oscillate at varying frequencies, in that way setting the pace for activities higher up, in the cerebral cortex.[32] When these cells oscillate at high frequency, the entire brain is awake and alert; at lower frequencies, the result is sleep—that is, when all is well.

In various brain diseases, Llinas has found that parts of the thalamus oscillate too slowly. Llinas theorizes that corresponding parts of the cortex then lose their link with the thalamus (the technical word is "decouple") and become overexcited because they do not get the pacing they need from the thalamus. Depression, obsessive-compulsive disorder (OCD), and Parkinsonism may all result from such decoupling, in Llinas's view.

This theory has not yet been fully tested. If true, however, it has far-reaching implications, since pacemakers implanted in the thalamus might then be able to reverse pathologies such as depression or mania. This is a good example of how investigating basic brain functions can pay off richly to improve lives.

The Bed Nuclei of the Stria Terminalis: An Anxiety Center

According to Michael Davis, professor of psychiatry and psychology at Emory University, the structures that bear this exotic name regulate anxiety, as distinct from fear.[33] Fear is an adaptive emotion that helps us respond to a specific threat and, as we have seen, the amygdala is necessary for a fear response. Anxiety, on the other hand, is a state of generalized fearfulness, often unconnected to any particular threat.

Davis has found that the bed nuclei (close neighbor of the amygdala) can induce conditions in animals that resemble anxiety in humans. Rats, which are nocturnal, show signs of anxiety (such as freezing stock-still) when placed under bright lights, even if there is no other reason for fear. Removing the bed nuclei, but not the amygdala, abolishes this response. The bed nuclei, then, may be at fault in people with anxiety disorders.

The Hippocampus: A Seahorse That Remembers

The hippocampus, another close neighbor of the amygdala, is named after the Greek word for "seahorse" because of its shape. Although traditionally regarded as part of the limbic system, its major function is the recording and storage of factual rather than emotional memory.

In normal people, both types of memory work hand in hand. For example, how can you truly enjoy seeing your lover walking through the gate at the airport unless you remember what he or she looks like—and all the wonderful times you have had together? Or on a darker note, how can you experience the pain of loss unless you remember what (or whom) you are losing?

Also, the hippocampus helps us remember the context for an event. In the example of a person once mugged by a tall man in a narrow lane at dusk, the amygdala would record the menacing elements of the approaching stranger, whereas the hippocampus would record the contextual details, such as the solitude and the approaching dusk. In this way, the amygdala doesn't fire off an alarm at every approaching stranger, only at a stranger approaching in circumstances that once produced danger.

Traumas, Tirades, and the Temporal Lobe

Julie, a woman in her early thirties who had once been a competitive ice-skater, developed a strange set of symptoms. Sometimes, while showering, she would once again smell the ice of the skating rink, once again feel the butterflies as she had just before a competition. During these spells, Julie's fiancé observed that she looked spacey, and she herself confirmed feeling detached, as though she were in another world. She wondered whether these experiences might have mystical significance, might represent evidence of some higher power. Julie became more religious over this time, attending church and praying more regularly. A neurological workup showed that Julie was suffering seizures in her temporal lobe, that part of the cortex that enfolds several of the limbic structures.

During a seizure, a large number of neurons fire away wildly. When the seizure occurs in a brain area responsible for movement, it results in disjointed motions of the arms, legs, and tongue. Wild firing in the temporal lobe, however, triggers memories, complete with their sensory and physical sensations and the powerful associated emotions. During a temporal-lobe seizure a person might feel anything from panic or rage to exaltation or mystical and religious experiences.

Julie was treated with antiseizure medications, after which she no longer had the déjà vu experience of competitive skating, nor any other symptoms of seizures. She has maintained her religious devotion, which has enriched her life.

Researchers have suggested that a seizure-type instability of the temporal-lobe neurons might also account for the extreme mood swings that afflict people with manic-depressive illness, also known as bipolar disorder. That line of thinking has led to the successful use of antiseizure drugs, such as Tegretol (carbamazepine), Depakote (valproic acid), and Neurontin (gabapentin), for treating this disorder.[34] Likewise, people with rage attacks may also suffer temporal-lobe instability and sometimes respond to antiseizure medications.

Researcher Martin Teicher, associate professor of psychiatry at Harvard University, and colleagues observed that children who have been abused physically or emotionally later show signs of "limbic irritability," reminiscent of people with temporal-lobe seizures.[35] For example, these children tend to space out at times and to have unusual bodily feelings or hallucinatory experiences. They might smell something that isn't there or imagine that someone is calling them by name. Their brains also generate abnormal electrical patterns, especially on the (analytical) left side.

While Teicher's patients had come to medical attention because of emotional or behavioral problems, it cannot be doubted that many others walk the streets in a similar condition, undiagnosed or relegated to special education. These findings offer important concrete evidence of the long-standing damage caused by child abuse.

The Cranial Nerves: A Hot Line to the Limbic System

What do the following people have in common (besides all being success stories)?

- Becky, a young woman, used to get depressed every winter. Now she basks in the dazzling rays of a light box for half an hour each day and feels well all year round.

- Rick, a middle-aged man, was depressed for years despite having been treated with many different medications and shock therapy. Then he had a pacemaker implanted under the skin of his chest and his mood is now completely normal.

- Ernie, an autistic boy, had a hard time even looking at another person. After listening to specially arranged music, he began to interact with others in a way that looks almost normal.

Becky, Rick, and Ernie have all been helped by innovative treatments that stimulate a particular cranial nerve. These paired nerves carry information between the brain and the body via holes at the base of the skull.

In Becky's case, bright lights reversed the sluggishness caused by seasonal affective disorder (SAD). The stimulus travels via the optic nerve from the retina directly to the hypothalamus.

In Rick's case, the nerve stimulated was the vagus, named after the Latin word for "wanderer" because it roves around so much of the body. Nerve fibers arising from organs in the abdomen, chest, neck, *and* head join together to form the vagus, a broadband nerve cable that transmits bodily data to many brain centers, some of which help regulate the emotions. En route, the two vagus nerves pass through the neck, where researchers can stimulate them with promising results for depressed people. The pacemaker in Rick's chest wall is connected to an electrode implanted close to the vagus on the left-hand side of his neck.

The nuclei of this important pair of nerves, the control centers that receive and transmit information, are located in the brainstem, the innermost, most primitive part of the brain. They constitute the center of what Stephen Porges, professor of human development at the University of Maryland, refers to as the *social engagement system*. Porges tries to modify the center by making it less reactive.

One way to modify the system is by music that has been specially adapted to stay in the range of the human voice. Ernie is one of Porges's patients in "The Listening Project," a novel program for treating autistic children by altering their environmental input.[36] Porges has found that playing tapes of this type of modified music to autistic children helps them engage better with their human environment. The sound is transmitted via the acoustic nerve to the brain stem, where, according to Porges, it helps children like Ernie engage with their environment. While the work is new and has not been fully tested, Porges shows a videotape of Ernie clearly in a world of his own, unable or unwilling to look at the adult sitting across the table. After listening to the tape, Ernie smiles and holds his hand out toward the adult, obviously enjoying himself. Though Porges is the first to admit that Ernie still does not behave like a normal child, I was impressed by the promise of this new approach.

Porges points out that when we socialize in a safe environment, we use many of our cranial nerves to read the smiles of friendly people, to listen to their soothing voices, to enjoy the warmth of the fireplace, and to savor good food. The result is a feeling of comfort and safety, orchestrated deep in the primitive brain. A mother mouse and her babies probably feel much the same, snuggled up in your pantry wall. Maybe Ernie and his autistic peers feel similarly comforted when Porges's special tapes soothe their social-engagement centers.

There are probably many ways to stimulate the vagus, such as that well-known soother of sucking on a lozenge. Porges is looking for more of these healthy ways to comfort and control ourselves via this nerve.

I think this approach is very promising, not only because of the experimental results so far, but also because the vagus is a two-way street. The outward-bound system of nerve fibers sends comforting signals throughout the body. This is called the parasympathetic nervous system, which opposes the functions of the sympathetic nervous system. Whereas the sympathetic nervous system galvanizes the body into action, the parasympathetic nervous system settles it down. It lowers the heart rate, promotes digestion, and conserves energy in a variety of ways.

People who are too tense can benefit from enhancing their parasympathetic nervous system activity. Stimulating your cranial nerves can relieve stress and enhance mood.

The following are some research-based suggestions:

- Stimulate your olfactory nerve with pleasing smells. The fragrance of citrus, for example, has antidepressant effects.

- Stimulate your optic nerve with bright light and with colors that enhance mood and provide energy when you need to be active. Conversely, when you need to relax, lie quietly in a darkened room to send messages along the optic nerve that release prolactin, a tranquilizing hormone.

- Listen to music, which stimulates the acoustic nerve. Most people have already discovered this common and reliable method to cheer themselves up, but systematic exploration will boost the effect. Experiment to find out what type of music helps you the most, and make sure you have music in your car and bedroom, as well as in your living area.

- Rock in a rocking chair or swing in a hammock. Rocking stimulates the vestibular nerve, which has a soothing effect.

- Get a facial massage and stimulate the trigeminal nerve, which supplies sensation to the face. Stimulating certain pressure points on the face can modify the social-engagement system, relieving anxiety and promoting relaxation. When you feel tense, try pressing gently on different points on your face to discover your own relaxation zones. Or better still, take a massage class, either alone or with someone special.

- Stimulate your parasympathetic nervous system by means of deep abdominal breathing. Porges points out the type of breathing taught in Prana Yama Yoga stimulates the vagus.

Porges is currently working on what he calls neurobiological yoga, composed of a cluster of approaches from Eastern traditions that activate the parasympathetic nervous system and foster relaxation. Besides breathing exercises, it might involve listening to music modulated to the frequency of soothing human voices.

The Agony and the Ecstasy:
Right and Left in the Cerebral Cortex

An esteemed colleague of mine, well known for his outstanding intellect and verbal expression, was the victim of a left-sided stroke while he was in his mid-forties. In a stroke, the blood flow to part of the brain is cut off, killing neurons in that area. Since the left side of the brain controls language, my colleague lost his ability to speak. In addition, he became partially paralyzed on the right side of his body and walked unsteadily, even with the help of a cane. Loss of speech was particularly cruel for this articulate man, recently remarried and in his prime. After some time he returned to work, but was a vestige of his former self. Not surprisingly, he became depressed, but his friends and colleagues only fully realized how much he suffered when he threw himself under the wheels of an oncoming subway train.

You might assume that anyone with an incapacitating stroke would become depressed, but that is not so. Take another eminent man, Supreme Court Justice William O. Douglas, who suffered a right-sided stroke that left him paralyzed and wheelchair-bound.[37] Although the Justice was at times depressed, overall he pooh-poohed the impact of his illness, much to the consternation of his colleagues on the High Court. He insisted on returning to work, though others thought him not mentally fit. Shortly after his return, Douglas summoned a group of reporters to tell them that resigning had never entered his mind, that "walking has very little to do with the work of the Court," and that he would soon walk again. He invited the reporters to join him on a hike the following month.

Such egregious optimism is not atypical of patients with right-sided strokes, many of whom minimize the consequences of their illness. Many seem unaware that their left side is impaired and may neglect that part of their body altogether. For example, they may not dress on the left side, leaving the left jacket sleeve empty, or may fail to shave the left side of the face.

Nor is Douglas's breezy manner, almost the opposite of depression, uncommon in right-sided strokes. In one study, 38 percent of right-sided stroke victims had the type of denial seen in the judge's case, as compared with only 11 percent of patients with left-sided strokes.[38] In contrast, 62 percent of patients with left-sided strokes were depressed or fearful, as compared with only 10 percent of right-sided stroke victims. The closer the damage is to the frontal pole of the left cerebral hemisphere, the severer the depression.[39]

New imaging techniques have shed a bright light on left-right differences, confirming what's been learned from strokes. The very front part of the left side of the brain, the left prefrontal cortex, is central to the experience of happiness, while the right prefrontal cortex handles negative feelings such as distress. And as you might guess, the Jeremiahs of the world consistently light up with more activity in the right prefrontal cortex and the Pollyannas on the left.

Richard Davidson, professor of psychology at the University of Wisconsin at Madison, whose research team performed many key brain electrical mapping and imaging studies, has extended the scope to positive and negative anticipation.[40] To generate positive anticipation, they took smokers who had refrained from smoking for twenty-four hours, showed them a lighted cigarette, and told them they could smoke in two minutes. As predicted, the subjects' left prefrontal cortices lit up before they did.[41] To generate negative anticipation, the team told people who were afraid of public speaking that they would soon have to deliver a public address. Not surprisingly, these unwilling speakers showed a surge in activity over their right prefrontal cortices.[42]

A propensity to experience and expect the best or the worst may be fundamental to personality, as it shows up at a very early age. Dr. Nathan Fox, professor of psychology at the University of Maryland, has found that 4-month-old babies who are easily stressed by novel stimuli, such as a mobile or an unfamiliar sound, show more electrical activity on the right than on the left side of their brains.[43] This right-sided predominance appears to persist into childhood and is not uncommon. This is the child who feels genuine fear and shyness even with a next-door neighbor, the kid for whom staying in kindergarten without a parent may take two weeks. Happily, psychologist Jerome Kagan's studies at Harvard indicate that if these children are not forced, but gently helped to interact with others, they eventually become bolder.[44] Fox suggests that exposing anxious children to a wide variety of novel stimuli may be beneficial, but points out that how this is done makes all the difference. Adults often fail to understand how scared these children are. Insisting, without taking the child's feelings into account, just makes it worse.

Feeling With the Right Side of Your Brain

The right side of the brain handles most of the perception and interpretation of emotional cues, whether these are facial expressions, tones of voice, or pictures of emotionally charged scenarios. Look at the two faces below and consider which looks happier.

Most people pick the face on the left.[45] But of course, the facial features match except that the smiling and frowning mouth is reversed in the two pictures. In the left picture, the smiling half of the face is on your left; in the right picture, the smiling half is on the right. Since your left visual field is processed by your right cerebral hemisphere, which senses emotions more acutely, the left picture looks happier to most people.

The Funny Zone

If you saw a sign in a tailor's shop in Hong Kong that read, "Please have a fit upstairs," or one in a Tokyo hotel that read, "Guests are invited to take advantage of the chambermaid," would you be amused? Would you at least recognize that someone else might be? If so, the chances are that you have a 2-inch by 3-inch area of your right frontal lobe that is working just fine.

Using jokes like these, a group of Canadian researchers have zeroed in on a "funny zone."[46] The research group studied twenty-one people with brain injuries, approximately half of which involved this "funny zone," to test their sense of humor. The people were asked, for example, to complete jokes such as the following:

> The neighborhood borrower approached Mr. Smith at noon on Sunday and inquired, "Say, Smith, are you using your lawn mower this afternoon?" "Yes, I am," Smith replied warily, to which the borrower replied:
>
> (i) "Oops!" as the rake he walked on barely missed his face.
> (ii) "Fine, then you won't be wanting your golf clubs. I'll just borrow them."
> (iii) "Oh well, can I borrow it when you're done, then?"
> (iv) "The birds are always eating my grass seed."

The lead researcher on the study, Dr. Prathiba Shammi, a psychologist at the University of Toronto, suggests that the ability to appreciate humor is a two-step process. The first step involves recognizing the element of surprise that all jokes have, while the second step requires the ability to see from two different perspectives. In the example above, the third and fourth answers are not in the running because they are, respectively, banal and a non sequitur. The first response is unexpected but slapstick—and that was the one chosen by the patients with a damaged right frontal lobe. Even though their capacity to reason was intact, they only got step 1, the surprise. The double-take effect of step 2 was beyond them. The second answer, the "right" answer, is unexpected and requires you to realize that the neighbor has figured out yet another way to cadge from the wary Mr. Smith. And that, of course, was the answer chosen by the people with intact brains and any injury but to the right frontal lobe.

The researchers do not suggest that humor is localized to one small brain area in the right frontal lobe, which they acknowledge would be "phrenological folly." Rather, they suggest that the right frontal lobe plays an important role in the neural network involved in appreciating a good joke.

A separate study suggests that there may also be a "funny zone" in the left frontal area. A.K., a 16-year-old girl, was to undergo surgery to control her seizures.[47] As part of the surgery, the girl's brain areas were mapped to understand their different functions and to minimize the impact of the surgery. The doctors found that whenever they stimulated a 2-centimeter by 2-centimeter area in the left frontal lobe, A.K. would laugh. Unlike the sham laughter that occurs with some forms of pressure on the brain, A.K.'s felt like genuine merriment. Each time she would laugh, the doctors would ask her what was funny and she would mention something in the environment, such as an object in the room, a paragraph she was reading, or the doctors themselves. On one occasion she responded, "You guys are just so funny . . . standing around."

Modern research has revealed that specific cortical zones are involved in the experience of all our emotions. The discovery of brain regions instrumental in humor and laughter is just one more example of how neuroscientists are unraveling the mysteries of where our feelings are stored, experienced, and expressed.

Chapter 4

Mixing Memory and Desire

> *I remember, I remember*
> *The house where I was born,*
> *The little window where the sun*
> *Came peeping in at morn.*
> —Thomas Hood (1798–1845)

MEMORY and feeling, and for that matter, identity, are deeply linked. We are largely who we remember ourselves to be— our mother's son, our father's daughter, the first person to walk on the moon, the parent of a particular child. Our strands of memories and feelings tie together the thousands and thousands of experiences that shape us.

You can readily see the link between feelings and memories in our popular songs. In "White Christmas," full of evocative details, for example, the singer remembers the nostalgic wintry landscape of his childhood Christmas. Recalling the passion of youthful romance, one lover remembers a night in September, while another, in a different song, pays tribute to a past steamy affair with a simple expression of gratitude, "Thanks for the Memory."

Memory, however, is a two-edged sword. Just as it can enrich our present and imbue it with significance, so it can haunt us, filling our every waking hour with dread and pain. Many people who have survived terrible traumas, such as the Holocaust, carry the burden of their memories with them every day of their lives. Their memories may announce themselves in nightmares, from which they jerk

59

awake sweating, or during the day, in flashbacks and painful, intrusive thoughts.

Such extreme consequences of trauma, collectively called *post-traumatic stress disorder* (PTSD), result from horrors, but the smaller upsets of everyday life can also take a toll, especially if they occur early in childhood or are repeated many times over.

Often, a good place to start when trying to understand a brain function is to examine instances where it is missing. So I begin my journey into the science of memory with cases of amnesia, some famous and others drawn from my own experience.

All About Eve: Doesn't One Have a Right to Withdraw Her Hand?

She is not named in the literature, so I will call her Eve. We know nothing about how she looked or the major details of her life. The only reason that we know anything about her at all, almost a hundred years later, is the curious nature of her amnesia, as described by the French physician Edouard Claparede.[1] Eve was 47 years old and had suffered from amnesia for the previous six years when Dr. Claparede began his observations.

Eve's past memories and her intellect remained intact. She was able to name the capitals of Europe and perform mental arithmetic. Yet she was unable to register any new facts. She did not know where she was, though she had been in the hospital for six years. She recognized neither the doctors she saw every day nor the woman who nursed her. When her nurse asked Eve whether she knew who she was, Eve revealed her good breeding by replying, "No, madame. With whom do I have the honor of speaking?" Eve could not name the year, month, or date although she was often told these facts.

Nevertheless, her ability to acquire certain *types* of memories was not completely lost. Here Claparede describes the first type of memory she was able to retain:

> When one told her a little story, read to her various items of a newspaper, three minutes later she remembered noth-

ing, not even the fact that someone had read to her; but with certain questions one could elicit in a reflex fashion some of the details of those items. But when she found these details in her consciousness, she did not recognize them as memories but believed them to be something "that went through her mind" by chance, an idea she had "without knowing why," a product of her imagination of the moment, or even the result of reflection.

Also, Eve could form new habits:

In the very halls of the institution which she claimed not to recognize (though she had now been there six years), she walked around without getting lost; she knew how to find the toilet without being able to say where it was, describe it, or have a conscious memory of it. When the nurse came, she did not know who she was, but soon after would ask her whether dinner time was near or some other domestic question. These facts prove that her habits were very well retained and active.

Finally, Claparede demonstrated that Eve retained a certain type of memory that is of particular interest to our present story. Here is how he describes his investigation:

I carried out the following curious experiment on her: to see whether she would better retain an intense impression involving affectivity [emotion], I stuck her hand with a pin hidden between my fingers. The light pain was as quickly forgotten as indifferent perceptions; a few minutes later, she no longer remembered it. But when I again reached out for her hand, she pulled it back in a reflex fashion, not knowing why. When I asked her for the reason, she said in a flurry, "Doesn't one have the right to withdraw her hand?" and when I insisted, she said, "Is there perhaps a pin hidden in your hand?" To the question, "What makes you suspect me of wanting to stick you?" she would repeat her old statement, "That was an idea that went through my mind," or she would explain, "Sometimes pins are hidden in people's hands." But never would she recognize the idea of sticking as a "memory."

There are several things we can learn from this famous case. There are different types of memory. The different types of memory are mediated by different parts of the brain. And we need to respect our emotional memory.

There Are Different Types of Memory

The type of memory that Eve lacked has been called *explicit,* or *declarative,* memory. Explicit memory allows us to recall newly presented information, such as a phone number or the latest news from the Middle East.

The type of memory that Eve had, at least partially, is called *implicit* memory. These memories are typically unconscious and cannot be recalled in any articulate way.

One type of implicit memory is *procedural* memory, which we use to learn procedures, such as driving a car or playing tennis. Explicit memory can help to begin with, but ultimately procedures can be learned by no other way than doing; one would hardly let a non-driver study a few manuals, then launch his car into downtown traffic. I often feel thankful for my procedural memory. It lets me brush my teeth, prepare a simple breakfast, eat, dress, and get to work—all with very little conscious attention. Procedural memory lets our "mind" go on automatic pilot, freeing it up to attend to other things.

Another famous amnesiac, known in the literature as H.M., had difficulties similar to Eve's when it came to recognizing his doctor and learning new information.[2] H.M. proved quite adept, however, at learning to draw a five-pointed star by looking at the movements of his hand and the pencil in a mirror. In other words, his explicit memory was impaired but his procedural memory was intact.

Eve also exhibited some ability in another type of memory called *priming.*[3] When elements of a story she had heard were repeated to her, she would recall other aspects of the story, even though she was unaware these facts came from her memory.

Priming may be intact even in people with impaired explicit memory.[4] In a classic experiment, researchers show amnesiacs a list of words including, let us say, "garden" and "cabbage." A little while later, the amnesiacs are given a list of word fragments, such as "gar" or "cab," and are asked to complete the sounds with the first words that come to mind. Invariably, they tend to offer words from the original list, such as "garden" and "cabbage," as opposed to words not on the list, such as "garbage," "Garfield," "cabbie," or "cabinet."[5] Priming shows that something of a memory can be retained even though it may not be available to conscious recall.

It is useful to know about priming—when taking a multiple-choice test, for example, or trying to become America's Next Millionaire. If you don't know the correct answer, but can get the choices down to just a few, you do well to guess. You have probably retained some element of the right answer unconsciously. Trust your first hunch, the thing that "feels" right. Or if you are struggling to remember a word, take a stab at it. Think of a sentence that requires the word, and you'll be surprised how often the right word shows up, once you've primed the pump with a context.

Emotional memory is a type of implicit memory. A single pinprick was all it took to condition Eve to fear shaking her doctor's hand, even though she could not say why. When she was pressed on this point, she improvised remarkably well when she asked, "Is there perhaps a pin hidden in your hand?" In some way the sensation of being stuck must have registered somewhere, associated with her doctor's hand. This type of memory is called a *body memory*, because it is as if the body remembers, though the mind may not.

Body memories are common in the victims of sexual abuse. For example, a young woman who attends a family event may feel nausea or an unpleasant tingling in her groin when she sees the uncle who abused her years before, even though she does not recall any specific details of the abuse. More happily, musicians count on body memories to perform. A pianist does not explicitly remember the thundering bass chords or the right hand's rippling cascade of thirty-second notes. His hands remember, while his mind and heart are caught up in the emotional flow.

Different Types of Memory Are Mediated by Different Parts of the Brain

Working at the turn of the last century, Claparede lacked the technology to image Eve's brain. Nevertheless, we can be reasonably sure that her hippocampus was damaged on both sides but that at least one amygdala was intact. H.M.'s hippocampus was surgically removed on both sides as a treatment for incapacitating epilepsy.

In a fascinating recent paper, researcher Antoine Bechara and colleagues teased apart the roles of the hippocampus and the amygdala in recording emotional memories.[6] They compared the results of fear conditioning in normal controls and in three different patients—one with bilateral damage to the amygdala but not the hippocampus, one with bilateral damage to the hippocampus but not the amygdala, and one with bilateral damage to both the amygdala and the hippocampus.

The subjects were shown slides of four different colors on several occasions. Each time they saw the blue slide (the conditioned, originally neutral stimulus), they were exposed to a loud blast from a boat horn (the unconditioned stimulus, unpleasant from the get-go). The slides of the other colors were not paired with any noise. The emotional responses were measured throughout by galvanic skin response, which is a standard component of lie-detecting machines.

Then came the moment of truth: How would the subjects react to the blue slide without the boat horn? Had they been conditioned to fear that patch of blue?

The person with a working hippocampus but no amygdala showed no skin change to the blue slide, no gut-level reaction. In other words, he did not acquire fear conditioning even though he was intellectually aware that the boat horn accompanied the blue slide. The opposite occurred in the person with the intact amygdala but no hippocampus: He feared the blue, sweating when he saw it, but had no intellectual awareness that the blue color and the blast went together. The person with bilateral damage to both the amygdala and the hippocampus could neither develop fear conditioning nor perceive the pairing.

Research in animals tells the same story. As measured by fear conditioning, the hippocampus remembers facts (declarative memory), while the amygdala registers emotional memory.

Respect Your Emotional Memory

The hippocampus matures slowly, which explains why few people have factual memories from before the age of 3.[7] The amygdala, however, lays down emotional information well before that age. This discrepancy is probably why some people who were abused in childhood have emotional and body memories—they cannot bear to be touched in a particular way, for example—but have no corresponding factual memories of the actual abuse.

The amygdala may also register less-dire unpleasant stimuli that the hippocampus ignores. For example, say as a child you visited an aunt who always made you feel bad, perhaps by commenting that you did not seem to be growing or that you had put on a lot of weight. You might be left with an overall bad feeling about your aunt without remembering exactly why.

This same type of experience can occur even with recent memories. Imagine that you look at your day planner and note your appointment for tomorrow morning. Later in the day you remember that you have an appointment, but forget with whom. But you do remember that it will be unpleasant, and your body registers a crawling unease. When you check your book again, you see that the appointment is with your dentist. Your amygdala, which had previously been conditioned to fear the dentist's drill, remembered the unpleasantness, but your hippocampus forgot the details. Contrariwise, you might wake up happy, knowing that the day holds something delightful, yet not remember it's a lunch date with a favorite friend.

When your amygdala gives you information, you should listen. Although sometimes it may cry out too loud or issue false alarms, as in people with anxiety disorders or depression, it is often a trusty messenger. That is the final important lesson we can learn from Eve's story.

Imagine for a moment how it must have felt to be a woman in the early nineteenth century, ignorant of her whereabouts or the date, hospitalized indefinitely, and unable to learn where she was in time or place. Her esteemed doctor was extending his hand and asking her to shake it. It must have been very awkward to refuse, but she did exactly that. And when confronted about her behavior, she had sufficient sense of her humanity to respond, "Doesn't one have a right to withdraw her hand?"

Although nameless, she lives on in the literature about memory and as an example to vulnerable people that, even in the absence of memory, it is possible to retain one's dignity. That is why I call her Eve—she is the first woman to teach us about memory. I give her a name in recognition of her gift to us.

Vanished Without a Trace

I had my first encounter with the mysteries of forgetting and remembering the day my uncle Leonard vanished. The car was packed and Leonard's wife and four children were ready to drive to the farm in the country where he was struggling to make a go of it, but Leonard was nowhere to be found. That morning he had drawn money from the family business and had not been heard from since.

A coordinated search began. Posters with Leonard's picture were sent to police stations all over South Africa, and newspaper advertisements offered a reward for anyone who could provide information leading to his whereabouts. A week later he presented himself, bearing one of these newspapers, at a police station about 1,000 miles from Johannesburg. The man in the picture looked like him, he said, but he wasn't sure if it was him. He gave as his current address the number and street name of the childhood home he had left some thirty years before. This was the only thread of memory he had.

Leonard was retrieved by his wife and younger brother, to whom he introduced himself politely as though they were strangers. They flew him back to Johannesburg, where he was admitted to a psychiatric hospital and found to have no discernible neurological damage. Yet he had lost his memory. His doctors treated him with high doses of insulin in the belief that putting him into a coma would restore him to his former self. Whether it helped or not, no one can say.

Gradually, over the weeks that followed, his memory came back to him, starting with his earlier years and progressing toward the present. At first he believed he was a child, then a teenager, then a young adult. When his children were permitted to visit, he could not bear to see them, as they were so much older than he believed them to be. When he saw his sister, my mother, he wept to find her so aged. And so it went, until his memory had all returned and he was discharged.

The diagnosis made was hysterical amnesia. He had gone into what is known as a fugue, a condition in which large parts of a person's past slip out of consciousness.[8] Although fugues are rare nowadays, they were formerly quite common, especially during wartime. In wars, fugues are often triggered by the traumas of shelling and bombing, physical and psychological exhaustion, loss of confidence, and the surrounding chaos and disintegration. Leonard had distinguished himself in World War II some years before. He had helped many of his comrades who suffered from shell shock or combat fatigue, including people in fugue states, but had himself returned from the war unharmed and in apparently good psychological health.

In peacetime, fugues can occur as a response to overwhelming stress and are often preceded by some sort of head injury.[9] In Leonard's case there were certainly conflicts enough in his work and family life to make it plausible that, unconsciously, he had literally wanted to run away and forget about his troubles. In addition, he had injured his head while working on a truck and had suffered a brief concussion and memory loss lasting for about a week exactly one year before the fugue occurred. From this he had supposedly fully recovered.

Whatever the causes, Leonard and many other fugue victims show that it is possible to forget large chunks of memory and then remember them again. Where do the memories go? What causes them to vanish and then to materialize again? Questions like these led Freud to explore the unconscious mind, but we still do not have adequate answers. Animal research shows that severe stress, which results in the release of high concentrations of cortisol, can cause the branching dendrites of the hippocampal cells to shrivel.[10] This mechanism may be one way that stress can lead to amnesia.

As a practicing psychiatrist for the past twenty-five years, I have seen many demonstrations of the unconscious mind at work, and of the power of forgetting and remembering, but none more dramatic than the disappearance and reappearance, the amnesia and recovery of my uncle Leonard.

Recovered Memories Versus False Memories

Although little controversy surrounds the loss and recovery of memory in fugues, there is another situation where similar events are passionately debated. I am talking of the so-called repressed and recovered memories that occur in the context of alleged child abuse. Consider these highly publicized cases:

- A former Miss America charged that her father abused her as a young girl. She said she had forgotten about the abuse for years, then remembered it again as a young adult.[11]

- A daughter claimed to recover memories of her father murdering her friend many years before, when she was 8 years old. The father was imprisoned entirely on the basis of her testimony, but the sentence was later reversed.[12]

- Two psychiatrists at a large Chicago hospital were successfully sued by a former patient who claimed they had persuaded her that she had been abused by a cult. She later disavowed any such experience, accusing them of having implanted false memories into her mind.[13]

- A New Jersey day care provider was accused of acts of depravity toward the children in her custody and was sentenced to 47 years in prison. The testimony of the preschoolers was later attributed to relentless questioning and dismissed, and after 5 years in jail, the woman's sentence was reversed.[14]

How can one make sense of the confusion that surrounds recovered memories and false memories? Can memories of child abuse really be forgotten and then retrieved, as occurs in a fugue? And can false memories be implanted? What does the science of memory tell us? Let us start away from the klieg lights of the media and look at a case with which I am personally familiar.

Phil: Memories of a Murderous Father and an Incestuous Brother

Phil, a doctor in his early forties, recalled growing up in a troubled household, a family that would be regarded as dysfunctional by any definition of the term. Throughout Phil's childhood his father's depression hung over the family like a thundercloud, at best dampening everyone's spirits, at worst filling them with dread. Phil always had the sense that his father didn't like him. He feared his father and, for that matter, all male authority figures, though he could not specify why that should be so.

At first, Phil's life was made easier by his closeness to his brother Jim, who was seven years older and whom he regarded as his best friend. But then something changed. This revered elder brother began to beat Phil up and generally act hostile. Phil attributed Jim's behavior to jealousy because the family was now better off financially than when Jim had been young, and Phil had more toys and games than Jim had ever owned.

When Phil was in his late teens, he was assaulted physically by an older boy. Although he suffered no lasting bodily harm, the months that followed were full of mental turmoil. Each night, as he lay in bed, bits and pieces of childhood memories would come back to him. He suffered severe insomnia and agitation and felt compelled, like a detective obsessed with a case, to put together the story of his childhood.

Over time, Phil recalled that when he was about 7 or 8 years old, his father had repeatedly threatened to shoot both himself and the rest of the family. Phil remembered going often to his father's bedroom, looking in the drawer where the gun was stored, opening the cardboard box and checking to see if the gun was still in its place. He remembered his mother and sister pleading for their lives, or at least for the lives of the younger children.

Then another set of memories returned to Phil—that he had been molested on numerous occasions by Jim. Under the guise of teaching Phil about sex, his brother had engaged him in all sorts of acts that left the boy confused and ashamed. Why was he unable to enjoy these acts that his brother said should be so pleasurable? he once asked his mother. She was horrified and violently disciplined Jim, who began to beat Phil regularly in retaliation.

After several years of grappling privately with these reconstructed memories, Phil set about trying to corroborate them. He approached his sister, who was eleven years older, and without cuing her as to his own specific memories, he asked whether any strange things had gone on at the time he was about 8 and she was about 19. She confirmed all his memories of his father's threats.

Then he set about testing his memories of Jim. First, he looked for other evidence of sexual abuse at his brother's hands. He spoke with his younger brother, who not only acknowledged having also been abused, but recalled an episode where a neighbor had called his mother to say that she never wanted the eldest brother to come anywhere near her young son again. Finally, in a letter, Phil confronted his elder brother, who acknowledged his acts of abuse. Even as an adult, however, he continued to justify them as an earnest attempt to teach Phil the facts of life.

Recovering these memories was accompanied by considerable emotional pain, including a suicide attempt and hospitalization. But after undergoing therapy, Phil experienced great relief. Now large portions of his childhood made sense to him. He understood for the first time why he feared all male authority figures, and in the years that followed, he was able to discriminate between benevolent and hostile bosses and supervisors. He developed good relationships with mentoring figures. He also now understood his discomfort with physical intimacy, and was able to establish intimate relationships for the first time in his life.

In Phil's case, we see a clear instance of traumatic events that were at first forgotten, but later recovered and corroborated. Such recollections are called *recovered memories*. To date, scientists do not understand how memories can be recovered this way—but they can. Ross Cheit, professor of public policy at Brown University, tells a story similar to Phil's in that he was abused as a child, forgot about it, later remembered the abuse, and corroborated it. He has since collected many other stories of corroborated cases of recovered memories, which he has published on his website.[15]

Representing the other side of the debate between recovered versus false memories are the members of the several-thousand-strong False Memory Syndrome Association.[16] This group asserts that a great deal of damage is done by therapists who attempt to help their patients recover memories of child abuse with such excessive zeal that they actually suggest "false memories," which their clients come to believe are true. In the process, according to this point of view, innocent people are accused, families are torn asunder, and patients end up traumatized by events that never happened.

Several cases of "false memory syndrome" have been brought to court, and judgments have been rendered against therapists. I could choose any of a number of cases to illustrate this phenomenon, but I may as well pick the one with the biggest financial settlement so far—$10.6 million levied against the hospital and the psychiatrists who treated the patient who brought the suit.

Of Human Meatloaf and the High Priestess of Satan

Patricia Burgus was referred to Rush-Presbyterian Medical Center in Chicago for the treatment of depression following the birth of her second child.[17] One of her treating psychiatrists had been a leader in a movement that emphasized the importance of recovering childhood memories. Burgus alleged that while undergoing psychiatric treatment including drugs and hypnosis over a six-year period, she was persuaded that she was a high priestess in a satanic cult, that she had been abused by numerous men, that she herself had abused her own children, and that she had eaten ground-up human flesh.

On one occasion, Burgus claimed, her therapists had agreed to test some hamburger meat brought in by her husband to determine whether it contained human parts. She was given to believe that her own children, who were 4 and 5 years old at the time, were in danger from the cult, and the children were admitted to the same hospital for almost three years, ostensibly for their protection.

Burgus was diagnosed as suffering from multiple personality disorder (MPD) and was told she had many different personalities. But she claimed that on more than one occasion, her psychiatrist confused her personalities with those apparently belonging to other patients. For example, she was played a tape of what she was told was one of her sessions, supposedly with her talking in a childlike voice. When the recorded voice reverted to a more normal speaking voice, however, she recognized it as belonging to another patient.

After a period of reflection, Burgus concluded that she did not suffer from MPD and that all the horrific events had not happened as she had been led to believe. She sued her two psychiatrists and the hospital, and on the day that the trial was to commence, her lawyers settled for $10.6 million, of which the hospital agreed to pay $3 million. The treating psychiatrists were responsible for the rest of the money, and the leading psychiatrist was removed from the state medical register.

Clearly the stakes are high on both sides of the debate. On the one hand, it would be sad to invalidate recovered memories of genuine early abuse, leaving a patient unable to trust his own mind and feeling crazy. That could also aggravate the lonely and isolated feelings related to the earlier trauma. On the other hand, false memories can also cause great damage, exactly as charged.

My personal understanding of this confusing situation, based on case histories and my own clinical experience, is as follows:

- Memories of trauma can be forgotten and recovered. Often they return spontaneously, not necessarily during a course of therapy.[18]

- It is impossible to know whether such recovered events really occurred unless they are independently corroborated. But even if they cannot be corroborated, they should still be respected. Even if a person gets the facts wrong, the memories may still contain a core of emotional truth that needs to be taken seriously.

- In some people with psychiatric problems such as obsessive-compulsive disorder, memories of early abuse disappear after their illness is treated.[19] So is the newly healthy mind repressing true but destructive memories? Or is the limbic news—and the story that goes with it—imaginary, a product of the illness?

- Memories do not have the accuracy of photographs and videotapes. They are subject to distortion by time, by new information, and even by the simple act of telling the story.[20]

- False memories can be instilled during therapy and in experimental situations. This is more likely to occur when hypnosis and other techniques involving imagery and suggestion are used.

The bottom-line message to patients dealing with the consequences of early abuse is *caveat emptor*. Choose a therapist who is respectful of early memories, but not overzealous in pursuing them. For the therapist dealing with a history of suspected abuse, it is a fine balancing act to support a person's memories—including bodily sensations and vague half-recollected fragments—yet avoid participating in the construction of false memories.[21] Two stories, one from my personal life and one from my case files, show my own struggle to do the right thing in such delicate circumstances.

When my son was a toddler, 3 or 4 years old, he liked all his babysitters except for Ellie. When he knew she was due to baby-sit, he would protest vigorously, and when she arrived, he was clearly unhappy. He never complained about any of the other sitters. I asked him what it was about Ellie that he didn't like. He couldn't say. Had she scolded him, hurt him, or touched him in an uncomfortable way, I asked. He said she had not. I never did find out why he didn't like Ellie. But the fact that he didn't like her was reason enough to stop asking her to sit.

I could have persisted in questioning my son, but I felt it would get me nowhere. In fact, it has since been found that children are highly suggestible and that repeated questioning will influence their responses. Regardless, the boy's limbic response was giving him and us the message, "Ellie is bad for me." That was his limbic truth and we respected it even in the absence of concrete evidence. We know that there are times when the amygdala stores information but the hippocampus does not. We have yet to fully understand all the circumstances under which this may happen.

In dealing with someone who might have been abused, we may never be able to establish exactly what actually happened. But that does not mean we should neglect the limbic truth, a person's core conviction that something bad happened, something that might have altered his or her life.

Alice was a patient of mine who had been in an abusive marriage for several years. Now, in a second marriage, to a husband who treated her well, she found herself obsessively wanting to reconnect with her abusive first husband. She had a persistent dream that a man was breaking into her home and attacking her. In the dream she berated her mother for not locking the front door and protecting her. An obvious interpretation of the dream was that Alice had been abused as a child and was angry at her mother for not having protected her. Her marriage to a violent man could be understood as a reenactment of her earlier abuse, which she was now perpetuating by hankering after him.

Well, I never did detect any evidence of such abuse. Alice and I worked together for several years. She began to recognize how awful her ex-husband had been and stopped obsessing about him. Instead she began to appreciate her current husband and focused her efforts on her second marriage and family. Rather than pursuing speculations about early abuse, I helped Alice tune in to her feelings and recognize what was in her best interest.

I was also influenced by the growing body of data indicating that memories retrieved under hypnosis are not necessarily true even though they may be held with great conviction (more conviction, in general, than those retrieved in a regular state). I was concerned about the possibility of implanting false memories, harming Alice and her relationships in the process. Yet had memories of past abuse emerged spontaneously, I would have listened to them and taken them seriously.

There may be times when someone feels as though it is important to find out the truth—the facts of what happened. But if that is to be accomplished, it cannot be done by memory alone. Corroborating evidence is required. Absent such evidence, one has only limbic facts, though in many instances limbic facts may be sufficient. The amygdala is imprecise, but it is quick. It might mistake a snake for a stick, but it can get you out of harm's way. And that is why it is important to listen to your limbic news, the amygdala and other parts of the brain where meanings are registered, because they may be giving you information that can save your life.

Turning away from rhetoric, let us examine the data, much of it quite recent, that supports these two very different phenomena, false memory and recovered memory.

We Can Remember It for You Wholesale: Evidence for False Memories

In the movie *Total Recall*, based on the short story "We Can Remember It for You Wholesale," by Philip Dick, memories are implanted into the brains of characters who then incorrectly believe that they have had certain experiences. An entertaining pretext for a science fiction movie turns out, bizarrely, to be quite feasible.

Ira Hyman, associate professor of psychology at Western Washington University, and colleagues quizzed college students about various events in their childhood, based on information provided by their parents.[22] Interspersed among the questions about real events were questions about events that never happened, such as an overnight hospitalization for an ear infection or a birthday party with pizza and a clown. Initially, the subjects did not recall the fictional incidents. But after being interviewed on several occasions, between 20 and 30 percent of them did evidence false memories. This finding is particularly important because, in the course of litigation, people are generally cross-examined many times over about the same events.

How might false memories occur? Apparently when you are asked whether an event happened, you run through the scenario in your mind to check it against your memory. The first time you do so, it may be clear that the event never occurred, but after thinking or talking about it several times, you create a "memory of it," based on visualizing the scenario. Later, it may be difficult to distinguish between this false memory and a true memory of something that actually happened.

The same type of situation can happen when you remind yourself that you need to tell somebody something. Afterward you may think you already did so, simply because you visualized doing so. In fact, Hyman has shown that telling people to imagine a fictitious event increases the likelihood of a false memory. He has also shown that the people most likely to create false memories either are highly suggestible, are highly skilled at creating visual images, or tend to have lapses of attention.[23]

Children are particularly suggestible when they are questioned repeatedly about an event. Stephen Ceci, professor of psychology at Cornell, and collaborators have questioned young children about events that never occurred, asking the same questions each week for ten weeks and encouraging them to think hard before replying. Some of the children began to remember the fictitious and unlikely events, such as getting a finger caught in a mousetrap. One young boy even provided extensive details, complete with a fictitious trip to the emergency room.[24] When they were later informed that the incidents did not occur, some of the children insisted that they had.

The technical term for remembering something but not remembering the source of the memory is *source amnesia*. In the case of the children and adults who were questioned several times, the memories presumably came from the questioning, rather than from the events themselves. Elizabeth Loftus, professor of psychology at the University of Washington, has conducted numerous studies on false memories. In one, students were shown a film of a robbery that involved a shooting.[25] Later they were shown a television report of the robbery that contained false details not included in the original film. When they were subsequently asked questions about the original film, many of them incorporated erroneous details from the report into their memories of the film. This is an example of source amnesia: The students remembered certain details, but not how they acquired them.

Modern Technology Defeats False Memories—Maybe

Plausibility appears to powerfully encourage false memories. In a study devised by Henry Roediger, professor of psychology at Rice University, a list of words was read to subjects. Afterward the subjects were asked to pick out the listed words from another list that was read to them. For example, one list included many words pertaining to sewing, not including "needle." Later, asked if "needle" was on the list, more than 80 percent thought it was and almost 60 percent were absolutely sure of it.[26]

In a more recent study, Roediger and colleagues successfully used position emission tomographic (PET) scans to discriminate between true and false memories.[27] Still reading out lists of words, the team examined which brain areas lit up when people identified words that really had been on the list—"true memories"—versus those that had not—"false memories." In both cases, an area close to the hippocampus known to be involved in recall lit up. But for true memories, an additional brain area glowed—a part of the cortex involved in the recognition of sounds.

Brain-wave patterns near the visual cortex may also pick out true from false memories. Ken Paller, associate professor of psychology at Northwestern University, found that people showed more electrical activity on the scalp near the visual cortex when reporting true (versus false) memories of words they had been shown.[28] These findings fit with other work suggesting, in general, that the visual cortex is more active during true than false memories.

In short, memories are often fragile and imperfect. They may change in the light of suggestion or later information, and certainly they cannot be automatically accepted as fact.

Evidence for Recovered Memories

People forget, and what they forget is often lost forever. In people with head injuries or Alzheimer's disease, for example, memories may be irretrievable, flatly gone. Lacking such a brain pathology, however, can highly charged emotional events be selectively blanked out, while other more neutral memories remain?

Yes, they certainly can, as evidenced by Phil, who completely forgot that his father had threatened to shoot the family and that his brother had molested him. Such a story seems commonplace to clinicians who deal with the victims of trauma, many of whom report having forgotten such incidents for years at a time. Researchers have found that between 20 and 59 percent of people who say they have been sexually abused also say there have been times in the past when they have forgotten either fully or partially the details of the abuse.[29] It may be that people avoid thinking of unpleasant events, which then fade from memory until some new event brings them to the surface.[30]

In a few studies researchers have confirmed a high incidence of forgetting by interviewing the subjects of documented abuse several years after the abuse took place. In one such study, researchers followed up on women and men who had been seen in hospital emergency rooms for sexual abuse in the mid-1970s.[31] Seventeen years later, 38 percent of the women and 55 percent of the men did not recall being abused. Even among the women who did recall, 16 percent reported a time in the past when they had forgotten. In a metastudy, between 32 and 60 percent of women and between 58 and 100 percent of men with a history of child sexual abuse *that had been corroborated by the courts* did not report that history when interviewed some twenty years later.[32]

Forgetting past trauma is less controversial than remembering what had previously been forgotten. Although it is impossible to know whether a recovered memory is true without independent corroboration, several corroborated cases are on record.[33] Since abuse often occurs surreptitiously, corroboration may not be available in many cases. For this reason, those cases where there is clear corroboration offer important evidence that memories can indeed be forgotten and then recovered.

Considering the importance and fragility of memory and the huge stakes involved in whether a memory is true or not, the question of recovered versus false memories is likely to be with us for a long time. As the technology that will enable us to discriminate between these two categories is developed, perhaps we will be able to look increasingly to science to resolve this perplexing issue.

Flashbulb Memories

Where were you when Kennedy was assassinated? That question is often asked of the members of the baby boom generation. Even though I was in South Africa, far away from the event, I clearly remember when I first heard the news. I was at a movie with a group of friends when the trail of words announcing the death of the great man flashed across the screen. I remember little about the movie, but it was unprecedented, in my experience, for a film to be interrupted in this way. What I do remember is the awed hush in the movie house as we digested the news. More recently, the attacks on the Twin Towers created flashbulb memories in the minds of the millions who saw the television images: the explosion of the first tower, the horrible moments of anticipation as the plane flew into the second tower, the ballooning flames, collapsing buildings, clouds of smoke, and flattened skyline, which represented a world changed in a single day.

Flashbulb memories are created not only by public events but also by important personal events. Click, flash, the thing is etched in your mind forever: the cap, the gown, the glowing face. That hushed circle at the bedside. The unmistakable sound of earth hitting a coffin. When these joys and sorrows are your own, you remember the details with far greater clarity than you do similar events you might have witnessed in the lives of your friends. It is your emotions that so intensify the details.

Imagine you heard a story about a boy who walks with his mother to a nearby hospital, where his father works as a laboratory technician. On the way, they pass a minor accident, which the boy finds interesting. At the hospital, the boy watches the staff as they go through a practice disaster drill. Now contrast that with another story that starts out the same way, but ends with the boy himself being involved in an accident. When he is hit by a runaway car, his feet are severed and he is critically injured. He is rushed to the hospital, where surgeons reattach his severed feet. Which story do you think would be more memorable? Which details would you remember best?

These two stories were used by researchers Larry Cahill and James McGaugh of the University of California at Irvine to test the impact of emotion on memory.[34] As you might expect, people remembered the emotional parts of the story far better than the neutral ones. So could it be, the researchers wondered, that the epinephrine and norepinephrine secreted in response to powerful emotions might strengthen certain memories? To find out, they used a common blood pressure medication, propranolol, which blocks the effects of epinephrine and norepinephrine.[35] And sure enough, when people took propranolol before being told the stories, they remembered the emotional details about the boy and the accident no better than they did the neutral, unemotional material. Emotional memories, then, are selectively strengthened when people are excited.

This research has important implications for people suffering from post-traumatic stress disorder, the long-term aftermath of trauma, who may benefit from propranolol. (For a complete discussion of this, see chapter 8). In general, people with PTSD have elevated levels of adrenaline and norepinephrine.[36] When experiencing traumatic memories, they release exaggerated amounts of these chemicals. Cahill suggests that these unfortunate people may be caught in a vicious cycle: Memories cause the release of these chemicals, which then strengthen the memories. He and his colleagues suggest that propranolol may interrupt this vicious cycle and are testing that idea currently.[37]

Another potential use of the drug propranolol is as a prophylactic in the immediate aftermath of a trauma—a rape, for example. Given in the emergency room, the propranolol might prevent the traumatic memory from being recorded so vividly that it leads to PTSD. The person would still remember the incident, but not with the extra intensity caused by the fight-or-flight hormones.

The amygdala coordinates the memory-enhancing effects of emotions, working hand in hand with its close neighbor the hippocampus.[38] We know that, because researchers have shown people horrifying movies while measuring the activity in their amygdala. The more active the amygdala, the larger the number of movies the subjects recalled.

I remember seeing one of the movies used in these studies while wandering around the exhibits at a professional meeting. The resourceful researchers had obtained authentic footage of a lion eating a tourist on the Angolan border in southern Africa. Although it had the grainy, bumpy quality of a home movie, it was riveting. The footage was credited to another tourist.

The group was watching lions feeding on a kill from the safety of their cars when a man holding a video camera got out of his car and kept shooting, presumably to get a close-up of the action. Someone in a nearby car waved a hand frantically through the window, urging him back in his car, but the man held up his free hand reassuringly, as if to say, "They are too busy working on the carcass. They won't mind me." What he didn't see was another lion close by, not involved in the feasting. The animal sprang at him, apparently out of nowhere, and felled him with a single graceful stroke of its massive paw. The last thing I recall was a leg going down the lion's throat, sock and shoe still in place.

This movie is all I can remember of the exhibits, an excellent illustration of how emotion consolidates memory.

Moods and Memories: The Story of the Prom Queen

Margaret was in her mid-thirties when she first consulted me. She was a striking beauty with jet black hair, a shapely figure, and a Marilyn Monroe smile. It was easy to see why she had been elected queen of the prom some twenty years before. Despite her good looks, Margaret's life had been hard. Her childhood was marred by a series of deprivations and traumas, and as a young adult, she lost a beloved brother to suicide. Since her teens Margaret had suffered from intermittent bouts of depression, brief but dark spells of sadness and despair that would alternate with short episodes of exaggerated good cheer.

While struggling to find a medication that would steady out her zigzagging moods, I encouraged her to talk about her life. She frequently discussed problems in her marriage, but it was hard to pin these down. Not only did her perceptions of her husband and their relationship change from week to week, but her memories of their past together kept changing as well. One week she would say that her marriage was hopeless, given all her husband's defects and the insults she had suffered at his hands. Yet the very next week, Margaret would insist that theirs was a match made in heaven. They were soul mates, and never again would she find someone who understood her so well or cared about her so deeply.

I pointed out these week-to-week inconsistencies to Margaret to no avail. When she was depressed, she could remember only the bad; when cheerful, only the good. And then finally I hit upon a drug that worked for her—the antidepressant Wellbutrin (bupropion), which was just being introduced into the United States at that time. Thereafter, Margaret's depressions dissolved, and her moods knit into a consistent state that was neither depressed nor ebullient.

Margaret was now able to evaluate her marriage in a more textured way. It was, she saw, neither terrible nor wonderful. Her husband was neither a rogue nor a saint. The couple separated, lived far apart for a time, and finally reunited. When I last spoke with her, they were living very happily together.

Margaret's story illustrates yet another aspect of conditioning, a phenomenon called state-dependent learning. Memories that are stored, or encoded, when someone is in a certain state of mind, such as depression, are most easily retrieved during that same state.[39] Margaret's memories varied so extremely because her moods were extreme.

The effect holds with less dramatic state changes, however.[40] A drug, a fragrance, a place—all will tend to bring back memories recorded in the presence of that same stimulus, especially emotional memories. A friend of mine, for example, recently visited the town where her late grandmother had lived. She is 52 and had last been to that town at the age of 8. Yet as soon as she got to the courthouse square, she found herself weeping, overwhelmed by painful memory, and she was able to drive directly to the place where her grandmother's house had been.

Here are some of the ways in which you can take advantage of state-dependent remembering:

- Fill your home and office with sounds, smells, and sights that are associated with the best times of your life. People do this instinctively, setting out photos of loved ones as well as mementos of fun adventures and happy times. You probably will not register these things consciously on a day-to-day basis, yet their presence will cheer and comfort you.

  To enhance the effect, move things around from time to time, so you see them freshly. Do this with scent, too. The smells of particular places and times can be surprisingly evocative—scented soap bought at a seaside resort, the lemon polish your mother used to use, cedar blocks. And some find pleasure in collecting things that remind them of happy days: seashells, coffee mugs, smooth stones, refrigerator magnets—whatever will bring back those memories.

- Do relaxation exercises such as deep breathing in the presence of a certain fragrance. Later, the smell alone will help you relax. This technique has been helpful for expectant mothers, who are given lavender to smell during their childbirth classes and then later during the delivery itself.

- Likewise, you can use a fragrance as a learning device. If you have something difficult yet important to memorize, try learning it while smelling a certain fragrance, then use the same fragrance as a memory cue.

Practice, Practice: Emotional Learning

Of course, you remember the old joke about a tourist in Manhattan who asks, "How do you get to Carnegie Hall?" The answer he's given is "Practice, practice." Everybody, it seems, knows that to get some-place you have to practice. In fact, modern technology has let us ob-serve large, physical changes in the brain when people practice.

For example, Thomas Ebert and colleagues at the University of Konstanz in Germany have imaged the brains of both violinists and nonmusicians.[41] In particular, they imaged those areas that regulate the function of the left and right hands. They picked those areas be-cause violinists require great skill to manipulate the fingers of their left hand, which they make dance over the strings very fast and in complex patterns. Their right hand they use simply to move the bow up and down. As expected, the part of the brain controlling the left hand was larger in the violinists than in the nonmusicians, whereas the right hand's brain area was similar in both groups.

Since these musicians build up that area over many years, you may well be wondering if there would be changes with less learning. Researchers Arvi Karni and Leslie Ungerleider and colleagues at the National Institute of Mental Health (NIMH) have tackled that ques-tion.[42] They taught people a simple motor task—touching their thumbs to their other fingers in a specific sequence, which activates the corresponding areas of the brain. After the subjects had practiced long enough to double their speed, the researchers found an expan-sion in the relevant parts of the brain, which persisted for many weeks.

These and other studies make it clear that when learning occurs, the brain reconfigures—not just one or two neurons, but tens or hun-dreds of millions of them, involving synapses by the billion. Neuroscientist Michael Merzenich, one of the leaders in this particu-lar field, and colleagues have described how New World owl monkeys can be taught the simple task of lifting food pellets out of a shallow well.[43] The skill was simple, one that the monkeys mastered in just a few days. Yet the new skill was accompanied by changes in fifteen to twenty separate areas in the cerebral cortex.

The researchers conclude that mastering a skill is accompanied by brain changes in all the specialized areas that handle the component subskills.

The tendency to grow new anatomical connections in response to experience turns out to be a ubiquitous feature of mammalian brains that can last a lifetime.[44] Already, this knowledge of brain plasticity is being used to help people with language disorders.[45]

These findings bear directly on emotional responses because emotional skills can be acquired and modified throughout life. If you have a pattern of emotional reaction that gets you into trouble, the good news is that *you can change it*, using the very same type of neurons and neuronal networks you use when acquiring any other skills. To learn how to respond appropriately, you will need to practice.

Good parents instinctively help their children develop good emotional habits. They teach their children how to comfort themselves when they are upset. They talk to them about feelings. They encourage them to cooperate with their siblings and to develop friendships outside the home. In a thousand ways a good parent helps a child expand those parts of the brain responsible for emotional skills. The development of such skills has been called *emotional intelligence* or *emotional competence*, which is the topic of the next chapter.

Unfortunately, not all parents are good ones, so many children acquire bad emotional habits. They may, for example, be unable to recognize or acknowledge their own feelings. They may be unable to comfort themselves. They may not be capable of empathizing with others, or may develop an exaggerated sense of their own importance in the world. There are many things that can go wrong with a child's emotional development. Happily, many of these problems self-correct in later life, when the person is exposed to healthier ways of living. Others may require specialized help, however, because even though the key to learning is practice, bad practice makes for bad learning.

Say that you are a golfer who is having persistent trouble with your golf swing, no matter how hard you practice on the driving range. What would you do? Probably you would seek out a coach. Without coaching, you'd keep making the same old mistake with every swing. People who develop bad emotional habits do exactly that, as mental health professionals see time after time. Some people repeatedly get into the same type of bad relationships. Others have the same type of trouble with their bosses, again and again, job after job. When a bad emotional pattern runs that deep, practice needs to be guided by an outside observer, someone with the expertise to help break the cycle: a psychotherapist, in a word. The essence of psychotherapy is to help a person recognize troublesome patterns and learn new habits of emotional response, ones that will make life easier, more joyful, and more productive.

The good news is that psychotherapy works for many different emotional problems. I am confident that, increasingly, imaging studies will demonstrate the brain changes accompanying clinical improvement. In a study conducted by Dr. Lewis Baxter and colleagues at the University of California in Los Angeles, patients with obsessive-compulsive disorder developed more normal brain patterns following successful psychotherapy.[46] Similar changes have also shown up after OCD symptoms have been reversed with medication. By illustrating the brain changes that accompany effective treatment, imaging studies may guide us to faster and better ways of helping those with emotional difficulties.

From Memory to Molecules

Fear conditioning, that great discovery of Ivan Pavlov, occurs in such humble creatures as the fruit fly and the sea slug. It was in this latter creature, distinguished by its small number of large neurons, that Eric Kandel did much of the groundbreaking work in memory and learning that earned him the 2000 Nobel Prize for Medicine and Physiology. By now, Kandel and others have mapped out in exquisite detail how the release of a neurotransmitter at a synapse creates a memory.

As I mentioned before, neurons that fire together, wire together, creating a neural network. If the firing exceeds certain thresholds, the network becomes so stable that it can persist for years. This type of memory is called long-term memory, as opposed to short-term memory, which lasts for only minutes or hours. To convert short-term memories into long-term ones, the genes of the relevant neurons turn on and synthesize new protein, which, in turn, forms new synaptic connections.

Any number of excellent books explain practical ways to help make that happen—review the material on the same day, practice in several short stints rather than one long session, and so on. For our purposes here, I just want to point to two things that *interfere* with long-term learning: alcohol and stress.

Think about the delicate biochemistry of synapses coordinating throughout the brain, assessing thresholds and turning on genes; then the delicate strings of amino acid folding into precise patterns that create proteins; then the proteins linking . . . well, you can see why research shows that alcohol interferes with memory. The famous blackout is an extreme example. But alcohol can damage memory long before blackouts begin.

Another thing that can inhibit long-term memory is stress. When stressed, the brain directs the adrenal glands to secrete adrenaline and steroid hormones, such as cortisol, and these in turn influence the storage of memories. Small amounts of stress—such as when you need to pay close attention, for example—result in a small burst of these hormones, which stimulates memory consolidation.[47] Massive stresses, on the other hand, cause huge amounts of these hormones to flood into the bloodstream, which can have the opposite effect, inhibiting the storage of memory. Anybody who has ever blanked out in a big exam knows exactly what I mean. Of course we did not evolve to take exams. Over the course of evolution, it might have been adaptive to consolidate memories of emotional significance, but forget anything so horrifying as to incapacitate.

Newly encoded memories are not very stable.[48] They can be disrupted by several means, such as electroconvulsive shock, and now by drugs that inhibit protein synthesis, thereby keeping short-term memories from converting to long.[49] Even memories already in storage, however, can be wiped out once they have been recalled. It would appear that when old memories are retrieved, they become once more labile and may need to be reconsolidated. In a recent study using rats, Joseph LeDoux and colleagues found that conditioned fear could in fact be disrupted by a protein synthesis inhibitor.[50]

This work has interesting implications for people who suffer from traumatic memories that they cannot escape. In the future, they may go to a psychiatrist to recall their painful memories, take a medication, and leave with the memories expunged—a sort of psychic surgery. If that were even possible, however, it would require great caution. We are, after all, very much a product of our memories, and removing a memory amounts to removing a part of oneself. It might well cause unanticipated harm.

Anticipating Freud by several centuries, Shakespeare, in the character of Lady Macbeth, depicts a woman enduring the painful aftermath of trauma. Some might say she brought it upon herself by egging on her husband to murder the King of Scotland. Nevertheless, the woman suffers. She walks in her sleep, trying in vain to wipe the blood from her hands. The king, concerned about his wife's sanity, asks her physician:

> Canst thou not minister to a mind diseased,
> Pluck from the memory a rooted sorrow,
> Raze out the written troubles of the brain,
> And with some sweet oblivious antidote
> Cleanse the stuff'd bosom of that perilous stuff
> Which weighs upon the heart?[51]

Current research suggests that such an antidote may be close at hand—another dividend of the Emotional Revolution.

Chapter 5

Emotional Intelligence or Competence

I MAGINE that it is the day after your twentieth high school reunion and you are reviewing what has become of your classmates. Some turned out just as you would have predicted, but others surprised you. Jack, for example, who was a mediocre student, has become a multimillionaire. At the reunion, he was overflowing with good cheer and seemed passionately engaged in his life. He has been much more successful than Henry, the class valedictorian.

Jack is managing a large number of people, several of whom have doctoral degrees, though he himself barely managed to squeak through college. It was a pleasure to chat with him as he asked after your family and career and seemed genuinely pleased with your accomplishments. Henry, on the other hand, was withdrawn. He spoke at length about his membership in Mensa, the society for people with high intelligence quotients (IQs), and complained about the unfairness of the world. You took the first opportunity to excuse yourself and get a drink.

While Jack and Henry are fictional stereotypes, we have all encountered people whose success seems out of line with their academic achievement. Observations such as these have led to popular enthusiasm about the concept of *emotional intelligence*, inspired in large measure by Daniel Goleman's best-selling book by that title. Emotional intelligence courses are being taken by people in all walks of life, from schoolchildren to business managers.[1] *Time* magazine even wrote a major story on the topic, asking on its cover, "What's your EQ?" and responding, "It's not your IQ. It's not even a number. But emotional intelligence may be the best predictor of success in life, redefining what it means to be smart."[2]

This type of public enthusiasm raises important questions. What exactly is emotional intelligence? Is EQ (emotional quotient) a reliable measure that should take its place alongside IQ in the pantheon of psychological measurements? Does emotional intelligence really predict success in life and, if so, to what degree? These are some of the issues I address here, based both on scientific studies and on my clinical and personal experiences.

What Is Emotional Intelligence?

The concept of personal intelligence was first introduced by Howard Gardner, a professor of education at Harvard University, who expanded the idea of intelligence from the traditional two forms, verbal and nonverbal, to seven forms.[3] Among the seven were two that deal with personal skills—one involving the capacity to look within at the workings of one's own emotional world, and the other an ability to perceive emotions in others.

The term "emotional intelligence" was coined by Yale psychologists John D. Mayer and Peter Salovey,[4] whose latest definition of the concept follows:

Emotional Intelligence (as Defined by Mayer and Salovey)

Perception, Appraisal, and Expression of Emotion

Ability to:
- identify emotion in one's physical and psychological states
- identify emotion in other people and objects
- express emotions accurately, and express needs related to those feelings

- discriminate between accurate and inaccurate, or honest and dishonest, expressions of feelings

Emotional Facilitation of Thinking

Ability to:
- redirect and prioritize one's thinking based on the feelings associated with objects, events, and other people
- generate or emulate vivid emotions to facilitate judgments and memories concerning feelings
- capitalize on mood swings to take multiple points of view; ability to integrate these mood-induced perspectives
- use emotional states to facilitate problem solving and creativity

Understanding and Analyzing Emotional Information; Employing Emotional Knowledge

Ability to:
- understand how different emotions are related
- perceive the causes and consequences of feelings
- interpret complex feelings, such as emotional blends and contradictory feeling states
- ability to understand and predict likely transitions between emotions

Regulation of Emotion

Ability to:
- be open to feelings, both those that are pleasant and those that are unpleasant
- monitor and reflect on emotions
- engage, prolong, or detach from an emotional state, depending upon its judged informativeness or utility
- ability to manage emotion in oneself or others

Source: P. Salovey et al., "Current Directions in Emotional Intelligence Research." in M. Lewis and J. M. Haviland-Jones (eds) *Handbook of Emotions,* © Guilford Press, 2000. Used by permission.[5]

Defined in this way, emotional intelligence is a series of abilities to perceive and make use of the full range of emotion, much as conventional intelligence consists of verbal and spatial skills.[6] Others have defined emotional intelligence more broadly, so that it overlaps with features that have typically been considered part of personality or temperament.

Personality traits such as optimism or extraversion clearly involve emotions and may also be important in predicting success in life. For that reason, I will consider them here. Combining these qualities with emotional intelligence results in a set of qualities that I will refer to as emotional competence. Although emotional competence has not been formally defined, the term has been used by such experts in the field as Peter Salovey and Daniel Goleman,[7] and in commercial programs designed to improve the emotional skills of business managers.[8]

Notice that the skills that compose emotional intelligence, as listed by Mayer and Salovey, are cleverly arranged hierarchically, so that it is necessary to be adept at those higher up on the list before mastering those listed lower down.

Emotional Intelligence Versus Emotional Competence

One of my patients, a highly successful architect, confessed to me with some embarrassment, "I don't listen to my wife, which makes her mad. I tend to get angry and loud with the kids. That causes trouble at home. My problem is that although I have a very high IQ, I have a very low EQ."

While I was pleased to see my patient thoughtfully considering the attitudes and behaviors that were landing him in trouble, it concerned me that he was labeling himself as emotionally unintelligent. Over the years professionals have been reluctant to divulge IQ scores to test takers on the grounds that the scores sound so final and fixed, as if nothing else matters. Knowing the number might discourage some from reaching their full potential and induce others to rest on their laurels. I wondered whether my patient was limiting himself with this notion of "a low EQ."

Researchers have begun to develop tests to measure emotional intelligence, but at present these tests are in their early stages. So far, no one can make solid predictions on the basis of such measurements (let alone without them), which is another good reason not to discourage oneself with a label. So I told my patient, "We don't know exactly how to measure EQ right now, nor do we understand what it can predict, but we do know that your competency in handling emotions could use some improvement. Let's work on it."

Listening to Your Feelings

In a secluded clinic in the Arizona hills with a commanding view of a vast and rocky desert landscape, a group of men sit in a circle and describe how they are feeling. "This morning I feel frightened, angry, and guilty," says one. The others listen attentively but say nothing in response. "Today I feel joy and passion," a second man says. "Right now I am feeling lonely and ashamed," admits a third. So it goes until each has had his chance to speak.

The men come from different parts of the country, are of widely divergent ages, and have different occupations—white collar, blue collar, no collar at all. All that unites them is a shameful secret: They are unable to control their sexual behavior. One compulsively seeks out prostitutes. Another is engaged in a torrid affair that threatens to unravel a marriage to a wife he loves very much. A third is able to see women only as sex objects and laments his inability to form a lasting relationship.

Clinicians who work in the field of sex addiction, and addiction in general, agree that a central problem for addicts is understanding their own feelings and expressing them. Instead, they medicate emotion with their drug or behavior of choice. Accordingly, a critical step in recovering from any type of addiction is learning to answer the question, "How am I feeling?"

Recent research on substance abuse among 205 seventh and eighth-grade students from culturally diverse backgrounds suggests a possible protective role of emotional intelligence in helping young people abstain from drug use.[9] Young people with high overall scores on a test of emotional intelligence designed specifically for adolescents were significantly less likely to have ever tried smoking or to have smoked recently. In addition, they were less likely to report having drunk alcohol in the previous week.

Of course, it is not only addicts who benefit from being aware of their feelings—we all can. Being able to identify emotion in one's physical and psychological states, which I call tuning in to your limbic news, is listed first in Mayer and Salovey's emotional intelligence skills roster for good reason. It is from this skill that all the other elements of emotional intelligence follow.

Once addicts identify a feeling, they (or anyone, for that matter) can begin to develop better strategies for living with it. If the emotion is positive, they need to enjoy it, enhance it, and build upon it. If it is negative, they might find addictive drugs and behaviors to feel good in the short run, but to compound their problems in the long run. Better strategies include reaching out to a friend, exercising, relaxing, meditating, and attending a religious service. It is hard to find healthy strategies to manage feelings, however, without knowing what the feelings are in the first place. I see many patients, for example, who do not even know that they are angry.

Many of today's adults were raised in an era when people were encouraged to conceal their feelings. One patient of mine, for example, a very sensitive man and a successful artist, had been told by his mother to "flush your feelings down the toilet." Another, a middle-aged woman, was cautioned not to tell the teacher when her beloved grandfather died. This type of harmful emotional education may require reprogramming in later life, which is exactly what psychotherapy, or emotional intelligence programs, seek to accomplish.

Ten Strategies for Tuning In to Your Limbic News and Improving Your Emotional Competence

When all the complications of psychoanalytic theory are stripped away, it may well turn out that the heart of the treatment is simply having someone listen empathically to the details of your life, particularly those with an emotional charge. It is impossible, of course, for everyone to have a psychotherapist. In our modern medical system, you might be lucky to have any mental-health-care coverage at all. But you can become your own analyst. After all, Freud analyzed himself. Although it may not be easy to listen to your feelings, learning to do so is highly worthwhile.

Here are ten strategies for developing the ability to listen to your own emotions, the first and perhaps the most important element in emotional intelligence.

1. *Don't interrupt or change the subject.* One of the difficulties that arises in listening to feelings, whether your own or someone else's, is a strong inclination to interrupt or change the subject. Freud was taken to task for doing just this by one of his earliest patients, a wealthy middle-aged widow, who angrily told him to stop interrupting.[10] If feelings are uncomfortable, we may want to avoid them by interrupting or distracting ourselves. This may sometimes be a good idea, but unless you know what you are feeling, you will not be able to decide whether to focus on the reason for the feeling or to distract yourself from it.

   I would recommend, as an exercise, that you sit down at least twice a day and ask, "How am I feeling?" Then wait for the answer. It may take a little time for the feeling to arise. Allow yourself that small space of time, uninterrupted. For many of us, just asking the question may be something new.

2. *Don't judge or edit your feelings too quickly.* Although popular belief asserts that there is no right or wrong way to feel, there are indeed some ways of feeling that are more helpful than others.[11] One of the ultimate skills in emotional competence is to use and manage your own emotions. To do so, you need to have a good idea of what your emotions are. Say, for example, that you are walking around all day feeling angry at your boss—an extremely wearing state of affairs. You may want to act quickly, either judging the feeling (I have no right to be feeling this way—it's a good job) or editing it (I am not really so angry—get over it). This does not do justice to what the feeling is telling you. Instead, review the feeling carefully and try to understand

more about it. How bad is it? What seems to make it better or worse? Try not to dismiss your feelings before you have a chance to think them through. Often healthy emotions rise and fall in a wave, rising, peaking, and fading naturally. Your aim should be not to cut off the wave before it peaks.

3. *See if you can find connections between your feelings and other times you have felt the same way.* Take the same example of an employee going around constantly angry at his boss. After establishing what he is feeling, his next question should be, "When have I felt this way before?" That is exactly the kind of question a therapist might ask. For many people, the answer might be, "With my last boss and the one before him." That might lead to a realization that he has a general problem with authority figures, rather than a specific problem with one boss. Or the answer might be, "My boss makes me feel just like my father did." That might help the employee realize that he is misinterpreting ordinary instructions for high-handed commands such as the ones his father used to issue.

4. *Connect your feelings with your thoughts using both your limbic system and neocortex.* When you *feel* something that strikes you as out of the ordinary, it is always useful to ask, "What do I *think* about that?" A woman friend of mine was very excited about a man she was dating. He was handsome, smart, and good company. One evening, however, she needed to run an errand that would require her to drive through a dangerous part of town. She asked her boyfriend to help, but he declined, offering what she viewed as a feeble excuse. My friend recognized that she was upset, hurt, and angry at her boyfriend's behavior. But it was only when she began to *think* about her feelings that she could use the information they were giving her.

My friend concluded that her boyfriend did not really care about her well-being. She could foresee other times when he might let her down, leaving her feeling as she did now or, worse still, exposing her to harm. When she connected her powers of reason with her feelings, she could reach only one conclusion: She needed to break off the relationship. And she did so, in short order.

Fear of the logical outcome of a feeling may discourage a person from recognizing the feeling in the first place. For example, my friend might have stopped herself from acknowledging her feelings about her boyfriend's behavior out of concern that she would then feel compelled to break off the relationship. People often confuse feelings and actions. Even if my friend were desperate to get married and have a family, she would still benefit from acknowledging her feelings. Once she brought them out in the open, she would be able to balance her hurt and anger against her desire for a family and her fear of being alone. She would be able to evaluate her options and determine whether this boyfriend was indeed her last best prospect for marriage. She could weigh how it might feel never to get married against how it might feel to marry this particular man.

Often one of our feelings will contradict others, and that's normal. Listening to all our feelings is like listening to all the witnesses in a court case. Only by admitting all the evidence will you be able to reach the best verdict. To recognize that feelings are often complex and not necessarily uniform is an advanced form of emotional intelligence, one well worth cultivating.

5. *Listen to your body.* The body, as we know, is an important repository of feelings. As you may recall, researchers using the gambling game were able to detect bodily changes, such as an increase in skin conductance (GSR), when subjects contemplated picking cards from risky card decks. These researchers noted that such bodily changes often occurred before any behavioral changes. You can use your bodily reactions as a clue to what is going on with your emotions.

For example, a gnawing pain in your stomach while driving to work may be a clue that your job is a major source of stress and anxiety. A tremor and flutter of the heart when you pick up a girl you have just started to date may be a clue that this could be "the real thing." Seeing your knuckles tense and whiten on the steering wheel as you approach your home may suggest that all is not well in your marriage. If you allow these bodily sensations to percolate through into consciousness, the underlying feelings that they signal will then be available to you to process with your powers of reason.

The intensity of your bodily sensations can help you gauge

the importance of particular emotions. Again, listen to your limbic news. J. K. Rowling, author of the fabulously successful Harry Potter series, describes how when she first conceived the idea of Harry Potter, she felt excitement throughout her body. This was an indication to her that she had hit upon an important creative idea, not just another ho-hum notion. When I first recognized the syndrome of seasonal affective disorder, my body registered that same type of excitement. I was reading through questionnaire responses from people with similar stories and similar reactions to environmental light when I realized that my colleagues and I had stumbled on a new syndrome with a potentially new type of treatment! I literally shivered with excitement.

6. *If you don't know how you're feeling, ask someone else.* The famous psychologist Donald Hebb observed that others are often better judges of how a person is feeling than is the person himself.[12] Sometimes I can tell that a patient is depressed just by glancing at his face and posture from across the waiting room, or by his tone of voice on the phone. This fact often surprises patients, who may be working hard to cover up (from themselves more than from me) how bad they feel.

People seldom realize that others are able to judge how they are feeling.[13] I have often been surprised at the transparency of my own feelings when I think I am doing a good job of concealing them. In this regard, I am not alone, even among therapists. In my first year of psychiatric residency I was assigned to a psychoanalyst, who was to supervise me in treating a patient with psychotherapy. He cordially asked me what my major interest was in psychiatry, and I replied, perhaps too candidly, that I planned to become a researcher. On hearing that, his face blanched, his lips narrowed, and hands trembling, he removed his eyeglasses and put them in their case. "If that is your major interest," he asked, "why on earth did you come to this program? Don't you know that Columbia is famous for its psychoanalytic teaching?" I muttered something and then said, "Excuse me, but you seem to be quite angry about this." He said slickly, "Not that I'm aware of." And I thought to myself, "So much for the value of insight."

The transparency of our emotions harks back to their evolutionary origins, because an important function of emotions is to communicate. In animals, for example, displays of anger are warning signals. Back off, that snarl announces, or risk a fight. At some level I was aware that my analytic supervisor was threatened. In fact, I later learned the department was in upheaval because power and resources were being shifted away from psychoanalysis toward biological psychiatry.

After that initial encounter I was more circumspect, and my supervisor and I got along quite well. Years later, when I met him at a departmental reunion, he greeted me in a very friendly way and told me how proud he was of my research. To his credit, this man had long since processed his initial anger and moved on to other, more constructive emotions. For my part, in the intervening years I had matured and become more respectful of the analytic tradition he represented.

If you have any question about how you are feeling, use the communicative function of emotions to clarify the matter. Simply ask someone who knows you (and whom you trust) how you are coming across. You may find the answer both surprising and illuminating.

7. *Tune in to your unconscious feelings.* Science has now confirmed not only that many of our emotions are unconscious, but also that conscious and unconscious fearful stimuli are processed differently. By bringing the unconscious into consciousness, we bring the power of the human neocortex to bear upon problems experienced by the more ancient part of the brain, the limbic system. How can you become more aware of your unconscious feelings? You can use the techniques pioneered by Freud, not by undergoing psychoanalysis, but by paying careful attention to certain ways that the unconscious can manifest.

- *Try free association.* While in a relaxed state, allow your thoughts to roam freely, but watch where they go. This will often lead you in useful directions. In particular, it may help you gain access to your unconscious feelings. Imagine, for example, that you are going about your day as usual, when all of a sudden, for no clear reason, you feel bothered and somewhat down. You consider all the obvious reasons for feeling down (hunger, anger, loneliness, fatigue), but none seems to apply. So you track back along a train of thought, wondering what was going on when you *first* felt down.

After a minute's thought you remember that just before your mood dropped, a friend was telling you about some expensive new item he had purchased—a car, house, motorboat, something you would love to have but cannot afford. You felt envious, then ashamed to be displeased at your friend's good fortune. So you buried the feeling—but it still pulled you down. As you identify this sequence of thoughts and feelings, you experience a sense of lightness and your bad mood lifts. You still cannot afford the item, you still envy your friend, but somehow things feel better. The workings of your mind make sense to you, and you get on with your day.

A friend of mine, a professor in a high-pressured academic department, once told me how for years he overworked to the point of exhaustion, which made his life so unpleasant that he sought help. In therapy, he realized that the reason he overworked was so he would not have to envy other people. "I thought that if my plate was overflowing with good things," he said, "I wouldn't have to envy my friends for having more on their plates." But the resulting exhaustion was ruining his life.

"So what did you end up doing?" I asked. "I decided it was easier to envy," he said, a look of contentment crossing his face. This friend later left the academic world and moved to a beautiful part of the country. When I last spoke to him, he was happier than he had ever been.

Sometimes unpleasant feelings are easier to live with than all the complicated maneuvers we undertake to avoid them. Ultimately, they may lead us to a better way of life.

- *Analyze your dreams.* Freud called dreams the "royal road to the unconscious." In my experience, they can be quite useful in understanding what is going on under the surface. Dreams are usually remembered best shortly after waking. If you are interested in recalling your dreams, keep a notebook and pen at the side of your bed and jot down your dreams when they are freshest, as soon as you wake up. Pay special attention to dreams that repeat or are charged with powerful emotion. Quite often, the dream's meaning is apparent and you don't need a psychiatrist to interpret it.

A friend of mine was up for a major promotion. The other leading candidate was an older scientist, a major figure in the field and much admired by my friend, who was in a dilemma. Should he run against this revered researcher? At that point he had a dream in which he was driving too fast and was stopped by a cop, who gave him a ticket. As he looked up at the cop's face, he recognized that it was the revered scientist. Upon reflection, my friend realized that his main concern was not that he thought the other man was a better candidate, but that he was afraid of retaliation by this father figure. Once that was clear, he realized that he did very much want the job and that he did not in reality have anything to fear from his competitor. His reluctance to compete evaporated and he ended up getting the job.

Once again, we see how access to all feelings, especially the difficult or embarrassing ones, allows the process of reasoning to help resolve a conflict.

- *Examine your behavior.* Professor Roger MacKinnon, former director of the Columbia Psychoanalytic Institute, used to teach that the unconscious is like the wind. You cannot observe it directly, but you know which way it is blowing because of its effects on the trees and the clouds. In the same way, your unconscious feelings affect you and the people around you. Observing those effects can give you useful clues to your unconscious desires and fears.

Research bears this out. A group of cocaine addicts was allowed to self-medicate with various solutions of cocaine of unknown concentration.[14] The subjects thought that the solution with the lowest cocaine concentration contained no drug. But when the researchers tallied up the number of times they had administered this low concentration to themselves, they found the number was far higher than for the drug-free control solution. The addicts' behavior was a better guide to what they really wanted than their verbally expressed desires.

The degree of insight that people have about their unconscious feelings varies widely. Let us take the example of a man who has had relationships with many women, all of whom ended up furious at him. It is highly likely that he does something to make his girlfriends furious. Perhaps he is secretly angry at all women and becomes provocative under certain circumstances, which triggers their fury.

One such man might say, "All women are bitches. No matter how hard you try, they always end up attacking you." That individual has no insight into the fury he provokes. Another man in a similar situation might say, "I don't know why it happens, but my relationships always end up with my girlfriends furious at me." This man is taking an agnostic position, not excluding the possibility that he is doing something to produce this outcome. A third man might say, "I must be doing something to make women angry because they always end up furious at me." This last person is the most likely to benefit from therapy, as he is taking responsibility for this event that continues to recur in his life.

Repeated self-defeating behaviors are the bread and butter of a therapist's practice. These include women who love too much and repeatedly get into abusive relationships with men; men and women who keep running into trouble with authority figures, which prevents them from realizing their potential; and competent people who work very hard to achieve something, only to run out of steam at the very last moment and let success slip away.

In all these cases, there is usually some unconscious force at work, like the wind, blowing the branches of their lives around and upsetting their most deeply cherished dreams and ambitions.

8. *Ask yourself: How do I feel today?* Just as you brush your teeth, floss, shower, and take care of yourself in other ways, you need to check in on your feelings for a few minutes at least once a day. Start by rating your overall sense of well-being, such as your feelings of joy, good cheer, energy, and vitality; and your overall negative feeling, such as sadness, irritability, fear, and anger. Give both your overall sense of well-being and your overall neg-

ative feeling a score of between 0 and 100, where 0 is the lowest possible and 100 is the highest possible. Write your scores down in a log book or journal. If your feelings seem extreme or out of the ordinary one day, take an extra minute or two to think about any ideas or associations that seem to be connected with the feeling.

Alternatively, you might want to use the slightly more complicated Positive and Negative Affect Scale (PANAS), developed by David Watson, professor of psychology at the University of Iowa, and colleagues (see page 105).[15] This questionnaire takes only a few minutes to complete. It consists of a list of 20 positive and negative feelings whose strength you rate using a scale of 1 to 5, where 1 is the least possible and 5 the most. To determine your score, add up all the numbers next to the positive items to form a total, then do the same with the negative items to form a second total.

Researchers have found that most undergraduates from Southern Methodist University in Texas scored between 22 and 38 on the positive items (the average was 30) and between 10.5 and 24.5 on the negative items (the average was 17.5). When similar students were asked to rate their feelings over the past week (instead of just today), their scores were on average about 2 points higher for both the positive and the negative items. The scores for the past year were about 5 points higher than the same-day scores for both the positive and the negative items. It makes sense that the longer the scoring interval, the more different types of feelings a person is likely to have.

Watson has used this scale in several research studies, as well as in a class in which students used it to monitor their moods. "If you want to manage and change your moods, you have to know where they are," he explains. "Most people don't do that naturally."

When mood shifts are large or sudden, Watson finds that most people notice. But when moods change in subtler ways, the shift is harder to pinpoint. Over time, changes may not be apparent even when they reach severe levels. Watson draws an analogy to the famous experiment of the frog in a jar of water: If the water is suddenly heated, the frog will jump out of the jar. But if the water is heated slowly, degree by degree, the frog will die because it does not notice how hot the water is becoming.

"If you're generally satisfied with your life, then tracking your mood probably doesn't matter," Watson says. "But if you think there is room for improvement, it can be extremely helpful." For best results, don't count on your memory, but track your moods in real time, because retrospective ratings are colored by general impressions. For example, women report greater premenstrual mood changes when asked to rate them retrospectively than when they track them day by day.[16] In another experiment, researchers asked people how they felt the previous Monday. Perhaps because many people associate Mondays with blue moods, they tended to rate their mood as low compared to the mood rating actually recorded on the Monday in question.[17]

In an analogous way, your daily ratings may reveal that things are not as bad (or as good) as you believe. For example, Watson finds that his students often expect their weekends to be more fun than they turn out to be. Observing such discrepancies can be very helpful. For example, you might decide not to worry about things that often turn out to be better than you expect, such as Monday mornings.

Watson and colleagues have found that positive feelings tend to be low early in the morning, high during the middle part of the day, and low again in the late evening. For this reason, you may get more useful results if you take your mood inventory in the midmorning (between 11:00 and 11:30 A.M.) or early evening (around 7:00 P.M.). Individuals differ, however, and it is helpful to know what times of the day are your best and worst. Then you can reserve the times when you function best for your most demanding tasks. Watson finds that until they track their moods systematically, his college students often misidentify their peak. For example, many believe that they are at their best in the late evening, which is seldom the case. Knowing your emotional rhythms can be vitally important for optimal time management.

One surprise from Watson's studies is that positive and negative feelings do not always change in tandem.[18] For example, just before exams, students often report more negative feelings, but their level of positive feelings may not drop. These results are consistent with what we know from brain imaging—namely, positive and negative feelings run on separate circuits.[19]

Once you know accurately how you are feeling, you can begin to ask why, which is critical to managing your moods. Watson encourages his students to be their own mood detectives. One useful question is, "Why am I not feeling good?" For example, are you sleep deprived, physically ill, hungry, or worried? If so, obviously you should attend to the cause of your low mood, not just the mood itself. Moods can be an important guide to what is going on in your world, your body, and your brain. You need to recognize and understand them if you want to function at your best and enjoy your life to the fullest.

In contrast, some people experience mood swings as part of a mood disorder. In these individuals, the moods themselves must be addressed directly, a subject I cover in chapters 11, 12 and 13.

9. *Write your thoughts and feelings down.* James Pennebaker, professor of psychology at the University of Texas at Austin, and his colleagues have developed a very simple technique for examining thoughts and feelings—have people write them down.[20] Research has shown that this simple exercise, which need take no more than a few hours spread over a week, can help profoundly. The details of this writing exercise and its benefits are described elsewhere in this book (on pages 201–205), as well as in Pennebaker's own book, *Opening Up*.[21]

10. *Know when enough is enough.* While self-knowledge is undoubtedly a good thing, there comes a time to stop looking inward and shift your focus to the world outside. In fact, it can be positively unhealthy to be too introspective. This often used to occur when depressed people went into psychoanalysis. They were encouraged to dwell on their depressive ruminations, consider the origins of their unhappy thoughts, and remember similar unhappy thoughts from the past. The net effect was to make them more miserable. We now realize that depressed people should be assisted in shifting their thoughts away from their depressed feelings and along more hopeful channels.

Several studies have shown that encouraging people to dwell upon negative feelings, such as anger, fear, or depression, can amplify these feelings.[22] To get the benefits of insight, without making matters worse, don't dwell on these feelings too much.

In the writing-exercise studies, for example, Pennebaker and colleagues encouraged people to deal with their feelings about a stressful event for twenty minutes only, then put the task aside. In addition, it is important to reflect on your thoughts as well as on your feelings. Embrace the balancing influence of reason. And any time you find your thoughts and feelings going round and round in an endless loop, stop them in their tracks. Emotional intelligence involves not only the ability to look within, but also to be present in the world around you.

The PANAS
(Positive and Negative Affect Scale)

This scale consists of a number of words that describe different feelings and emotions. Read each item and then mark the appropriate answer in the space next to that word. Indicate to what extent you have felt this way *today*. Use the following scale to record your answers:

1	2	3	4	5
very slightly or not at all	*a little*	*moderately*	*quite a bit*	*extremely*

_____ P _____	interested		_____ N _____	irritable
_____ N _____	distressed		_____ P _____	alert
_____ P _____	excited		_____ N _____	ashamed
_____ N _____	upset		_____ P _____	inspired
_____ P _____	strong		_____ N _____	nervous
_____ N _____	guilty		_____ P _____	determined
_____ N _____	scared		_____ P _____	attentive
_____ N _____	hostile		_____ N _____	jittery
_____ P _____	enthusiastic		_____ P _____	active
_____ P _____	proud		_____ N _____	afraid

P = Positive Affect item   N = Negative Affect item

Perceiving Emotions in Others

Be you man or mouse, you need to be able to perceive emotions in others. Should you flee? Should you approach? We all need to be able to send and receive the relevant clues, a task for which the brain has specialized regions. The amygdala, for example, responds to frightening cues, which is why people with a damaged amygdala have difficulty recognizing untrustworthy faces. As one would expect for hard-wired brain functions, certain facial expressions, such as grief, rage, surprise, or disgust, are recognized universally in all cultures. (Darwin was the first to observe this.)[23] Chimpanzees can also recognize basic emotions such as anger and fear in the facial expressions of other chimps, and even in their human keepers.[24]

Humans have dozens of different muscles devoted to facial expressions.[25] By using them in different combinations, we communicate nuances of feeling. Consider, for example, the many different types of smiles there are, and how easily most people can tell a social smile from one of pure joy. That's because a joyful smile involves both the mouth and the eyes, but while the mouth is under voluntary control, the eye muscles are not. When we force a smile, therefore, it looks fake because the widening mouth is not accompanied by changes in the eyes. The ability to produce a radiant smile on demand is one of the great assets of such highly paid actresses as Julia Roberts.

A slight curl of the lip will detract from the joyful quality of a smile, making it look sardonic or contemptuous; that may relate to the upturning lip we see in the typical expressions of disgust. A slight droop at the corners of the mouth, on the other hand, will imbue a smile with a bittersweet, slightly sad, or mysterious quality. As for the mysterious smile of Mona Lisa, a new theory holds that her smile is ambiguous because it looks sad when viewed directly, but happy when seen with peripheral vision.[26] People wait in line to see that smile—a testimonial, I would say, to the depth of our long-evolved need to read faces right. The Mona Lisa's smile fascinates us because we can't quite get it.

Even highly intelligent people misread faces, thus misinterpreting the feelings of others. One young patient of mine, a boy who had been caught in a flagrant lie, came to see me together with his father.

Although his father was clearly both hurt and embarrassed by his behavior, the son was unable to read the pain in his face. Once I showed him how to see it, however, he understood the hurt he had caused, became remorseful, and promised to be honest in future. It is possible that some people have a type of facial dyslexia, while others are especially gifted at detecting subtleties of expression.

Reading body language is another valuable skill. When someone is ashamed, for example, he may lower his head and hunch his shoulders, as though trying to look smaller. A gracious person, reading these cues, might then go easy, even without any conscious thought. Very few of us enjoy giving pain. It's also true, at the tit-for-tat level, that adding to the pain of others is a poor policy. The tables may turn sometime.

Each of the major emotions can be detected by properly deciphering the combination of facial and bodily expressions. Reading her husband's angry demeanor, a prudent wife might wait for another occasion to raise a contentious issue. Detecting his wife's tense posture and clenched knuckles whenever he drives fast, a wise husband will slow down so that they are both able to enjoy the ride.

The capacity to read body language is, once again, separate from conventional intelligence. One of my patients, a young woman, has an IQ score of 84, well below average. She is so successful at reading people's bodily responses, however, that she has become a much-sought-after massage therapist. She has succeeded in helping people with aches and pains after others have failed, because of her special talents.

It is important to remember that the range of most human talents, including reading others, can probably be described as a bell-shaped curve, and that talent is only part of the ability. Even if we will never be able to play golf like Tiger Woods or read bodies like my patient, most of us can improve with effort and practice.

I Feel Your Pain: The Value of Empathy

"I feel your pain," was an expression used by President Clinton early in his first term. Later it was appropriated by comedians, who loved to say it in an Arkansas accent, and with a glee that suggested, perhaps unfairly, that the original sentiment was less than genuine. I would suggest, though, that part of President Clinton's enormous political success was his capacity to convey to others that he really did share their pain and would address their concerns.

Empathy means something beyond the ability to perceive accurately what another person is experiencing.[27] Empathy implies that one actually picks up something in others, like a vibration, and feels it too in some way. However it occurs, empathy involves some degree of sharing the emotion, as well as a compassionate response. It is an important element in emotional intelligence.

I remember once calling various people while searching out a day care provider for my son, who was six at the time. The first few candidates sounded quite unsuitable. Then I reached a woman who articulately and intelligently outlined the type of day-care services she provided. As she talked, I could hear a child screaming in the background. "Excuse me," she said politely, "but I have a very tired boy here. Can you hold a moment while I settle him down?"

I heard her murmuring some reassurances to the boy. Perhaps she gave him something to eat or drink. Within a few minutes all was quiet and she returned to the phone and continued with the conversation, unruffled. That was someone whom I wanted to have looking after my son, I determined, because of the empathy she showed toward her own son. She realized that he was tired, not misbehaving. She placed his needs before mine. I liked that. She turned out to be a great day-care provider and remains a good friend many years later.

Neuroscientist Paul MacLean suggests that empathy evolved in mammals along with the long period of immaturity, the months to years during which young mammals need care.[28] It's essential to respond to young ones' distress—and we do, even across species. So empathy is to some degree biologically programmed. Even newborn infants will respond to cries of distress from another infant.[29] Researchers have found that infants cry less, however, in response to other equally unpleasant noises or to tape recordings of their own cries.[30] So there is, it would seem, something innate about the capacity to respond to others.

As infants begin to distinguish themselves from other people in the second year of life, their expressions of empathy move outward. Researchers who have studied the way children behave toward adults who appear injured have found that prosocial acts such as hugging or patting the "victim" start at the beginning of the second year. The capacity for concern and caring increases with age, and girls show these qualities to a greater extent than boys.[31]

The capacity of young children to show caring is an amazing thing to witness. I remember observing with delight a small child in a stroller eating ice cream with a spoon that she could barely manipulate. I was amazed when she scooped out some ice cream and extended the spoon toward her mother. It struck me as remarkable that someone so young would be willing to part with something so delicious in the interest of some higher need, perhaps empathy.

There are wide individual differences in the ability to experience and express empathy. Psychopaths, for example, show low levels of empathy.[32] Psychologist Carolyn Zahn-Waxler, a researcher in the Section on Developmental Psychopathology at the National Institute of Mental Health, suggests that such low levels of empathy may be related to low activity levels in the sympathetic nervous system.[33] Research suggests that a low resting heart rate at age 3 predicts high aggression levels at age 11.[34]

At the other extreme, too much empathy can also be bad. Research shows that children who have too much empathy are at an increased risk for developing depression later in life.[35] Several of my adult patients have developed excessive empathy as an early sign of relapse into depression, for example crying at the sight of a dead squirrel at the side of the road or at a television image of a hungry child in a distant country. While these images are undoubtedly sad, these same people do not generally respond so powerfully when they are feeling well.

In addition to innate capacity, environmental influences also play a role in empathy. Harsh, abusive parenting impairs a child's ability to show concern for others.[36] For example, maltreated two-year-olds are more likely to be aggressive and unempathic toward distressed peers, a trend that can develop over time. In hostile environments, by the time children reach elementary school, their teachers report that many show abnormally low levels of concern for others.

How to Raise an Empathic Child[37]

According to research, the following six actions will help parents encourage the development of empathy in their child.

1. *Model empathy for your child.* Every time you "kiss a boo-boo better," you are showing empathy. When you respond with concern to someone in pain or distress, you are modeling empathy for your child.

2. *Reinforce displays of empathy.* Be sure to join with your child every time he shows appropriate concern or empathy for someone else. Acknowledge that it is a good thing to do.

3. *Include discussion of other people's feeling in your conversation with your child.* If something bad happens to someone your child knows, ask her, "How do you think that made him feel?" Prompt her if she has difficulty coming up with the words. "Do you think he may be sad? Do you think it made him cry?" Then, you can go a step further by asking, "What do you think he can do when he's feeling sad?" Or, "Do you think there is anything we can do to help him feel better?" Be sure to include your child when you do something thoughtful such as order flowers or make a casserole for a sick friend. Ask, "What kind of flowers do you think Helen might like?" While empathy itself may be largely innate, the corresponding behaviors are learned because they are specific to a culture.

   Some parents believe that their children should be sheltered from emotional distress, especially that of their parents. In my own experience it is valuable for parents to express their feelings to their children, in a way that is natural and not overwhelming. It is not advisable, of course, for parents to burden their children with difficult feelings that they themselves have yet to process, such as raw anger at the other parent, to take a common example. But children are sensitive to their parents' feelings and usually know, at some level, what is happening emotionally in the home anyway. If feelings are appropriately expressed, that can foster a child's growing emotional competence. It's good for a child to be able to realize when a parent is sad and can use a hug.

4. *Consider role-playing games in which empathy is relevant.* Children enjoy playing imaginative games, which can easily include feelings. Acting out stories, for example, can be used as exercises for

> working through emotions. Cinderella has every reason to cry, and Jack's mother has a right to stomp around when she learns that he has sold the cow for two beans. Ask how the various characters might feel in different situations.
>
> 5. *If your child does something thoughtless, make sure to ask how it will affect others.* Research has shown that mothers who gave their 1- to 2-year-olds clear explanations of the consequences of causing harm to others were repaid with children who showed more caring behavior toward others in distress.[38]
>
> 6. *Maintain a family atmosphere of nurturance and affection.* As you may have noticed, children are born mimics. Just as babies will mirror your facial expressions, so they will play back to you the treatment you mete out to them. A loving and nurturing atmosphere is therefore key to raising an empathic and considerate child.

Researchers Robert Levenson and Anna Ruef of the University of California at Berkeley set out to study whether people can accurately identify emotions in others.[39] They asked thirty-one volunteers to view videotaped sessions of married couples interacting and to describe what they thought one of the spouses was feeling. While the volunteers watched, the researchers measured various physical functions known to change with emotion, such as heart rate and skin conductance. The results: People vary widely, from 100-percent accuracy in assessing emotions in others all the way to 0 percent.

The people who could best rate negative feelings in the videos showed physical changes like those of the people they were rating, such as increased pulse rate or skin conductance. So the key to empathizing with people who are suffering may literally reside in the ability to feel their pain, or at least some of its bodily features. In a similar way, the people who accurately rated positive feelings in the videos showed reduced arousal of their cardiovascular system.

Perhaps the big surprise from this study was that the subjects turned out to be very bad at estimating how empathic they were. There was no relationship between self-rated empathy and actual success in identifying the feelings of others. These findings suggest that if you want to know how empathic you are, ask someone else!

Advanced Emotional Intelligence Skills

The abilities to identify and label feelings in yourself and others are basic emotional skills on which more advanced skills are built. (See "Emotional Intelligence [as Defined by Mayer and Salovey]" on page 89.) Let's now consider a few of the more advanced skills of emotional competence.

Making the Most of Your Moods

Salovey and colleagues have pointed out that our different moods offer us the chance to see the world in various ways, which may help us solve complex problems.[40] That may be one reason why many of the world's most creative artists, writers, and musicians suffer from mood disorders.[41] In working with people who experience a wide range of moods, I am often impressed by the way some of them use their ups and downs to advantage.

People with seasonal affective disorder often use the high energy, high spirits, and expansiveness of their summer months to kick off new projects. When winter arrives, in contrast, they use their less energetic, more sober mood to carry out their plans. Complex tasks often require meticulous attention to detail, which they find better suited to their plodding winter mode than to their summer ebullience.

One of my female patients, a senior business manager, used her premenstrual mood swings to handle different aspects of her administrative responsibilities. During the midcycle, when she was laid back, mellow and easy to be around, she would encourage her staff and praise those who had performed particularly well. When she was premenstrual, however, she used her predictable irritability to deliver unpleasant but necessary feedback. By using her self-knowledge in this way, she developed the reputation for being a tough but fair boss.

Understanding and Analyzing Emotional Information

Although many emotions are simple and predictable, some are more complicated, requiring greater skill to understand and interpret. Imagine, for example, the complex blend of feelings you might have if you were to visit your childhood home for the first time in many years. You might remember both happy and sad times and realize that they cannot be recaptured. The resulting feeling might be nostalgia, a combination of wistfulness and bittersweet emotions. Then you might think of the years that have passed since you left your earliest home. You might consider the many good things that have happened in those years and feel gratitude, or remember the people you have lost along the way and feel a mixture of sadness and resignation. Finally, you might experience a sense of integration, the past and the present sitting comfortably side by side in your mind. Integrating such complicated skeins of feeling involves both self-awareness and analytic skills.

Regulating the Emotions

If we are not to be passion's slaves, we need to learn how to regulate our emotions. And for those who do, each emotion brings a gift. Anger can lead to strength, fear to wisdom, pain and trauma to healing and recovery, loneliness to reaching out and connecting with others, guilt to better values, shame to humility, passion to creativity, and joy to growth. In the chapters on the individual emotions, I go into some detail on how to use your emotions and how to rein them in when they threaten to overwhelm your judgment.

Temperament: Teflon-Coated or Tempest-Tossed

Anyone who observes the different children in a large family will come away amazed that the same two parents can produce offspring of so many different temperaments. One child may have a sunny disposition, rolling with the punches, while another is fussy and easily derailed by the small disruptions of daily life, from which he is slow to recover. Researchers who work with humans and other animals have documented such differences in temperament for decades, both psychologically and physically.

People who experience more anxiety and stress have higher base-line levels of the stress hormone cortisol than those who feel less anx-iety. Jerome Kagan, professor of psychiatry at Harvard University, has found that shy and inhibited children have higher heart rates both at rest and when they are under stress, and higher blood levels of the stress response chemicals epinephrine and norepinephrine.[42] These differences are apparent in children just a few days old. As infants, those who will later be shy react more strongly to changes in light and sound than do the more emotionally robust. Kagan speculates that these temperamental differences probably result from the bal-ance between more than 150 different molecules in the brain. The re-sult of this balance is that some infants giggle and coo, while others are irritable and sullen.

Children also show differences in baseline cortisol levels, with shy children having higher levels. In one study, researchers measured cor-tisol levels in children who were settling into the school year.[43] Those whose cortisol levels were low after the settling-in period were judged to be more outgoing, competent, and well liked, while those whose levels stayed high tended to be more isolated and sad.

Studies with other primates reveal similar differences between in-dividuals. Dr. Stephen Suomi, a primate researcher at the National Institute of Mental Health, has identified rhesus monkeys that react very strongly to stresses such as being placed in novel situations or being separated from a loved one.[44] These monkeys are easy to iden-tify because they are timid and withdrawn. Suomi has shown that the monkeys' behaviors may have both genetic and environmental influ-ences. For example, their high reactivity can be completely reversed by fostering them with extremely nurturing mothers in the first six months of life.

In studies of baboons in the wild, Stanford neuroscientist Robert Sapolsky has found that baboons that are proactive have lower levels of the stress hormones.[45] If these animals sense a threat, they don't wait to be attacked. Instead they take charge. They make a preemptive move. Sapolsky can actually predict a baboon's cortisol levels based on his behavior after fights. Less-stressed baboons, with lower cortisol levels, are more likely to have two sets of behaviors, one for winning and one for losing: grooming a friend after he wins, for example, or beating up a smaller animal after he loses. Baboons with higher cortisol levels tend to behave the same way after a fight, whether they win or lose.

As you can well imagine, whether a person is Teflon-coated or tempest-tossed will influence his emotional competence. In the workplace, for example, someone who smolders for hours after a small slight by his boss will register stress in his body, lose productive work time, and feel miserable. Contrast such a person with one who shrugs and says, "I guess the guy is having a bad day." Or, "She doesn't realize what a great job I do. I'll show her." Or, "Maybe I need to be someplace where my talents are better appreciated." Whether a person shrugs or smolders may reflect his temperament more than his emotional intelligence.

In contrast to the "shrug-smolder factor," some behaviors that seem innate are almost certainly acquired. Woody Allen has noted that 80 percent of success is just showing up. Members of Alcoholics Anonymous often remind one another to "just show up." Over the years I have seen many patients fired from their jobs because they have not followed this simple doctrine. For some people, difficulty getting to work is a direct result of a psychiatric problem such as depression, obsessive-compulsive disorder, or attention deficit disorder. In other cases, however, people just have not acquired the habit of getting to places on time. Punctuality and other important social habits such as courtesy, respect for others, and honesty—in whatever forms your particular subculture prefers—are largely learned and not preprogrammed. We refer to these qualities, collectively, as "character."

Robert Cloninger, professor of psychiatry at Washington University in St. Louis, has suggested dividing temperament and character into different elements on the basis of biological evidence, as follows: Temperament, he suggests, is a blend of different tendencies, such as to avoid harm, to seek novelty, to depend on reward for motivation, and to persist in a task. Character, on the other hand, involves such traits as the ability to direct yourself in tasks, to cooperate with others, and to develop a vision and goals that go beyond your own immediate self-interest.[46] All of these elements combine together to form personality.

Temperament is at least 50-percent inherited and is rather stable from early childhood through adulthood.[47] Temperament is said to consist of "habit systems" because it generally involves more-or-less automatic responses to the world. Some people are naturally fearful and prefer the safety of familiar environments, whereas others are innately adventurous and need novelty and excitement to feel alive. According to our latest scientific understanding, these elements of temperament are biologically based. Fundamentally, harm avoidance relates to brain serotonin, novelty seeking to brain dopamine, and reward dependence to brain oxytocin. Of course, all these three systems—and others too—interact.[48]

As you can imagine, we have much to learn about temperament, beginning with questions such as, "Can temperament be altered by medications?" To explore this topic, a team led by neuroscientist Brian Knutson, currently at the National Institute of Alcoholism and Alcohol Abuse, administered Prozac to fifty-one healthy volunteers over a four-week period. Although the subjects showed no increase in positive emotion, they did show less hostility while on the drug.[49]

At this time I see no way to justify using drugs to alter temperament in a person with no clear problem. First, there is no evidence that they would be helpful, and second, they may cause side effects. At present, I think that drugs such as Prozac should be reserved for people whose emotions cause them significant trouble. What we mean by "significant" may be in flux, however. Some people who we once would have thought of as having a troublesome temperament we now view as having mild variants of psychiatric disorders. Such people may benefit from the same medications that help more full-blown disorders, in much the same way that painkillers can help both ordinary headaches and full-blown migraines.

In contrast to temperament, character ripens over the lifespan. It includes our ethics, our philosophy of life, and our ideas of who we are as people. Self-directedness is about how you deal with yourself, your goals, and your ambitions; cooperativeness is about how you deal with others; and self-transcendence is about your vision of how you fit into the universe. Like a rudder on a boat, character provides a person with direction in life. It lends value to action. Without it, emotional intelligence can be useless or even dangerous, as in the case of charming Ted Bundy, a serial killer who murdered at least thirty-six women in the 1970s.

An older but still useful way to describe personality is by the so-called Big Five personality factors: extraversion versus introversion, neuroticism, openness, agreeableness, and conscientiousness.

The extraversion-introversion dimension is one of the best-studied personality variables. Extraverts are more gregarious; they are energized by interactions with others. Introverts tend to prefer their own company and often find interactions to be draining. Extraverts are more likely to seize opportunities; introverts are more likely to perceive pitfalls and avoid them. Extraverts are more likely than introverts to experience positive moods.[50]

Neuroticism is composed of a mixture of qualities, including the tendencies to be anxious and impulsive. As you might predict, a high neuroticism score goes with lower moods.[51] Openness to new experience is related to high levels of *both* positive and negative moods, presumably because both these experiences might be either good or bad.[52] Those individuals who are more conscientious and agreeable also seem to be happier, perhaps because these qualities result in the satisfaction that comes with accomplishment and with richer personal relationships.[53]

How Important Is Emotional Competence for Success in Life?

One reason emotional intelligence and EQ have captured the public imagination is that they're touted as keys to success in work and life. Granted that intelligence alone is not enough to predict success, to what degree does emotional intelligence explain the rest? Salovey and colleagues, though enthusiastic about a concept they themselves created, are careful to temper what they refer to as misleading media claims for emotional intelligence.[54] For example, in response to such popular claims as, "if intelligence predicts 20 percent of success, emotional intelligence can fill in the 80-percent gap," they say, "not true." That is too huge a claim, one that research does not support. They point out that no single psychological entity contains all the personality elements necessary for success.

In 1991, psychologists Murray Barrick of Michigan State University and Michael Mount of the University of Iowa conducted a meta-analysis of how the Big Five personality dimensions predict success in the workplace.[55] Their analysis pooled results from 117 studies of almost 24,000 people. They concluded, surprisingly, that agreeableness (one of the Big Five) had little effect on job performance even in sales and management. The best predictor was conscientiousness, not even part of emotional intelligence. Overall, Barrick and Mount concluded that only 3 percent of job success is predicted by personality, a far cry from the claims of some media reports.

In a recent study of success by Albert Mehrabian, professor emeritus of psychology at the University of California in Los Angeles, however, personality variables did tend to predict success.[56] Mehrabian had 302 university students each bring along a relative or close friend, who rated the student's degree of success in various spheres. Then the students themselves completed a battery of personality tests.

Mehrabian found that what he called *relaxed temperament* was quite highly correlated (0.57) with overall success in life as judged by the subjects' friends and relatives. This dimension also correlated highly with success in relationships, work, and finances. Key attributes for relaxed temperament were the tendency to seek out pleasure, to be optimistic, to score low in anxiety and depression, and to have high self-esteem.

One caution: In evaluating traits such as self-esteem, we need to view them in context. Salovey and colleagues point out, for example, that Hitler and Stalin probably had high self-esteem, but would hardly be called good role models.[57] In my practice I frequently encounter parents who are so eager to promote their children's self-esteem that they forget the need for its partners, character traits deserving of esteem. Unconditional love is not enough. Parents should also foster socially responsible behavior and expectations of reasonable accomplishment. In short, parents need to help build their children's character.

Mehrabian found that success at work is best predicted by a factor he calls *disciplined goal orientation*, which includes patience, the ability to delay gratification, and low levels of impulsivity and procrastination. Although the ability to control one's emotions is necessary to focus on a job, disciplined goal orientation does not strictly fit into emotional intelligence.

One measure in the Mehrabian study that predicted low levels of success in *all* spheres of life was *emotional thinking*, by which Mehrabian means an excess of emotions in one's thinking. Emotional thinking can result in selective, distorted judgments of situations and relationships.

In summary, emotional intelligence is quite important for success both in work and in life, but it works best in conjunction with other important factors, such as conscientiousness, good character, and regular intelligence.

Can Emotional Intelligence Be Learned?

As with all skills, emotional skills can be learned and improved. People differ in their emotional aptitude, just as they do in their verbal and calculating aptitudes. Everybody has some emotional aptitude, however, just as everybody has some verbal and motor skills. Of course, there are people with deficits in emotional intelligence, such as *alexithymia*, which is an inability to put feelings into words. This defect may be neurological.[58] Researchers speculate that these people may have inadequate communication between the right cerebral hemisphere, where many emotions are registered, and the left hemisphere, which handles language. Other deficits in emotional skills, such as difficulty interpreting the emotional elements in facial expressions, voice tones, or gestures, may yet emerge.

Society recognizes the need for people to learn basic skills, such as the "three R's" (reading, 'riting, and 'rithmetic). What is most exciting to me about the concept of emotional intelligence (or competence) is the growing awareness that everyone can benefit from being taught emotional skills. Such teaching, along with the homework that all learning requires, can improve the emotional skills regardless of a person's natural abilities. Just as a poor golfer can reduce his golf handicap, so a person with impaired emotional abilities can learn to reduce his emotional handicap. Although the golfer may never be able to play professionally, he may still learn to enjoy a social game of golf, and so it is with emotional skills.

To take the analogy a step further: Even Tiger Woods, the greatest of all modern golfers, needs to practice his golf swing for many hours a week. So it is that even those with outstanding emotional skills can benefit from coaching and practice. Psychiatrists and psychologists used to undergo psychotherapy as part of their training, and it certainly was useful. I remember that in my residency, when I first began to treat people with psychotherapy, I had the bad habit of changing the topic when the talk got painful. For example, a young woman might confide her worries about the state of her mother's health, and I would find myself asking how things were going with her children. Unaware of what I was doing, I was directing the therapy away from an unpleasant subject (her sick mother) toward a pleasant one (her vibrant children), which did not help the patient. I realized finally that when my patient spoke about her sick mother, it made me worry about *my* mother, so I'd change the subject. After training made me more aware of my own feelings (both conscious and unconscious), I became a better listener and more emotionally competent.

Understanding how the emotions relate to each other—an advanced emotional-intelligence skill—can also be learned. Arlene, a lawyer, was understandably angry when she discovered that her husband, Martin, had had an affair with someone she had thought was a friend. Even though the affair had ended four years before, she berated him for his infidelity. He was contrite and apologetic, and she felt comforted to some degree by his guilt and remorse. But she was unable to let go of her anger and continued to remind Martin of his past transgressions at every opportunity. How do you think that made Martin feel? His guilt turned to anger, which led to counterattacks and, finally, withdrawal. That is what you can expect if you keep making someone else feel guilty. In therapy, Arlene realized that what she really wanted was to heal the wound in her marriage, and that would be possible only if she let go of her resentment. She was encouraged to focus instead on what she wanted from her marriage, and to let Martin know what he could do to help her trust him again. Martin learned that although the affair was over as far as he was concerned, he had to let Arlene go through the stages of healing, and to be loving and supportive in the process.

Research on Emotional Intelligence

Researchers are just learning how best to measure emotional intelligence, and until you can reliably measure something, it is difficult to study it. As you can imagine, research in emotional intelligence is in its very early phases. There are currently more than 300 programs in the United States designed to teach social and emotional learning.[59] Since the introduction of these programs into schools, some have observed that school violence and feelings of hopelessness have declined.[60] Although researchers cannot say for sure that these favorable changes are due to the programs, it makes sense that teaching children emotional skills will pay off. If children can learn algebra and history, why would they not be able to learn that their feelings—and those of other children—matter? Surely they can be taught that feelings work according to certain predictable rules, much like math or language; and just as you can solve an equation or write an essay, so you can figure out what is going on emotionally and find a solution to it.

Many programs have been developed to improve emotional competence in business and the medical profession. In one such program, the American Express Financial Advisors, those financial advisors who took part in the program had greater business growth than others.[61] But here again, properly controlled studies are needed to be sure that the programs, rather than other factors, are making the difference. Again, though, it would come as no surprise to anybody who has had an unempathic doctor or dealt with rude business people that many could stand to benefit from training in emotional competence.

Emotional Competence in the Workplace

Although more research is needed, I predict that emotional skills will indeed prove to be extremely valuable in the workplace. Here are a few examples of situations where handling things in an emotionally competent way could make a difference.

Imagine that you are a manager whose newly acquired supervisee proves to have what is known on the street as "an attitude." She is sullen toward you, slams doors, and follows directions with apparent reluctance, though she never defies you openly. You conclude, probably correctly, that she is angry about something. What do you do?

If you ignore the problem, it will continue, and will create morale problems in the office. You cannot allow this behavior to become entrenched. At the same time, it doesn't pay to shoot from the hip; it is better to wait long enough to observe a *pattern* of behavior, several clear examples that you can point out. As a psychiatrist, I have learned the value of detecting a pattern of behavior before intervening. If you comment on someone's behavior too soon, you will probably meet with denial. Waiting for several examples to accrue will put you on more solid ground.

You call your employee into your office and point out to her that she appears to be unhappy. This is affecting both her work and the atmosphere in the office, as indicated by examples x, y, and z. You invite her to discuss what is bothering her. If you know what the problem is, you explain, you and she will be able to address it directly. She denies that anything is wrong. What do you do now?

The denial was to be expected, as she has already shown that she is uncomfortable dealing directly with anger. Instead she has developed a pattern of expressing her anger indirectly. Further confrontation will probably fortify her passive aggression. At this point some managers might choose to fire the employee, but since that is not always either feasible or desirable, let us say you choose to retain her. How do you proceed?

You might say, "It still seems to me that something is bothering you. Why don't you give the matter some thought and let's meet next week [specify the day and time] to review things. But even if nothing in particular is bothering you, I would still be interested in your thoughts as to how things might work better around here." This strategy may accomplish several things. Although you have not backed down on your message that there is a problem, you have spared her a confrontation, which will be a relief to her.

By planning a follow-up meeting that is independent of how she functions over the next week, you lessen the chance that the next meeting will be perceived as a further complaint against her. She may work better over the next week to ensure that the meeting does not take on an unpleasant tone. Most important, however, you have reframed the situation, offering her the opportunity to change her perception of her role in the office from that of a powerless underling to someone who can help work collaboratively to improve the way the office functions.

Gentle reframing does not, of course, guarantee a successful outcome, but it improves the likelihood. In handling matters this way, you will have exercised several elements of emotional intelligence—empathy, knowledge of how other people function emotionally, ability to control impulse (to chastise her or fire her prematurely), and marshaling your interpersonal skills to achieve your long-term objectives.

Emotional intelligence in work situations is valuable not only for managers but for supervisees as well. I remember one lesson I learned as a young manager from Jim, a research assistant of mine. Jim was in his mid-thirties when, as a result of a bureaucratic shuffle, he was assigned to work for me in a position far below his previous level. He was good humored about it and began to apply himself to the tasks I had assigned. After the first week, Jim asked to meet with me and explained that I had given him too much to do in the time available. Would I be good enough to set priorities, he asked, so that he could determine which tasks to do first and which to leave undone?

I realized that Jim was correct. As a result of my inexperience as a manager, I had in fact assigned him too much work. I took certain tasks away from him and told him what my priorities were. The important lesson Jim taught me was that, even from a subordinate position, there are ways to change things that are respectful of both yourself and your supervisor. By acting in an assertive but respectful way, you can save yourself a great deal of unnecessary stress without loss of standing in your job. Jim had shown, once again, the value of emotional intelligence.

Improving Emotional Competence in Intimate Relationships

There has been a great deal of emphasis on the value of emotional competence in the more public aspects of life. But nowhere are emotional skills more valuable than in intimate relationships. Although emotional-intelligence research has yet to deal with this area, let us consider some situations in which emotional competence is necessary for success in love and marriage.

It has been said with some truth that opposites attract. But they can also drive each other crazy. Michael and Jennifer got married as a result of that sort of attraction. He is an accountant, careful, meticulous and measured in his ways. She has a dramatic flair, which she employs to good effect by playing minor roles at the local dinner theater. When out in company, he is generally considered stuffy, though he has a dry sense of humor. She is the life and soul of the party, often has one drink too many, says outrageous things for which she later apologizes, and is generally regarded as "a character." At first, the two seemed like an answer to each other's prayers. He would provide her with the organization and structure her life desperately needed. She would breathe vitality into his otherwise dull existence. But somewhere along the way things went wrong. Now she sees him as parsimonious, nitpicking, and dull. She feels he constrains her. He regards her as irresponsible and flighty. Her disorganization and extravagance drive him to distraction.

Michael and Jennifer are stereotypes, composites of many people I have seen over the years. Much has been written about their type of relationship in the professional literature, which has described these two personality styles as obsessional and hysterical. They view their worlds in different ways. Many of Michael's actions are governed by reason and calculation. Jennifer's actions are governed by impulse and feeling. There was some wisdom in their first instincts to become a couple—they have much to learn from each other. But now they are too angry to listen. They have driven each other into opposite corners of the room, caricatured each other's flaws, and disavowed each other's feelings. To make a go of their relationship, they will have to change the way they perceive and treat each other.

Incidentally, this type of relationship is not confined to heterosexuals. Such a union is depicted in the movie *The Bird Cage*, where the rather controlled and well-modulated owner of a nightclub is driven crazy by the self-dramatizing antics of his partner, a drag queen.

Another type of attraction between opposites involves one partner, let us say the husband, who is extraverted, and one who is highly anxious and introverted. At first, the wife's anxiety made the husband feel strong, masculine, and protective. His confident, gregarious manner made her admire him and lean upon him. Now he complains that she hardly ever wants to go out and he is forced to stay at home against his will. She, on the other hand, feels that he pushes her too hard. Resentful, they have become silent and withdrawn.

Here is where emotional intelligence comes into play. What these individuals need to do first and foremost is to empathize with each other. To do so, they must:

- *Understand each other's world.* If you traveled to a foreign land, the ways of the local people might seem strange, but you would presume that there was some logic, structure, and organization to them even if they were not readily apparent to you. That is how you should view someone with a different temperament or emotional style. If you want to understand what it is like to live in that person's world, you need to ask questions, then sit back and listen.

  Chronicles of travels to foreign lands typically fall into two types. In one, the writer pokes fun at the locals. Their customs are quaint and odd in comparison to ours, the writer suggests, inviting the reader into a conspiracy of superiority. In the other type, the writer tries to understand how the local people experience their universe. The former approach is distant and unempathic. This is the approach being taken by the two we just met. The latter is empathic, which is the approach for which our two couples need to strive.

- *Look beyond the anger.* Anger is just the surface of what people in an estranged relationship feel. It is obvious. Dwelling on it at length is uninformative. The more interesting question is what other feelings there are besides the anger. To find this out, the couple should look at each other in a fresh way. They should try to remember what attracted them in the first place and to appreciate those qualities that are still there.

  If they do this, Jennifer will realize that Michael is not just a human calculator. He has a lot of feelings, though he is not as facile at identifying and expressing them as she is. Yet he would love to be able to do so if only he felt safe from her anger and derision. And Michael, if he would look beyond Jennifer's spending and histrionics, would find a woman who would like her life to be more orderly and who wants to be respected. She feels inadequate, however, and tries to distract herself from that painful feeling and deflect others from observing her inadequacy by her dramatic behavior.

In just the same way, the extraverted husband will understand that his wife is not willfully trying to curtail his social life. He should observe how anxious she becomes in public settings and recognize that it is painful for her to socialize. She, in turn, would do well to understand that he is champing at the bit sitting at home when he wants to be out and about.

- *Cultivate the art of listening with a nonrebutting mind-set.* One exercise that can help couples such as Michael and Jennifer is called listening with a nonrebutting mind-set. This means sitting back and listening to how the other person feels about his or her day without jumping in and contradicting. This can be difficult, and couples would do well to start with very short periods, say just five minutes per person per day. One way to do the exercise is for the couple to sit back to back. Take a few moments to decompress from the day's activities and to reflect on how you are feeling. Then, gently, one person begins to talk, focusing on feelings and moods, rather than leaping right into a complaint about the other. Once the ice begins to melt and the couple starts to relate to each other as friends, they can slowly begin to address the more difficult issues.

Therapists encourage what they call "I" statements, such as "I feel anxious, sad, or lonely when thus and such happens," as opposed to "you" statements, which blame and distance the other person. Be careful not to cheat by turning the "I" statement into a dumping "You" statement, such as "I feel bad when you behave like a pig."

The funny thing about empathy is that it changes the way you see the other person, which can change your own behavior. Jennifer may find herself becoming more respectful and less derogatory of Michael. He may once again begin to enjoy her capacity for fun and feel less need to rein her in. As she begins to understand his concerns about finances, she may curtail her spending. Or perhaps they will decide to change the way they handle their finances so that each has an independent budget to manage in his and her own way.

The extravert-introvert couple can similarly work together to find solutions that respect and accommodate their differences. With her husband's support, the wife may seek out help to overcome her social anxiety. She may be surprised to find herself enjoying her social life more than ever before. Or they may decide together that she does not need to accompany him to all social events. Once they feel closer, she may encourage him to go out with the guys once a week, which might ease the tension resulting from their different needs.

Researchers Jacobson and Christensen have come up with a novel form of marital therapy that they claim is far more effective than traditional therapy.[62] Rather than encouraging the two parties to change to meet each other's expectations, they instead emphasize the need for each to understand and accept the other one as he or she is. According to these researchers, once people feel more loved and accepted exactly as they are, they may spontaneously change! In contrast, when each partner focuses on changing the other's long-standing patterns of behavior, the natural tendency is to dig in and resist.

The findings of Jacobson and Christensen correspond well with my own experience. People have a fundamental need to be understood and accepted, particularly by those they love. After all, if two people decided to enter a committed relationship in the first place, there must have been strong forces pulling them together. It is worth trying to recapture those forces. The unanticipated (and unwelcome) baggage that came along with the traits one loved may look less troublesome, even endearing, in the larger context.

I have two dear friends, both highly successful professionals, who have been married for a long time. The husband tends to be laid back and optimistic, whereas his wife tends to be anxious and pessimistic. I ran across the husband in the airport once when we were traveling to the same conference. The plane had been delayed because of bad weather. He was reading his newspaper as we waited for the clouds to clear and visibility to improve. I asked him how he was feeling about the delay and he replied, "I'm fine, but Marcia is really having a hard time with it. You know," he said, "traveling is much harder for some people than for others." I could tell that behind the comment there must have been many, many trips that had been far easier for him than for her. Another person might have complained at having to put up with a difficult wife, but there was no sense of this in his comment. Rather, his tone was one of empathy for her difficulties and acceptance of their differences. I came away with a feeling of deep respect for my friend. His attitude seemed to transcend emotional competence. It looked more like wisdom.

Emotional Competence in Everyday Life

Emotional skills are useful in every aspect of our lives. I was reminded of this recently when I was standing in a long line to buy lunch at a food court. I noticed that things had slowed down at a booth where speed of service is one of the major attractions. I craned my neck and recognized that the irate customer was a scientist who worked on the same campus as I did.

"You ought to have the right kind of crackers!" he shouted. "And if you don't, the least you can do is give me an extra packet of the second-rate crackers that you do have!"

The young man behind the counter was adamant. "All you can get is one helping of crackers," he insisted, apparently indifferent to the special circumstances of the situation.

"I will not move until you make good the lack of your usual crackers!" the scientist shouted. His face was turning beet red, and the veins bulged and stood out on his forehead.

Then another person offered the clerk 25 cents for an extra packet of crackers, which he readily handed over. End of story.

As you will see later in the book, anger can kill. I am sure that during the course of this exchange, my colleague's blood pressure must have jumped many points, his heart must have beat faster, and his coronary arteries might well have gone into spasm. I wondered how often during the course of a day or week he becomes excited over trivial matters, and what the long-term health costs to him will be.

During this short exchange my colleague revealed several problems in his emotional competence. He allowed himself to be provoked by a trivial setback, reacted with disproportionate anger, and was unable to turn off his rage once it was in full swing. Allowing himself to lose control in this way subjected him to public humiliation and put his health at risk, and all for a packet of crackers!

The incident gave me pause. It made me aware of the importance of emotional competence not just in intimate relationships or at work but in our everyday lives. Each day presents many situations that call for understanding the emotions, which we can handle either well or foolishly. How we do so, played out thousands of times as the years go by, may determine whether we end up like the underachieving valedictorian at the class reunion or the happy multimillionaire who barely squeaked through his college examinations.

Chapter 6

Emotions That Kill and Cure

A merry heart doeth good like a medicine.
—Proverbs, 17:22[1]

A s this biblical quote indicates, the idea that feelings can influence health is not a new one. The ancient Greeks believed that an imbalance in the body's "humors" could result in both physical and mental afflictions. In recent times there have been many attempts to use this connection between mind and body to advantage. Popular authors have written extensively about the potential healing powers of the mind. Some have issued grave warnings of the health consequences of negative emotions or made extravagant promises about the benefits of maintaining a positive attitude. Can emotions really kill? Can improving your attitude really save your life? These are some of the questions I address here.

Margaret and the Mystery of Voodoo Death

Margaret was an elderly woman who lived all of her life in a small city in the Midwest. By the time she reached the age of 100, she was so well known and loved that her friends, family, and neighbors threw a party in honor of her special birthday. Overwhelmed with happiness, Margaret stood up to address the crowd. "You cannot imagine how wonderful it is for me," she said, "to be surrounded by so many friends and loved ones. In fact, if I were to die right now, my life would be complete." At that very moment, she keeled over dead.

The timing of Margaret's death might, of course, have been pure coincidence, but there are many reports of people dying suddenly from an overabundance of excitement. In the well-recognized phenomenon of voodoo death, the shaman points out the person who is destined to die, and in many instances, the person does. The cause of death in such cases has been a matter of speculation among physiologists for the better part of a century.

Since there is no good medical documentation in voodoo deaths, it is always possible that some trickery, for instance poisoning, is involved. But the real explanation may be suggested by the following exchange from Oscar Wilde's *The Importance of Being Earnest*.[2] At a certain point in the play, one of the protagonists is attempting to explain the disappearance of Mr. Bunbury, a friend he had invented:

> *Algernon:* The doctors found out that Bunbury could not
> live . . . so Bunbury died.
> *Lady Bracknell:* He seems to have had great confidence in
> the opinion of his physicians.

That, in essence, is our best understanding of what happens in voodoo death. The victim has such faith in the shaman that the terror engendered by the shaman's dire prediction overwhelms him physiologically, to the point of death. Our current best understanding of exactly how this might occur implicates an excessively powerful response of the sympathetic nervous system.

The sympathetic nervous system, as you may recall, plays a major role in the body's response to what we call stress. Stress evolved to deal with emergencies: "That cave looks occupied. Run! It's a cave bear!" When a stress or threat appears, the news is instantaneously registered by the amygdala and other limbic centers, which send alarm signals to the rest of the brain and throughout the body. The alert spreads via the sympathetic nervous system, an almost ubiquitous network of nerve connections.

Because of the sympathetic nervous system, by the time the mind has a chance to register warning emotions, such as fear, rage, or sadness, the body has already been galvanized into action. The bloodstream has been flooded with adrenaline and norepinephrine, and the heart is already beating faster. The blood pressure rises to drive blood into those parts of the body that need it most, such as the muscles involved in fight or flight.

When powerful emotions are experienced suddenly, the force of the sympathetic system, especially in someone who is old or frail or has heart disease, may prove to be too much. The person may die from a heart attack, an irregular heart rhythm, or a stroke, owing to the blood-pressure spike.

In Western societies, overwhelming emotions do cause sudden deaths from time to time. In a study of 170 sudden deaths reported in newspaper articles, the emotional triggers included suddenly hearing of a death, mourning on an anniversary, loss of status or self-esteem and threat of being injured.[3] But some of the subjects also died of extreme triumph or joy.

This is why it is prudent to break news, even good news, gently to people who are elderly or infirm. We see an example of such a strategy in The Odyssey. When Odysseus returns to Ithaca after twenty years, long after most people thought he was dead, he seeks out his aged father in the fields.[4] But he does not identify himself right away. Instead, he pretends to be a friend of Odysseus's, and he gently leads the old man through a discussion of his son before finally revealing the good news. This was smart strategy, especially since cardiopulmonary resucitation was thousands of years from being invented.

In modern times, we have medical strategies to prevent death from powerful emotions—if you can predict when the emotional surge will come. One colleague of mine took propranolol, a medication that blocks the effects of the sympathetic nervous system, before going to his father's funeral.

Since stresses (and the need for extra strength and alertness) often persist over hours or days, the body has evolved hormonal responses that are longer lasting than the initial burst. The adrenal glands, located in the abdominal cavity just above the kidneys, are responsible for both early and delayed hormonal responses.

The initial adrenal response, triggered by the sympathetic nervous system, involves releases of the hormones epinephrine and norepinephrine into the bloodstream.[5] The slower response is initiated by the hypothalamus, a structure at the base of the brain, which releases a substance called corticotropin-releasing hormone (CRH). CRH in turn stimulates the pituitary, a gland that sits just behind the eyes, to release another substance called corticotropin. Corticotropin courses through the bloodstream to the adrenals, where it causes the release of other hormones, notably cortisol, which helps us deal with longer-term stresses.

As you might expect, the emergency stress-response system is best adapted to deal with emergencies. Like firefighters or a SWAT team, it is geared to rush in, take care of the problem, and go home in short order. Imagine how a town would work if its firefighters and SWAT team were occupied round the clock. Likewise, when stress persists for too long, it can damage the body in many ways. One reason the topic concerns us here is that negative emotions, such as anger and depression, if they persist over time, signal persistent stress, and recent research indicates that they damage the heart and blood vessels, which can prove fatal. (For further discussions of this, see chapters 9 and 11.) In addition, recent studies point to harmful effects of stress—and negative emotions—on the immune system.

The Sixth Sense: The Immune System and the Brain

The immune system is known as the Sixth Sense because of its capacity to sense danger—viruses, bacteria, allergens—and communicate with the brain via chemical messengers. In one of the first studies to show that the brain affects the immune system—a startling idea at the time (1975)—Dr. Robert Ader, professor of psychiatry at the University of Rochester in New York, and colleagues gave rats a type of drug that suppresses the immune system, along with an artificial sweetener.[6] Later the researchers found that giving the rats the artificial sweetener alone was enough to suppress their immune function: The immune system could be classically conditioned! This discovery opened up a whole new field of research, which has since shown that stresses of all kinds can affect immune function, as measured both in the laboratory and in people.

Some of the most important work in this field has been done by Ron Glaser, professor and chair of immunology at Ohio State University, together with his wife, psychologist and fellow professor Janice Kiecolt-Glaser. A hard-nosed scientist, Glaser was at first skeptical that the mind could play any significant role in immune response. But he was persuaded by an early study done in collaboration with Janice Kiecolt-Glaser and James Pennebaker. The trio showed a long-lasting benefit to health from writing down thoughts and feelings. Over the ensuing six months, students who kept a Pennebaker-style journal (see pages 201–205) had fewer medical visits to the student health clinic than the controls.[7]

As Glaser points out, healthy students don't need the health clinic very often anyway. To cut the number of visits still further by a psychological intervention was therefore quite impressive. Since then, Glaser, his wife, and other colleagues have thoroughly explored the role of stress in immune functioning—a big one, as it turns out. For example, high stress can make a wound slow to heal.

The wounds in question were made on the forearms of 26 people by means of a punch biopsy of about 3.5 millimeters in diameter (a procedure commonly used in dermatology).[8] Thirteen of the people at the time were caring for a relative with dementia, a stressful and depressing task, while the other thirteen had no major sources of stress in their lives. The Glaser team found that in the caregivers, the wound took an average of nine more days to heal.[9] In a later study, biopsy wounds on medical students healed faster at the end of summer vacation than during exams.[10]

Stress also increases susceptibility to infection. For example, compared to noncaregivers, people taking care of demented patients have more respiratory-tract infections and take more days off sick.

Susceptibility depends, however, not only on the stress itself, but also on how the individual views the stress and on individual vulnerability. For example, one study looked at the number of head colds in children under roughly equivalent stress.[11] It turned out that those who reacted to stress with greater increases in heart rate and blood pressure were also more likely to develop sniffles. (High emotional reactivity is a largely genetic trait, as discussed on page 113–117). Similarly, in work by Sheldon Cohen, professor of psychology at Carne-gie Mellon University, and colleagues, a group was exposed to cold viruses.[12] Those who came down with colds tended to have negative mood states, to be under high life stress, or to rate their stress as high—not the same things by any means. Most of us, for example, would find boot camp at West Point highly stressful, to say the least. But Glaser and his colleagues found the actual cadets, young athletes all, more immunologically stressed during finals. Boot camp did not perturb their immune function in the least.

Stress also plays a major role in the way we handle latent viral infections, which everyone has. Many viruses that infect us are wrestled into submission by our immune system, but are not eliminated. Instead they lie dormant, like an army of terrorists, biding their time for a moment of weakness—stress, in a word. Then they attack the ruling government. Common hidden saboteurs of this kind are the herpes simplex viruses, which cause cold-sore blisters when the immune system is weakened by a cold, and the Epstein-Barr (EB) virus, which is responsible for infectious mononucleosis.

These dormant viruses appear to be reawakened by the release of cortisol and other steroid hormones during times of stress. Then the immune-system cells respond, producing antibodies to seek them out and mark them to be killed by other immune cells. By measuring levels of antibody, scientists can obtain a very precise measure of the immunological effects of stress for a particular person. Using this measure, researchers have shown increased EB-virus activity in people under stress, such as students taking exams and caregivers for people with Alzheimer's disease.[13]

Stress plays a role in the course of infection with a more sinister virus, human immunodeficiency virus (HIV). Researchers found, for example, that HIV infection progressed faster in infected gay men who stayed in the closet.[14] Infected men who were open about their gay identity did better. In other respects, in this particular study, the men's lives, personalities, and coping styles were similar. It makes sense to conclude that the stress of concealing an important part of one's identity is bad for health.

In general, researchers agree that negative moods are bad for immune functioning, while positive moods enhance it, even on a day-to-day level. In fact, the latest research indicates clearly that *mood is what matters:* Life events impact immune function by altering mood.[15] In other words, it is not just what happens to us that fine-tunes our immune responses, but how we react emotionally.

Love, Medicine, and Miracles: Fact or Fiction?

Lily, a patient of mine, had been married for many years to Dave when his colon cancer was diagnosed. Lily was a devoted wife, and she did whatever she could to help Dave manage his illness. But she herself was overwhelmed—with sadness at the prospect of losing him, fear of being alone, and anger at her situation, which seemed especially unfair as Dave had maintained a meticulously healthy lifestyle. She kept her feelings under wraps, however: She was terrified to express any anger, irritability, or negative feelings in front of Dave lest she "Bernie Siegel" her husband to death. Lily was referring, of course, to the author of *Mind, Medicine and Miracles*, who has suggested a powerful link between cancer and the patient's state of mind.[16] Siegel links a person's attitude with both his likelihood of getting cancer and his prospect for recovery.

Some physicians and scientists have criticized this approach as blaming the patient for the illness. They argue that Siegel places an unfair responsibility on the patient to recover miraculously.[17] To some degree this criticism is justified. There are so many types of cancer and so many factors involved. It is bad enough to learn that one has cancer. Why make it worse by taking on feelings of guilt and responsibility for the affliction—especially when there's no way to know the "truth."

"We would rather feel guilty than helpless," observes David Spiegel, professor of psychiatry at Stanford University, and I agree. In addition, who wouldn't want to believe that we can overcome potentially fatal illnesses by an effort of will?

Such a hope would seem harmless, even helpful, were it not for its dark corollary. What happens if the illness gets worse, not better? Is it the patient's fault? Has he not wished or tried hard enough? It is wrong to hold those who have battled cancer bravely responsible for their own demise.

Human Studies of Psychological Treatments in Cancer Patients

Spiegel has thought long and hard about these issues, and no wonder: It was his landmark study, conducted with colleagues at Stanford

University, that brought the debate about the psychological effects on cancer into respectable medical circles. In a 1989 study of women with metastatic breast cancer, Spiegel's team found that those women who received weekly supportive group therapy survived almost twice as long as those who did not, specifically 36.6 months versus 18.9 months.[18]

Spiegel's study galvanized both cancer patients and cancer specialists to consider emotional support as part of the treatment for breast cancer. Given what we know about stress and the immune system, this is a good thing. Yet the awkward fact is that no one has been able to replicate Spiegel's original success.[19] He himself is in the tenth year of an attempt at replication.

Is it something about the type of therapy or the skill of the original therapists that accounted for the success of the original study? Or is it simply that all the publicity about the Spiegel study has empowered breast-cancer patients everywhere to reach out to their friends and family, and express their feelings freely. Maybe today's "control groups" are getting their own "group therapy" at home. In any event, nobody knows at this time whether group therapy can prolong the lives of cancer patients.

Based on his extensive experience, however, Spiegel suggests seven important psychological strategies for managing cancer:

1. *Express your emotions.* Expressing emotions serves several vital functions. It helps people come to terms with the critical life issues presented by illness, and it is crucial for mobilizing social support. People who are able to hang in despite the negative feelings they have about their illness and express themselves in a direct way seem to do best. There are unpleasant aspects of serious illnesses that one might understandably prefer to ignore, but they are best discussed. For example, a person might have concerns about whom she can count on if unable to take care of herself or how she would like her body handled after death.

2. *Build bonds and social supports.* Spiegel notes that social isolation can be as great a risk factor to general health as smoking. He recalls one breast cancer patient, a beautiful model, who was thinking of taking her life because she was losing her beauty. The emotional support she received from her support group helped her reevaluate how much she still had to live for.

3. *Detoxify the fear of death and dying.* Again, once you express and face your fears, you will be able to take action. For example, do you have a living will? Do your family and doctors know what it says? Does it say everything you want it to? I know a nurse whose living will specifies that she be fed chocolate ice cream. What a great way to detoxify your fears of dying!

4. *Reorder your life priorities.* If there is something you have to do, do it now. Leave the rest for later.

5. *Improve your family relationships.* If you live another thirty years, you will be glad you stayed close to your family. If you die next month, your family will be glad you made peace with them.

6. *Improve communications with your physicians.* A good bond between you and your doctor is critical for getting the best treatment. If you are unable to communicate with your physician, consider finding another one.

7. *Control your symptoms, for example, by learning self-hypnosis.* Remember, you are not helpless to exert some control over your symptoms.

Spiegel emphasizes the value of hoping for the best while preparing for the worst. He advocates balance in dealing with issues of truth about a patient's disease. He favors telling patients the truth, even when the news is bad, because it helps them come to terms with reality. But he disapproves of what he calls "truth bashing," the indiscriminate all-at-once communication of a person's predicament, regardless of time or circumstance. Instead, he advocates tact and consideration for how much information a person can handle at a given moment.

"Find something to hope for within the context of what is realistic," Spiegel recommends. Of course, hopes may change over the course of time. Initially, one might realistically hope to survive. If it becomes apparent that the illness is progressing, the focus of hope can shift—for example to staying alive as long as possible, or to attaining some special goal, such as a child's wedding. Hope can literally keep people alive, which is why people are more likely to die after birthdays or holidays than before them.[20] It is as though their minds will their bodies to hold on just that little bit longer so they can enjoy the special day.

Setting aside the replication issue, Spiegel's study is by no means alone in finding value to intervening psychologically with cancer patients. A 1993 study by Dr. Fawzy Fawzy and colleagues at the University of California School of Medicine investigated the effects of psychotherapy on sixty-eight patients who had malignant melanoma, a virulent form of skin cancer.[21] After all the patients received standard surgical care, over a six-week period, half of the patients received six structured group-therapy sessions. In these sessions, they learned about their illness, stress management, and how to improve their coping skills; and they received emotional support from other group members and staff.

Six years later, 10 of the 34 members of the control group (29 percent) had died as compared with only 3 of the 34 members of the treatment group (9 percent). It is well known that immune functioning is critical to the course of malignant melanoma. In fact, an important form of treatment for this particular cancer involves administering the naturally occurring substance interferon, which boosts the immune system's attack against the tumor. It is quite likely that the psychological intervention in this study improved the outcome by enhancing immune function.

A curious secondary finding to emerge from this study is that those patients who initially showed the *least* emotional distress were *more* likely to suffer recurrence and death. On the surface this would seem contradictory: Doesn't distress injure immune function? Yes, it can. But the researchers suggest that when one is that seriously ill, a ho-hum attitude amounts to minimizing the problem, which is a bad way of dealing with it. As you will remember, Pennebaker's writing studies are quite clear: There is value in probing difficult feelings. As Spiegel points out, "Don't pretend that everything's OK. Once you address painful feelings, you can take whatever steps are necessary and make the most of the time that you have left." That is wise advice, not just for cancer patients but for all of us.

Basic Studies Suggesting a Link Between State of Mind and Cancer-Fighting Potential

Cancers often begin with damage to the DNA, the genetic code, by carcinogens such as those found in cigarette smoke. Once damaged, the altered cell begins to reproduce too fast, and so do its daughter cells, and on and on. The result is cancer. DNA damage occurs quite often, and the body has enzymes that repair it. Unfortunately, it seems that DNA repair is one more body function affected by stress. In a study of psychiatric patients, for example, Kiecolt-Glaser and colleagues found that X-ray damage to the DNA of lymphocytes (a type of immune cell) of psychiatric patients was less readily repaired than similar damage to the lymphocytes of healthy people.[22] In addition, the more depressed the patient, the worse the repair.

Nor is that all. Another part of the immune system, the *natural killer cells*, which seek out and destroy abnormal cells, become less active when a person is under stress.[23] And stress can throw off a process known as *apoptosis*, cell suicide triggered by the cell's genetic program when something is not quite right. Apoptosis is very handy when it comes to tumor cells.

In summary, basic immunological studies show that stress can impede DNA repair, natural killer cell function, and apoptosis, all of which are important in halting cancers while they are still just one or two cells. As a friend of mine likes to say, "If you have to wrestle an alligator, wrestle it while it's small."

Let us return then to Lily, my patient who feared that she might aggravate her husband's cancer if she were not continuously nice to him. I knew much less about the topic then than I do now. Indeed, some of the studies I've mentioned here had not yet been done. But I don't think my advice to her would be substantially different today. I advised her not to worry about minor aspects of their communication, pointing out that she cared deeply for her husband, Dave, *and* he knew that, and it was a comfort to him.

The doctors had given Dave less than a year to live, but he was a fighter. A highly intelligent man, he sought out experimental treatments for his form of cancer and would travel to other cities to participate in various treatment protocols. Lily was always there, keeping him company, driving him around, attending to his nutrition, dealing with his health-care professionals, and taking care of his many small daily needs. He defied the predictions of the doctors and went on to live for more than six years after receiving the diagnosis, during much of which time he was able to enjoy his life with Lily and his family.

As one definition of the word "miracle," *Webster's Dictionary* offers, "a wonder or wonderful thing." By that definition, Dave's longevity, several-fold greater than his doctors had predicted, certainly qualifies as a miracle. It is hard to believe that Dave's brave and intelligent fight did not contribute to this outcome. Nor could he have beaten the odds without the many ways in which Lily lovingly helped him through.

In some ways, therefore, Bernie Siegel had an important point. Miracles of this kind can happen, and when they do, they are often a tribute to the strength of the human spirit and the power of love. This is an excellent basis for hope. But had the tumor been of a different type, maybe all of Dave and Lily's best efforts would have been in vain. Would that have made his fight any less worthy or her love and wisdom any less profound? That is why it is very important not to place the burden of recovery on the patient's attitude. Diligent care of an illness, which includes attention to stress and emotional well-being, will often improve both the quality and the quantity of life, but there are always factors beyond our control. To quote Spiegel, the best strategy is to hope for the best and prepare for the worst.

Managing Your Emotions to Lead a Healthier Life: Thirteen Research-Based Suggestions

Considering the important influence that the emotions have on physical health, how can you use this knowledge to best effect? When the emotions are seriously disturbed, for example in disorders of mood, anxiety, or anger control, certain specific measures are needed. (For further discussions of this, see chapters 8, 9, and 12.) But even for those who have no emotional disorder, it pays to deal effectively with the feelings that accompany the everyday ups and downs of life. Here are some suggestions to help you do so, based on the latest research findings.

1. *Use your emotions and bodily responses to recognize when you are under stress.* Although you may think it is simple to tell when you are under stress, it is by no means always obvious, especially

over the long term. Many people are so *used* to feeling stressed that they can't imagine life any other way.

Taking a daily inventory of your emotions takes only a minute or two, yet the payoff can be big. An emotional inventory will draw your attention to negative feelings that you might otherwise brush aside. Once you know you are upset, you can better pinpoint why and what to do about it.

Listen to your body, which often gives off early warning signals. A racing pulse, dry mouth, aching stomach, tight muscles, or muscle pain may all indicate that something is amiss in your emotional world.

2. *Write down your thoughts and feelings about what is stressing you.* Research indicates that if you sweep your feelings under the rug, your body will pay the price. Actively suppressing emotions, *even positive ones*, overworks the cardiovascular system.[24] When health plans offer psychological services, several studies have found that the use of medical services drops.[25] It's a fact: Handling your negative emotions well can pay off in fewer doctor visits.

While going to a therapist may be helpful, it is not always possible or necessary to do so. You can be your own best therapist by writing down your feelings about painful or traumatic experiences, as well as the thoughts that go along with them, for short periods over several days. The details of this method are described in full on pages 203–204.

This technique, which involves a total of one to two hours of writing time, has been thoroughly researched by many groups. Among the results:

- After college students used the method, they needed fewer visits to the student health clinic.
- Several studies, each measuring results by a different method, all found improved immune response after the writing exercise.[26]
- Seventy-one patients with either asthma or rheumatoid arthritis were asked to write briefly about the most stressful events of their lives.[27] Four months later, they were doing significantly better medically than similar patients who wrote

about neutral events. Both asthma and rheumatoid arthritis involve abnormalities in the immune system, so the observed improvements may have resulted from enhanced immune functioning.

If so little time to examine feelings and thoughts can help so much, possibly an ongoing journal might work even better. But for the writing to pay off, you have to write about difficult or painful experiences, not just superficial activities. It is also important to write about the thoughts that go with the feelings.

3. *Don't make mountains out of molehills.* Robert Sapolsky, professor of biological sciences at Stanford University, has studied stress in baboons in the wild.[28] He finds that the male baboons who can discriminate a threatening gesture from a neutral one have lower circulating levels of the stress hormone cortisol than baboons who are unable to make this critical distinction. If you want to live a low-stress life, don't get all worked up over trivial matters.

When difficult situations arise, it is important to assess how bad they really are before going into panic mode. One of my good friends, a psychologist, often asks, "What is the worst that could happen?" That's a good question to help put minor stresses into perspective.

4. *Control whatever aspect of the stress that you can.* Even in situations that you can't control, there may be some piece you can change—and that can make all the difference. For example, I remember a time in a doctor's office when a nurse said to me, "Put on the robe and lie down facing the wall. The doctor will be with you in a moment." The piece of crepe paper she handed me bore little resemblance to a robe.

In the past I might have followed instructions. Now I am aware that if I lie down facing the wall and the doctor walks into the office from behind me, I will feel out of control and, therefore, will be far more stressed. For that reason, now I put on the crepe paper and sit up facing the door, ready to greet the doctor face to face. I still don't have control over the medical procedure, but at least I feel like a person rather than an object.

Life presents many such situations every day, and you should not view them in black-and-white terms—those you can control versus those you cannot. Look for the shades of gray—elements you *can* control. I bet you will feel much less stressed that way.

Closely related to control is predictability, which is another way to reduce stress. When you know what's going to happen, your nervous system can gear up to handle it. Have you ever been in a dentist's chair and wondered, "How long is this drilling going to go on?" Ask the dentist. Just having that knowledge will make you feel better. Do this to lessen other types of stresses, too, such as tax audits, litigation, and surgery. In each case, ask the professional involved what you can expect. How long will it take? What are the exact procedures? What extensions are available if necessary?

Many experiments with both humans and other animals have shown how much control and predictability matter. For example:

- Caged rats were given shocks under two conditions—without warning and preceded by a warning bell. Although all the rats suffered the exact same number of shocks, those that knew what to expect developed fewer stomach ulcers. Not only could they predict when the shocks would come, but the rest of the time they could relax, knowing they would not be shocked. There was no need to be hypervigilant.[29]
- Nursing home residents were divided into two groups. The subjects in one of the groups were encouraged to make their own decisions about their daily activities, such as their choice of meals and social activities, whereas the members of the other group had their decisions made for them. The first group was not only happier and healthier, but also had only half the death rate of the second group.[30]
- People suffering from severe pain were initially required to ask a nurse for the powerful and potentially addictive pain medications they needed. Then researchers decided to see what would happen if the patients had ready access to these medications at all times and were permitted to determine their own medication needs. Paradoxically, medication use decreased, presumably because the enhanced sense of control helped the patients relax and do with less medication.[31]

5. *Redefine the problem.* Shakespeare, an early spin doctor, noted that "There's nothing that is good or bad but thinking makes it so."[32] Your attitude to a stress can affect your health more than the stress itself can.

Sally was a teller at an extremely busy bank. She came to me for treatment because she felt like "a nervous wreck." She found her job overwhelming and blamed it for her chronic backaches and stomach ulcers. One problem was that there were too few tellers. As a consequence, the lines were long and the customers were often angry and rude by the time they finally reached the window. Sally caught the brunt of their complaints, and she kept working faster and harder, faster and harder, to keep the line moving. Complaints to management fell on deaf ears, and no new tellers were added.

These trying conditions continued until one day, Sally had an epiphany. If there were long lines in front of her window, she thought, surely that was the bank's problem, not hers. The next morning she opened up for business and went about her tasks in a brisk and cheerful manner. The line soon began to grow, as usual. Sally looked out at it and thought, "My, but the bank has a problem today." After a short while the customers began to complain, but instead of apologizing and working harder, Sally responded cheerfully, "I don't blame you a bit. It really is a shame that there are not more tellers. Perhaps you want to mention it to the manager."

She repeated this refrain all day. By the very next day, Sally began to feel her stress level dropping, and within weeks both her back and stomach felt better. Within a month, management decided to add extra tellers and the lines became noticeably shorter.

Sally's story is an excellent example of how redefining a problem can help. Sally was literally shouldering the bank's burden, and she felt it in her body. By placing the burden where it belonged, she relieved her stress and obtained the extra help she needed.

So important is the influence of thoughts, or cognitions, on the way we feel that there is a whole form of therapy devoted to changing them, namely cognitive therapy, or cognitive-behavior therapy (CBT). This form of treatment, which has been shown to be effective in helping people suffering from depression, anxiety, and excessive anger, can have physical benefits as well. (For further discussions of this, see chapters 8, 9, and 12.)

6. *Develop behaviors that distract you from stress.* We know that caged rats exposed to electric shocks develop ulcers. But if the shocked rats are able to run over and gnaw on a piece of wood after being shocked, they develop fewer ulcers.[33] This experiment shows what many of us have already discovered—that it helps to have an outlet for your frustration, especially a physical one. Go for a walk, chop wood, pull weeds out of the garden. Anything you do that distracts you from your stress for a while is probably helping physically as well.

7. *Reach out to a friend or family member.* There is a group of rhesus monkeys in Sri Lanka called the Temple Troop that has been observed by filmmakers for some time.[34] These journalists caught on film an amazing tale of three monkeys: Hegel, Jeeves, and Ducci. Hegel led the troop for five years, far longer than the average three-year tenure of a leader. He showed kindness and consideration to the other monkeys in the troop and was much loved and respected. Then a younger monkey, Ducci, made a play for the top position. After months of aggressive moves by Ducci, it was clear that a battle for dominance was imminent. Although Jeeves, Hegel's good friend, attempted to intervene, the law of the troop prevailed. The fight between the two principals took place.

The day after, the filmmakers found Hegel mortally wounded, with all the members of the troop except Ducci stopping by to pay their respects. Jeeves even tried to help his friend by licking the blood off his gaping wound. But Hegel died, and Ducci took over leadership. Ducci proved to be a harsh leader, however, and after a mere three months, the filmmakers found him deposed and isolated. In his place, the troop had installed Jeeves, renouncing a bully in favor of a friend.

All primates, it seems, need friends, as indicated by the following studies:

- People with spouses or close friends have longer life expectancies than those who do not.[35] When a spouse dies, the risk of death for the remaining spouse increases greatly.
- Patients with severe heart disease had a three times higher rate of death if they lacked a spouse or close friend, according to a study by Redford Williams, professor of psychiatry at Duke University, and colleagues.[36] In fact, half of the loners in the study died within five years. Domestic companionship probably protects by lowering the levels of stress hormones. These hormones increase the blood pressure and promote clotting and damage to arterial walls.
- Beyond significant others, just plain friends can also lower stress. In one study, people were stressed with challenging tasks such as doing mental arithmetic, either on their own or with a friend present. Blood pressure rose less in those with friendly support.[37] In a similar study, researchers found that a supportive stranger was better than no one, but not as soothing as a friend.[38]
- Having different *types* of social relationships is also good for your health. Categories might include your spouse or partner, parents, children, other close family members, close neighbors, and friends. In an experiment in which people were exposed to cold viruses, those who reported having only one to three types of relationships were four times more likely to develop a cold than those with six or more.[39] In fact, diverse social ties outweighed more obvious factors such as exercise or smoking.

Many other studies all point in the same direction. Friends and loved ones not only enrich the quality of our lives but are good for our health. Being alone is stressful but reversible. Look at your own social network. If you find it lacking, think of ways to expand it. There is no shortage of groups, clubs, and other opportunities to meet people and develop relationships. Many people find it easiest to meet others during a shared activity, which provides (if nothing else) something to talk about. People who enjoy doing the same things that you enjoy are good candidates for friendship.

Cicero observed thousands of years ago that sharing your life with a friend doubles your pleasure and halves your suffering. This is worth bearing in mind if you ever find yourself wondering whether a particular person is truly a friend. And it is also a good prescription for your half of the transaction—being a friend. When friends are together, they should feel the relaxing benefit of spending time with someone who is solidly in their corner.

For many people, the unconditional love offered by cats and dogs provides much joy, greatly relieving feelings of stress and loneliness. In addition, pet owners live longer, and people out walking with their dogs become acquainted with other dog walkers. A puppy is a virtual people magnet.

Some people have turned to the Internet as a source of friendship, but the data so far suggest that the Net is a mixed blessing. Although I know at least one person who met his soul mate through the Net, a Carnegie Mellon University study found that heavy Internet use was associated with higher levels of depression, perhaps because the people on the other end of the line were not really friends.[40] It is far better to depend on the kindness of friends than the kindness of strangers.

8. *Exercise regularly.* Regular exercise is good not only for the cardiovascular and immune systems, but also for emotional well-being. (For further discussions of this, see pages 188 and 330.)

For those of us who are not superathletes, it is a comfort to know that even moderate amounts of exercise can help. In embarking on an exercise program, you would do well to choose a type of exercise you enjoy because you are much more likely to stick with it. My favorite exercise is walking, which is a way for me to feel connected to my neighborhood and the changing seasons. Some people like to exercise alone, but others, like myself, prefer company. On my regular walks with a friend, we often see a group of women from the neighborhood, striding along briskly and obviously having a great time—an excellent way to combine two stress-reducing strategies, exercise and social support.

9. *Meditate and relax.* Meditation, the Eastern practice of actively stilling the mind, has favorable effects on both the mind and

the body.[41] It is well known, for example, that meditators are able to decrease their heart rate and skin conductance while meditating. Once you have caught the knack of meditation, you can use it to calm yourself down in stressful situations. And of course, meditation classes are one more place where you can meet new people.

Studies of medical students and residents of independent living facilities have found that hypnosis and relaxation can enhance immune functioning in both the young and the old.

10. *Try a healthy dose of humor.* There is a story of a short Jewish man who was walking along a narrow lane in a small town in Eastern Europe when a burly soldier from the Czar's army hurried by and knocked him off his feet. The small man picked himself up, dusted himself off, and turned to the soldier. "Did you do that out of spite," he asked, "or just as a joke?"

"Out of spite," the soldier replied.

"Good," replied the little man, "because I don't like those kinds of jokes."

Over centuries of persecution, the Jews have developed a finely honed sense of humor to temper their feelings of powerlessness. If they could not stop the persecution, at least they could view it in an ironic, distancing way. In telling stories about their hardships, in some small fashion, they capture the storyteller's sense of control over events. In Yiddish there is a term that means "a bitter laugh" that is used to indicate a humor wrenched out of sad circumstances. Many other peoples in the role of the underdog have also resorted to humor.

It now emerges from scientific research that humor actually has health benefits. For example:

- Laughter produces changes in the heart rate, blood pressure, and respiration similar to those seen after vigorous exercise.[42]
- Exposure to funny stimuli reduces feelings of anger, aggressive behavior, anxiety, learned helplessness, and depression.[43]
- The blood from volunteers who had viewed a humorous videotape showed fewer metabolic signs of stress and enhanced immune function as compared to the blood from people who did not view the tape.[44]

- Need one have a good sense of humor to enjoy these benefits? Apparently not. In research by psychologists Michelle Gayle Newman and Arthur Stone of the State University of New York at Buffalo, forty people who were judged to have a good sense of humor (based on standardized tests) watched a stressful silent movie about industrial accidents. Half of the subjects were asked to provide a humorous running commentary, whereas the other half was asked to comment seriously. Another forty subjects who scored low on sense of humor went through the same protocol.[45]

  The results: The humorous narrative was associated with a less negative mood, less tension, and less stress-related physical change. Better yet, the scores on the sense-of-humor tests had no bearing. So you need not be a stand-up comedian to derive health benefits from humor.

As part of your stress-management program, find something that makes you laugh and take a few moments to enjoy it—*regularly*. Alternatively, take whatever it is that stresses you, and as an exercise, deliberately set about finding a humorous angle to it. Perhaps imagining your Scrooge-like boss in a pink tutu will lighten your heart the next time he glowers. I recall a certain government bureaucrat who seemed to delight in blocking my initiatives and those of my colleagues. When I heard her voice on my answering machine, it was never good news. I would feel my blood curdling even before I knew exactly what she wanted. Then, one day over lunch a friend told me of a mental trick he had devised to help deal with her. "Imagine that you are playing a video game," he suggested, "and that she is the last major obstacle. You go through this labyrinth and slay all the monsters, and finally you have to do battle with the dragon lady before you can win the game." I found his strategy not only amusing but very helpful, and I have little doubt that it reduced my heart rate and blood pressure in my further dealings with her. Next time you are confronted by such an adversary, try the imaginary video-game strategy. You may be surprised at how well it works.

11. *Temper your temperament—or change it.* Like so many of my contemporaries, I have dabbled in the stock market over the years. I

would buy a few shares on some hot tip and watch the stock closely, riding the predictable highs and lows as it rose or fell. Like most people, I was energized by bull markets and bought, and I was demoralized by bear markets and sold. This strategy, driven by my temperament, resulted in buying high and selling low. Something different had to be done. I had to temper my temperament.

I did this by retaining a financial analyst who had helped a friend of mine succeed during my period of stock market experimentation. To paraphrase the language of twelve-step programs, when it came to investments, I made the decision to turn my will over to the care of my financial analyst. Henceforth, I would neither buy nor sell stocks without his approval. It soon became clear that he was to be as much a therapist as a financial consultant. In one conversation he gave me his clinical formulation. "There are nerves that go between the stomach and the brain," he said. "When markets move up and down, these nerves send signals to the brain and people act on those signals. In my case those nerves are severed. You have a double set of them. My job is to help prevent you from acting impulsively on those nerves when they begin to fire."

As we know, temperament is largely genetic, rather stable during adult life, and difficult to change. If you know that you have a certain type of temperament that causes you stress, repeated difficulties, or unhappiness, don't beat up on yourself and promise to "reform." Instead, reach out. For example, if your problem is making yourself sit down and pay your bills, find someone with whom to share the chore. Or hire someone to come in once a month to get your checks ready to sign.

If you are in the market for romance, find someone with a different temperament whom you trust to offset your less desirable traits. People instinctively tend to do that, which is why optimists tend to marry pessimists, highly emotional people marry more controlled people, and so on. And this is a good thing too, provided they continue to appreciate each other.

Some people with worrisome or pessimistic temperaments probably suffer from lesser forms of the altered brain chemistry that causes full-blown anxiety attacks or depression. These people may benefit from the medical remedies that are so helpful for their more afflicted counterparts. (For discussions of this, see chapters 8 and 12.)

12. *Hope for the best.* Optimism is associated with numerous health benefits. In one study of men undergoing bypass surgery, the optimists were more likely to cope by focusing on their goals following surgery.[46] Five years later more optimists than pessimists had adopted healthier habits, such as eating a low-fat diet, taking vitamins, or participating in a cardiac rehabilitation program.

Optimistic people are more likely to stay informed about health-related issues[47] and more likely to schedule screening procedures for the early detection of skin or breast cancer.[48] Whereas a pessimist, fearing the worst, might tend to avoid such visits, an optimist is more likely to reason, "If something negative turns up, it's better to catch it sooner than later. Then I can take care of it more effectively."

13. *The healing power of faith.* Any seasoned doctor can call to mind cases that went sour, sometimes fatally so, because the patient sought out some form of faith healing instead of using conventional medicine. After the disease progressed, many of these patients turned back to conventional medicine, but often too late. You can see why doctors tend to bristle at the words "faith healing."

At the same time, there is evidence that faith can heal. I am not myself convinced by the few studies supporting the healing power of prayer or "healing touch." Yet astonishing things do happen—that's another thing any seasoned doctor has seen. Certainly researchers would agree that about one-third of all patients will respond to placebos, such as sugar pills or some other treatment that theoretically "should" have no effect.[49] That shows how powerful it can be to believe that something will help, or even merely that it might help. Belief seems to turn on the body's ability to heal itself.

You can use this effect to your advantage. If you believe that a certain treatment might help you, *and* if you are not harming yourself by using it, such as by putting off starting a treatment of proven efficacy, then why not pursue it? In my own practice, if there are two treatments that have a roughly equal chance of helping, I will almost always start with the one preferred by the patient.

I should also say that the alternative practitioners whom I know prefer the word "complementary" because they see their work as an adjunct, not a stand-alone. "I want my patients to have the best that Western medicine can offer," says one acupuncturist. "If your readers come across someone who wants them to disobey their doctor's orders, tell them to run in the other direction. That's unethical. Also, beware of anyone who promises a cure. That's the hallmark of a quack."

Faith is an important element in all religious beliefs. Many studies have shown that people who participate in religious activities enjoy longer and healthier lives. Those who attend church services regularly have lower rates of cardiovascular disease, emphysema, and cirrhosis of the liver. They also tend to live longer.[50]

Of course, religious people lead healthier lives for reasons other than their beliefs. They may smoke and drink less than nonobservant people, and they may socialize with the members of their congregation. One study of religious and secular kibbutzes in Israel, however, suggests that the social element cannot explain the health benefits of religion. Kibbutzim are a communal form of living, by definition. Yet between 1970 and 1985, the mortality rate was almost double for those living on secular versus religious kibbutzim, even though the level of social support and contact was similar in both.[51]

Why is religion good for health? Nobody knows for sure. But the explanations include the transcendent feeling of connection with a higher power, the security of a belief system that can explain the curious contradictions in life; and the sense of comfort, in some religions, from believing that you will be rewarded somewhere down the line for your belief or for living a good religious life.

Religion can be of enormous comfort to people facing tragedy that is beyond their control; I have seen that often. No wonder, then, that nonobservant people turn to religion in hard times. I recall one elderly man who became religious when confronted with a potentially fatal disease. When his friends inquired about his late conversion, he replied ruefully, "I'm cramming for finals." Besides considerations of faith, his decision might well have been wise from a medical point of view.

To summarize the central point of this chapter, stress and negative emotions can result in illness and premature death. There are many ways to reduce stress, and much to be gained by using them. To quote Ron Glaser, a distinguished immunologist, "stress is a public health issue." A highly driven personality himself, he has taken his data to heart and has incorporated stress-management behaviors into his own life. After considering the data presented in this chapter, you, too, may be persuaded, as I have been, that feelings exert a potent influence on physical health.

PART TWO

FEELINGS

Chapter 7

What Doesn't Kill You Makes You Stronger

I N this next group of chapters, I talk about specific emotions: fear and anxiety, anger and rage, love and lust, sadness and depression, and happiness and euphoria. Before going on, I'd like to point out a few facts about emotions, so big that sometimes it is hard to see them, for the same reason (to borrow a Zen parable) that fish can't see water: To them, it's everywhere. They swim in water as we swim in emotions.

Fact 1: Our Emotions Tend to Push Us Forward or Drive Us Back

When our slimy forebears first slithered out of the sea (and probably long before), they were confronted at every turn with both menace and opportunity, which required decisions. Each new creature they encountered triggered the basic question: "Food or foe? Am I his next meal or is he mine?" To seize or to run—the decision often needed split-second timing, and creatures that were slow to make the right call and act on it did not live long enough to pass on their genes.[1]

Scenarios like that one help me imagine how our emotions evolved as forces that motivate us, quicker than thought, either toward something or away from it. Researchers refer to this directional quality of the emotions as valence and speak of positive and negative emotions. Those terms do not mean good or bad, but have to do with direction. Positive emotions urge us forward, to approach something beneficial, such as an opportunity or an object of delight. Negative emotions drive us back, to withdraw from something menacing, dangerous, or disgusting.

Positive emotions, such as happiness and love, tell us that we are in a safe environment that offers opportunities we should pursue. Love and lust, for example, drive us to approach the object of our desire, to mate and procreate, to spend time with our loved one and raise a family to give our genes the best chance of survival. Happiness arises at the prospect of food, territory, success, or opportunity; it propels us to seize, venture out, conquer, and accumulate those resources that we need to flourish.[2] Whether you are a hunter-gatherer, setting out to bring food back to your family, or a modern worker, making a cold call from a cubicle in a fourteenth-floor office, it's all about resources. Bringing down a mastodon probably didn't feel all that different from making the first million-dollar sale—happiness. The joy of accomplishment, though wonderful, is usually transient, giving way to new goals and further striving.

Fact 2: Our Emotions Did Not Evolve to Make Us Happy

As I mentioned, by positive and negative feelings, I do not mean feelings that are good or bad for us. Negative feelings, such as fear and sadness, are good for us when they tell us something important about our world. For example, if a person is threatened by a lion, he should feel afraid; if he loses a loved one, he should grieve. Conversely, positive emotions are not always good for us. Falling in love with a dangerous stranger can spell disaster. Being blissfully happy from snorting a line of cocaine is a sign of trouble. Our emotions did not evolve to make us happy. They evolved to save our lives and ensure that we could successfully pass on our genes.

But like everything else, emotions don't always work as they should; and when they fail or falter, we need help. In the coming chapters, I'll discuss each emotion in its healthy form, which evolved as a survival tool, and in its negative form, when it goes haywire. Emotions in their healthy form constitute our limbic news; we must pay attention to them. When emotions go haywire, however, they can cause unspeakable misery, so we must learn to heal them.

Fact 3: Mixed Emotions Are the Norm, Not Necessarily a Problem

In this book, for the sake of organization, I have separated the emotions into chapters of their own. In real life, though, an emotion is almost never pure. Sometimes people are most angry with the ones they love, and most violence occurs between people who know each other, often intimately. As Holocaust survivor Elie Wiesel has said, "The opposite of love is not hate, it's indifference."

Work by psychologist John Gottman bears that out. Gottman found that withdrawal, rather than argument, is more likely to presage the end of a marriage.[3] In other research, John Cacioppo, professor of psychology at the University of Chicago, and colleagues examined positive and negative attitudes toward donating blood.[4] It turned out that the people with neutral attitudes, those who could take or leave it, were less likely to donate blood than those who were ambivalent, expressing both strong positive and negative attitudes (as in, "The blood bank saved my mother's life, but I hate needles").

Success does not depend on being consistent in our feelings. A marriage can succeed even when love is mixed with anger. We can perform good deeds even toward those for whom we harbor darker sentiments as well. We can do good work, such as at Los Alamos, even if we predict it will have harmful consequences. Often the most successful people are those who can accept and work with the ambiguities and complexities of their emotional landscape.

Fact 4: Positive and Negative Feelings Operate Independently

The fact that positive and negative feelings operate independently, which emerges from recent research on emotions, is extremely interesting to me because I would not have predicted it. Certainly, many people act as if life were otherwise. We somehow think that we'd be happy if we could get rid of the negative—if only our boss would quit, or we got a new car, or the other political party would win the election.

This turns out not to be true. The absence of fear, anger, and grief does not guarantee happiness, though it certainly helps clear the way for positive feelings. In fact, fear can sometimes even boost happiness, as in bungee jumping or climbing Mount Everest: Fear intensifies the pleasure of the accomplishment.

Research consistently bears out that positive and negative emotions are independent. For example, in a 1994 study, researchers administered a questionnaire designed to measure the positive and negative feelings in college students on three successive class days. On the middle of these three days, the students received their grades from a major exam.[5]

Sure enough, the students with good grades showed an increase in their positive feelings, but no decrease in their negative ones. Apparently, getting an A does not compensate for having your roommate eat up all of the pizza, any more than a trip to Hawaii can save a dead marriage. The pattern also held true in reverse. The students with poor grades had increased negative feelings, but no loss of their positive ones. In other words, despite getting a D, falling in love still feels good. Other studies produced similar results: Positive and negative feelings do not mirror each other. The two do not correlate.

Brain-imaging studies tell a similar story: Happy feelings light up different parts of the brain than do sad ones.[6] Although antidepressants, as their name implies, reverse sad, depressed feelings, they do not increase happiness in those who are not depressed. To me, the number of "normal" people who respond to Prozac and its cousins simply shows how much undiagnosed depression there really is.

Why, then, do we humans keep having this feeling that life would be wonderful if only . . . Well, perhaps because of the following.

Fact 5: We Are Amazingly Optimistic Creatures

All things being equal, healthy people (and other animals) have a positive emotional bias toward the world. We generally expect the best.

Researchers have tested this, asking people to assess the outcome of unknown future events,[7] or to give their impression of neutral, unknown, or ambiguous situations.[8] The findings are consistent: an unrealistic optimism. Curiously, people who are not depressed believe they have more control over their world than they really do. This distorted sense of reality gives them an extra boost in approaching the world, making them more willing to venture out and take risks even when the odds are against them. In general, optimists are more likely to succeed.[9] Depressed people, by contrast, sometimes have a more realistic view of what they can and cannot control.[10] They, therefore, do not get the extra boost that comes from unrealistic optimism, which constrains their actions—a research finding that has been called "the sadder but wiser effect."

Cacioppo suggests that the normal tendency toward optimism (even when unwarranted) has been helpful, over the eons, in motivating us to explore the world.[11] If we don't expect the best, there would be little reason to venture into unfamiliar territory.

Fact 6: The Negative Tends to Outweigh the Positive

It makes sense, from an evolutionary point of view, that at any given moment, negative events will seem more urgent. Mating can wait another five minutes (or five hours) if our lives are in jeopardy. So can eating, for that matter. It would be much more important to escape that cave bear or hit the brake.

Again, research bears that out. In study after study, negative events evoke stronger and more rapid bodily, cognitive, and emotional reactions than do neutral or positive ones.[12] This applies to such disparate fields as forming impressions and memories of people, blood and organ donation, hiring decisions, and voting behavior. Cacioppo suggests that this tendency to greater responses to negative events counterbalances the basic optimism of animals and humans. All things being equal, we venture forth into the world expecting the best, hoping it will make us stronger. But if we encounter the worst, we are quick to regroup to make sure it doesn't kill us.

Chapter 8

Fear and Anxiety

But thy throat is shut and dried, and thy heart against thy side
Hammers: Fear, O Little Hunter—this is fear!
—Rudyard Kipling, "The Song of the Little Hunter"[1]

The thing I fear most is fear.
—Michel Eyquem de Montaigne[2]

The Gift of Fear: Tales of the City

ONE summer evening, a patient of mine named Alix and her friend Jeannie, two single lawyers, were walking home through downtown Washington, D.C., when Jeannie suggested they take a shortcut through a park. "I don't think that's a good idea," Alix said. "You see those two men sitting on the park bench? They're probably just waiting to mug us."

"Don't be silly," Jeannie laughed. "There are people all around. Come on, I'll lead the way." Alix looked at the bench again. One of the men, tall and slender, could barely have been twenty. The other, fat and squat, looked older and more sinister. Not wanting to appear neurotic, Alix reluctantly followed Jeannie into the park.

As the women passed the bench, the men jumped them. The tall young man pointed his gun at Alix, while the other turned on Jeannie.

Alix fought the urge to freeze and took command of herself. "What do you want?" she asked.

"Get there behind the shed," the tall young man replied, gesturing with his gun. Alix glanced to the side and saw that the squat ugly man was riffling through Jeannie's pocketbook. Jeannie herself had vanished.

"Look, he has her bag," said Alix to the young man. "Why don't you take mine?" She threw her bag some distance away. It seemed to Alix to take the young man forever to make his decision, the dilemma playing out on his frowning face. Should he go after the bag or zero in on her? Both knew that others could enter the park at any moment.

As the young man turned and ran to retrieve her pocketbook, Alix seized the chance and ran back to the street. There, in front of a Starbucks, she found Jeannie, anxiously looking back toward the park.

Alix's mistake was to ignore her feelings of fear and apprehension, primitive messages from her limbic system that warned her to avoid the park. Once in the park, though, she tuned in to those feelings with perfect pitch and refused to go behind the shed. Had she followed the mugger's instruction, she might have been killed.

Fear is the legacy of millions of years of evolution, a gift that can save your life if you listen to it. Ignore it at your peril.

The mean streets of Washington, D.C., are scary to those who know them well, such as James, a fitness instructor in his mid-forties who grew up in one of the toughest neighborhoods in the city. "In the 'hood," says James, "you survive on your instincts, and instincts are nothing other than fear. When you grow up in the 'hood, fear is a constant feeling. A confrontation can brew up anytime you step outside, and especially when you step out of your territory, which could be no more than a street away." James tells story after story of all the men he knew as a child who had come to grief, like casualties of war. No wonder people now refer to that part of the city as "Little Vietnam."

In his twenties James used to hang out with a man named Showboat. Initially Showboat seemed like a regular guy to James, fun to be with, always lots of laughs. Then drugs began to filter into the neighborhood and Showboat became an enforcer, beating up people who owed the dealers money. He began to wear fancy clothes and behave differently. "He would look right through you when he talked to you," James remembers.

One evening several young men were due to play basketball. James and a friend had planned to meet Showboat in an alley behind Showboat's house. "I have a funny feeling about this," James confided to his friend. "Let's not go there. Let's just meet him at the playground."

"We went on to the playground," James recalls, "but Showboat didn't show up. Someone must have snitched to his enemies that Showboat was going to be in the alley at that time, someone who was there that night when we made plans to meet. I found out from a police buddy of ours that when Showboat went out to the alley to get his motorbike, someone came up behind him and blew the top of his head off. He showed us the police pictures. There was Showboat, still on the motorcycle like he was ready to take off, except the upper half of his head was gone and the crows were perched on the rim of his skull picking at his brains.

"If it hadn't been for my instinct of fear, I would have been killed that day," says James. "They would have killed all of us, thinking we were Showboat's cronies. I found out later that he not only was an enforcer, but was also robbing other drug dealers, which is a no-no. I didn't know all those details at that time, but I just had a bad feeling about it."

The central lesson from these two stories is that fear is a highly adaptive emotion that evolved over millions of years as a response to environmental threats. We may feel fear even when we don't fully understand what's causing it. We should never ignore fear, though in some cases, after careful consideration, we may judge it to be unwarranted.

Scientists have focused their attention on fear and anxiety more than on any other emotion, in large part because there are good animal models. Much of what we know about certain critical limbic structures, such as the amygdala, has come from studying fear. (See chapter 3.) In response to a threat, the amygdala receives input from the senses and other parts of the brain, processes the information, and signals an alarm, firing messages back to the rest of the brain and the body.

While it is true that animals (including humans) are born with certain instinctive fears, such as the fear of snakes, other fears are conditioned. If a rat is repeatedly foot-shocked when it hears a certain tone, it will cower at the sound of the tone even without any shock. Fear conditioning is regulated by the amygdala. Conditioning to a context, such as a park at night or a place where drug dealers meet, also requires a functioning hippocampus, that part of the brain that stores explicit, or cognitive, memories.

We process some warning signals very quickly. A copperhead rearing to strike or a vicious dog with fangs bared will evoke an instinctive response so quickly that you will jump out of harm's way even before you know why you are jumping. Such signals reach the amygdala via "the low road," the thalamus, a primitive structure that sits below the cerebral cortex. Although signals that travel this "low road" are imprecise, they are lightning fast.[3]

Other danger signals take a more complicated route, traveling via the cerebral cortex, the "high road" to the amygdala. When James decided not to meet with Showboat in the alley, many conscious considerations might have gone into that decision—a knowledge of Showboat's recent activities, an understanding that he must have enemies, an ability to predict that he himself might become a collateral target for a gunman. Instinct was clearly not sufficient. These considerations required input from the cerebral cortex to the amygdala. Joseph LeDoux, in his excellent book *The Emotional Brain*, has pointed out that there are far more neural projections from the amygdala to the cerebral cortex than the other way round, which perhaps explains why emotions such as fear can so often dominate intellect.[4]

To make the most out of the gift of fear, it is important to use both gut instinct and thoughtful consideration. Experienced motorists, for example, combine danger cues that enter their awareness almost unconsciously from their peripheral vision with an understanding of driving conditions and the behavior of the other motorists (conscious cognitive information) to reach their destination safely.

Wait Until Dark: Fear and the Startle Reflex

In the 1960 thriller *Wait Until Dark*, Audrey Hepburn plays a blind woman harassed by a man who is trying to steal her doll. (The doll, unbeknownst to her, is full of drugs.) Desperate when she will not give it up, the man tells her on the telephone to "wait until dark." She unscrews the lightbulbs in her apartment and waits for night to fall. Since she is used to living in a world of darkness, she hopes this will give her the upper hand. And it does. When he attacks, she strikes back, stabbing him, and he falls, apparently mortally wounded. But just as she (and the audience) relaxes, the assailant leaps across the room in a last desperate attack. I distinctly remember when I first saw the movie how I literally jumped out of my seat, as did half the people in the movie house.

The technical term for that reaction is *the startle reflex*, which has been studied extensively by Michael Davis of Emory University, and which is closely related to fear.[5] This reflex can be elicited by exposing animals (including humans) to a sudden, unexpected stimulus, such as a loud noise, a blast of air, or a murderer leaping across a movie screen. The reflex is so basic and primitive (it is thought to involve only three neurons) that it can be elicited even in animals with no cerebral cortex.[6] Davis and colleagues have found that, when frightened, an animal will jump higher and startle more easily.[7] In other words, a state of fear potentiates the startle reflex. This insight goes a long way to explain a fundamental benefit of fear—heightening our responses. Fear prepares us to act in split seconds.

Davis describes, for example, a combat veteran who, dressed in a white tuxedo, was standing next to his bride outside the church on his wedding day. When a passing car backfired, the groom dropped flat on his belly behind a bush, covering his finery with mud. In Vietnam, he had been conditioned to respond defensively to loud noises, a reflex that no doubt served him well. But now he was unable to ignore the backfire, and his startle reflex caused him to dive for cover— a victim of Pavlovian conditioning.

Inappropriate startle responses are found in people with posttraumatic stress disorder, such as war veterans, rape victims, Holocaust survivors, and people who were abused in childhood.[8] All these people live in a state of heightened vigilance and arousal, which makes them more likely to overreact, especially to stimuli that resonate with their earlier trauma.

Happily, Davis and colleagues have shown that fear-potentiated startle responses can be deconditioned as well.[9] Take the rat that has been conditioned by foot shocks to fear a bright light. When the light is on, the animal is like the veteran—*very* jumpy. Its startle response is potentiated. However, when the rat is later exposed repeatedly to the light with no foot shock, the conditioning gradually wears off. The animal will learn that the light is no longer a signal that a foot shock is about to occur, and it is no longer afraid. Now when it hears a noise while the light is on, it shows only a normal startle, not a potentiated one.

Davis's work may explain why seeing an apparently dying villain leaping across a movie screen is no longer as scary as it once was. When viewing a similar scene from *Fatal Attraction* in which the vindictive lover bolts out of the bathtub, knife in hand, movie-goers did not generally leap from their seats. We have been deconditioned since *Wait Until Dark*. Ostensible corpses have risen from the dead so many times that we are no longer afraid of them. In addition, the denouement in the earlier movie occurs in a darkened room, whereas the fashionable bathroom in *Fatal Attraction* is brilliantly illuminated.

Davis's group found that average people, not just those with PTSD, show enhanced startle responses to noises when they are in the dark.[10] The opposite is seen in nocturnal animals (such as rats), which show more fearful behavior when in bright light. The fearful response of rats to bright light appears to be intrinsic, not conditioned. In a similar way, we humans may be intrinsically afraid of the dark.[11]

This type of generalized fearfulness, increased arousal, and hypervigilance is more akin to anxiety than to fear. Fear is a response to a *specific* environmental trigger, such as shady characters lurking in a park, whereas anxiety is a *generalized* state. Clinicians see many people with what we call "free-floating" anxiety, an emotional and physical state of fearfulness that has no clear point of reference in the outside world.

Some states resembling anxiety can be adaptive. For example, the way nocturnal animals react to bright light, and daytime creatures to the dark, seems to have evolved along with the two types of vision, regular and night. For diurnal animals (such as humans), nighttime is a dangerous time to venture out because we are disadvantaged in relation to predators with good night vision. A little extra alertness is all to the good. In addition, our behavior and experience are heavily oriented to the daytime world. To us, the night is like a foreign country. The reverse applies for nocturnal animals.

So when children fear the dark, they are feeling a natural biological propensity. A good parent will help the child learn that darkness can be safe by associating bedtime with comforting stimuli, such as a soft toy, soothing music, or a night-light.

Sadly, for some children, this natural fear of the dark is enhanced by a scary home life. I have treated several patients who grew up in homes where shouting and slamming doors were routine late at night, and where physical violence seemed always just a moment away. No wonder that children from such families often grow up anxious and hypervigilant. Even decades later, the smallest noise at night makes these people awake with a jump, unable to get back to sleep.

Recent research on rats by Davis and his colleagues suggests that whereas fear centers on the amygdala, the unconditioned fearfulness that rats experience in very bright light principally involves the bed nucleus of the stria terminalis.[12] This discovery has led Davis to suggest that while fear is mediated by the amygdala, anxiety may be mediated by the bed nucleus. This is another clue suggesting that fear and anxiety are separate emotional states.

Flying into the Sea: The Genetics of Fear and Fearlessness

It was twilight when they set off to fly across the ocean, a strikingly handsome man, his beautiful wife, and her sister. They were the golden people, their activities minutely chronicled in newspapers and popular magazines under photos of their glowing youthful faces. I am referring, of course, to John F. Kennedy, Jr.; his wife, Caroline Bessette Kennedy; and her sister Lauren Bessette, a broker at a major New York firm.[13]

His leg just out of a cast from a recent hang-gliding accident, Kennedy limped across the tarmac to his private plane. They were late in leaving, a haze was settling in, and the sky was darker than usual for that hour. Without clear visibility, instruments would be needed to navigate and Kennedy was only recently trained to use these instruments. A seasoned pilot with years of flying experience watched the Piper Saratoga take off for Martha's Vineyard. Even for himself, he had determined that flying conditions that evening were too risky.

In the weeks preceding the fatal crash, a friend had cautioned Kennedy against his recklessness.[14] The friend suggested that he should see the hang-gliding accident as a warning to slow down and be more careful. The friend referred specifically to Kennedy's flying. What was in the young man's mind the night of the fatal plane crash, we will never know. Did his friend's warning cross his mind even briefly, before being brushed aside? Did he underestimate the dangers? Or was he instead like the Irish airman in Yeats's famous poem who foresaw that he might die but went ahead anyway because of the thrill of flying?

The Greeks understood the importance of caution, as we see, for example, in their myth of Icarus, who flew so high that the sun melted the wax that held his wings together. On that fateful day near Martha's Vineyard another young man flew too high. According to radar images of Kennedy's plane, the pilot appeared to lose his bearings, turning sharply in the wrong direction before plummeting into the sea. Perhaps the simplest and most useful way to understand the fate of both Icarus and Kennedy is as a failure of fear—a fear that older and wiser men understood and heeded, thereby saving their lives.

Of the many reactions to this latest Kennedy tragedy, a common one was "Not again." We all recognize the uncanny profusion of tragic deaths that has beset the clan, and many commentators have speculated about hubris, learned behavior, and a high value placed on taking risks. The new science of emotion, however, points to a genetic trait known as *harm avoidance,* which is heritable to a high degree.

A person's level of harm avoidance appears to be related to his brain-serotonin activity.[15] People with lower levels of serotonin activity seem readier to take risks. Another genetic variation related to brain-serotonin transmission is connected with the tendency to have anxiety. A full understanding of the genetics of anxiety, however, will probably point to a number of genes acting together.

An opposite picture emerges with the neurotransmitter dopamine, which has to do with novelty-seeking in humans. A gene responsible for coding one of the dopamine receptors is associated with novelty-seeking behavior in some studies.[16] Several studies also connect variants of the dopamine system to attention deficit disorder, which is often characterized by easy boredom and a high level of novelty-seeking.[17]

These studies in humans are consistent with studies in mice, in which certain genes were either knocked out, resulting in "knockout mice," or replaced with other genes, resulting in "transgenic mice." Knockout mice that make no dopamine at all, for example, sit around in a lethargic state, showing no interest in anything, even food or drink.[18] Eventually the mice die of starvation, not because they cannot eat but because they simply do not care. In the words of Dean Hamer, behavioral geneticist at the National Institute of Health and coauthor of *Living with Our Genes*, "That is what I call very low novelty seeking."

At the other end of the novelty-seeking spectrum are transgenic mice, which have an excess of dopamine transmission. According to Hamer, these mice "run around frantically like crack addicts on speed . . . so the whole story fits perfectly with what we and others find in humans."

As far as the serotonin system in mice is concerned, Laurence Tecott, a researcher at the University of California in San Francisco, and colleagues have shown that a knockout mouse that lacks a certain type of serotonin receptor shows both heightened anxiety and fearfulness.[19] Summing up what is known of the genetics of neurotransmitters and behavior, Hamer observes only half tongue in cheek, "One neurotransmitter makes you optimistic, curious and active . . . the other makes you bitter, hostile and sad. Isn't it pathetic how our entire life hinges on the balance of a few little chemicals?"

Although behavioral genetics is still young, it's clear that someday we will understand in far greater depth how genes drive our behavior. It might be possible for each of us to obtain a snapshot of our genetic profile that could help us plan our lives better. Although gene therapy for exaggerated behavioral traits is some way off, each of us can already benefit by understanding our basic temperament, so that we can factor it into our plans.

As for the train of tragedy in the Kennedy clan, it may be that many Kennedys carry a high genetic loading for novelty-seeking and a low loading for harm avoidance. Since both entrepreneurs (such as the patriarch Joseph Kennedy) and leaders (such as John and Robert Kennedy) require courage, adventurousness, and derring-do, perhaps the very same genes that propelled some of the Kennedys into dazzling celebrity and high accomplishment might also have driven them to destruction.

Such a genetic view of fearlessness versus caution no doubt oversimplifies the issue, as training and experience clearly modify the way our genes are expressed. Still, I like to think that someday the philosopher's admonition to "Know thyself," may be extended to, "Know thy genes." A dopamine receptor here, a serotonin transporter there, may make all the difference in whether you fly off needlessly into a darkening sky or stand back and watch, concluding, "I'll wait for sunrise. Better safe than sorry."

Nothing to Fear But Fear Itself

So far we have considered fear mostly as a life-saving gift and asset, but it is not always so. An estimated 19 million Americans suffer from anxiety disorders, conditions in which fearfulness is the problem rather than the solution.[20]

Jerilyn Ross, president of the Anxiety Disorder Association of America (ADAA), and author of *Triumph over Fear*, clarifies the use of the word "fear" in connection with anxiety disorders. "It's not ordinary fear," she says emphatically. "A phobia is an involuntary fear reaction that is inappropriate to the situation and usually leads to avoidance of common, everyday places and situations, even though there is no real threat. I have a height phobia, not a fear of high places. If I'm in a high place and have a panic attack, I will feel trapped and unable to escape. I'm afraid that if I don't see an escape route, I'll 'go crazy' or may lose control."

Anxiety disorders come in different forms, and much research over the last few decades has aimed to sort them into meaningful subgroups according to symptom patterns and treatment response. One of the first such subgroups was carved out in the 1960s by Donald Klein, professor of psychiatry at the New York State Psychiatric Institute.[21] While working on an inpatient psychiatric ward, he observed one man who kept coming to the nursing station in fits of anxiety, afraid he was going to die. Standard anti-anxiety drugs such as Valium did not seem to help, so Klein thought he would try imipramine, an antidepressant.

Within a few weeks the nurses reported that the panic-stricken man was no longer bothering them with his attacks. But Klein found the man still to be anxious, afraid that he would have further panic attacks, and *this* anxiety did indeed respond to Valium. Such observations inspired Klein to carve out the syndrome of panic disorder as distinct from generalized anxiety disorder without panic attacks. He found that people with panic disorder first develop panic attacks, then anticipatory anxiety, and later agoraphobia, a fear of venturing away from home lest they get a panic attack someplace where they cannot escape.

Each phase requires its own treatment. Klein found that panic attacks respond to antidepressants. (Initially, he used the older antidepressant imipramine, but now psychiatrists use members of the Zoloft family, which have also been shown to work well.) Anticipatory anxiety responds to members of the Xanax or Valium family of drugs. And the phobia itself responds to behavior therapy—the patients are exposed to the feared condition, which helps them deal with it.

Recent research using both animals and humans suggests that fear and panic run on separate neural pathways.[22] Under normal circumstances, the panic pathways help mediate feelings of separation, loneliness, and grief. So-called school phobia, a form of panic disorder in children who are afraid to be separated from their mothers, may involve a disturbance of the same neural pathways. The phobic children may respond to the same medications that help adults with panic disorders.

Other forms of anxiety include obsessive-compulsive disorder, posttraumatic stress disorder, and social phobia. For some reason not as yet understood, most of the anxiety disorders affect women more frequently than men.[23] Some of these other anxiety disorders also respond well to antidepressants.

Panic on the Bridge

Jeff was in his mid-thirties when it first struck him. It happened while he was driving across a bridge over the Susquehanna River. Suddenly and without warning, terror surged through his body like a tidal wave. His heart pounded as though it was about to burst, and sweat rolled off his forehead. He felt as though a magnet was pulling him off the edge of the bridge, and it took everything he had to resist going over.

He slowly eased his car across the bridge. Once on the other side, he pulled over, exhausted as if he had just run a marathon. He was also terrified. Was he losing his mind, or was he suffering some horrible illness, such as a heart attack or brain tumor? All he could think was, "I have got to get to the nearest emergency room."

At the hospital, the doctors investigated him extensively and sent him home with a clean bill of health. Nevertheless, Jeff had a lingering feeling that something really was terribly wrong. Even though the doctor had told him it was "all in his head," Jeff found that hard to accept. The pounding in his chest, the sweating, and the terror had been so physical that he could hardly believe they did not have a physical basis. He almost wished that the doctors had found some physical problem to explain his symptoms. "Imagine the worst fear you have ever had," Jeff said to me, "then multiply it by a thousand. That's what it felt like."

Thereafter, Jeff remained fearful, and he avoided crossing all bridges. He also started to develop panic attacks in innocuous places such as grocery stores and his child's school. Soon he was reluctant to go anyplace where there was no easy route of escape in case he had an attack.

Jeff's problem was exacerbated by poor medical care. His panic disorder was not properly diagnosed, and it was years before he was given cognitive behavior therapy or an appropriate drug, in his case Prozac. As Don Klein had recognized years before, antidepressants can abort panic attacks, which the Xanax family seldom does. Still on Prozac today, Jeff is free of panic attacks. He crosses bridges, even the notorious Chesapeake Bay Bridge, practicing what he learned from cognitive behavior therapy when he needs to.

As Jerilyn Ross says, the scariest part of the phobia is the feeling of being trapped and having a panic attack. Many people who are afraid of bridges, for example, get some relief when they are far enough across that they can see the other side, which provides a sense that escape is near. Ross has noticed that when she is on a high floor, she fears a panic attack much less if the door into the hall is ajar, so she can see the exit sign.

I once flew with a colleague who specializes in research on anxiety disorders. I was assigned the window seat, while he was on the aisle. He asked me if I cared about sitting by the window, and when I replied that I did not, he asked if we could switch. He confided that he was very anxious about flying, but that being able to see outside the window gave him the illusion of an escape route, which eased his anxiety. He knew that this illusion had no basis in logic, yet it calmed him. This is another example of what can happen when fear, a normally adaptive mechanism, goes awry, and also of the resourcefulness with which many fearful people work out ways to help themselves.

The cause of the fear is not always apparent. For example, many people who are afraid of flying are not really afraid of crashing, but rather of losing control, of putting their lives in someone else's hands. Often this sense of not being in control can trigger a panic attack. One patient of mine, an executive who travels extensively for his business, would dose his intense fear of flying with several stiff drinks and Valium. This strategy was problematic as he was addicted to sedative drugs and alcohol. This man was helped by using the telephone on the airplane to call his office and issue instructions. By shifting his focus from the flying of the plane, over which he had no control, to the management of his office, where he was commander in chief, he was able to ease his fear of flying. A more common treatment for flying phobia is to help the person accept that he is not in control, then help him let go of his fears by a combination of modifying thought processes and self-soothing techniques, such as deep abdominal breathing.

Looking back, Jeff, the man whose problem began when he was crossing a bridge, realizes that he had three harmful beliefs about his phobia that tend to be extremely common among anxious patients:

- I thought I was the only one with the problem.
- I thought it was my fault.
- I thought there was no way for me to be helped.

All of these beliefs proved to be dead wrong.

The recent surge of scientific interest in anxiety disorders is welcome in two ways. Not only does it promise new treatment breakthroughs, but also it legitimizes these disorders. According to Ross, "People with anxiety disorders are often viewed as hypochondriacs. Their disorders have been trivialized by the medical establishment and they and their families have been blamed for their problems—wrongly. Recent brain imaging studies suggest brain abnormalities in patients with panic disorder.[24]

Although we are far from understanding exactly which nerve pathways are disturbed in panic disorder, Ross notes that patients already see some research payoff. Looking at their scans, research subjects can see the abnormal wiring in their brains. This helps them understand how they can feel as though something terrible is happening even though it is not. It helps them accept that medications and rewiring of their brains through cognitive-behavior therapy may be necessary. It helps them let go of shame.

One recent study showed that anxiety disorders take a heavy toll not only in the workplace but also on the health-care system. The total annual cost of anxiety disorders in the United States has been estimated at about $42 billion, half in estimated medical costs and half in absenteeism.[25]

Researchers believe that certain neural circuits are hypersensitive in patients with panic disorder, so that attacks are triggered by stimuli that would not bother normal individuals.[26] While some have speculated that the hypersensitive neural circuits involved in panic normally regulate feelings of attachment and loss, Donald Klein's latest theory holds that the relevant circuits may be our "suffocation alarm," the one that makes sure we panic when we are about to suffocate.[27] This response must certainly have been adaptive to our cave-exploring ancestors. The ones that did not rush out of the cave fast enough would surely have died of oxygen depletion and been less likely to pass along their genes.

Klein first came up with his theory when he noticed that patients with panic disorder are extremely sensitive to carbon dioxide.[28] They show a panic (suffocation) response even when the levels of carbon dioxide are unnoticeable to normal people. It is possible that, in panic-disorder patients, the suffocation alarm is set to go off at abnormally low levels of carbon dioxide.

Klein and colleagues have recently found an association between panic disorder and smoking in the general population.[29] He suggests that smoking may trigger panic by increasing the amount of carbon dioxide inhaled. For those with panic disorder who smoke, this is one more good reason to quit.

Exposure, Exposure, Exposure: Turning Off the Panic Button

To paraphrase a slogan used in real estate, the three most important principles in treating anxiety disorders are "exposure, exposure, and exposure." The anxious patient must be exposed to that which is most feared to be cured, or deconditioned. This principle has been observed in both animal experiments and human studies.

However, even after a subject has been deconditioned, he will retain a certain vulnerability to the former bugaboo. Under stress, then, the panic may reemerge. It is observations such as these that have led researcher Joseph LeDoux to observe that "fear is forever."

Avoidance behaviors may also persist. There is a joke about a boy who is taken to a psychiatrist because he keeps snapping his fingers. When asked why he does it, the boy says, "To keep the polar bears away." "But the polar bears are thousands of miles away," the psychiatrist counters. The boy smiles, still snapping his fingers. "It's effective, isn't it?"

A classic experiment illustrates the behavioral principles at work in this boy.[30] In this experiment, researchers placed dogs on a grid, exposed them to a musical tone, and then applied a shock to their feet. Next to the grid was a low hurdle that the dogs quickly learned to jump, to escape the shock. Later, the same dogs were placed on the grid again and exposed to the tone only—and they continued to jump over the hurdle. For these dogs, the tone became a scary stimulus in its own right, and jumping over the hurdle served to decrease their level of fear. In fact, unless the dogs were forced to stay on the grid, they would continue to avoid the tone indefinitely.

Experiments like this one provide the theoretical basis for the exposure therapies now used in all forms of anxiety disorder. *The basic premise is that unless the avoidant behaviors are stopped, they will continue indefinitely. If a person can be helped to wait out the anxiety without using his defensive maneuvers, however, the uncomfortable feelings will subside, and the patient will master the anxiety disorder.*

Here is how exposure therapy works in practice. It's a busy afternoon on the Washington Beltway, and Jerilyn Ross is out driving with her patient Marge, who is terrified of this notorious roadway that handles a large percentage of the D.C. metropolitan traffic. Eighteen-wheelers whiz by, seemingly indifferent to the little vehicles all around them. Aggressive drivers dart from lane to lane, thinking nothing of cutting off a fellow driver. And every lane is dense with cars.

Marge sits quivering in the driver's seat. Idling at 30 miles per hour, she hugs the right lane and waits for the panic attack that she is sure will hit at any moment. The first thing Ross teaches her is to evaluate her level of anxiety, to rate it from 0 to 10, and to notice what makes it better or worse. Marge rates it at an 8. "Let's see how many red cars we can spot," Ross suggests, and Marge begins to notice the red cars and to count them. Within a few minutes, her anxiety level drops to a 5, but it then shoots up to an 8 when she asks, "What if I lose control and drive into the wrong lane?" Ross points out that when Marge stays in the present, she feels less anxious. When she thinks catastrophic what-ifs about the future, her anxiety soars. Now Ross suggests that Marge turn on the radio. An old show tune is playing, and Marge begins to hum along. As you might expect, her anxiety level drops once again.

Marge has already learned several important lessons. First, she has learned that she can control her anxiety by what she chooses to think about. The more she dwells on imaginary fears, the more anxious she becomes. The more she remains in the present, the less panicky she feels. Second, Marge has learned the value of distraction. Third, Marge has learned that she can keep going, making headway toward her destination despite her anxiety. Finally, and most important, she realizes that staying with her anxiety, rather than leaving the situation that causes it, is the key to overcoming her problem.

Next Ross teaches Marge how to breathe with her diaphragm, letting her belly expand and contract as she takes deep slow breaths. Marge finds this soothing, then learns to use the breathing to help herself endure the anxiety, for example, to wait to the count of 10 before she pulls off the road. When Marge shows that she is able to wait that long, Ross suggests that maybe the next time she feels anxious, she should count to 20. Each time Marge is able to stay with her anxiety long enough to watch it subside, she gains confidence that she can keep driving, even when she feels anxious and desperate to get off the road. On the other hand, if she pulls off the road as soon as she wants to, that action will reinforce the notion that she cannot drive when she is anxious. Her behavior will resemble that of the dogs that keep jumping over the hurdle long after the shocks have stopped.

Sometimes during their sessions, when Marge's anxiety reaches a high point, she asks Ross, "Will there be a time when I am no longer plagued by anxiety?" Ross replies, "I don't know the answer to that. What I do know is that I can teach you skills that will enable you to lead a normal life. The goal of treatment," Ross explains, "is not to eliminate anxiety, but to function in spite of it. Eventually the anxiety will die of neglect."

Ross and Marge draw up a hierarchy of fearful situations, ranging from the least to the most fearful. The least fearful is driving in the right lane with Ross sitting beside her. The next is having Ross sit in the back, and the next is driving in the middle lane. After a while Marge drives alone and Ross meets her at the next exit. And so it goes, until Marge is fully able to drive on the Beltway by herself. She may still be anxious, but she has methods for decreasing her anxiety without the use of drugs. She understands the anxiety for what it is—not a fear based in reality but a fear of fear itself, a misfiring of the fight-and-flight response. Most important, she can now go where she needs to go and lead a full life. Her anxiety is no longer disabling.

I have used the term "limbic news" to describe the informational value of emotions. In anxiety disorders and other emotional disturbances, an individual's limbic news is faulty. One function of cognitive-behavior therapy, such as Ross used with Marge, is to help people override their limbic news when it misleads them, and the more we work with CBT, the better it looks. A recent landmark study of more than 300 patients over a fifteen-month period is particularly impressive. This study compared cognitive-behavior therapy with medications for the treatment of panic disorder. A team led by David Barlow, professor of psychology at Boston University, assigned patients to five different treatment groups:

1. antipanic medications (in this case imipramine)
2. panic-control therapy (a special form of CBT)
3. placebo
4. medications plus panic-control therapy
5. placebo plus panic-control therapy[31]

The panic-control treatment used by Barlow and colleagues in this multicenter study bears some resemblance to that used by Jerilyn Ross in treating Marge. Patients learned various methods to soothe themselves during the all-important exposure to what they feared. In addition, they were exposed to the symptoms of panic (for example, to dizziness, by being spun around in a chair) and deconditioned. The researchers took away all their little comforters—medication bottles (even empty ones), teddy bears, and prayers of comfort. Panic-disorder patients tend to accumulate these things; however, comforters help patients avoid the fear of what they truly fear—their panic attacks—thereby making it harder for CBT to help them.

After three months of treatment, all active forms of therapy proved superior to the placebo, a difference that increased over six months of maintenance treatment. At that point it seemed that medications and therapy together were superior to either treatment alone. In addition, those classified as medication responders tended to do better than those who responded to CBT. Then all treatments were discontinued and six months later, the participants were again evaluated.

Surprisingly, those who had received only CBT tended to retain the benefits of their treatment. But those who had received medications, with or without CBT, tended to lose ground. Perhaps in the combined treatments, the soothing medications prevented the patients from experiencing their anxiety fully, thereby making the deconditioning less effective.

That makes sense based on animal studies showing that one neurotransmitter involved in deconditioning is GABA, the transmitter influenced by Xanax and its cousins. These drugs have been shown to interfere with the process by which an animal unlearns a fear response, which supports the idea that anti-anxiety drugs lessen the power of CBT.[32]

Based on what we know about learning, CBT probably helps to rewire abnormal brain circuits, and medications may interfere with this rewiring. Nevertheless, if panic is severe and disabling, medications may be essential and needed indefinitely.

I Want to Be Alone: Understanding Social Phobia

The incomparable Greta Garbo was famous for her sultry beauty and unsmiling hauteur, and for the words for which she is best known: "I want to be alone." To my knowledge, she never explained why she wanted to be alone. But whatever the reasons, her words are sure to resonate with the estimated 6 million American adults who suffer from a disabling form of anxiety known as social phobia.

In his recent biography, singer Donnie Osmond describes the painful social phobia that he had to confront to relaunch his singing career. Despite his celebrity, Osmond had such anxiety about ordinary human interactions that he was unable to return a shirt to a store where he had bought it. That was one of the tasks he had to do as part of his cognitive-behavior therapy with therapist Jerilyn Ross.

As Osmond's case makes clear, social phobia can affect anybody, even celebrities, even those who appear to all the world as enviably self-confident. Women are affected slightly more frequently than men, though men more often seek treatment. Dr. Michael Liebowitz, professor of clinical psychiatry at Columbia University and a pioneer in the diagnosis and treatment of social phobia, speculates that the condition may be more disabling for men. Men in our society are expected to be more assertive and socially forthcoming than their female counterparts.

Joe, a patient of Dr. Liebowitz, was one such man. An accountant in a large New York firm, Joe worked best when he was at the lower echelons and able to do most of his work on his own. As he became more successful and was expected to attend company lunches, meet with potential clients, and bring in business, Joe's secret problem became harder and harder to conceal. He was terrified of social interactions, and now his anxiety mounted with every passing day. Just having someone walk into his office and stand next to his desk was a trauma. Joe was afraid that his hand would tremble and that his colleague would see the tremor.

Eventually getting to work became such an ordeal that Joe quit his job, retiring to his apartment. He became increasingly reclusive and afraid of meeting anyone, so much so that he would wait until 3:00 A.M. before taking his garbage to the incinerator.

That was when Joe first went to see Liebowitz, who put him on the antidepressant Nardil. Nardil belongs to that family of medications called monoamine oxidase inhibitors (MAOIs), which are rarely used these days because they restrict the diet and have unpleasant side effects. Nowadays, the medications of choice for social phobia would be those in the Zoloft family. In fact Paxil, a member of this family, was the first drug the Food and Drug Administration (FDA) approved specifically for social phobia.[33]

Gradually Joe's anxiety decreased. After three months he felt better, and after six months he returned to work. He started with the more solitary aspects of accounting, but soon he was tackling the social interactions that had previously been unthinkable. At that point, cognitive-behavior therapy was added to his treatment, and with its help, Joe was able to reduce his medication.

As with panic disorder, CBT can be extremely useful for social phobia. The therapist systematically helps the patient reinterpret the many cues that trigger his anxiety. For example, a patient who regards his shaking hand as a major embarrassment will be invited to consider that other people might not even notice it. And if it is noticeable, the therapist might encourage the patient to ask, "Why is that such a big deal?" In this way CBT will address the black-and-white thinking by which the social phobic views every encounter as either a total success or a hopeless failure, and the patient will learn that not every social encounter has to be a total success.

How does such therapy stack up against medications? Liebowitz and colleagues recently published their comparison study of daily medications (Nardil) versus weekly CBT sessions administered over a twelve-week period.[34] They used two control groups, one given placebo pills and the other given "educational support," both of which were encouraged to meet weekly, mix with one another, and find out about their illness. The two control treatments had a response rate of 25 to 30 percent, whereas the active treatments each showed about a 60-percent success rate. Although this would imply that the active treatments were equally good, in those who did in fact respond, the medication responders appeared to do better than the CBT responders. (Do these results begin to sound familiar?)

In a six-month follow-up study, the medication responders continued to take their Nardil daily while the CBT responders received booster sessions once a month. The good news was that both groups remained well throughout, indicating that the benefits of effective treatment continue over time. Then the researchers stopped both treatments. And once again, the effects of CBT endured, with none of the CBT group showing relapse, as compared with half of the medication group.

It would appear that over time CBT does better at rewiring the brain than medications do, for both panic disorder and social phobia—and in some people, medications may prevent the CBT from producing enduring effects. For many people with social phobia, CBT alone may be the best treatment. For others, especially those with severe symptoms, taking medications along with CBT may be preferable.

Researchers are also making inroads into the biology of social phobia. It looks like a dopamine problem. Brain images of people with social phobia show lower levels of dopamine and dopamine-related structures.[35] This is not surprising, given that dopamine helps regulate the desire to engage in activities with others.

Stagefright: A Special Form of Social Phobia

We have all heard of it—and many of us have experienced it. The curtain is going up, the audience is waiting in hushed silence, and you are on next. Maybe you have to sing, act, give a speech, or play a musical instrument, but whatever it is, you are paralyzed. You would rather die than have to walk out there. You are suffering from performance anxiety, a special type of social phobia.

Researchers believe that this type of social phobia may be due to overactivity of the sympathetic (fight-or-flight) nervous system. For this reason, drugs that oppose that part of the nervous system, such as beta-blockers, are very successful for this condition. As Liebowitz points out, the more evidence there is of sympathetic arousal, such as rapid pulse, sweating, and cracking voice, the more likely the condition is to respond to beta-blockers.

While it is well known that concert musicians often use beta-blockers to curb stage fright, it is less well known that people from all walks of life can benefit from occasional use. I recall helping a typist who had such severe performance anxiety that her fingers froze every time she was required to take a typing test. After taking a small dose of a beta-blocker, she was delighted to find that she was able to test at her usual 80 words per minute. Likewise, a patient of mine who is an elementary school teacher was surprised to find that with the help of a beta-blocker she could now teach in front of the principal without breaking a sweat or stumbling over words.

In short, beta-blockers can relieve anxiety related to all forms of social performance, including job interviews and presentations. Do talk to your doctor before you try them, however. Certain medical conditions, such as asthma and low blood pressure, can be aggravated by beta-blockers.

I Just Can't Stop: Obsessions and Compulsions

Matt was in his early teens when his parents brought him to see me. He was a handsome but serious-looking young man, with subtle facial tics and a lean, but extremely muscular build for reasons that soon became clear: Matt could not stop exercising. He ran up and down hills until he was exhausted and did push-ups, first two-armed and then one-armed, until his arms could no longer hold up his slender body, chastising himself if the left and right arms did not perform equally well. One error in his exercise sequence would make him feel compelled to start all over again.

When I asked him why he was doing all this rigorous exercise, Matt said that it was to prevent bad things from happening, but he could not specify what these bad things might be. He knew his behavior made no sense, but knowing was of little help. He just couldn't stop.

I treated him with Prozac, which is known to help people with obsessive-compulsive disorder, and he responded quite well. I then referred him for CBT, and for a while he was able to cut back on his exercise rituals. But after returning from summer camp, he underwent a serious relapse. All the rituals were back in full force.

That bothered me. Why should someone relapse so suddenly and completely? I wondered. He said he had enjoyed summer camp and there was no evidence that it had been stressful. On the contrary, his strength, endurance, and athletic abilities had made Matt shine at camp. Then I remembered that my colleague Susan Swedo, chief of the Developmental Neuropsychiatry Branch at the National Institute of Mental Health, was doing research on connecting streptococcal infections with obsessive-compulsive behavior.

I called Sue at home to discuss Matt's story, and she recommended I send him for a throat swab, even though he had no sore-throat symptoms. I did so, and to my astonishment, the swab came back positive for Type A hemolytic streptococcus, the bacterium responsible for rheumatic fever. Swedo had been working on the theory that in some people the symptoms of OCD might be caused by antibodies that the patient makes to the bacterium, which attacks a part of the brain known as the basal ganglia. Abnormalities of these ganglia had previously been associated with OCD.

To test her theory, Swedo admitted Matt to her program at the NIMH, drew his blood, and had his brain scanned. Sure enough, Matt had high circulating levels of antibodies to Type A streptococcus, while his brain scan revealed swelling of the basal ganglia. She then put Matt through an experimental protocol that involved replacing his plasma with fresh plasma that was free of antibodies. To everyone's relief, Matt's symptoms subsided once again.

Swedo estimates that about one quarter of all children with OCD may be infected to begin with or may relapse because of the Type A hemolytic streptococcus. A key to diagnosing OCD due to infections is sudden onset. Parents whose children acquire obsessions or compulsions seemingly overnight would do well to take their children for throat swabs.

After treating Matt, Swedo and her colleagues went on to show that people whose OCD symptoms were the result of streptococcal infections responded better to plasma exchange treatment (of the type

Matt received) or infusions of immune globulins than to control treatments.[36] These globulins presumably attach to the antibodies that attack the brain, thereby neutralizing their toxic effects. As of 2001, this type of treatment is still experimental, not yet generally recommended for people with OCD. If conventional treatments do not work, however, one might seek it out, perhaps at a university medical center.

Like other anxiety disorders, OCD usually responds to CBT, antidepressant medications, or both. Drugs that act on brain serotonin, such as the Prozac family, seem to work best. Therapists who specialize in the behavioral treatment of OCD take a great deal of time with patients to identify *all* their obsessions and compulsions. If only some symptoms are identified and deconditioned, the unidentified symptoms tend to get worse.

In cognitive-behavioral treatment for OCD, as for panic disorder, patients are encouraged to hold in mind whatever makes them anxious, but refrain from their old ways of dealing with it. For example, people with OCD should stay with their thoughts while going about their daily lives. If they do, the anxiety begins to ease, sometimes within minutes. In one study of compulsive patients, both Prozac and CBT tended to correct the abnormalities originally seen in brain scans.[37]

Seeking Help Versus Treating Yourself for Anxiety

Anxiety symptoms vary greatly from one person to the next, both in nature and severity. If your anxiety is severe enough to disrupt daily functioning, either in your relationships or in your work life, it would pay to consult a professional. I have seen many people, however, manage to treat their own mild anxiety once they understand how— a good thing, because professionals who are up-to-date specifically on anxiety can be hard to find.

One frequent mistake that I see nonspecialists make is to prescribe the right medication but in too high a dose. People with panic disorder are extremely sensitive to these drugs, and the overdose can make the panic worse, not better. For panic disorder, it is essential to start with very low dosages, even as little as 1 milligram of Prozac per day, moving up gradually as tolerance builds. The same is true for the herb St. John's wort, which should be started in very low dosages in people with panic disorder. People with other forms of anxiety disorder, such as OCD, may be far less sensitive to medications and may actually require high dosages.

As for therapy, research shows that what works is systematic exposure to the triggers that provoke anxiety and concrete assistance with managing the responses, of the sort Marge received on the Washington Beltway. Simply sitting with an empathic person and talking about your anxiety is unlikely to be successful. Those who choose to seek out therapy for an anxiety disorder would do well to shop around. Look for a skilled psychopharmacologist or a therapist with specific training in cognitive-behavior therapy.

Important: Before embarking on a course of treatment for anxiety or panic disorder, be sure to get a complete physical examination and blood work because anxiety resembles several medical conditions, such as cardiovascular disease and overactive thyroid functioning. Be sure that your doctor checks your blood for thyroid hormone levels.

Meanwhile, here are eight research-based suggestions:

1. *Cut out caffeine in all forms.* On several occasions I evaluated people for what appeared to be an anxiety disorder and told them that my major recommendation was that they cut out all caffeine—coffee, tea, and colas. This is not a popular piece of advice. They plead, they negotiate. Can an exception be made in the case of Starbucks? they ask. Unfortunately, people with panic disorder are so sensitive to caffeine and other stimulant drugs that even decaffeinated coffee can be enough to cause them generalized anxiety or full-blown panic attacks.

   Dean, a friend of mine and a Wall Street broker, suffered continuous anxiety from early in the morning to late at night, when it interfered with his sleep. Sometimes the anxiety was so bad that he felt as though he were having a heart attack. This was not good news, especially for someone who has to advise billionaire clients on a daily basis about what they should buy or sell. Dean could have spent endless hours analyzing the sources of stress in his life—there were plenty to choose from—but the simple answer lay in caffeine. He quit coffee and has never looked back. He can now stay calm and collected even when billions of dollars stand to be won or lost on the basis of one of his trades. Contrary to his fears that stopping coffee would cost him his edge, Dean has been more successful than ever, now that he is free of severe anxiety.

If you choose to cut out caffeine, remember to taper down your intake over a period of about a week. Otherwise you risk unpleasant withdrawal symptoms such as headache, lethargy, and difficulty concentrating.

In several cases, the same individuals who looked so appalled at my cruel and simple-minded solution to their complex problem have returned very pleased. You, too, can be a genius in the treatment of your anxiety using this simple strategy.

2. *Do aerobic exercise.* This all-purpose emotional toner is helpful for anxiety, as it is for stress and depression. Research shows that exercise reduces anxiety, as do meditation and relaxation.[38]

Regular exercise over a period of time, such as twenty minutes three times per week for ten weeks, is necessary for full benefit. Moderate exercise appears best.[39] For example, some studies have found that the improvement in anxiety peaks when the exercise sessions are forty minutes long.[40] Aerobic exercise works better than weight training or stretching regimens.

The relationship between exercise and anxiety disorders is complex. Exercise may produce symptoms of a panic attack, such as sweating and increased heart rate, which can trigger anxiety. ("Oh no! Here comes a panic attack!") But assuming you are in reasonably good physical condition, persistence pays off. Among other benefits, regular aerobic exercise stabilizes the cardiovascular system by increasing its reserve and efficiency. This might act as a buffer against the tendency to develop a common trigger for anxiety.

3. *Be sure to get enough sleep.* People with panic disorder, especially nighttime panic disorder, are more vulnerable to attacks when they are sleep deprived. Proper sleep hygiene dictates that you

go to bed at a regular time, allotting enough hours for sleep so that you need not doze off right away. Many people need time to unwind. Keep the bedroom dim and free of distracting stimuli (such as a television or computer). If at all possible, do nothing in your bedroom except sleep and make love. That practice will condition your body to relax and prepare for sleep the moment you walk into the room.

4. *Eat regular meals.* People with anxiety disorders tend to be very sensitive to bodily sensations. When they skip meals, their blood sugar drops and they often feel light-headed or queasy. Then they worry that they might be developing a panic attack. Regular meals will prevent that. For emergencies, many people find it helpful to keep protein-rich bars tucked away in their cars or at work to prevent hypoglycemia.

5. *Manage stress as well as possible.* People who suffer from anxiety often have difficulty separating what is within their control from what is not. Make a comprehensive list of the sources of anxiety in your life and divide them into those you can and those you cannot do something about. When those stresses that are beyond your control arise, talk to your emotional brain. Persuade it to accept that difficult fact. When you worry about things you cannot change, you waste precious brain and bodily energy. Why not spend this energy where you can influence the outcome?

Next, divide those matters that are under your control into "urgent" and "those that can wait." Take care of the urgent things directly so that they won't be a worry any longer. The others, by definition, can wait. Keep the list up to date and check it twice a day. By dedicating this time, you will get some relief from having to worry the whole day.

When you are presented with difficult problems, solutions are seldom obvious. The problems sit in your unconscious, and your creative mind plays around with them. It commonly happens that solutions come when they are least expected, such as in the shower or while driving. Many people find that a notebook or the electronic equivalent is useful for jotting down these inspirations as they crop up.

By having a mechanism for keeping tabs on your day-to-day

responsibilities and a way to trap useful thoughts before they are lost, you will find yourself less anxious and more productive.

6. *Practice relaxation, meditation, and yoga.* Some technique for relaxation is included in most behavioral programs for managing anxiety. Some people with panic disorder, especially those with nighttime panic attacks, tend to feel anxiety rising the moment they start to relax. It is as if the panic comes as soon as they drop their guard. As with exercise, however, this is no cause for alarm. Persist with the techniques and the panicky symptoms will generally pass. Meditation may work by boosting the soothing effects of the parasympathetic nervous system, which counteract the fight-and-flight properties of the sympathetic nervous system.

7. *Try your own cognitive-behavior therapy program.* Although people with marked anxiety are generally best served by seeing a qualified therapist, one is not always available or affordable. The key to CBT is to identify those thoughts and behavior patterns that are part of the problem and to modify them. Those people who want further information on how to implement the methods of CBT on their own should see "Further Reading" on page 421.

8. *Try herbal remedies for panic and other anxiety disorders.* The two most popular herbal remedies for panic and anxiety are St. John's wort and kava-kava.

Despite a lack of systematic studies on using **St. John's wort** for panic or anxiety, it is logical that this flowering herb might be helpful, since it works well for depression. St. John's wort enhances some of the same neurotransmitters, notably serotonin and norepinephrine, as do antidepressants. (Extracts of the herb inhibit the clean-up phase of both serotonin and norepinephrine transmission, causing these neurotransmitters to linger in the synapse for longer durations. This biochemical action, which is shared by many antidepressants, is thought to reverse anxiety as well as depression.)[41]

Judy was a woman in her mid-thirties who had suffered panic attacks for the previous ten years. These attacks occurred specifically when she visited restaurants. In the middle of a meal, her hands would begin to sweat, her heart would start to pound, and she would be unable to swallow. This caused tension with her husband, whose favorite recreation was dining out at fancy restaurants.

Her husband's fortieth birthday was approaching and the couple planned to spend it in Bermuda. Judy knew that he would want to eat out a lot and dreaded the prospect of all those public meals. She had previously been treated with Prozac for her anxiety but it had made her feel edgy, and she was now disinclined to try any other medications. She was, however, willing to try St. John's wort, and within a day of taking the first 300-milligram tablet, felt calm and relaxed. She increased the dosage to 300 milligrams twice a day for several weeks until it was time to leave for Bermuda. The trip was a complete success and she was astonished that she was able to dine out without any symptoms for the first time in many years.

St. John's wort may also be helpful for social phobia. Jack, an economist in his early fifties, is a case in point. His doctor suggested that he try St. John's wort for his chronic low energy and inattentiveness, and indeed it did boost his stamina and ability to concentrate. In addition, Jack was delighted to find one more unexpected benefit. As long as he could remember, he had always shrunk from interacting with others both at work and socially. Yet after starting St. John's wort, he was surprised to find himself greeting people who parked their bicycles next to his. Even more surprising, he became more assertive in meetings, offering opinions that once he would have kept to himself. He was delighted when others began to treat him with more respect and friendliness. Serendipitously, his social phobia had been treated without ever having been diagnosed. Perhaps this effect of St. John's wort derives from its influence on dopamine transmission, which is disturbed in people with social phobia.

The last form of anxiety I have seen respond to St. John's wort is obsessive-compulsive disorder. I prescribed the herb for Jackie, a generally anxious young woman who complained that she could not stop checking things. It was impossible for her to leave the house without checking that she had turned off the stove, locked all the doors, and switched off all the lights.

Anything that could be checked she would need to check dozens of times over. This behavior kept her from leading a normal life. She had previously been treated with antidepressants, but they had caused her to gain an unacceptable amount of weight. Treatment with St. John's wort greatly reduced her symptoms without any major side effects.

A recent open trial of St. John's wort in twelve patients with OCD found improvements that were comparable to those found with synthetic medications.[42]

Currently, however, there are no published recommended dosages for St. John's wort in the treatment of anxiety. The dosages that are used are based on the dosages of antidepressants used for the treatment of anxiety disorders.

If you suffer from panic disorder, start with low dosages of the herb, such as a few drops of tincture, and build up gradually to the full dosage of between 600 and 900 milligrams per day. People with obsessive-compulsive disorder often need high dosages of antidepressants in general and may therefore need as much as 1,800 milligrams of St John's wort per day. They can start their treatment with 300 milligrams per day and build up the dosage as rapidly as they can comfortably handle.

Note: For information on which brands of St. John's wort to buy and possible interactions between the herb and various medications, see page 336.

While some people like St. John's wort for panic and anxiety, others prefer **kava-kava.**

Jim was a lawyer with a driven personality and a fiery temper that he struggled to control. He was often anxious and would dwell on work-related matters ad nauseam. I had tried him on various synthetic antidepressants and antianxiety agents, but the side effects he suffered were intolerable. Then he discovered kava-kava and started taking 250 milligrams three times a day. He experienced rapid relief of his anxiety, which has been sustained now for many months. The herbal preparation enabled him to cut the synthetic medications to doses he can tolerate.

Kava-kava is derived from the rhizome of a Polynesian plant, that the natives learned long ago would induce a pleasing sedation if mixed with coconut milk.[43] In several controlled studies kava-kava has beaten placebos in the treatment of anxiety and, in at least one study, performed just as well as a standard Valium-type drug.[44] Kava-kava is the only herbal product that is approved in Germany specifically for the treatment of anxiety. Some researchers have claimed that kava-kava has advantages over most tranquilizers in that it can be stopped without withdrawal symptoms and produces fewer memory problems. Such claims, if borne out by further testing, would be extremely exciting. Animal studies have shown that kava-kava influences the neurotransmitter GABA, the very same relaxing neurotransmitter that is affected by drugs such as Valium or Xanax.[45]

The typical dosage recommendations for kava-kava range from one to three 250-milligram capsules per day of the whole herb preparation, which corresponds to 75 to 225 milligrams of the active extract. For anxiety, the herb is generally taken two or three times a day; for insomnia, one hour before bedtime.[46]

Catch-22: Post-Traumatic Stress Disorder

Felix was a firefighter in his mid-thirties when his therapist referred him to me for his depression. It soon became clear that depression was only one of his problems. A Vietnam veteran, Felix lived each day as though he were still in combat, even though the war had been over for a full ten years. During the day, as he went about his work, he often had flashbacks. Shadows that crossed his face in a certain way made him feel as if he were back in the jungle. His heart would pound and his muscles tighten as if the enemy were about to jump him. His sleep was disrupted, and he kept a knife under his pillow at all times, ever ready for a surprise sortie by the Vietcong.

Felix was suffering from post-traumatic stress disorder, a condition that was called "shell shock" after World War I and "battle fatigue" after World War II, but was more or less forgotten until the Vietnam War. In the classic American novel *Catch-22*, the hero Yossarian, a bombadier, keeps having flashbacks to a flight during which one of his comrades was mortally wounded.[47] Memories of the incident come back to him in fragments until, piecemeal, he reconstructs the event in its full horror. In the final version of this reconstruction, he remembers pulling back his comrade's flak jacket and seeing the abdominal wall peel away to reveal his vital organs.

That is how trauma is often reexperienced, bit by bit, until a story emerges. *Catch-22* is a term that has entered the language to describe the crazy endless loops in which we can find ourselves. Post-traumatic stress disorder is such a loop in which a past trauma continues to be reexperienced as though it were happening in the present, an endlessly complex and repetitive maze of painful experiences that twist and turn upon themselves, resulting in a type of suffering from which there appears to be no escape.

Felix had been assigned to rescue downed pilots on the Ho Chi Minh Trail. The crew would lower him from a helicopter to retrieve the wounded or the dead, sometimes in several battered pieces. He never knew what he would find when he reached the ground, nor if there would be enough room on the helicopter for both himself and the wounded soldiers. If not, he would have to stay behind surrounded by enemy fire.

When he returned from his tour of duty, Felix had a hard time distinguishing between what had really happened and what he had only imagined. Fireworks looked to him like the flares from gun ships, and he had a recurrent nightmare that he was picking up the helmet of a downed pilot. As he turned it over, he would see, time and again, the dead man's half-shattered skull still in the helmet, the eyes staring back at him. Inside, Felix felt dead, without feeling. He felt different from everyone around him, alienated and old. As he puts it, "There is a wall that goes up inside you that makes everything out there feel unreal; you become unfeeling. Dead people become numbers, patients, enemies; no longer human. I was twenty when I went there; when I came back, I was a million years old."

In therapy, Felix said, "I had to learn why people cry; what a tear of joy is. When I was finally able to experience feelings, I was so confused, I didn't know how to deal with them. Warm fuzzy feelings bothered me. It was as though I was crying out to the world, 'Don't touch me.' I guess in Vietnam we learned not to get close to people. There was an expression there: 'Don't get close to the new guy' cause he'll be the first to get killed 'cause he doesn't know what he's doing.'"

Felix grew up in a family of alcoholics and had sworn never to touch alcohol. "But when I saw my best friend in a body bag, I picked up my first beer and didn't stop drinking for sixteen years." Indeed Felix's family had been terribly troubled. When he was six years old, his mother doused herself with lighter fuel in front of him and set herself on fire. His older brother put out the fire by rolling their mother in a blanket. She died after six months in the hospital. Not surprisingly, perhaps, both Felix and his brother ended up as firefighters, rescuing people. Felix's father, an abusive alcoholic, committed suicide when Felix was 18. Despite the horrors of his childhood, it was only after Vietnam that Felix developed PTSD. It has been shown that people with a history of early trauma are at greater risk for developing PTSD when they are traumatized in later life.

Felix dates the true beginning of his recovery to his getting off alcohol, which he did by means of an inpatient detoxification program and membership in Alcoholics Anonymous. He worked hard in therapy, became active in veterans affairs, and found solace and companionship in the company of fellow veterans. To anyone who wants to conquer PTSD, his first advice is to "get off the booze."

But Felix could not fully recover until he had retired from the fire department. Working there, he had kept facing again the traumas of his childhood and of the war. He could no longer tolerate the terrible injuries he saw. He would say to himself, "If I see one more dead child, someone will have to institutionalize me." Yet he acknowledges that there was a certain thrill in the drama of the job. "You get to be an adrenaline junkie, living on the edge, being a risk taker," he says. "As a fireman, you're like Pavlov's dogs. You're in bed and the bells go off and you're up and running. Then you stop and it's all gone. You get addicted to the adrenaline high."

After his retirement, one of the hardest adjustments was giving up the excitement of living on the edge. "It was boring for a while," he says. "But now I'm as content as all get-out."

PTSD is found in the victims of all types of trauma, not only war but also natural disaster, rape, and child abuse. The symptoms are as follows:

- Reexperiencing the trauma in the form of intrusive thoughts, flashbacks, images, memories, and nightmares.

- Emotional numbing and flatness, loss of interest and motivation, and avoidance of any place, person, or topic associated with the trauma. There may also be dissociation, a feeling that the trauma happened to somebody else, or amnesia for aspects of the trauma.

- Increased arousal, which includes startle responses, poor concentration, irritability and jumpiness, insomnia, and hypervigilance.[48]

Sometimes, attempting to come to terms with their past, people with PTSD may seek out circumstances that recall the earlier trauma and, in doing so, may compound their problems. This process, which therapists call "reenactment," is not uncommon in people who were sexually abused as children. As adults, they may exhibit self-destructive patterns of sexual behavior, such as promiscuity, seeking out prostitutes, or sadomasochism. In most such cases, I have found that the adult behaviors incorporate elements of the early trauma.

The curious thing is that people with PTSD may reenact as well as avoid—two completely opposite patterns. One woman with PTSD, for example, had been abused as a child by an uncle who was a physician. In her adult life, she alternated between being excessively suspicious of doctors and not being suspicious enough. Although a highly educated and intelligent person, she underwent unnecessary operations at the hands of an unscrupulous surgeon, whom she later successfully sued for malpractice.

It is not surprising that people with PTSD should want to avoid situations that might trigger their symptoms—the sweating, heart-pounding state that accompanies the detailed memories of the trauma. Reenactment, though harder to understand, may occur because some aspect of the trauma has been connected with feelings of comfort or safety. For example, an abused child may learn that she needs to put up with her parent's abuse to be cared for. Later, she may seek out abusive people to replicate the mixture of comfort and pain. On a neurological level, circuits that cause pain and pleasure might have become connected in a neural network at an early age. In later life, activating one aspect of the neural network (such as the need for affection) may also activate the other aspect (seeking out painful re-abuse).

New ways of imaging the brain and recording brain activity are beginning to shed light on these murky matters. For example, electrical studies of the brain find that people with PTSD have a hard time sorting out relevant from irrelevant information.[49] Relevant information, if it has no emotional load, does not catch their attention as much as it does that of normal people. According to Bessel van der Kolk, professor of psychiatry at Boston University and an expert in PTSD, research suggests that these patients have difficulty neutralizing any trauma-related stimuli—noises, shadows, smells, tones of voice—to attend to daily life. As a result, they are either hypervigilant (an unpleasant state) or shut down to compensate for the overarousal. The price of shutting down is detachment, an eerie remove from community.

Brain structure is clearly altered, perhaps forever. Three separate studies have shown a shrunken hippocampus in Vietnam veterans and survivors of child abuse.[50] In one study of veterans, the men with the most intense combat exposure had suffered the most marked decrease in hippocampal volume.[51]

Remember, the hippocampus is very important for recording explicit or factual memories. Researchers believe that this hippocampal shrinkage comes about in response to the flood of stress hormones, such as cortisol, that are released during trauma. It is a way to adapt, an example of the brain's amazing resilience and plasticity. It's as if the system says, "Too much! Let's shut down some of the capacity to remember!" In that way, having less hippocampus may protect the trauma victim from being overwhelmed by horror. As a side effect, however, it could produce emotional flatness once the trauma has passed.

Importantly, PTSD patients have abnormally low levels of cortisol in their urine, according to work by researcher Rachel Yehuda, professor of psychiatry at Mount Sinai Medical School.[52] Yehuda's group found low circulating cortisol in both Vietnam veterans and Holocaust survivors with PTSD. One function of cortisol is signaling the body to stop putting out stress hormones, a signal that seems to trip prematurely in people with PTSD.[53] Yehuda suggests that this tendency to shut off the stress response too soon may be part of the physiological abnormality in PTSD patients.[54] In normal people, following trauma, it may be necessary to mount a cortisol response large enough to turn the fight-or-flight system off once the trauma has passed. The low cortisol levels in PTSD patients may therefore partly explain why they have such difficulty recovering from their traumatic experiences. In support of this theory, researchers have found that those people with the lowest levels of urinary cortisol following traumatic experiences such as car accidents or rapes are at highest risk for developing PTSD.[55]

Interestingly, the stress-response profile seen in PTSD is the opposite of that seen in depression, which is marked by elevated blood cortisol levels and no ability to turn off the stress response.

Right brain–left brain communication also suffers in these people, a research group at Harvard has suggested. Brain-imaging researcher Scott Rauch and colleagues read detailed descriptions of their trauma to PTSD patients while scanning their brains.[56] Regions of the right hemisphere lit up, particularly the areas that process emotion, notably the amygdala. At the same time, the activity dropped in the left frontal lobe and in Broca's area, which handles language.

These findings suggest that PTSD patients experience their memories very intensely in the right side of their brain, but are not good at expressing or analyzing them, functions that require input from the left cerebrum. In addition, the left frontal area is important for placing events in time, so a shutdown there may explain why people with PTSD relive their trauma again and again, seemingly unable to pack it safely away in the past. As a final insult, the left frontal lobe is also responsible for generating positive emotions. If it shuts down in patients with PTSD, no wonder these individuals have a hard time countering painful feelings with more positive ones.

In some circumstances, continual vigilance might be adaptive; for example, when a stress is ongoing. In PTSD, however, the trauma is over, so continued vigilance and hyperarousal causes nothing but trouble.

Recovering From Trauma and PTSD: Five Suggestions

To some extent, fear is forever, as Felix, the Vietnam veteran, can testify. Yet just as torn flesh and ruptured organs resolve, the traumatized mind can also heal, albeit with some scars. In that process, a skilled therapist is invaluable, as PTSD can seem intractable. At the same time, I have known individuals who made remarkable headway on their own. If someone you know is struggling with the aftermath of a trauma, whether or not a therapist is involved, the following research-based guidelines may help:

1. *Clarify the connection between the trauma and the symptoms.* In many instances, a person knows precisely how the trauma and the symptoms connect. Veterans and rape victims, for example, might be fine before their trauma, but emerge from it hobbled by PTSD. The cause-and-effect relationship is clear. But with childhood traumas, such as sexual or physical abuse, the child may grow up not connecting the later symptoms with the earlier abuse. Often a person will seek treatment because of trouble with intimacy and only later discover the connection to an early trauma. According to Rachel Yehuda, "It is important to help people recognize that there is a relationship between their trauma and their behavior. Sometimes a lot of exploratory work is needed to get them to that point. By the time people can make this connection, they are ready to work on the problem."

2. *Find a safe place and a trustworthy person or group of people.* Understandably, people who have been traumatized feel unsafe, and without safety, they cannot work effectively on their problems. Political prisoners and battered spouses, for example, rarely feel safe until they are beyond the reach of their tormentors.

   For that reason, the first goal for a person with PTSD is to find a safe place or a person in whom to confide. Be careful not to explore the details of the trauma until you feel safe. A good therapist will understand and will take the time to establish trust before tackling the particulars of the event.

A recent meta-analysis of treatment studies found that only 14 percent of PTSD patients dropped out of psychotherapy, but nearly a third (32 percent) quit taking medications—a significant difference that reflects the importance of the therapeutic relationship to these people.[57] They suffer greatly, yet can be emotionally inaccessible, and their lives are often so chaotic as to put off therapists who don't understand PTSD. Psychotherapist John Schlapobersky, himself tortured by the South African Apartheid regime, now specializes in treating trauma victims. He recalls an Iranian torture victim who told him, "Yours is the hand of humanity that reaches out to save me from drowning in my sorrow."

Victims of trauma face a complex set of issues. "Shameful feelings often occur," Schlapobersky told me when we met in his London office, "especially in trauma that occurs within families or when there has been a personal violation. The victim often blames herself and needs help to shake free from inappropriate feelings of responsibility. Finally, trauma always involves some loss—of family, innocence, a vision of a future, a sense of bodily integrity. The traumatized person needs help in grieving these losses. People who are unable to grieve their losses hold on to them forever."

While he sees no substitute for a qualified, empathic, and trustworthy therapist, Schlapobersky suggests that trauma victims also seek out self-help programs that involve other victims. "However much people have lost," he says, "they have not lost the capacity to be generous, to be of use to others; and this often becomes the fulcrum of reconstruction." Schlapobersky has learned this from personal experience. He sees his own efforts on behalf of refugees and victims of political abuse and systematic cruelty as part of his ongoing recovery from his own trauma.

3. *Think about it, talk about it, write about it.* While some patients with PTSD avoid dealing with their symptoms, other traumatized people are eager to tell their story to professionals, family, and friends. That turns out to be a good thing. Edna Foa, professor of clinical psychology at the University of Pennsylvania and an expert in the treatment of PTSD, encourages patients to tell their story.

"It takes time and effort to process this information properly," Foa emphasizes. "You have to get really engaged in it. Go over the details of the trauma in your mind, but do so in a deliberate way." Foa finds it important not to think about the trauma with detachment, as though it happened to someone else. Instead, review the memories in tandem with the feelings they arouse and pay attention to each painful detail. "Don't think about an important detail of the trauma for just a minute," says Foa, but rather for several minutes at a time. In this way, the trauma victim directly confronts the memory of the trauma, as opposed to running away from it. By sitting with the details of the trauma—both the feelings and the thoughts—the fear response related to the trauma can be deconditioned.

Although Foa advocates thinking deeply about the trauma, she cautions against obsessing over it, by which she means getting stuck on a single detail and grinding it round and round in your mind. She also finds that it does not help to dwell on what might have been. She counsels people to avoid such thoughts as, "If only I could have it happen over again. What would I do?" Instead, successful recovery requires the processing of traumatic memories and associations in such a way as to change them. That is why, in reflecting on the experience of a trauma and its aftermath, it is important to think about it in different ways and not to repeat the same old story again and again. One must get the left brain involved, so the event can recede into the past. Other experts agree. Yehuda points out that the ultimate goal is to detoxify the trauma by putting it into words.

One of the best ways to detoxify a trauma is to write about it. As we have seen, James Pennebaker has shown that written self-disclosure has many benefits, even improving physical health in groups ranging from laid-off workers to victims of crime. Immediately after writing, Pennebaker notes, people often feel worse, but they feel better weeks later. (For James Pennebaker's writing exercise, see pages 203–204.)

John Schlapobersky recalls that during his two months of solitary confinement, he kept a diary on a roll of toilet paper, using a pen he had stolen. When his guards read the diary and learned of his deep despair, they encouraged him to commit suicide by leaving naked razor blades lying around in his cell when he left to exercise and shower. He resisted the temptation by continuing to write, which he credits for saving his life.

Pennebaker and colleagues examined the impact of written self-disclosure on the career progress of Texas Instruments workers who had been laid off without warning and in a rather harsh manner. As you might expect, the laid-off engineers were deeply angry. Although they were not men given in general to writing about their feelings, they were encouraged to do so as part of the study.[58]

Even rather terse notes proved helpful. For example, one engineer wrote on the first day, "Thinking about getting new job. Have to tell girlfriend." The next day he wrote, "Writing exercise yesterday was very helpful." How could those few simple statements be helpful? It turned out that the man was considering taking a job in another town. He needed to discuss that with his girlfriend, as leaving town would probably end the relationship, and he had been avoiding that discussion. But the writing exercise forced him to confront his avoidance and tackle the problem head on. In the end, he took the job and broke up with his girlfriend.

Those laid-off engineers who wrote about their feelings and thoughts were rehired significantly sooner than the ones who were asked to write about superficial matters. Why? Pennebaker could detect no difference in the men's activities, such as the number of calls made or job interviews attended. He suspects that the writing exercise might have helped diminish the men's anger, making them more appealing to prospective employers.

Clearly there is an important connection between language and recovery from trauma, a topic that Foa and colleagues have studied. Working with twelve rape victims, they found that immediately after the event, the victims commonly told what happened in a fragmented, incoherent way. But the more articulate the women were in those early descriptions of the rape, the fewer PTSD symptoms they showed three months down the line.[59]

In another study these researchers found that as rape victims progressed through treatment, their stories of the trauma became longer. Perhaps the victims felt less anxious and therefore were able to stay with the painful material. Over time, the women spoke more about their thoughts and feelings, and less about the actions and dialogue related to the incident. And as the women's stories became more coherent, their symptoms eased in proportion. In addition, as the women thought more about the trauma—as opposed to just dwelling on their feelings—they became less depressed.

James Pennebaker's Writing Exercise[60]

1. For the best results, take the exercise seriously and make a commitment to follow through on all the phases of the exercise. The goal of the exercise is to reveal your deepest secrets to yourself in an honest way. To do this, you need to "get into" your writing as deeply as possible.

2. Even though the total writing-time commitment is less than 90 minutes, it is important to take this time commitment seriously. Be sure to schedule four 20-minute undisturbed blocks of time into your schedule on four consecutive days.

3. If at all possible, find a quiet place that is away from the ordinary hurly-burly of your life, away from telephones and other sources of distraction. The idea is to immerse yourself in your writing for these few short blocks of time. The best results are obtained when you find a special place where you can focus exclusively on your writing.

4. The only rule of the writing exercise is to write continuously for the entire 20 minutes. If you run out of things to say, just repeat what you have already written. In your writing, don't worry about grammar, spelling, or sentence structure. Just write.

5. Sometimes people feel a little sad or depressed after writing. If this happens, it is completely normal. Most people say that these feelings go away in an hour or so.

6. Be sure that your writing is completely anonymous and confidential. If you have any concern that someone else will find your written material, it may constrain what you say and how you say it, which may make the exercise less effective.

7. What you should write about over the four days is the most traumatic, upsetting experience in your entire life. In your writing, you should really let go and explore your very deepest emotions and thoughts. You can write about the same experience on all four days or about different experiences each day. In addition to a traumatic experience, you can also write about major conflicts or problems that you have experienced or are experiencing now. Whatever you choose to write, however, it is critical that you really delve into your deepest emotions and thoughts. Ideally, you should also write about significant experiences that you have not discussed in great detail with others. Remember that you have four days to write. You can tie your traumatic experience to other parts of your life. How it is related to your childhood, your parents, the people you love, who you are, or who you want to be. Again, in your writing, examine your deepest emotions and thoughts.

8. When you finish the writing exercise, you can keep the written materials or throw them away. Remember, the key to this strategy is the exercise itself and not the quality of the finished product.

Source: James Pennebaker. *Opening Up*, Guilford Publications, 1997.

James Pennebaker has used a computer program to analyze what sorts of words people use in his writing exercise to describe their unpleasant experiences. He was curious about what words distinguish those who have come through their trauma well. It turned out that the more words denoting positive feelings were used, the better the outcome was. No surprise there. But "the real action," according to Pennebaker, comes from *cognitive words*—words that indicate an understanding of cause and effect—and *insight* words—words such as "realize," "understand," and "know." These studies, once again, indicate that what helps in processing a trauma is a cognitive change. That's why, in Pennebaker's view, people who tell the same story again and again don't seem to improve.

Nobody knows exactly what it is about language that soothes the roiling emotions of a trauma victim. Perhaps a clue to the power of words lies in the imaging studies of PTSD patients, that show that the language centers on the left side of the brain shut down. This abdication may leave the emotional centers overactive with no means of expression. Telling the story, either orally or by writing it down, activates the language centers, which may help connect the right hemisphere (which feels the pain) with the left (which tries to analyze and make sense of it). The use of language may also be a way to bring into play the positive emotional influence of the left cerebral hemisphere to help alleviate the pain associated with the traumatic memories and put the best cast on an unfortunate situation.

4. *Seek therapy.* Self-help can do a great deal to assuage the pain of trauma, but when the symptoms of PTSD disrupt one's life, there is no substitute for therapy. While all good therapies include that trustworthy and empathic person, two specific forms of therapy have been shown to be more effective than simple comfort and support.

According to one meta-analysis, the most effective therapies for PTSD are cognitive-behavior therapy and a new form of treatment known as *eye movement desensitization and reprocessing* (EMDR).[61] Both work well overall, though EMDR seems to be more efficient. It required an average of only 4.6 sessions over 3.7 weeks versus 14.8 sessions over 10.1 weeks for CBT.

EMDR was developed by psychologist Francine Shapiro, currently a senior research fellow at the Mental Health Research Institute in Palo Alto. While walking in a park one day, Shapiro became aware that some troubling thoughts seemed to simply drain away, leaving her feeling inexplicably better. In reconstructing the event, she realized the relief came while she was moving her eyes rapidly from side to side. Since that day, Shapiro has developed the technique of side-to-side eye movements into a form of therapy that has now been widely taught and tested for the treatment of PTSD.

In an EMDR session, the patient concentrates on a traumatic memory, while at the same time giving full rein to matching unpleasant thoughts and shuttling her eyes from side to side. For example, a rape victim might remember details of the actual rape while thinking "I am powerless, helpless to defend myself against whoever might want to assault me," and moving her eyes. (It helps if the eyes can track an object, such as the therapist's hand or lights from a special machine.) The patient observes her bodily sensations throughout. Later the exercise is repeated, but this time the person is encouraged to relate the trauma to positive thoughts about herself. For example, "I am safe now," and "There are many things I can do to protect myself from being raped again."

EMDR has been quite controversial. Although everyone now agrees that it works better than placebo treatments, fans of CBT have suggested that it is only the cognitive elements of EMDR that make it work.[62] A recent review panel, however, concluded that EMDR is effective in its own right.[63]

How EMDR works is unknown at this time, though theories abound. Both deconditioning and reconceptualizing do seem to occur—but the same is true for all the effective treatments for PTSD. What is different about EMDR, is that you are alternately stimulating the left and right cerebral hemispheres. When you look to the left, your right cerebral hemisphere is activated, and when you look to the right, your left cerebral hemisphere is activated. It is tempting to speculate that moving the eyes from side to side engages both the cerebral hemispheres and helps them to communicate with each other. Time and more research will tell.

Cognitive behavior therapy for PTSD has many of the usual elements, including:

- Educating the patient about the common reactions to trauma
- Teaching the patient some form of deep breathing
- Prolonged, repeated exposure to the memory of the trauma
- Repeated exposure to trauma-related situations that the patient avoids out of fear, *provided this is objectively safe.*

This last point is crucial and requires judgment. If a woman was raped in a dangerous neighborhood, it would be foolhardy to teach her not to fear that neighborhood. On the other hand, if she was raped in a car and is now unable to drive even in safe neighborhoods, this would constitute a disabling symptom, and helping her to drive again would make sense.

As Foa puts it, in CBT for trauma, one foot should stand in the safety of the present, while the other should step into the past where the trauma occurred. Studies find that after a course of treatment, most people no longer qualify for a diagnosis of PTSD.[64] Best of all, studies by Foa and colleagues suggest that people from the community, even those with no special counseling background, can be taught to use CBT with only light supervision. These trainees enjoy results roughly equivalent to those the experts obtain.[65]

5. *Take Medications.*

A meta-analysis of PTSD-treatment studies suggests that medications are less effective than psychotherapy, but more effective than placebos.[66] In addition, fewer people dropped out of psychotherapy studies than out of drug studies. The problem with drugs, the authors speculate, may be that PTSD patients are hyperaroused, therefore hypersensitive to medications.

Of the medication studies, antidepressants such as Prozac and Zoloft showed the most impressive results, far better than the Xanax family.

Another type of drug that may be effective in treating PTSD is a beta-blocker. As you may recall, powerful emotions help us form memories by causing the release of stress hormones, such as adrenaline. This effect can be blocked by beta-blockers, drugs that are widely prescribed to treat high blood pressure. Researchers James McGaugh and Larry Cahill in Irvine, California, have suggested that PTSD is essentially a vicious cycle: Flashbacks release adrenaline, which consolidates memories of the trauma, which in turn cause more adrenaline to be released, and so on.[67] Their current research will tell us whether the beta-blockers can interrupt this circle by blocking the effects of the adrenaline.[68]

As of 2001, the results are still pending. However, if you suffer from PTSD, you and your doctor might like to try a beta-blocker, especially if other treatments have not helped.

So we reach the end of the first great pair of feelings, fear and anxiety, which are ubiquitous in the animal kingdom. We see them in cats and rats and even lizards as they dart into crevices and bushes. Fear and anxiety are part of our animal legacy without which *Homo sapiens* would not have survived to the present. When we feel them arise by the tingling of our nerves, the quickening of our breath, or the palpable beating of our heart, we need to pay attention.

But the machinery of fear and anxiety can also lead us astray. If, after measured thought, we realize that our fears or anxieties have run away with us, we need to still the trembling and the beating, correct the messages of unreasoned doom, and focus our attention where it best belongs.

Chapter 9

Anger and Rage

Anger is never without a reason, but seldom a good one.
—Benjamin Franklin

"I'll be judge, I'll be jury," said cunning old Fury.
"I'll try the whole cause and condemn you to death."
—Lewis Carroll[1]

Commandeered by Rage

O NE evening my friends Mark and Dan were over and we sat around chatting as we had done many times before. Everything was pleasant enough until I made a comment that Mark found insulting. What followed was nothing short of extraordinary. His face turned blood-red, his eyes narrowed into slits. He fixed me with a murderous glare and screamed, "You! You! That's it!" Then he jumped up and ran out of the house. Dan followed and retrieved him, still shaking with rage ten minutes later. I was rather shaken myself, but we all sat down and discussed what had happened.

Mark had mentioned his problem with rage attacks before, but it was only after I had been on the receiving end that I could truly appreciate their impact on the people around him. Although Mark apologized immediately and obviously felt ashamed and remorseful, and although I formally forgave him, for many weeks I felt mistrustful of him and kept my distance. I finally understood how his rage attacks had gotten him fired from several jobs and had cost him four marriages.

During rage attacks like Mark's, those parts of the brain that are central to feeling and expressing anger, such as the amygdala and the hypothalamus, commandeer the rest of the brain.[2] In this wholesale takeover, the cerebral cortex is overwhelmed and restraint and reasoning are impossible. Such a rage attack can be destructive, not only to its targets, but also to the goals and interests of the enraged individual. Although rage—by which I mean anger that is extreme, immoderate, or unrestrained—may be adaptive as a response to severe threat, in most situations it destroys much more than it accomplishes.

The Value of Anger

Under normal circumstances, anger has an important communication function. It lets others know that they have encroached upon you or your territory, and it warns them to back off . . . or else. A mother whose infant is threatened will become angry, and as we all know, it is unwise to get between a mother bear and her cub. A baby whose arms are restrained shows signs of rage, and adults feel enraged if their freedom is constrained.[3]

Like all emotions, anger provides important limbic news. When there is not enough to go around, anger lets us know that we had better seize whatever resources we can. Anger can also regulate how we are doing in relation to our goals. In the course of everyday life, we develop expectations of ourselves. Then, if we do not reach them, our frustration—a form of anger—spurs us on.

When anger or rage builds to a certain point and is not restrained by countervailing forces, aggression ensues. Aggression refers to the overt expression of anger toward an object or individual, as when an animal snarls or a person curses. In humans, aggression is often verbal. The legal term "fighting words" speaks to the idea that words can be equivalent in some ways to a physical attack. Too often aggression is expressed as physical violence.

In stable primate societies, including human ones, communications of anger take place every day, usually without overt aggression.[4] A frown, a hostile glance, or a menacing posture all send a signal clear enough to maintain social stability. Sometimes, however, when the individual senses that a threatening gesture is too weak, he attacks. People who suffer from rage attacks have too low a threshold for such outbursts, as well as inadequate mechanisms for controlling the attacks once under way.

Knowing when to attack is a critical life skill for both humans and other animals. It is so important, in fact, that we can assume evolution has programmed such judgment calls into the nervous system. Circumstances have changed for humans, however. In prehistoric times, when threatened by a beast of prey, it would have been fatal to dither about what to do. But in modern times, in Western societies, trouble more often comes from expressing anger too hastily. In modern times our evolutionary legacy of anger is often more a liability than an asset.

In most everyday situations we are more likely to pay a greater price for losing our temper than for not getting our licks in quickly enough.

The Cost of Anger

Helen, a married woman who has been in treatment with me for some time, told me one day how she had recently lost her temper with her husband, regaling him with a bitter litany of his flaws and weaknesses. "I'm not going to be treated like a doormat," she declared. "Finally I am learning to assert myself. You would have been proud of me." Indeed, I was not. I winced inwardly, anticipating a backlash. Sure enough, two months later Helen's husband walked out.

Jack, a businessman, was having trouble with his business partner, who was concealing certain critical information from him. "I let him have it in no uncertain terms," he told me with some satisfaction, describing how he had cowed his partner into silence. Unfortunately he misinterpreted the silence as a victory for himself. Jack's attack proved to be no victory, but only an early skirmish in a war that ended with Jack being ousted from the business.

In the long run, Helen might well be better off out of her marriage, and Jack may be well rid of his partner. Both would agree, however, that the transition would have been far less traumatic had they been able to check their rage. A temper tantrum may feel good for a short while, but most people wish later that they had been less hotheaded.

An old myth is that it is best to let your anger out when you feel it. New evidence, however, suggests that releasing it only makes it worse.[5] To your nervous system, the release may be more a rehearsal, enhancing the neural pathways involved. It is far better for your health to find ways to let the issue go, or to channel the anger in a constructive way.

In one of the many studies that have reached this conclusion, the subjects were deliberately provoked. They were then either given some distracting task or encouraged to express their irritation. When later asked to evaluate the person who had provoked them, those subjects who had expressed or pondered their anger gave more negative ratings than the subjects who had been distracted. In real life, if you dwell on angry thoughts about someone, you are likely to be hostile the next time you encounter that person. You are at risk of starting a vicious cycle, with each of you ratcheting your anger higher and higher.

Rage Attacks May Be Part of a Larger Problem

It has been estimated that 40 percent of people with clinical depression also suffer from rage attacks.[6] For men, in particular, it may seem stronger and more acceptable to express painful feelings as anger rather than as depression, which may be viewed as weak or feminine. If you suffer from rage attacks, ask yourself whether you may be depressed. If so, treating the depression may resolve the rage attacks.

A case in point is heavyweight boxer Mike Tyson. In the boxing ring, Tyson's aggression (except when he bit off a piece of Evander Holyfield's ear) has paid off handsomely. In his private life, however, Tyson's unbridled aggression has been a disaster.

According to newspaper reports, Tyson has been on the antidepressant Zoloft, which can reduce aggression by affecting serotonin transmission. While preparing for a fight, Tyson stopped his Zoloft. Shortly afterward, he viciously attacked two men who had the misfortune of getting into a traffic accident with him. According to news reports, his bodyguards had to restrain him from seriously injuring the men.[7] In a recent interview, Tyson told reporters, "I'm on Zoloft to keep me from killing y'all. It has really messed me up, and I don't want to be taking it, but they are concerned about the fact that I am a violent person, almost an animal. And they only want me to be an animal in the ring."[8]

Zoloft affects aggression because brain serotonin, the neurotransmitter it modifies, shores up the brain circuits responsible for exercising restraint. Animals whose serotonin pathways are damaged or underactive show unrestrained aggression, while violent and impulsive people have been found to have low levels of serotonin-breakdown products in their spinal fluid.

Rage attacks may be part of post-traumatic stress disorder.[9] Dr. Martin Teicher and colleagues at Harvard have found that adults who were abused as children, whether verbally, physically, or sexually, show brain-wave changes over the temporal lobe of the cerebral cortex. These changes resemble those seen in people with documented seizures in the temporal lobe, which surrounds the limbic-system structures. Teicher suggests that early traumatic experiences might kindle seizure-type activity in this area, resulting in a storm of electrical activity in an emotional part of the cerebral cortex.[10]

The term "kindling" describes the process in which part of the brain is stimulated at intervals with an electrical current that is not initially strong enough to cause a seizure. After several such stimuli have been administered at intervals, a seizure will occur.[11] It is possible that repeated abuse may resemble repeated electric stimuli. Each abusive episode may not in itself trigger a seizurelike rage attack, but the end result could be a brain that is cocked and all too ready to fire off a limbic storm.

My friend Mark, whose rage attack I described at the beginning of this chapter, had been abandoned by his father at an early age and was later shamed and ridiculed by his stepfather. In adult life, his rage attacks were frequently triggered when he felt belittled, as he did on that evening at my house.

Unlike seizures, however, which are truly outside a person's control, rage attacks can often be prevented. Serotonin-boosting medications can help,[12] as can behavioral training, separately or together.[13]

Lessons from Attacking Cats: The Anatomy of Rage

While anger is an emotion, aggression is an action. Aggression is the way that anger is often expressed. Aggression can be observed in animals but we don't really know if the animal is angry. Rage attacks can be induced experimentally in cats, for example, by electrical stimulation of the brain (ESB) in certain anatomical areas, such as the amygdala. Here is a description of one such experiment by neuroscientist Jaak Panksepp:

> Within the first few seconds of ESB the peaceful animal was emotionally transformed. It leaped viciously toward me with claws unsheathed, fangs bared, hissing and spitting. It could have pounced in many different directions, but its arousal was directed right at my head. . . . Within a fraction of a minute after terminating the stimulation, the cat was again relaxed and peaceful, and could be petted without further retribution.[14]

Researchers believe that such stimulation is an unpleasant experience for the animal because given the opportunity, the animal will turn off the stimulation. When humans are stimulated in comparable brain areas—for example, when they are undergoing brain surgery—they report feelings of anger. This suggests that an animal is probably experiencing anger during a rage attack, such as the one described above.

Based on animal experiments, the brain circuits involved in experiencing and expressing anger have been mapped out in some detail.[15] Critical circuits begin in the amygdala, travel through the hypothalamus, and end in the midbrain. These rage circuits receive input from other parts of the brain that interpret what is going on in the animal's

world. Sensations of pain and hunger, the vocal tones of other animals, and visceral cues (such as heart rate and bowel activity) all feed
into these anger circuits. That is why pain relief, good food, and calming music can all soothe the savage breast. The frontal lobes also connect with the rage circuits, and it is these connections that need to be
strengthened in people who have anger problems.

In passing, I should note that not all violence is associated with
anger. When a cat kills a mouse, there is no evidence that the cat is
angry.[16] On the contrary, he appears to be enjoying himself, sometimes playing with the mouse before killing and eating it. This type of
violent activity appears to be mediated by different circuits from
those responsible for the feeling of rage. This type of behavior in cats
may find its human analogy in hunting. A deer hunter may enjoy the
sport of locating a deer, waiting for it to move within range of his
rifle, and shooting it—without any trace of anger.

The Hazards of Hostility

Hostility expresses a mindset in which the world looks menacing. To
this mind-set, anger in thought and feeling is considered a necessary
baseline state for dealing with outside threats. "Hostile" certainly describes Frank, a middle-aged, highly successful businessman who saw
me for psychotherapy. As long as I knew him, Frank was embroiled in
some feud or spat. He would ponder night and day how best to exact
revenge, and it was the unfortunate man or woman who crossed his
path in a legal skirmish. Brilliant and highly organized, Frank would
bring a laser focus to his legal battles, mowing down the opposition
after months or years of bruising litigation.

For some reason, there remained those who sought to cross swords
with Frank. Invariably they met a sorry outcome. I recall one man
who was a particular target, as he had double-crossed Frank several
times. On one occasion, while visiting the French Quarter in New
Orleans, Frank consulted Sister Liz, a practitioner in the voodoo arts,
about this man. She gave him a candle and advised him to write the
name of his enemy on a piece of paper and put it under the candle.
Then he must light the candle and blow it out, she counseled, and

that would take care of the matter. Frank followed her advice diligently. Within a matter of months his enemy dropped dead of a heart attack.

They say that revenge is a dish best served cold and Frank was certainly able to wait before he dished his out. But he was also given to sudden outbursts of anger. He could not tolerate being cut off in traffic, for example. On one occasion after this happened, he shifted lanes so his car was alongside that of the offending driver. When they got to the next red light, he opened his window and spat into the face of the other driver before speeding on his way.

As you can imagine, Frank was not an easy man to live with and I met on several occasions with his wife and children to help them deal with his anger. Frank's hostility was poisoning his home, as well as raising his blood pressure. Unfortunately, the years of hostility took their toll. At a relatively early age, Frank had a heart attack that required quadruple bypass surgery.

There is a happy ending to this story. His cardiac problems were a timely warning to Frank. He worked with me to find ways to manage his anger, using many of the techniques outlined later in this chapter, and over time, he changed his view of the world. Now he realizes it is more important for him to be happy and healthy than to be right. He has learned to recognize his anger when it first begins to rise, then to cut it off by changing either his environment or his thoughts. He understands better what triggers his anger and avoids such triggers wherever possible. There is reason to hope that with these changes Frank will live not only a longer life, but a richer one. The changes he has made are also good news for the people in his personal and professional life.

The way the association between hostility and coronary artery disease was discovered reads like a medical detective story. The first clue came from a man who was hired to reupholster the waiting-room chairs of two San Francisco cardiologists, Meyer Friedman and Ray Rosenman.[17] This upholsterer observed that the chairs had been worn in a very unusual way—disproportionately toward the front.

In reflecting on that observation, the physicians realized that their patients were unusually driven people. Perhaps they were literally sitting on the edges of the chairs, ready to rush into the doctors' office, so they could return more quickly to their driven and pressured lives.

Friedman and Rosenman coined the term "Type A" to denote this driven type of personality, which, they suggested, might be a risk factor for coronary artery disease.[18] The typical Type A person is aggressive, ambitious, and competitive, and has a chronic sense of time urgency.

Friedman and Rosenman first published their research in the late 1950s to a startled world. Scientifically, connecting personality with illness was a new idea. Over the next two decades, other studies refined this association, noting certain aspects of the Type A personality that were especially toxic to the heart, with hostility in the lead. In one study in the early 1980s, Professor Redford Williams and colleagues at Duke University administered a scale for hostility, derived from the commonly used personality inventory, the Minnesota Multiphasic Personality Inventory (MMPI), to patients undergoing angiography for coronary artery disease.[19] They found that the degree of arterial blockage could be predicted even better by hostility than by Type A personality. The essential difference between those with high and low hostility scores, these researchers found, was that the high scorers viewed other people as bad, selfish, and exploitative, whereas the low scorers did not.

These findings inspired other studies in which groups who had completed the MMPI were followed up decades later, to see how individual levels of hostility (as measured by the MMPI) influenced physical health. Two of the most dramatic early studies were conducted by John Barefoot, now research professor of psychiatry and behavioral sciences at Duke University. In one, Barefoot followed up physicians who had completed the MMPI while studying at the University of North Carolina (UNC) Medical School.[20] Twenty-five years later, those who had scored in the more hostile half of the class had a cardiac-death rate almost five times that of their less hostile classmates. Even more surprising, all types of death were related to high hostility. Out of the 22 doctors who had died in the 25 years since completing the MMPI questionnaire, only 3 had scored below the median.

In a study of 128 lawyers who filled out MMPIs while at UNC Law School, Barefoot and colleagues again found that the hostility scores were a strong predictor of survival 25 years later. Those who scored in the top quarter of the scale had more than a fourfold chance of dying, compared with those in the bottom quarter.[21] In his studies, Barefoot found three aspects of hostility to be particularly harmful to health—cynicism about other people, hostile feelings, and a tendency to respond aggressively.

From that early work and other studies since, almost all researchers in the field concur that hostility is an important risk factor for coronary artery disease (CAD).[22] In fact, a review panel on coronary-prone behavior and CAD concluded that the effects of hostility are equal to or greater than those of high serum cholesterol, high blood pressure, and cigarette smoking.[23] Research shows that hostile people are more likely to smoke and eat fatty foods, which compounds their CAD risk. Yet even when these factors are accounted for, hostility is a risk factor in its own right.

The simple lesson is that hostility is very bad for your health. Hostility includes having a cynical attitude toward people in general; regarding others as mean, selfish, and exploitative; feeling angry, disgusted, and contemptuous; and responding to setbacks and obstacles with aggression.

If you are a hostile person, it may be as important to your health to reduce your hostility as it is to stop smoking or avoid fatty foods.

How can hostility poison the heart? There are many competing theories. Hostility may be associated with a heart that reacts more strongly to events.[24] Williams has suggested that each episode of anger releases more epinephrine and raises the blood pressure.[25] High blood pressure damages the walls of the arteries much as a turbulent river erodes its banks. But when platelets attempt to repair the damage, plaque forms because the platelets are extra sticky due to the high levels of epinephrine.[26] Foamy cells full of cholesterol are then attracted to the plaque, which grows, progressively blocking the flow of blood and depriving the heart (and other organs) of oxygen, without which tissue dies.

Support for this theory comes from Edward Suarez and colleagues at Duke University, who found that men with high scores on the MMPI-derived hostility scale also have exaggerated cardiac responses when provoked.[27] In their ingenious experiments, the researchers built on the fact that harassment evokes hostility in susceptible individuals. They asked their subjects to solve anagrams under one of two conditions, either without disruption or while being harassed by a technician whom the subjects were led to believe was obnoxious.

When harassed, the hostile individuals had a dramatic response in their fight-or-flight system. They showed increases in heart rate, blood pressure, and circulating levels of norepinephrine, cortisol, and testosterone, all chemicals involved in gearing up for a fight. Their less hostile counterparts, however, were far less aroused. The hostile group also reported more negative feelings, such as anger. Neither group was thrown into flight-or-flight simply by working to solve anagrams.

The effects in hostile women are probably much the same, though modified by estrogen. In a separate study, Suarez and colleagues showed that women who scored high on measures of antagonistic hostility had higher blood levels of cholesterol, including the more toxic low-density lipoprotein (LDL) cholesterol, than less hostile women.[28]

In general, people who score high on measures of cynicism, hostile feelings, and the tendency to express aggression will react to everyday hassles with exaggerated fight-or-flight responses.[29] Over time, the result may be cardiovascular disease.

There are other factors that complicate the picture. Hostile people alienate others. They have generally high levels of interpersonal conflict and low levels of social support.[30] This is unfortunate, as supportive relationships are known to buffer the health consequences of stress. A stressed immune system may explain why, in some studies, hostility is associated with a higher death rate from all causes, including cancer, in which the immune defenses are critical.[31]

Hostile people make bad patients, ignoring medical advice while complaining about its cost.[32] Many studies have shown that hostile people are more likely to smoke, drink alcohol, and overeat.[33] And to top it all off, rude people are more likely to meet with rude or unhelpful responses. They create stresses for themselves that others do not suffer. In this way a hostile attitude becomes a self-fulfilling prophecy, creating a world that justifies cynicism. My hostile patients are always quite surprised at how easy life can be when they let go of their anger.

How Hostile Are You?

Given the major health hazards of hostility, it is useful to answer that question, just as it is to know your blood pressure or blood cholesterol level. Most people underestimate how angry they are.

The following questions will help you assess your level of anger. In answering the questions, try to be as accurate as possible. Also, leave aside the issue of whether your hostility is justified.

Because your hostility affects those around you, others are often a better judge of your hostility level than you are. It may be useful to ask someone who knows you well to answer these questions independently. You may be surprised at the answers.

- *Do you experience cynical mistrust of others?* Answer yes or no. Do you think that most people:

  1. cannot be trusted?
  2. are out mostly for their own personal gain?
  3. would lie to get ahead?
  4. know less than they pretend to know?
  5. use people chiefly for what they can get from them?
  6. exaggerate their misfortunes?
  7. whom you come across don't really care what happens to you?
  8. do the right thing only when it suits them?

If you answered yes to 5 or more questions, you are very cynical. A score of 3 or 4 means you are reasonably cynical, while a score of 0 to 2 puts you at the low end of the scale.

Cynical people have a poor opinion of others. They do not believe that people are fundamentally honest. They are likely to think that others will lie to get ahead, and that it takes a lot of work to convince others of the truth. If they hear a hard-luck story or see a homeless person or panhandler, they are more likely to think, "He is probably exaggerating his plight," rather than, "The poor guy seems down on his luck." If others are honest, the cynic tends to think that they are telling the truth out of fear of being caught in a lie, not because it is right.

According to the cynic's view, most people will cheat to get the upper hand and will choose their friends for advantage. The cynic believes that others dislike to put themselves out, and that they feel entitled to more respect for their own rights than they are willing to grant others. The cynic thinks that so-called experts and authorities often know less than he does.

For all of these reasons, the cynic believes that others do not really care about him and that it is safer to trust nobody. The cynic's world contains few genuine friends and close connections, and consequently lacks the many health benefits that come with close personal connections. Several studies have found that those who endorse a large number of cynical statements have proportionately more health problems.

To some extent, the opposite of cynicism is trust, and not surprisingly, trust correlates with physical health. Barefoot and colleagues studied 100 men and women between the ages of 55 and 80 and found that high levels of trust in others were associated with better self-rated health and more life satisfaction. Those who were more trusting had a higher survival rate over the following fourteen years.

These results do not mean that we should indiscriminately start trusting everybody, as do people with bilateral damage to their amygdala. Obviously, judgment is required to determine whom we should trust, when, and with what. If we are generally mistrustful without specific reasons, that burden can manifest in our health.

Examine your level of cynicism and trust and ask whether it is justified. If you are excessively cynical about people in general, you might consider reevaluating your worldview for the sake of your health, if for no other reason.

- *Do you attribute hostile motivations to others?* Do you think that most people:

  1. are likely to misunderstand the way you do things?
  2. are nice to you only when they have an ulterior motive?
  3. have something against you?
  4. treat you unfairly?
  5. are critical of you?
  6. talk about you in a negative way?
  7. are jealous of your good ideas?
  8. don't give you appropriate credit for your contributions?

If you responded yes to 5 or more questions, it suggests that you have a very strong tendency to attribute hostile motivations to other people. A score of 3 or 4 suggests that you have a reasonably strong tendency to do so, whereas a score of 0 to 2 puts you at the low end of the scale.

It is very stressful to live among people who you believe, rightly or wrongly, do not wish you well or actually wish you ill. It is no wonder, therefore, that attributing hostile motivations to others has been found to predict ill health.

• *Do you experience feelings of hostility?* Every person has a certain image of himself or herself. Describe yourself in reference to the following sets of words. The right- and left-hand qualities are opposites of each other. There are five lines between the opposites. Circle the line that best fits your concept of yourself.

Answer according to your real self-opinions, not according to your ideal or other people's opinions. Use the extreme when appropriate and circle the middle line only when it really best indicates your character

	1	2	3	4	5	
Seldom get into arguments	——	——	——	——	——	Quite often get into arguments
Do not get angry easily	——	——	——	——	——	Get angry easily
Do not get irritated easily	——	——	——	——	——	Get irritated easily

To determine your score, use the point values shown above the lines (for example, the extreme left line is worth 1 point, while the extreme right line is worth 5 points). You will get a total between 3 and 15.

These are the actual questions used in a Finnish study of 3,750 men between the ages of 40 and 59.[34] The researchers found that those who scored in the highest range on hostility (13–15) were almost three times more likely to have symptoms suggesting cardiac troubles, such as chest pain, than those who scored in the lowest range (3–5).[35] Over a three-year follow-up period, for the men who had symptoms of cardiac disease or high blood pressure, hostility levels were a strong predictor of subsequent heart attacks.

A closer relationship between health and hostility emerges from studies using personal interviews rather than self-rated question-naires.[36] John Barefoot, who has conducted many studies on hostil-ity, illuminates this discrepancy. In response to the commonly asked question, "What would you do if you were stuck in traffic behind a slow driver?" he points out that two people might provide the same answer: "I would pass the driver as soon as possible." But the answer can sound very different, depending on the hostility level. A nonhos-tile person might be neutral in tone, simply answering the question. A hostile responder might be contemptuous, "I'd pass him, you idiot!" The tone of voice might imply, "Isn't it obvious? Why are you bother-ing me with such a stupid question?" Even though the hostile person may be unaware of the contempt, listeners are sure to pick it up.

Causes of Anger and Hostility

Given the hazards of hostility, it is of some interest to inquire how this emotion comes to prevail. Although nobody can say for sure what makes any one individual hostile, science has several sugges-tions. Among them are an unhappy childhood, angry genes, other emotional disturbances, hormones that provoke, and an angry brain.

Unhappy Childhood

We know from working with patients that hostility may begin in childhood, stemming from feelings of insecurity and negative atti-tudes toward others.[37] These feelings and attitudes can result from parenting that lacks genuine acceptance, is overly critical and de-manding of conformity, and is inconsistent with regard to discipline.

In rhesus monkeys, too, a stressful childhood (for example mater-nal deprivation) produces an aggressive adult[38] whose impaired mothering is likely to lead to abnormal development in her own off-spring.[39] In this way environmental stresses can lead to behavioral problems that are passed from one generation to the next.

Angry Genes

Some research suggests that hostility may have a genetic basis. In troops of rhesus monkeys, about 5 to 10 percent of the young male monkeys show abnormally high levels of aggression and impul-sivity.[40] When studied, these monkeys have genetically reduced levels of serotonin transmission, as measured by serotonin-breakdown products in their spinal fluid. In the wild, as with their human counter-parts, their aggression is not well accepted, and these monkeys tend to be expelled from the troop before they are three years old. Too young to fend for themselves or join with other monkeys, most of them perish.

Researchers have recently created genetic variants of mice that show aggression—for example, knockout mice that lack the gene that codes for the enzyme that produces nitric oxide in nerve cells.[41] The males in this line constantly attack other mice and keep trying to mate with females that have rejected them. Curiously, female mice that lack the gene are not aggressive, but are less vigorous in defend-ing their young than is the wild strain. Although nitric oxide is known to be a neurotransmitter—a surprising and novel finding, considering that nitric oxide is a gas—these findings were quite unex-pected, revealing just how much we have yet to learn about the biol-ogy of anger and aggression. We do not at this time know of any similar genetic variation in humans.

Other Emotional Disturbances

Hostility may arise as a symptom of emotional disorders such as de-pression, post-traumatic stress disorder, attention deficit disorder, and paranoia. All of these are worth treating in their own right.

Hormones That Provoke

The male hormone testosterone is clearly associated with aggression in humans and other animals.[42] In almost all mammals, males are more aggressive than females.[43] Spotted hyenas are an exception, and sure enough, in that species the female has more circulating testosterone than the male.[44] In humans, testosterone is at its highest levels during adolescence, which may go some way to explaining why young men commit a disproportionate number of violent acts. Blood levels of testosterone also rise to their highest levels during the summer, when rapes and other violent acts tend to peak.[45] The neural tracts that mediate aggression in animals are richly supplied with receptors for testosterone.[46]

Testosterone has many beneficial effects.[47] It is involved in sexual arousal and functioning, as well as in the type of striving that leads to socially useful victory. Success in itself, such as graduating from law school or medical school and winning at tennis, increases blood levels of testosterone.[48] So there may be a positive-feedback loop in which testosterone promotes victory, which in turn increases testosterone levels, and so on.

Considering the central role of testosterone, it would hardly be desirable to suppress the effects of this hormone in most people. For extremely aggressive individuals, however, it might be worth considering.

Other hormones have a soothing influence on the brain. These include the female hormones estrogen and progesterone and the hormone oxytocin, which has been found to promote attachment and nurturance.[49,50]

Angry Brain

It was 1966, an ordinary August morning at the University of Texas at Austin, until the peace was shattered by rounds of gunfire. Bullets began to tear through the bodies of people who just happened to be in the vicinity of the 300-foot clock tower that dominates the campus. One young woman was shot, and when her boyfriend ran to her aid, he was shot too. Both died on the spot. A serviceman driving a van stepped out to see what all the fuss was about and became another victim of a well-aimed bullet. The sniper's accuracy was alarming. One man, a full three hundred yards from the tower, was reading a magazine at a newsstand when a bullet pierced him, killing him instantly.

By day's end, the death toll stood at fourteen, with another thirty-one wounded. The killer turned out to be Charles Whitman, a handsome, square-jawed former marine. Whitman had been one of the youngest men in his state to achieve the rank of Eagle Scout, had served as an altar boy in his church, and was an accomplished pianist. He had killed his wife and mother the day before to spare them the embarrassment of his shooting spree.

The various factors that might have triggered his act of lunacy have been summarized in *A Sniper in the Tower* by Gary Lavergne.[51] Of particular relevance here are excerpts from the note he wrote the evening before the murders:

> I don't quite understand what it is that compels me to type this letter. Perhaps it is to leave some vague reason for the actions I have recently performed [the murder of his wife and mother]. . . . I don't understand myself these days. . . . I have been a victim of many unusual and irrational thoughts. . . . I talked with a Doctor once for about two hours and tried to convey to him my fears that I felt some overwhelming violent impulses. . . . After my death I wish that an autopsy would be performed on me to see if there is any visible physical disorder. I have had some tremendous headaches in the past and have consumed two large bottles of Excedrin in the past two months.

Whitman goes on to request that his dog be given to his in-laws with the message that their daughter had loved the animal, and that arrangements be made for the disposition of his meager assets. He requests that after his outstanding debts are settled, "Donate the rest anonymously to a mental health foundation. Maybe research can prevent further tragedies of this type. If you can find it in your heart to grant my last wish," he concludes, "cremate me after the autopsy."

At postmortem the pathologist found a walnut-sized malignant tumor deep within Whitman's brain, in a location where it might well have exerted pressure on the amygdala and other circuitry responsible for mediating violent impulses. In Whitman these emotional parts of the brain appear to have been uncontrolled by those regions responsible for proper judgments, such as the prefrontal cortex. Whitman seems to have been aware of this disconnect and saddened by it, but awareness was insufficient to moderate his impulses.

If someone with Whitman's problems, including severe headaches, were to consult a physician today, a routine MRI would show up a brain tumor of far smaller size than Whitman's with no difficulty. A potential tragedy could be averted.

Whitman's case raises the question as to how many people who have problems controlling their violent impulses might actually be suffering from brain lesions. A lesion could reside either in areas that mediate feelings of rage or in areas involved in restraining aggressive impulses, such as the prefrontal cortex.

Adrian Raine, professor of psychology at the University of Southern California, has explored the brains of people given to violent actions.[52] In one study, he and his colleagues compared the PET scans of twenty-four murderers with those of forty-one nonmurderers. They found that murderers had more activity in the deeper centers of the brain, lying underneath the cortex. In addition, impulsive murderers showed reduced activity in their prefrontal cortex, a deficiency not seen in those who had murdered with premeditation.

In a more recent study, Raine and colleagues looked at the MRI scans of twenty-one individuals diagnosed with antisocial personality disorder (also known as sociopathy) and a history of violence. They found that the violent sociopaths had 11-percent less gray matter in their frontal lobes as compared with the normal group, again implicating the control area.[53]

The antisocial individuals had another biological abnormality as well: Their emotions were blunted. When asked to prepare and deliver a speech about their faults, they showed less increase in heart rate and less sweating than the normal controls. In the absence of such bodily signals, sociopaths may not appreciate the impact of what they do, which may help explain their impulsiveness and reckless disregard of others.

It is likely that as our imaging and other diagnostic techniques become more sophisticated, many people who show immoderate anger and violent behavior will turn out to have brain abnormalities. Although these may explain their behavior to some degree, it will still be up to society to decide how to assign responsibility and deal with the disruptions that these people cause.

Managing Anger

> *Anger is a momentary madness, so control your passion or*
> *it will control you.*
> —Horace[54]

So far we have encountered nothing but bad news about anger. As with all emotions, however, anger brings important news from the limbic system, shouting that something is amiss. But when anger shouts *too* loudly, it is like static on a radio: It blocks out the quieter voice of reason. The good news is that excessive anger can indeed be modulated so that we can hear the signal beneath the noise and act appropriately on it.

Raymond Chip Tafrate, a psychologist in the criminology department at Central Connecticut State University, recently conducted a meta-analysis of over fifty controlled studies of anger management in adults.[55] Encouragingly, he found that overall the strategies studied are quite effective. Many of these studies were performed by Jerry Deffenbacher, professor of psychology at Colorado State University, who has been studying anger management in college students for the past twenty years.[56] The following ten-step program for managing anger is based on the suggestions of these two researchers, as well as on my own clinical experience.

Before you start this or any other anger-management program, consider whether your anger attacks might be related to a medication you are taking. If the attacks began at a particular time, as opposed to being a lifelong problem, check and see whether they coincided with starting the medication. Several drugs—including caffeine, steroids for asthma or bodybuilding, other antiasthmatic medications, diet drugs, and antidepressants—can make a person more irritable and prone to anger. If you think your medicines may be making matters worse, be sure to review them with your pharmacist or physician.

Step 1: Recognize That Your Anger Is a Problem

Many angry people do not regard their anger as a problem. In the minds of angry people, rage is a logical and justifiable response to those around them. Other people, not them, have the problem—which is why many angry people do not seek therapy. Before an angry person can be helped, he must recognize that he has a problem.

A patient of mine frequently ran afoul of his wife and family because of his temper tantrums. With antidepressant medications and some behavioral help, he was able to bring these under control. On reflection, he observed that "the key to getting a handle on myself was recognizing I had a problem. The most important insight was to realize that I wasn't just this average Joe with a bit of a temper. I had a problem with rage attacks. And that caused problems for everybody else. Until I took responsibility for that, I couldn't expect things to improve."

Step 2: Monitor Your Anger Level

The second step toward changing any emotional response is to keep tabs on it, accurately and as it occurs. Any pocket-size notebook will do. Make two columns by drawing a line down the middle of the page. Then, at intervals throughout the day, note in the left column the time and your level of anger (rated from 0 to 100). In the right column, jot what is happening, especially when your anger level is high. In Deffenbacher's experience, most people find anger a problem when it exceeds 40. Try to make at least one recording per day when your anger level is high.

Step 3: Look for a Pattern

Different triggers provoke different people. Bad traffic, slow waiters, an insensitive boss, an incompetent employee, or an inattentive spouse are all common provocations for angry people, some of whom might endorse all of the above as triggers. Try to find a pattern in what triggers your episodes. Sometimes the pattern that emerges will involve the time of day or month rather than the nature of the trigger. Working mothers, for example, often feel irritable just after they get home from work. The time when they feel the greatest need to unwind may also be the time when the demands on them are at a peak. Many people are most vulnerable when their blood sugar is low.

Your anger log may also reveal behaviors that protect you against angry outbursts—for example, exercising, feeling happy, or eating a snack.

Step 4: Take a Time-Out

Thomas Jefferson advised, "When angry, count ten before you speak. If very angry a hundred."[57] Mark Twain parodied this, suggesting instead, "When angry, count to four. If still angry, swear."[58] The insight embedded in these epigrams is that a time-out often provides the angry person with an opportunity to calm down and collect his thoughts.

People who suffer from rage attacks, such as Frank, the businessman I mentioned, report that these attacks are physical, sweeping over them in waves. They sense an attack coming on, sometimes starting in the pit of the stomach, and sweeping upward as a feeling of heat and pressure in the head. Blood rushes to the head, causing the face to flush. (It is not without reason that people given to such bouts are known as hotheads.)

As with any other wave, the peak will pass as the wave runs its course. But that takes a certain amount of time, the duration of which varies from one person to the next. For some people, counting to ten is sufficient; others need longer to settle down.

I have advised several patients with anger problems to literally turn the other cheek, physically moving away from the person who is provoking the anger. In my observation, it is almost impossible for someone in the grip of a rage attack to modulate his response while also engaging with the person who provoked the attack. There might be many appropriate responses to a provocation, witty, diplomatic, noncommittal, or properly assertive. But the rage-prone individual is unlikely to find them in the heat of an attack if the *agent provocateur* is in his face. It is better to turn away, taking time to form a modulated response. If something must be said, "Let me think about it and I'll get back to you," can be a useful way to buy time until you cool off.

One of my patients, a middle-aged man who is repeatedly in trouble for what he calls "my big mouth," readily admits that nothing improved until he learned to turn away when his wife or children were annoying him. "Then I can gather my thoughts and get myself together and the outcome is invariably better." Interestingly, chimpanzees consider a direct stare to be an act of aggression and respond in kind. During rage attacks people are like angry apes in this regard.

If a person's anger attacks are generally directed toward someone in particular, it is best to discuss this strategy in advance. A man who has outbursts toward his wife at the dinner table, for example, might try to contain his anger by leaving the table. Misunderstanding, his wife might feel abandoned or insulted and go after him to resolve matters there and then, adding fuel to the fire. Obviously, things go better when a husband and wife have discussed his rage attacks and the proposed solution ahead of time.

One desired outcome might be for the husband to recognize when an anger attack is building and excuse himself, and for his family to leave him alone until he is calm enough to return of his own accord. At that point it would be best to talk about neutral topics, leaving the bone of contention to be revisited at a later time. Such a strategy will give the couple a far better chance at resolving their issues, including the rage attacks.

Step 5: Challenge Perceptions and Thoughts That Fuel Your Anger

Anger researchers have found that anger is very often driven and reinforced by mental impressions, ideas that feed the angry feelings. There are several common misperceptions that fuel anger.

SEEING HOSTILITY WHERE IT DOES NOT EXIST.
Research has shown that aggressive children misperceive other people's intentions and overestimate the threat that they pose. People with post-traumatic stress disorder tend to be hypervigilant about their surroundings. Depressed people often believe—incorrectly— that others feel hostile or critical toward them. Working from their misperceptions, all these people tend to defend themselves, and provoke hostility as a result. This feeds their misperceptions, and so a vicious cycle can develop.

Here again your notebook may be helpful. Is there a pattern in what you are thinking when your anger rises? It may help to check with others whether your perceptions are correct. For example, you might ask your spouse, "When you said that, you seemed angry. Were you?" Jot your spouse's answer in your notebook.

THE HIGHWAY DOES NOT BELONG TO YOU

The thought "I should not have to put up with this" often goes along with a semiconscious notion that the world should be other than it is. When it isn't, the person becomes enraged—by a delay in traffic, for instance, or at an airport. For that reason, whenever you notice yourself thinking, "I shouldn't have to put up with this," ask yourself, "Why not? What is so special about me that I should be exempt from the ordinary hassles and inconveniences of everyday life?" Such ideas of entitlement often justify anger and aggression and prevent people from taking responsibility for their emotional state and their behavior.

Deffenbacher sometimes points out to drivers who become angry as they wend their way along Highway I-25 that the name of the highway does not stand for "I and my 25 friends." In other words, the highway does not belong to them and they need to realize, emotionally as well as rationally, that public places belong to everyone and that sometimes they get crowded. It's nothing personal. The husband of a friend of mine tends to get very angry and curse at long red traffic lights. His wife reminds him gently that the red light doesn't care, so he might as well save his fury.

BLACK-OR-WHITE THINKING

Former British Prime Minister Margaret Thatcher, in summing up Britain's position in the Falklands War, declared the issue to be quite simple: "They were wrong and we were right." While that type of absolutist thinking might work for a politician, it mostly gets angry people into trouble. Watch out when you begin to think in black-or-white terms as it may mark the beginning of an anger attack.

One variant of black-or-white thinking is the worst-case scenario. For example, a small criticism of a report submitted by an angry person can be heard as an outright rejection, not only of the writing but of the writer, which can light the anger fuse.

Thinking about matters in a polarized way feeds a sense of righteous indignation. "I'm either a winner or a loser," an angry person might argue, "and I don't want to be a loser, so I'd better fight back."[59] Instead, listen to the other person and try to understand his point of view. If you don't see everything in terms of right or wrong, win or lose, you can lessen your feelings of anger.

NOT HAVING A TANTRUM DOESN'T MEAN YOU'RE GIVING SOMEONE PERMISSION TO ABUSE YOU

A common misperception among people who are given to angry outbursts is that if you do not get your licks in right away, you are essentially giving the provocateur permission to offend again and again. It is important to realize that you will have other opportunities to put your foot down and make it clear that you are not willing to accept certain types of behavior.

EVEN IF YOUR ANGER IS JUSTIFIED, IT CAN STILL COST YOU

The evidence that anger and hostility are harmful to your health does not take into account whether they are justified. For example, researchers called in to help New York City traffic cops deal with their anger went to great lengths to point out the legitimacy of the cops' feelings, given the abuse they receive from motorists they ticket.[60] In giving a ticket, after all, the cops are simply doing their job, enforcing the law. Yet, the insults these traffic cops receive are astonishing in their meanness. Cops are the butt of all manner of humiliating slurs and serious threats.

An important part in treating the abused cops was to acknowledge the injustice of the slurs, the seriousness of the threats, and the legitimacy of the cops' anger. Only then was it possible to help the cops recognize that their angry responses, justified or not, were damaging to them. Only then was it possible to help them modify these responses.

IT IS GENERALLY EASIER TO CHANGE YOUR EXPECTATIONS THAN THE WORLD

A major aspect of managing anger involves recognizing that life is often neither fair nor easy. Anyone who thinks otherwise will be angry a great deal of the time. Simply shifting our expectations can go a long way to mollifying our anger.

Step 6: Dig Deeper to Understand the Roots of Your Anger

Once you recognize a pattern in the types of events that tend to trigger your anger, ask yourself when in your past you have experienced similar reactions.

Joe, for example, would become enraged when his son brought home poor test grades or report cards. On reflection, he realized that he was spending a great deal of money to send his son to a top-notch private school, whereas he himself had gone to an inferior public school in an impoverished school district. He was determined that his son would have better opportunities in life, and he expected the boy to have a similar level of determination. When the boy's report card fell short, Joe became resentful. He was not receiving a satisfactory return on his investment. How could his son fail to appreciate this wonderful opportunity?

After making these connections, Joe realized that it was not his son's fault that he, Joe, had been deprived as a child, nor had his son asked to go to a private school. While it was important that his son should make the most of his opportunities, Joe realized that it was unfair to saddle the boy with baggage from his own past. These realizations helped Joe restrain his ill-temper and lighten up around his son. He and his son began to have more fun together than they had had in years.

Step 7: Change the Messages You Give Yourself

An anger-management strategy called *self-instructional training* is highly effective.[61] This strategy involves changing the messages you give yourself when you are angry. Take Ken, for example, a young man whose outbursts at work had cost him three jobs in five years. When angry at his boss, Ken would say to himself, "It's unfair. I don't have to take this crap from him! He needs to be put in his place!"

In therapy the young man learned that these self-statements amplified his feelings of anger. He was taught to replace them with statements such as: "I can handle criticism from my boss. Blowing up just makes the situation worse. It's better to let it go than to tell him off. Stay calm." Ken was encouraged to rehearse these alternative messages, both silently and out loud, while thinking about his boss and the situations that made him angry.[62]

Later, in the actual workplace, that practice helped him stay cool. It was also useful for Ken to recognize that some of what happened at work was not personal and that his boss had his own problems. Ken could say to himself, "My boss's behavior does not necessarily mean that there is anything wrong with me." That helped Ken get less upset when his boss became irritable.

It was common for the abused cops to say to themselves, "If people aren't polite to me, it means they don't respect me. It is impossible for me to work when I am not respected."[63] Many angry people have that reaction. If you feel that way, you might try an alternative message along these lines: "Some people are rude, but I don't have to let them get to me. I respect myself for being a competent and polite professional. I am not going to let anybody take that self-respect away."

In developing your own new self-messages for your trigger situations, you can learn from those around you. Ask those you know and trust what thoughts help them stay cool in the face of provocations.

This method may not work for you right away if you have spent many months or years practicing how to be mad. If you want to change, you need to practice how not to be mad. And "practice" is the key word. The more often you rehearse your new self-messages, the more easily they will come when you need them. Some people find it helpful to write these messages down on flashcards and read them again and again. Just as other forms of learning can increase the size of relevant brain areas, learning and practicing new emotional skills will surely develop new neural circuits in the part of the brain that governs these responses.

Step 8: Use Exposure and Relaxation

Anger-management researchers have adapted methods from effective anxiety treatments, reasoning that both anger and anxiety are unpleasant emotions with a state of high arousal. Joseph Wolpe, a pioneer in behavioral-therapy research, was the first to reason that it is impossible to feel highly aroused and relaxed at the same time.[64] If you get a person to relax while at the same time exposing him to an unpleasant stimulus, he suggested, you might be able to decondition him. The nervous system can be taught to greet that stimulus with relaxation, not the old unpleasant emotions.

In research since then, attempts to treat anger by simply teaching a person how to relax have been shown to be much less effective than combining relaxation with exposure to the trigger stimuli.[65] The triggers differed from person to person. The relaxation techniques included slow, deep abdominal breathing, contracting and relaxing various muscle groups, and several meditative techniques. Many currently available books are devoted to teaching these relaxation techniques.

Coupling relaxation with anger triggers is difficult to practice on one's own because the stimuli are so unpleasant that people with anger problems are understandably reluctant to expose themselves to the pain of reliving them. For this reason, most people don't like to do this sort of work at home. Those with serious anger problems are advised to consult a therapist with some expertise in anger management. A skillful therapist can be very helpful both in pointing out your strengths and in putting the anger-inducing insults in perspective before starting the exposure therapy. Essentially the treatment involves thinking about the anger triggers, feeling the bodily sensations of anger, and then going through a relaxation exercise that helps you settle down those angry feelings and bodily sensations while still holding in mind the unpleasant situation.

Whether you work on your anger with a professional or on your own, remember that every time you get triggered is an opportunity to practice. So, an ideal time for Ken to work on his anger at his boss might be while he is sitting at his desk, shoulders hunched, and jaw clenched, ruminating over the latest indignities. For example, he could think about his boss's behavior, breathe in deeply, using his diaphragm, and murmur to himself, "Be calm." On the exhalation he could say, "Let the anger go," and visualize it flowing out of his system in a stream of colored light. This exercise can be repeated as long and as often as needed.

Letting go of your anger is important to the success of this exercise. If you are not vigilant, you can easily lapse into your angry thoughts again, which would make the exercise worthless.

Step 9: Use Humor

Humor is an excellent antidote to anger. Some of the things that people think or say when they are angry are quite funny. If you are angry at someone and think, "What an asshole!" imagine him with a pair of buttocks sitting astride his shoulders. Take the natural humor inherent in your hostility and milk it for all its worth. Recently a friend and I were in a hurry and found ourselves stuck behind a very slow driver on the highway. Just as I began to feel hot and bothered, we read her license place, which said, "1ST TWIN." That led us to speculate as to whether the experience of holding up the second twin in the birth canal might shape later behavior, inducing a sense of pride and pleasure in obstructing others. As we laughed, our anger seemed to just evaporate.

Step 10: Listen to Your Limbic News—And Act Appropriately

Once your anger has calmed down, you will find it possible to think more clearly. Now ask yourself, What is the message from my anger, and what do I want to do about it? Is your anger justified by the event that triggered it? If so, it is providing you with important information about your world. Sometimes the cause of the anger may need to be addressed; at other times it might be better left alone. That is a judgment call, one best made with a cool head.

Recently someone owed me money and had obviously decided not to make good, even though he could well afford to do so. I asked my lawyer, a good friend, what he thought I should do. He responded in his typical flowery style, "I think that to pursue it would be a misapplication of your limited and precious remaining days on earth," adding hastily, "though I certainly wish you a very long life." In less than a minute he had put the whole matter in perspective and left me with a smile on my face. His advice is encapsulated by the popular expression that "living well is the best revenge."

Sometimes, however, it is desirable or even necessary to act on the cause of your anger. Perhaps an important principle is at stake or a wrong needs to be put right. An abusive action may be unacceptable and may need to be addressed. Anger outbursts and temper tantrums—your old way—were ineffective, self-defeating responses. They left you looking unreasonable and out of control, which distracted everyone from your point. Now you need to learn new ways to communicate a problem and suggest solutions.

A dissatisfied employee can bring her grievances to her supervisor's attention in a way that is respectful but firm. She can point out which of her supervisor's behaviors are causing her difficulty and show how these behaviors are defeating their mutual goals. Then she can point out a better way to resolve difficulties. Say her boss is in the habit of barging into her office several times a day and barking out criticisms. The employee might say: "If you are unhappy with the quality of my work, I need to hear about it. But perhaps we can confine that feedback to a regular supervisory meeting. That will help me to work more effectively the rest of the week."

Anger transformed in this way, modulated and tempered by reason, is known as assertiveness, an extremely useful skill both at home and at work.

The question of retaliation or even revenge is a morally complex one. Certainly, retaliation and threats of retaliation are major strategies used for constraining aggression in others. Retaliation is routinely administered by our justice system in the form of punishment or by governments in the forms of sanctions and warfare. Quite aside from these official forms of retaliation, however, people get even with one another on a daily basis in all sorts of ways, such as lawsuits. Retaliation or revenge is a tricky strategy, however. As the Chinese proverb goes, "When you plan revenge, be sure to dig two graves."

The great counterpoint to revenge is forgiveness, which involves letting go of the anger. The issue of revenge versus forgiveness is an ethical question of mammoth proportions that goes beyond the scope of this book. Chronically angry people, however, have more to gain both emotionally and physically from embracing the latter rather than the former.

Creating a Program That Blends the Ten Steps of Anger Management

Most patients with anger problems who find their way to my office—and to the offices of most other mental health professionals—have some additional problem as well, such as a mood or anxiety disorder. To illustrate how the ten steps of anger management can be blended to help people whose *primary* problem is anger, I have turned to my colleague Jerry Deffenbacher, an expert in anger management, who has kindly shared the following examples, drawn from his case files.

Sally: An Angry Mind in an Angry Body

Sally was a middle-aged woman who drove forty-five minutes to and from work each day. Throughout her commute she would be furious, cursing under her breath at the "idiots" who hogged the road. Though she tried to conceal her rage from others, she could not hide it from her own body, which responded with headaches, stomach-aches, and fatigue that carried over into her work and home life.

Sally was helped by relaxation techniques that calmed her highly reactive body. Her excellent sense of humor was recruited to help her take the road hogs less seriously. She was encouraged to create funny nicknames for them and to imagine hogs' heads nodding away on their necks. Questioning her about her anger revealed that she resented people who delayed her, considering them to be stealing precious minutes from her life. She came to realize that being angry so much of the time was degrading the quality of her life more than her fellow commuters were. Her therapist encouraged her to find a way to make her commute time enjoyable. She decided to rent some audio-taped books, which enabled her to listen to the classics she had always wanted to read.

Sally's aches and pains subsided over time. She became an easier person to be around and, more important, reclaimed her sense of pleasure, even during her dreaded commute.

Hurricane George

George was the owner of a consulting firm, a bright, energetic, and creative man whose business would have been very successful were it not for his temper tantrums. His employees nicknamed him Hurricane George because of his tendency to storm about when their work fell short of his perfectionistic standards. Then he would become as loud and intimidating as a storm at sea. As a consequence, he lost good employees and his business faltered. He realized that he needed help.

George was taught that he had to take a time-out when a "hurricane" came over him. He was advised that when he felt an anger outburst coming on, he should stay away from his staff until he cooled down. Knowing that George was an ardent Republican, Deffenbacher decided to use some humor with him, instructing him to wear a CLINTON FOR PRESIDENT button on his lapel for half an hour whenever he went into one of his rages. Not wishing to be seen wearing such an adornment, he would slink off into his office, where his reflections on his political anathema reminded him that his anger was his worst enemy.

While in his office cooling off, he was encouraged to tense and relax his muscle groups in sequence as he let go of his rage. He was taught to relax in response to certain triggers, such as contemplating an error that one of his employees might make. While thinking of such irritants, he was instructed to breathe in and out deeply, using his diaphragm instead of his chest muscles, counting with each breath, as he let go of his anger.

George was also taught to challenge the cognitive assumptions that were at the basis of his anger. He was inclined to black-or-white thinking, judging a report turned in by one of his employees to be either excellent or trash. Even a comma in the wrong place could consign it to the latter category. George learned instead to appreciate the shades of gray, to see that some elements of the report might be good whereas others might need work. He was taught to recognize that yelling would not get the job done and to rehearse saying that to himself, so that he could look past his anger and address the problem at hand.

Once he managed to bring his anger under control, George's business thrived. While he retained the nickname "Hurricane," it now took on a respectful connotation among his staff, suggesting his energetic dynamism rather than an attack of foul weather.

Brent: A Victim of Righteous Indignation

Brent, a vice-president of a large corporation, was one of the most productive senior officers in the company. Imagine his shock, therefore, when he was called in by the president of the company, who informed him that they had reluctantly decided to ask him to leave because of his problem with anger. Unlike Hurricane George, Brent's anger was quiet and smoldering but equally destructive to those around him. When enraged, Brent's lips would narrow and he would adopt a cold, steely, penetrating glare toward all who crossed his path. Even though he might not say anything, his quiet rage was unmistakable and the atmosphere it generated was deadly.

Realizing that his job was in serious jeopardy if not already lost, Brent asked his supervisor to give him another chance and for the first time sought help for his problem. His therapist's questions revealed two main triggers for his anger: when he thought that someone was questioning his integrity and when fellow managers criticized those working on the front lines who provided the fuel that made the company run.

Brent was asked to examine the assumptions behind his anger. When people questioned what he said, were they really questioning his integrity? What motivation would they have for doing so? Was it not possible that rather than accusing him of lying, they were actually checking on the quality of his information and determining how accurate it was? In a similar vein, when they complained about the line people, were they really impugning their competency or just engaging in the commonplace activity of blaming others when things go wrong?

Digging into Brent's past revealed that he had been brought up in a very stern family that treated the slightest shading of the truth like a dastardly lie. As a result, Brent learned to believe that unless he was scrupulously honest to the last detail, he was guilty of a heinous crime that would be punished with cold, harsh silence. It was that same cold harshness that he exhibited toward others whenever he became angry.

Brent needed to learn that the kind of treatment he had received as a child and that he now exhibited to others was unacceptable. He was taught other ways to express his angry feelings. When others questioned him, he learned to ask them first why they doubted what he had to say. At times he might say, "It seems as though you are questioning my integrity and that bothers me." That provided an opportunity for resolving the issue openly so that it did not fester and corrupt the atmosphere. When the line people were being criticized, he learned to say, "I don't think it is really fair to blame them. They are working very hard. Perhaps there are other reasons productivity is down." By expressing his opinions calmly, he felt less burdened by anger, and that helped everyone who had to deal with him. In the end, Brent was able to keep his job and actually managed to enjoy it more once he learned alternative strategies for dealing with his anger.

Medication: A Novel Approach to Anger Management

As we saw in the case of Mike Tyson, a little medicine can go a long way. I have successfully treated several angry people with Zoloft and similar medications that enhance serotonin uptake. Other medications that inhibit the fight-or-flight response, such as beta-blockers, have also been successfully used in people with rage attacks.[66] In addition, I have had luck with antiseizure medications, such as Depakote.

In some clinical studies, a problem with anger has been treated as part of another condition. For example, researchers Maurizio Fava and Jerrold Rosenbaum at the Massachusetts General Hospital in Boston found that anger attacks disappeared in about one-half to three-quarters of the depressed patients treated with standard antidepressants.[67] There is a need for research into the value of antidepressants in treating rage attacks even in those who are not clinically depressed.

If the ten steps for anger management are not sufficient to bring your anger under control, consider using medications. Of course, a prescription should always be supervised by a properly qualified physician, preferably following a psychiatric consultation.

Don't Let It All Hang Out

A popular method for treating anger has been "letting it all hang out." Vocalize your anger, talk it out, punch a pillow or a punching bag, goes the theory. Like a good bowel movement, it will purge your system. The technical term for "letting it all hang out" is *catharsis*, a concept that has been around since classical times.

In fact, there is no evidence that catharsis is helpful. On the contrary, many studies show that dwelling on anger makes it worse.[68] One recent study found that even when subjects were tricked by means of a bogus news article into believing that catharsis would help, expressing anger by hitting a punching bag still left them feeling more, not less, aggressive.[69]

Angry Children: A Powder Keg Waiting to Burst

They are small towns, scattered across the United States. Their names, formerly unknown to most Americans, have now become household words—Littleton, Colorado; Jonesboro, Arkansas; Springfield, Oregon. These words conjure up images of children or adolescents whose anger reached such monumental proportions as to explode in murder and carnage. Each case left classmates, parents, teachers, neighbors, and fellow citizens asking: "How could it have happened? What could we have done to prevent it?"

For every child who is angry enough to kill, there are no doubt thousands of others whose anger is a problem to themselves and others. Rather than discussing violence as a major societal issue, however, I'd like to focus on the risk factors for anger in individual children and how to manage these young people. Consider these research findings:

- Both bullies and their victims are more likely to be clinically depressed than are children not involved in bullying behavior, according to school surveys in Finland and Australia.[70] In the Australian study, both bullies and those who were bullied were more likely to smoke, and bullies suffered from significant physical symptoms. The take-home lesson is that bullying behavior is a cry for help. intervention is called for.

- Conduct disorders are estimated to occur in between one in ten and one in twenty young children.[71] This problem is defined as "a repetitive and persistent pattern of behavior in which the basic rights of others or major age-appropriate societal norms or rules are violated." Generally these children are very unhappy and have low opinions of themselves. Two out of every five go on to become hardened delinquents in their teenage years. However, if they are treated before age 10, many can be helped.[72] One famous example of a badly behaved 9-year-old who went on to make good was the young Winston Churchill, whose school report card noted that he was a "constant trouble to everybody." To turn around aggressive behavior, it is important to intervene when a child is young; adolescents are far harder to treat.

- Five aspects of parenting style repeatedly associated with aggressive behavior are poor supervision; harsh, erratic discipline; disharmony between the parents; rejection of the child; and little parental involvement in the child's activities.

- Early prevention can have long-lasting effects. One of the most dramatic illustrations of the benefits of early intervention is the Perry/High Scope project, which gave educational input to deprived children at ages 3 to 4. Follow-up at age 27 showed that those who had participated in the program had better relationships with their peers, received fewer state benefits, and had a far lower rate of repeat arrests than their untreated peers.[73]

- A meta-analysis of forty treatment studies aimed at helping angry and aggressive children and adolescents, by psychologists Denis Sukhodolsky of Yale University and Howard Kassinove of Hofstra University in New York, found that teaching children how to handle angry feelings was more effective than helping them get in touch with their feelings. For children who cannot manage their anger, aggression may appear to be the only available option, the analysis showed. The children often lacked the interpersonal skills to address their needs in other ways.[74]

Eva Feindler, professor of psychology at Long Island University who has been working with angry children and adolescents for many years, observes that anger is a central component of aggression in young people. She provides the following guidelines for recognizing when help should be sought:[75]

- *Temper tantrums that extend beyond "the terrible twos."* A 6- or 7-year old who cannot tolerate the word "no" has a problem.

- *Mood disturbances,* which may present as sullen, grim, or hostile responses.

- *Aggressive behaviors.* Most children learn to inhibit angry impulses. Children with anger disorders don't know when to stop being aggressive.

- *Hostile thinking as a pattern.* When things go wrong, angry children tend to blame others rather than take responsibility or show remorse. They feel as though they are victims, an idea with which they justify their aggressive behavior. Normal children do not have these thought patterns, which can be recognized as early as age 7.

- *A lack of empathy or concern for others,* which is often present in children with anger disorders.

Guidelines for Dealing With an Angry Child or Adolescent

If you detect signs of anger in your child, here are eleven guidelines to help you deal with the problem and prevent it from getting out of control:

1. Play with your child and be sure to have enjoyable times together. When you are dealing with an angry child, so many of your interactions take on a critical or disciplinary quality. This often serves to make the child angrier, feeding a vicious cycle. To

break this cycle, it is important to create a positive atmosphere and a sense of bonding that the child will not want to lose by his angry behavior.

2. Make it clear what you expect from the child and what is off limits. Avoid vague criticisms and sarcasm, such as "Stop raising hell," or "Why do you always have to make trouble?" Instead, be specific.

3. Be calm when responding to angry behavior. Many parents scream back at their children, which sets a bad example and creates an atmosphere in which it seems legitimate to ventilate anger. When parents make threats that are not carried out, they leave their children with a sense that there are no real consequences to misbehavior. This simply encourages the children to wait out the storm of their parents' anger.

4. Respond positively to good behavior. Even the small accomplishments of daily life should be recognized and rewarded. This will encourage the child to behave well the next time.

5. Be consistent in setting limits. Erratic standards of discipline reinforce bad behavior. The child may say to himself, "Maybe I didn't get away with it this time, but I will if I keep trying."

6. Help the child distinguish between feeling angry and behaving aggressively. If a child's little brother grabs his toy from him, it is legitimate for him to feel angry, but inappropriate to hit his brother over the head for doing so.

7. Help the child generate options other than aggression for dealing with anger. Often a child with an anger problem can think of only one way to deal with an insult—aggression. It is important to help the child find other ways. The child whose brother steals his toy, for example, can choose to ignore it, complain to a parent, offer the brother some other toy, or leave the scene. Later, after calming down, he can reclaim the stolen toy. Help the child find acceptable ways of expressing his anger, such as writing or talking about it or drawing a picture.

8. Teach the child calming skills. Just like adults with anger disorders, angry children tend to explode when provoked or frus-

trated. These children benefit from learning to take a time-out. A "calming chair" or other special spot in the home can give the child a place to go and calm down when angered. A movie or videotape can help distract the child long enough to let the anger settle. Deep-breathing exercises may also help, as can sitting in a comfortable position. All these techniques are geared toward helping children learn to soothe themselves and settle down the hyperaroused nervous activity that seems to affect angry children.

9. Encourage the child to swim or take a run or brisk walk to help dissipate his anger. Exercise can help settle anger, just as it can help settle anxiety. The martial arts are good for children with impulse problems, as they teach discipline and self-control along with providing a physical release.

10. Point out to the child that anger can be a positive emotion, providing energy and the impetus to change. Were it not for anger, many important social and political changes would not have occurred. Children should be taught to channel their anger in positive ways. If there is something a child does not like at her school, writing a letter to the principal will surely do more good than setting a fire.

    Children should be taught the difference between healthy competition and aggression. The first is about winning but not about harming another person. A child should learn that even when competing, empathy toward one's opponent is important. One important lesson that organized sports teaches is that you shake hands with the opposing team after beating them rather than kicking them in the shins.

11. Help the child to learn empathy. Involving children in community service is one way of teaching them to deal with disadvantaged people in a positive way.

Angry children, like angry adults, are often uninterested in getting help for their problems because they don't see themselves as the problem. They may need to be motivated, at least initially, by paying attention to that aspect of the problem that bothers them or prevents them from getting what they want. If a child is upset because he has no friends, for example, it might be useful to point out that children would enjoy playing with him more if he were nicer to them. Later on, the other problems that anger causes can be addressed.

As with adults, encouraging children to vent their hostility in a physical way exacerbates their anger. Studies have shown that children who are encouraged to punch a Bobo doll (a large inflatable doll that rocks when hit) show more aggression than those who are not.

A Last Thought About Anger

The pros and cons of anger have been debated since ancient times, so perhaps it is fitting to give the last word on this important emotion to two important classical thinkers. The Greek philosopher Aristotle made strong claims for the value of this emotion, arguing, "Anger is necessary, and no battle can be won without it." Taking a polar opposite view, the Roman sage Seneca wrote a treatise "On Anger" in which he had nothing good to say about the emotion. Compared to anger, he stated, "no plague has cost the human race more dear."[76]

Modern research supports both of these perspectives. Clearly an emotion that has been conserved over millions of years of evolution must play an important role in survival. On the other hand, we know that anger can damage not only those at whom it is directed, but also those who harbor the emotion. It is critically important to notice our anger as a signal that some problem exists in our world. But it is equally important to address the problem skillfully. Those who indulge their anger frivolously pay a heavy price for such entertainment in the form of poor relationships, failed ventures, and ill health. Therefore, it is good news indeed that there are strategies for managing anger that actually work. Those who walk around angry much of the time would do well to adopt them.

Chapter 10

Love and Lust

*Love is a canvas furnished by Nature and
embroidered by the imagination.*
—Voltaire

*Love is the answer, but while you are waiting for the answer,
sex raises some pretty interesting questions.*
—Woody Allen

THE woman climbed the fence into the narrow path between the dense bristling young firs. She was a ruddy country-looking girl with soft brown hair and a sturdy body, and slow movements full of unusual energy. The man, moderately tall and lean, who stood in her path, barring her way, looked at her curiously and searchingly with his blue eyes. They exchanged only a few sentences before he led her through a wall of prickly trees into a clearing. There he threw down a few dry boughs, put his coat and waistcoat over them, made her lie down on them, and undressed her. And then:

> He too had bared the front part of his body and she felt his naked flesh against her as he came into her. For a moment he was still inside her, turgid there and quivering. Then as he began to move, in the sudden helpless orgasm, there awoke in her new strange thrills rippling inside her. Rippling, rippling, rippling, like a flapping overlapping of soft flames, soft as feathers, running to points of brilliance, ex-

quisite, exquisite and melting her all molten inside. It was like bells rippling up and up to a culmination. She lay unconscious of the wild little cries she uttered at the last. But it was over too soon, too soon.

She clung to him unconscious in passion, and he never quite slipped from her, and she felt the soft bud of him within her stirring, and strange rhythms flushing up into her with a strange rhythmic growing motion, swelling and swelling till it filled all her cleaving consciousness, and then began again the unspeakable motion that was not really motion, but pure deepening whirlpools of sensation swirling deeper and deeper through all her tissue and consciousness, till she was one perfect concentric fluid of feeling, and she lay there crying in unconscious inarticulate cries.[1]

The woman in this story is, of course, Lady Constance Chatterley; her lover, Mellors, the gamekeeper. The tale of their love affair, first published in 1928, marked the rude eruption of lust out of the jungle and the unspoken recesses of society into the drawing rooms of civilized men and women throughout the Western World. Years later, Alfred Kinsey would document the many ways in which lust expresses itself, and later still, researchers William Masters and Virginia Johnson would measure and describe the bodily responses involved in sexual arousal, intercourse, and orgasm.

Lust can exist independent of romantic feelings, as any viewer of pornography can attest, but is also an integral part of romantic love. However, with or without "love"—whatever we mean by the many varieties of experience encompassed by that word—lust is an emotion of enormous importance for propagating an individual's genes. Without knowing it, Lady Chatterley and Mellors were acting out a behavioral script that has been programmed into the DNA of humans and other animals through the course of evolution as a necessary way to ensure the survival of their genes.

What can science tell us about what might have been going on in the brains of Lady Chatterley and her lover as they made love under the trees on that spring day?

Molecules of Desire

Studies in animals have found that sexual activity is accompanied by increased electrical activity in widespread areas of the brain, particularly the limbic system.[2] These activated areas communicate with the hypothalamus, which stimulates the pituitary gland to pour a stream of hormones into the blood. These hormones contribute to the mounting intensity of the type of satisfying sexual encounter experienced by Lady Chatterley.

Two hormones that are important in mediating sexual response are oxytocin and vasopressin. These hormones, which are chemically very similar to each other, are secreted by the back part of the pituitary gland, a structure that lies at the base of the brain. During sexual activity in men, more and more vasopressin is pumped into the circulation as sexual pleasure mounts.[3] At orgasm, a burst of oxytocin is released into the system.[4] Oxytocin also seems important for orgasmic pleasure in women.[5] In multiorgasmic women, for example, there is a direct relationship between the intensity of the orgasm and the amount of oxytocin released.[6] Oxytocin is also secreted in women during the earlier phases of courtship, such as flirting.

Oxytocin and vasopressin are versatile hormones. In general, oxytocin is associated with typically female behaviors, such as childbirth and nurturing the young,[7] whereas vasopressin is associated with male behaviors, such as territorial aggression.[8] There is more oxytocin in the brain of female animals and more vasopressin in the brain of males. Both oxytocin and vasopressin have important functions in both sexes, however. For example, oxytocin may be responsible for the afterglow of orgasm in both men and women, a state of peaceful relaxation.[9] The production of oxytocin in the brain is controlled to some extent by estrogen, the predominantly female hormone,[10] whereas the production of vasopressin is controlled by the male hormone testosterone.[11]

The hormones testosterone and, to a lesser extent, estrogen also seem to enhance sexual activity in men and women respectively. Men with a low libido and low circulating levels of testosterone may benefit from regular testosterone injections or gels applied to the skin. Recently it's been learned that some women with low sex drives can also benefit from testosterone.[12] However, women who use testosterone need to watch out for the masculinizing side effects of this hormone, such as facial hair or deepening of the voice. (In female singers, this deepening may be irreversible; they may lose those high soprano notes forever.) Men who use testosterone need to be aware that it can stimulate the development or progression of prostate cancer.[13]

During sexual activity, the choreographed discharge of these sexual hormones is accompanied by a dance of neurotransmitters released into the limbic system. Although we are far from knowing the fine details here, we can identify the most important chemicals. They are the usual suspects: dopamine, endorphins, norepinephrine, epinephrine, and serotonin.

Dopamine is thought to be a major mediator of many types of pleasure, and sexual pleasure is no exception. Dopamine is released during mating in rodents and presumably in people.[14] We know that because the antidepressant bupropion (Wellbutrin), which acts mostly by enhancing dopamine transmission—in contrast to the serotonin-enhancing antidepressants—is unlikely to reduce sexual desire or functioning.[15] In fact, Wellbutrin has even been used to counteract the sexual-dampening effect of the serotonin-enhancing drugs. Several patients to whom I have given Wellbutrin alone have reported increases in both arousal and libido. One reported a welcome increase in sexual activity, while another, a married man, was embarrassed to find himself sexually aroused by several women in his office.

How do we know that rats enjoy sex? Once they have had sex, they prefer going to the places where they had it as opposed to neutral locations.[16] I suppose it is the rodent equivalent of revisiting the secret haunts of one's adolescent explorations. Sexual pleasure—and all pleasure, for that matter—involves the release of endorphins, the body's own endogenous opiates.[17] We know that from experiments using endorphin antagonists, drugs that occupy endorphin receptors and thereby block the endorphin effects. A rat's preference for places where he has had sex can be inhibited by giving him an endorphin antagonist,[18] while in humans, the pleasure of orgasm can be inhibited by similar drugs.[19] On the other hand, powerful orgasmic and erotic feelings are described by some drug addicts after they inject themselves with opiates such as heroin.[20]

Norepinephrine and epinephrine, agents of the sympathetic nervous system, are both associated with arousal. Released by the adrenal gland, the former acts in the brain, while the latter is secreted into the bloodstream. They orchestrate the tingling flesh, pounding heart, and other sensations that accompany sex. Decades ago in medical school, we were taught to warn cardiac patients that the sympathetic nervous system activity associated with sex could be as risky as working out. According to one professor, having sex with one's spouse was equivalent to climbing one flight of stairs, while having sex with a lover was like climbing two flights. I doubt that anybody ever did a controlled study to explore this question, but the point remains. Having sex involves the activity of the sympathetic nervous system, and the more exciting the sex, the more active this system is likely to be, and the greater the strain on the heart. For this reason, heart patients should consult their cardiologist about "safe sex."

The role of serotonin in sexual drive seems to be largely a restraining one.[21] Perhaps it is serotonin that helps prevent men from accosting every object of desire and women from acting in a similarly brazen way. Animals with lesions of serotonin pathways in the brain show increased sexual urges and less discrimination in their choice of partners—for instance, males more often mounting males.[22] It is easy to see the evolutionary importance of choosing an appropriate mate with whom to reproduce, and serotonin may be critical in this regard.

It is only since the introduction of the selective serotonin reuptake inhibitors (SSRIs), the Prozac family of antidepressants, that I have become fully aware of serotonin's power to influence sexual experience. Although the impact of the SSRIs on sexual functioning varies from one individual to the next, it is not unusual to find global decreases in sexual desire and functioning in both men and women.

Drew is a case in point. Before I gave him Prozac for his depression, he enjoyed a healthy sexual appetite. Within weeks of starting the drug, that changed. Now he no longer enjoyed looking at pretty women as he walked to work. He still recognized that the women were beautiful, but his bodily response, the sexual charge, was missing. He also became less inclined to approach his wife for sex. When he and his wife did get around to making love, he was able to get an erection, but the sensations in his penis were less pleasurable, so much so that he found it difficult to achieve orgasm. His wife enjoyed his long-lasting performance, but for Drew, when he finally did achieve orgasm, it was disappointing. It lacked intensity. Women on SSRIs also complain of decreased arousal and sexual pleasure.

Antidepressants that enhance norepinephrine, such as desipramine and Serzone (nefadozone), do not seem to dampen sexual drive and functioning as much as the SSRIs. Nor does the herbal antidepressant St. John's wort, which enhances norepinephrine and dopamine as well as serotonin.

Before I go on, I'd like to remind you that much of what we know about brain functioning before and during sexual activity comes from work done on other mammals. We need to be careful in assuming the same facts are true of humans. Even so, I think it's valid to compare different species because the functions of many important biological molecules and nerve tracts have been conserved over the course of evolution. As an example, take oxytocin and vasopressin, hormones that are extremely important for arousal and orgasm in men and women. A close chemical cousin of these hormones coordinates the egg-laying behavior in sea turtles, and the hormones themselves are important in orchestrating monogamous behavior in certain types of voles.[23] So it makes sense that we can learn about the mechanics of our own lusty natures by studying the sexual and reproductive behaviors of other animals.

Vive La Différence

From an evolutionary point of view, why have two sexes? After all, amoebae seem to do perfectly well with only one (they reproduce by splitting in half) and many other species have survived for millions of years with only one sex. Yet when it comes to more complex creatures—reptiles, fish, birds, and mammals—two sexes are the norm. Why? What's the advantage?

People who study these things agree that the first benefit comes from the mixing of genes that occurs when a sperm fertilizes an egg. Mixing produces a genetically unique individual who inherits his genes from both his parents in roughly equal measure, and that keeps the population diverse. Diversity promotes the survival of a species because the environment changes over time. Certain mixtures of genes will deal better with a change in climate, predators, or viruses, increasing the likelihood that at least some of the population will survive.

The second major benefit comes from the different functions or roles that the two sexes play in the production and care of offspring. In complex animals, raising offspring can take years, as any parent can testify. Infant creatures with two parents on the job are at a distinct survival advantage.

Just as the two sexes differ physically, so do their brain structures. How much the brains differ may vary, but in general, the more the males and females of a species differ in physical appearance, the more different their brains look.[24] In the case of humans, the brains of males and females look very similar. Only careful and microscopic analysis can reveal the critical differences.

One major difference shows up in the corpus callosum, a large bundle of fibers that connects the left and right cerebral hemispheres and is larger in women than in men.[25] Presumably this physical difference accounts for the different ways in which men and women coordinate the activity of the two hemispheres. A woman's left and right hemispheres stay in touch more, notably in language processing, where women use both cerebral hemispheres to a greater degree than men. This may explain why after a left-sided stroke, women as a group recover the ability to speak more than men do.

Many microscopic differences have been found in the primitive regions of the brain, including in parts of the limbic system. The most famous of these is in the preoptic area (POA) of the hypothalamus, where several clusters of cells differ substantially.[26] In rats these clusters have been called the sexually dimorphic nuclei, while in humans the corresponding areas are called the interstitial nuclei. Neurons in the POA exert a major influence on sexual behavior in all the mammals studied so far. For example, when a male primate approaches a female, his POA neurons begin to fire away furiously and continue to do so throughout copulation.[27]

The differences between the brains of men and women also involve the cortex, the area responsible for complex thought processes. Recent imaging studies that compared men and women at rest found that the male brains showed more activity in the temporal lobes, areas that help regulate aggression, whereas the female brains lit up more in the cingulate areas, which are important for nurturing and social functions.[28]

Given these differences in the brains of men and women, it is not surprising that their sexual fantasies should differ too. As Richard C. Friedman and Jennifer Downey, clinical professors of psychiatry at Cornell and Columbia Universities respectively, have pointed out, men's sexual fantasies generally focus on graphic details of the sexual act, the actions that lead up to penetration, the thrusting and pounding of body parts, and the thrill of consummation. Women, on the other hand, generally fantasize about sex as emanating from a loving relationship. That is why pornography is created and consumed predominantly by men, whereas romance novels are written and read predominantly by women.

The vast industries of both pornography and romance bear witness to the ubiquity of both types of sexual fantasy. According to one videotape rental store clerk whom I interviewed, his store, which stocks both X-rated and regular videotapes, brings in much more revenue from the former than the latter. "The usual customer," he said, "is a man who comes in after eleven P.M. and takes out about five videotapes at a time." Note also the thriving pornography business on the Net, which allows both ease of access and anonymity. According to one source, $1.4 billion worth of pornography was sold over the Internet in 1999.[29]

In a typical pornographic movie, a man meets a woman in an uncomplicated way, and after a brief exchange, his sexual overtures are readily gratified. What follows is a series of different scenes involving a variety of sexual acts, positions, and people. Often the same character or characters couple with a variety of individuals, and the story line is typically thin. For example, in the old favorite *Debbie Does Dallas*, the entire plot concerns a team of cheerleaders who sell their sexual favors to make enough money to go to Dallas and support their football team. Gone are the days of the bake sale, it would seem.

A completely different picture emerges from the plot lines and characters of romance novels. The story is usually told from the point of view of a particular woman, who is attracted to a particular man. According to Janice A. Radway's 1987 study of the romance novel, the typical heroine is a feisty and independent woman who wins over the aloof and powerful man by dint of her irresistible charm.[30] The final goal of the book is the consummation of their love and the story typically involves the obstacles they have to overcome to get there.

Such obstacles typically revolve around mutual misunderstandings that temporarily alienate the would-be lovers or people who wish to thwart the couple's union, particularly other women. These latter may be jealous rivals or spiteful older women who bear some grudge toward the nubile new focus of the hero's attention. In Daphne du Maurier's classic love story *Rebecca*, for example, the evil housekeeper, Mrs. Danvers, falls into this second category.

Of recent years, many plots have come to include at least some sex, of a soft-porn, emotion-laden sort—often as a flashback or fantasy—but the orgasm supreme awaits the final clinch and is powered less by sights and actions than by love. A quote from *Fire in the Blood* by the late Dame Barbara Cartland, who authored over 700 romance novels, provides the typical atmosphere of the genre: "All she knew was that she was close against him and he was kissing her wildly, passionately, demandingly and the world stood still."[31] Romance novelists like Cartland know their business, however. In 1999, romance fiction comprised 58 percent of all popular paperback sales and generated $1.35 billion in revenues.[32]

These differences in the sexual fantasies of men and women can easily be understood in evolutionary terms because, over the course of evolution, locating a suitable object of lust has been more critical for the female. A healthy male can depend upon a steady flow of sperm, allowing him to spread his genes far and wide until advanced old age. Because of this, he is able to fertilize as many females as are willing, thereby giving him many shots at passing on his genes. The female, on the other hand, has only a limited number of eggs, which are released over just three or four decades. But even during her fertile years, she is taken out of the mating pool for months to years, during and after each pregnancy, as her energies are devoted to bearing and nurturing her latest child. For these reasons the stakes are far higher for a woman than for a man when it comes to choosing the proper mate.

Attraction: In the Eye of the Beholder

A great deal has been written about what attracts men to women and vice versa. Beauty is of great importance as an initial attractor, especially for men. For example, one study found that girls who are beautiful in high school are ten times more likely to marry in later life than their plainer counterparts. Another study showed that men are more willing to go out of their way or take risks for strange women whom they consider to be beautiful. According to social psychologists Elaine Hatfield and Susan Sprecher, "at the beginning of a romance there is nothing that counts more" than beauty.[33]

Over the longer haul, good looks are by no means the only trait that makes for an attractive mate. Psychologist David Buss found that kindness is a highly valued trait among both men and women in many different cultures.[34] While good looks are more important overall to men than to women in most cultures, good financial prospects are more important to women. This makes sense: You'd expect a woman to value a man's ability to provide for her and their offspring. In tribal societies such men might have been the best hunters, whose skills could be predicted by their strength, forcefulness, and athletic prowess.

Initially, however, attraction is about beauty. Why should this be so? According to modern theorists, because the features that we consider beautiful are also the ones that suggest good physical health and therefore a partner who will produce healthy offspring. For example, a smooth complexion, which is one sign of good health, specifically youth and the absence of parasites, is regarded as beautiful by people of all cultures.[35] Facial symmetry is also prized, not only by humans but by other animals as well.[36] Presumably symmetry signals the normal parallel development of the left and right sides of the body.

To some degree, believe it or not, we like average faces. Several research teams have used computers to blend faces into a composite, and all over the globe, both men and women rate the composites as more attractive than the faces from which they were composed.[37] So, the average is beautiful, perhaps because deviation from the norm may imply physical or mental problems. Great beauties, however, are by definition not average-looking, and research has shown that shift-

ing facial features away from the average in particular ways can enhance attractiveness.[38] For instance, large eyes combined with small
chins provoke a desire to nurture in both men and women.

Turning now to the body, men over the centuries have preferred
curvaceous women, as reflected by a waist-to-hip ratio of between 0.6
and 0.7.[39] What do the famous Venus de Milo and movie star Sophia
Loren have in common? An identical waist-to-hip ratio of 0.68.
Marilyn Monroe's voluptuous hips made for a slightly lower ratio of
0.66, while Twiggy, the slender British fashion model, scores a
slightly higher 0.69. Yet all these appealing women fall into this narrow range, which may signal to men a woman ripe to bear their progeny: large-hipped enough to deliver their babies and fleshy enough to
be fertile.

Women prefer well-nourished tall men with V-shaped bodies.[40] In
general, well-muscled men with square jaws and prominent brows
succeed in life to a greater degree than would be predicted by their
other abilities.[41] The development of these physical features is influenced by testosterone secretion and they are generally perceived as
signs of dominance. For example, in one study of West Point cadets,
their pictures alone were predictive of the rank attained by candidates
at the academy and their success in later life.[42] Good-looking men are
also more successful sexually. They begin to have sex at a younger age
and have more sexual partners.[43] Studies even suggest that better-
looking men are better lovers, more likely to bring their women to orgasm and to give them simultaneous orgasms, perhaps because they
have had more practice.[44]

Obviously a firm jaw and financial prowess will outlast a woman's
youthful bloom, and many have commented on the "double standard" that is applied to aging men and women. While older men can
still be considered sexually desirable, older women seldom are.
Consider the continued popularity of older male movie stars such as
Harrison Ford, Sean Connery, and Clint Eastwood. Though in their
fifties and sixties, they are paired with women twenty to thirty years
younger. Where are their female counterparts?

Again, these observations make sense in terms of evolution. Age reduces a woman's fertility beginning in her mid-twenties, then shuts it
off completely at menopause. A man, on the other hand, stays fertile
into the last decades of his life. An older man is more likely to appeal

to a younger woman if he has wealth and power, evidence that he will be able to provide for any children they might have. And even for people who do not plan to have children, the biological triggers of attractiveness still hold sway, the residue of millions of years of evolution.

In addition to visual appearance, new research suggests that attraction may also be governed by smells, which help animals choose mates with immune systems that are different from their own. This may be yet another means by which genetic diversity has been promoted in the course of evolution. The selection of mates with different immune-system properties, previously described in rats, has recently also been described in humans.[45] In one European study, women sniffed T-shirts that had been worn by men for several days and were asked, on the basis of smell alone, which men they would most like to go out with. They almost always chose the shirts worn by men whose immune systems were most different from their own.[46]

In selecting a mate, one dilemma women have always confronted is whether to choose an extremely masculine man or one with some feminine qualities. While the former might be a better hunter, yielding hardier progeny, the latter might be a better helpmate, a more nurturing father to her children. How do women weigh these trade-offs? With the help of computer graphics, researchers have addressed this question scientifically. By morphing a man's photograph to make his chin and brow more or less prominent and his bone structure more or less angular, his face can be made more or less masculine. What version would women prefer?

In several experiments, Scottish researcher David Perrett and colleagues instructed women to morph computerized images of faces to the point they considered most attractive.[47] The researchers found that women in Britain and Japan generally settled on faces that were 15 to 20 percent more feminine than the extreme masculine end of the spectrum. The preferences varied, however, depending on the phase of the menstrual cycle. During the weeks when the women were least likely to become pregnant, they preferred the male faces that were 15- to 20-percent feminized. Around the time of ovulation, however, when they were most fertile, the same women preferred the male faces that were only 8-percent feminized. The women on birth control pills preferred the feminized faces throughout their cycle.

These studies suggest that women would prefer to mate with more masculine men but, at other times, prefer men with some feminine qualities.[48]

For both sexes it seems fair to conclude that our innate sexual preferences remain much as they were programmed over eons of evolution. Men prefer women whose youthful and curvaceous appearance suggests fertility, while women prefer healthy-looking men who will be powerful and nurturing fathers.

Of course, cultural factors can change or even outweigh the "natural" choice. In cultures where marriages are arranged, women may have no choice of mate, and most cultures strive to restrain the natural lust of both men and women. So in our attempts to understand lust and its expression, we need to acknowledge both our biological heritage and the powerful cultural forces that modify it.

The Science of Being Gay

No discussion of love would be complete without acknowledging that not all romantic love is between men and women. All the elements of love and lust that I describe in this chapter could apply equally to men who love men and women who love women.

One of the more controversial social issues of our times is how to view gay men and lesbians. What rights should they have as couples and as individuals, and is their sexual orientation anybody's business but their own? At the heart of much of this controversy is a central question: Is homosexuality a choice? Or is it rather, like skin color or gender, an essential part of a person's biological makeup, just one more example of natural diversity? To date, science leans toward the latter view, based on evidence from genetic studies and an understanding of the way fetuses develop while still in the uterus.

The Genetics of Being Gay

What is known about the genetics of male homosexuality in humans? Since identical twins share all the same genes, whereas fraternal twins are no more alike genetically than regular brothers, twin studies have long been used to identify genetic traits. Recent reputable studies show that if one male twin is gay, his identical twin has a 50-percent chance of being gay as well.[49] If the twins are fraternal, the likelihood drops to 20 percent. Very recent sophisticated analyses of twins show that the tendency of boys to show feminine behaviors is influenced by their genes.[50]

Geneticists have found that gay men have more gay relatives than would be predicted by chance alone.[51] Some but not all of these researchers have found a selective increase in the number of gay relatives on the mother's side of the family.[52] Since a son necessarily inherits his X chromosome from his mother, the next question researchers asked was: Could homosexuality be connected to the X chromosome? Researcher Dean Hamer and colleagues at the National Institutes of Health, in two studies published in the mid-1990s, studied the families of gay men who had an excess of gay maternal uncles and cousins.[53] They found that a particular genetic locus on the X chromosome matched for gay brothers more often than for brothers of different sexual orientation.[54]

Some subsequent researchers have been unable to replicate this finding.[55] Although there is no consensus among geneticists, it remains possible that for some gay men, a gene on the X chromosome may account for, or contribute to, their sexual orientation. On the other hand, as with many complex behavioral traits, the genetics of male homosexuality in humans may result from the interaction of many different genes. Within the near future, the question of the genetic basis of homosexuality and many other behaviors will become much clearer as the human genome is translated and the genes corresponding to the various human traits are deciphered.

Are there any situations in which a specific genetic variation has been definitively shown to result in homosexual behavior? Yes, but so far only in the fruit fly. When a male fruit fly sets out to mate with his lady love, he performs a little courtship song, which involves vibrating his wings to produce a sound that will hopefully prove irresistible. Then he moves to the rear of the female and licks her, and if he is lucky, she will permit him to mount and mate with her. Researcher Jeffrey C. Hall of the University of Washington in Seattle has found that a specific variation in the fruit fly gene (he named it "fruitless") results in homosexual behavior.[56] Males with the fruitless variation court and mount other males.

Although research into the biology of male homosexuality is far from comprehensive, we know still less about lesbianism. In contrast to male homosexuality, lesbianism does not appear to run in families and animal models are lacking. It is possible that lesbianism is less strongly influenced by genetic factors than is male homosexuality.

Becoming Gay in the Womb

Even if a male fetus is not genetically programmed to become gay, important developmental influences in the uterus may help determine his sexual orientation in later life. In the first weeks after conception, every fetus has a female appearance. At first, no one can tell just by looking whether a particular fetus carries two X chromosomes and is destined to become a girl, or carries one X and one Y chromosome and is destined to become a boy. The weeks that follow are marked by a series of changes, which I will discuss first for boys. A gene on the Y chromosome called testis determining factor (TDF) is activated and causes the testes to develop.[57] The testes in turn secrete testosterone, which triggers the fetus to develop a male body and a male brain—most of the time, but not always.

Variations can occur because the fetal testosterone is converted into masculinizing chemicals, one for the body and one for the brain, by two distinct biochemical pathways.[58] In the pathway that molds the developing brain toward typical masculine features, testosterone becomes estrogen, which in adult functioning is associated with women rather than men. It is easy to see how a small genetic variation in this pathway might lead to a brain with some feminine qualities despite a masculine body.

The development of a masculine body, on the other hand, involves converting testosterone into yet another hormone, dihydrotestosterone (DHT). A genetic variation in the enzyme that catalyzes this conversion can lead to a feminine body that houses a masculine brain. One extreme variation of this type is seen in a small group of boys in the Dominican Republic who are born looking like girls, with some enlargement of the clitoris, and their testes undescended.[59] They don't grow a proper penis until puberty, when the adolescent spurt of testosterone does the job. At that time, they also begin to show the typical male pubertal facial hair and are typically attracted to girls.

Although these Dominican boys are an example of the development in the uterus of a masculine brain in an initially feminine body, they provide an example of how the pathways that masculinize the fetal brain and body may become uncoupled from each other as a result of hormonal variations. These boys provide us with a model for how some boys may be born gay as a result of uterine influences that masculinize their bodies but not their brains. As yet this remains a theoretical possibility that awaits scientific investigation.

What factors in a mother's environment might influence her hormonal responses in such a way as to affect her child's sexual orientation? The leading contender is maternal stress, which has been associated with homosexual behavior in male rats.[60] Of the males in a normal rat litter, about 80 percent are sexually active and about 20 percent are inactive.[61] When experimenters stressed pregnant rats by giving them foot shocks or forcing them to remain immobile in bright light, the same 20 percent of the male pups were sexually inactive, while 60 percent showed homosexual or bisexual behavior. (In the case of male rats, homosexual behavior is defined as behaving like a female rat, arching the back toward the ground while raising the rear end when mounted by another male rat.)

Researchers have suggested that the hormonal milieu in the uterus is altered by maternal stress in such a way as to feminize developing male fetuses. Several researchers have suggested that homosexuality in humans may also be related to maternal stress as well, but thus far, good data are lacking. Are women who are under stress either at home or in the workplace more likely to give birth to homosexual sons? That question has yet to be studied, but given its importance, it certainly warrants further research.

Maternal exposure to environmental chemicals might also influence the sexual development of her fetus. For example, the drug Propecia, which prevents baldness by counteracting the effects of testosterone in men, comes in bottles with prominent labels warning women who might be pregnant to avoid exposure to the chemical. Given what we know about the importance of testosterone to the developing male fetus, would it be any surprise if a mother who was exposed to this drug gave birth to a boy who later turned out to be gay?

In female fetuses—usually—the presence of two X chromosomes ensures a female mind in a female body, a girl who will become a heterosexual woman. The chemical environment in utero is also important, however. For example, the female fetus must produce substances to prevent her mother's circulating estrogen from masculinizing her.[62] Don't forget, in the XY fetus, it is estrogen that masculinizes the mind. If the fetus cannot produce enough of these neutralizing substances, or if there is too much estrogen in the fetal environment, the female fetus may become masculinized in body, mind, or both.

The one demonstrated instance of hormonal exposures resulting in sexual-orientation changes occurred in girls. A hormone called diethystilbestrol (DES), which mimics the effects of estrogen, was given to pregnant mothers around the middle of the last century to prevent miscarriages.[63] The use of the hormone was later found to be associated not only with physical abnormalities in women and men, but also with homosexuality and bisexuality in women. It is worth noting that many environmental chemical pollutants resemble estrogen in their biological effects. It remains to be seen whether exposure to these widely distributed pollutants will influence the prevalence of male or female homosexuality.

In an attempt to explore the possible influence of intrauterine hormones on the development of homosexuality, neuroscientist Marc Breedlove and colleagues from the University of California in Berkeley were inspired by the observation that men tend to have shorter index fingers than ring fingers, whereas in women these two fingers tend to be roughly the same length.[64] Reasoning that the relative length of these two fingers might be influenced by the intrauterine hormonal environment, the researchers interviewed people at street fairs in the San Francisco Bay Area, noting their sexual orientation and measuring their index and ring fingers. They found that compared to heterosexual women, the fingers of lesbians showed a pattern more similar to that of men (with index fingers shorter than their ring fingers).

The key point about the hormonal effects on sexual orientation in both sexes is that the sex hormones operate on the growing fetus and on the pubertal male and female in different ways. Sexual preference is not influenced by adult hormone levels, which have not been found to distinguish gay from straight men or women.[65] What matters is hormonal exposure in utero, which imprints the sexuality of the growing fetus before birth. At puberty, the normal hormonal surges act on this imprint, resulting in adult homosexual or heterosexual orientation.[66]

Can Sexual Orientation Be Changed After Birth?

This question remains controversial. Although mainstream psychiatric and psychological associations have long since stopped regarding homosexuality as an illness, some practitioners continue to view it as such and claim to be able to "cure" it. After sexual imprinting in the womb, however, what happens to a child after birth may have little influence, as a dramatic case from the medical literature illustrates.

John was a normal boy who had the serious misfortune of having his penis cut off as a result of surgical error when he underwent a circumcision before he was one year old.[67] His parents took him to see an expert in the field of sexual development who reasoned that since it would be traumatic for a boy to grow up without a penis, it would be easier for the child to become a girl. At that time, the premise was that all children are born neutral and that a child's gender-specific and orientation behaviors could be shaped by a combination of hormonal and cultural influences. So the expert recommended that John become Joan, and his parents agreed.

John's testicles were removed, a vagina was constructed and Joan was treated in every way like a normal girl. Around puberty the child was given estrogen supplements so that she would develop breasts and look like a burgeoning young woman. For years, as far as the sex experts could see, everything was going according to plan. Joan's case was written up and widely reported in the popular media as a vindication of the theory that gender is neutral and malleable at birth. But a subsequent report by the local doctors who took over Joan's care from the experts indicates how wrong the experts had been.

It turned out that from early childhood, without knowing anything about her medical history, Joan had rejected being treated as a girl, not quietly but with vehemence. One day, when her father was shaving, she imitated him, and when her mother tried to encourage her to put on makeup instead, she replied, "No, I don't want makeup. I want to shave." She rejected dolls in favor of gadgets and tools, dresses in favor of pants. On one occasion she went to the store to purchase an umbrella, but left with a toy machine gun instead.

Among her peers Joan was a misfit, teased by the other girls for her unfeminine behaviors, like trying to urinate standing up. In fact, at times she would go to the men's room to urinate. Joan was extremely unhappy as a girl, and at one point actually considered suicide. Eventually when Joan was 14, her local doctors overruled the experts.

Joan's father now told her what had happened in her first year of life and the teenager experienced a feeling of intense relief at learning the truth: "All of a sudden everything clicked. For the first time things made sense and I understood who and what I was."

Joan now became John. He had surgery to construct a penis and went on to date, marry, and become the adoptive father of his wife's children. He has no question that he is happier living as John than he ever was as Joan.[68] He feels anger at his original doctors for not listening to him all those years and for using the presence or absence of a penis as the sole determinant of how he should be raised.

For John, sexual preference was not a choice. It was a biological imperative that fought through the best-intentioned efforts of parents and doctors to persuade him otherwise. Most gay men and lesbian women feel similarly about their sexuality. To most of them it does not feel like a choice, but rather like their destiny, which they may fight or deny but must ultimately accept.

While scientists cannot exclude the possibility of postnatal environmental influences on sexual orientation, most mainstream clinicians have long since given up on trying to change it. They tried to do so for decades and failed. The memoir *Cures* by Martin Duberman is a good example of a gay man who endured several unsuccessful "therapeutic" attempts at changing his sexual orientation.[69] Today most gay men and women don't even try.

Regardless of the causes of homosexuality, the vast majority of clinicians who have dealt with homosexuals agree on certain key points. First, by the time a person reaches adulthood, his or her sexual orientation appears to be largely fixed, especially in the case of men. Second, there is no evidence that attempts to change this fundamental trait are of any value. Third, there is no evidence that homosexual men and women are any more likely to harm others in any way to a greater degree than heterosexuals. Pedophiles are more likely to be heterosexual than homosexual. Fourth, homosexuals in general are neither interested in converting others to their "way of life" nor could they even if they tried.

Understanding more about homosexuality offers us an opportunity to learn more about the biology of gender and love. There is reason to hope that this expanding knowledge will also bring new levels of tolerance to this aspect of the human condition.

Eros: The Power of Romantic Love

> *When one of them meets with his other half, the actual half of himself . . . the pair are lost in an amazement of love and friendship and intimacy.*
>
> —Plato, *Symposium*[70]

The ancient Greeks had six different words for the various types of love that exist between people. *Agape* was altruistic love. *Storge* was the love between comrades in arms or brother and sister, those who have been through much together. *Ludus* was the playful love of children or casual lovers, while *pragma* was the companionate love that develops between two people who have been married for a long time. *Mania* was the obsessive love that takes over one's being and it was associated with *eros*, sexual passion.[71] As psychologist John Alan Lee has pointed out, these ancient concepts also describe the different styles of love that people experience either singly or in combination with one another.[72]

To the ancient Greeks, Eros was also the god of love, known by the Romans as Cupid, who would fly around with his bow and quiver. When he fired his arrow directly into the heart of a man or woman, the person would fall helplessly under the heady spell of love. How apt an image for the passion that enthralls the ardent lover. We talk of "falling in love" to denote the loss of control we feel when overtaken by romantic passion. We are struck suddenly and mysteriously, perhaps the very first time our eyes lock upon the stranger who shortly becomes the center of our life, the object of our most powerful desire. When Shakespeare's Romeo, that star-crossed lover, first lays eyes on his beloved Juliet, he confides to a serving man:

> O, she doth teach the torches to burn bright!
> It seems she hangs upon the cheek of night

Like a rich jewel in an Ethiop's ear—
Beauty too rich for use, for earth too dear![73]

So powerful and pleasurable is the experience of romantic passion that it is not surprising that most people actively seek it—though many will settle for sex in the meanwhile. Romantic love gives life a sense of focus and purpose—to be with the object of your love, now and forever. You think of her for much of the waking day, till your friends laugh when you mention her name. You turn on the radio and listen to love songs that the disk jockey seems to be playing especially for you. "I've Got You Under My Skin." "Can't Fight This Feeling." "Ain't No Cure for Love." "I Wanna Hold Your Hand." "I'm Happy Just to Dance With You." "All You Need Is Love."

When we are in love, we feel more alive. Our senses are more acute. Colors are more vivid, smells more intense. We may feel more loving toward the whole world, wanting everybody to be as happy as we are. We count the time till we can be in the arms of our beloved. In the words of the famous *West Side Story* song, the minutes seem like hours and the hours drag by slowly. But when we are finally together . . . the hours zoom by. Where did the evening go? you ask yourself. To illustrate his Theory of Relativity when speaking to the public, Albert Einstein often used the image of how quickly time seems to pass for lovers.

As with all powerful emotions, we feel love in the body: the pulse quickens, the pupils dilate, and the breathing speeds up. You sleep less but don't feel drowsy. On the contrary, you are souped up, energized, even frenzied—and the energy all goes to spending as much time as possible with your loved one.

The elements that make up erotic or romantic love have clearly evolved to serve a function—survival of your genes. The tracking mechanisms that zero in on a particular person, the sensory acuteness with which you take in every clue, the persistence in thinking about him or her, the directed focus and tenacity of purpose, all are geared toward mating and reproducing your genes with a suitable match. Love is a state of mind in which that goal can best be met.

When it comes to choosing a mate, the would-be lover considers not only physical appeal but also courtship skills, which are ritualized in many species. Male birds, for example, may perform fantastic feats of swooping, parading, and preening, showing their athletic prowess and brilliant tails, fans, crests, or wattles to best effect.[74] To show what a fine provider he is, the courting male may feed the female tender morsels from the sea, or may carry blades of grass in his beak to show what a fine nest he plans to build for their offspring.

Since such courtship requires a well-functioning nervous system, it essentially allows the female to assay the brain of her prospective mate. Similarly, in humans, a woman assesses her would-be lover by watching his behavior. Can he dance? Is he smooth? Is he generous, thoughtful, and capable? Does he observe all the right protocols—or does he brilliantly and originally break with protocol to innovate a form of courtship behavior all his own?

Often the person's wooing words are as important as his looks. That is the tragicomic premise of the French drama of Cyrano de Bergerac, a poet with a grotesque and laughable nose of which he is so self-conscious that he does not court his love, the beautiful Roxanne. Instead, he writes Roxanne passionate letters and speeches to be delivered by his friend, the handsome but stupid Christian. Roxanne marries Christian, who is promptly killed in battle. Only after a lifetime of mourning does Roxanne realize that the soul she has loved belongs to Cyrano, not to the man for whom she wears black.

Throughout early courtship, each party is acutely aware of the other's words, actions, and body language. Is she tipping her head? Showing more skin? Tossing her hair? Leaning toward me? Do our gestures begin to match? Other cues, such as smells, contribute to the way a person chooses a mate. That may explain the multi-billion-dollar fragrance industry.

Love and Chocolate: The Chemistry of Love

Before turning to the chemistry of love, let me tell you the little we know about its anatomy—at least at the level of the brain. Despite the widespread availability of imaging techniques, little has been done to date to elucidate what pathways and parts of the brain are responsible for mediating the experience of romantic love. Semir Zeki and A. Bartels, researchers at University College in London, studied this question in seventeen women who acknowledged being "truly and madly in love."[75] Zeki and Bartels had their lovestruck subjects look at pictures of their beloved, then at pictures of ordinary friends, and performed functional magnetic resonance imaging (fMRI) throughout. The researchers found that when the women looked at the pictures of their sweethearts, specific areas in the limbic system, notably the anterior cingulate, lit up. This part of the brain is known to be associated with attachment behaviors.

As to the chemistry of love, Michael Liebowitz, professor of psychiatry at Columbia University, noted some years ago that the heady, compulsive, delightful experience of erotic love feels like being under the influence of a stimulant drug, such as an amphetamine.[76] Liebowitz speculated that romantic love may unleash in the lover a superabundance of the body's own amphetamine-like chemicals. That would explain many of the signs and symptoms of being truly, madly, deeply in love: euphoria, a racing pulse, an increased sense of focus, a decreased need for sleep, and an excess of energy and drive.

Liebowitz suggested that the stimulating brain chemical phenylethylamine (PEA) might be one of the candidates responsible for the power of love. And since PEA is found in high concentrations in chocolate, some wondered if this traditionally romantic gift might work its charms literally as a love potion. (I recall a box of chocolates from my youth called Black Magic, a name that aptly conveyed the spell of the confection.) Alas, a study performed by Dr. Richard Wyatt and colleagues at the National Institute of Mental Health found that people who ate large amounts of chocolate failed to show any increase in PEA levels in their blood.[77] A beautiful theory was thus laid to rest by dreary facts, and now, 20 years after Liebowitz's initial speculations, there is still no evidence that PEA plays any role in the chemistry of love.

Nevertheless, researchers agree that Liebowitz was probably on to something. Internal chemicals released into a lover's brain may well explain the intense experience of being madly in love. In current thought, dopamine and the endorphins look like candidates for that role, as both mediate pleasure, including sexual pleasure.[78]

Neuroscientist Thomas Insel and colleagues at Emory University have very recently mapped out the brain circuitry involved in the powerful monogamous attachments that develop in a certain species of voles. The researchers found that these brain circuits are very similar to—if not the same as—the ones involved in reward. These circuits contain dopamine neurons, which are responsible for the euphoriant effects of drugs such as cocaine and amphetamines. "Falling in love is a lot like getting addicted," observes Insel. "The same pathways are involved, which may explain why, when people become addicted to drugs, they lose interest in human relationships. Maybe that is why one thing that helps people recover from drug addiction is to get into a deep relationship."

It is tempting to speculate that romance may also involve internal hallucinogens, given the euphoric fantasies in which lovers engage. And indeed our bodies do produce chemicals called anandamides that act on the same brain receptors as the active ingredients in mari-juana.[79] And guess what food contains anandamides—chocolate.[80] So perhaps the theory that connects love and chocolate is not com-pletely dead after all.

The more we look at the details of romantic love, the more plausi-ble the self-drugging analogy becomes. For example, if romantic love is one of the sublimest of human emotions, loss of love is certainly one of the most painful. In attempting to explain the depth of lovesick suffering, Liebowitz points out that if drugs that cause plea-sure are abruptly discontinued, people ricochet into a painful state of withdrawal.[81] With amphetamines, for example, withdrawal causes a sharp drop into lethargy and sometimes into acute depression. Opiate withdrawal, as neuroscientist Jaak Panksepp has pointed out, results in a state that resembles the distress of grief and separation from a loved one—crying, loss of appetite, depression, sleeplessness, irri-tability, and a profound feeling of loneliness.[82]

Finally, the idea that the human brain in love makes its own eu-phoriant chemicals explains one more thing about romantic love—why it does not always last. Liebowitz points out that if euphoriant drugs are given on an ongoing basis, the brain develops tolerance for them. In other words, the chemicals of love become less potent. Liebowitz uses the concept of tolerance to account for the fact that heady romance usually lasts no more than a few years. After that, the lovers will either seek romance elsewhere or the quality of their love changes, moving into a phase in which companionship and attach-ment, rather than passion, are the glue that holds the pair together. *Eros* becomes *pragma*, at least to some degree.

Helen Fisher, anthropologist and author of *The Anatomy of Love*, has reported on data that are consistent with Liebowitz's two-process model of love.[83] On analyzing divorce statistics between 1947 and 1988 from sixty-two different societies, Fisher found that the frequency of divorce peaked between the third and fourth year after marriage. She offers the evolutionary explanation that three to four years is about the length of time needed to raise a human infant into toddlerhood, a reasonable state of self-sufficiency in societies where there is some form of communal child care, as in a hunter-gatherer village. At that point, the individual's genes might be better served by moving on and mating with a different partner.

If love is to survive such evolutionary pressures, couples will need to develop bonds of affection to replace the waning black magic of their erotic love, the "voodoo that you do so well." As Helen Fisher puts it, "We're put on earth to reproduce; if we want to find lasting happiness in love, we have to work at it to make it for ourselves."

Addicted to Love and Sex

Given the pleasure-inducing power of the erotic brain chemicals, it is small wonder that some people become addicted to love, much as to any other drug. In love addictions, the brain's biology has gone haywire, producing situations that are very painful to the addicted people, as well as to their romantic partners. Three forms of love addiction we commonly encounter in psychiatric practice are:

1. A type of mood disorder known as hysteroid dysphoria
2. Obsessive love fantasies
3. Compulsive sexual behavior

Jean was an attractive and vivacious actress who was struggling to be discovered by a Broadway producer. At her day job as a waitress on the Upper West Side of Manhattan she was a favorite among the clientele (especially the men) because of her sassy charm and striking looks. Jean's cheerful demeanor at work, however, belied the continual turmoil in her private life. After the latest of many failed romances, Jean sought help from a psychiatrist. Only the week before, she explained between sobs, her boyfriend was professing eternal love. Then she didn't hear from him for days, even though she left numerous messages on his answering machine.

Finally, Jean went round to his building, managed to get past the doorman by means of charm and a plausible lie, and went up to the man's apartment. Through the door she could hear conversation and high-pitched laughter. Jean knew he must have another woman there—but even so, she could not restrain herself from ringing the doorbell. When he asked who it was and she told him, he said he was busy and couldn't talk. When she got home, there was a message on her answering machine. He said, "Listen, Jean, it's over. It just isn't going to work out."

Jean plunged into the most dismal despair that she could remember. She slept nonstop and gorged on candies. It was hard to believe that only the week before she had been giddy with joy. How could life be so cruel? How humiliating it was to think of that woman behind the door, laughing and discussing her with that subhuman creep. She felt like killing herself.

When asked about her previous relationships, a clear pattern emerged. Jean would fall madly in love. He would be perfect, the most wonderful man she had ever met, different from all the others. And her love would be returned—or so it seemed. There would follow a period of bliss. Then something would go wrong, the man would break off the relationship, and Jean would fall into a horrible depression that would reverse only when she found a new romantic prospect, the most wonderful man she had ever met.

Donald F. Klein, professor of psychiatry at Columbia University, was the first to describe this pattern of recurrent depressions in the context of romantic losses.[84] He called it *hysteroid dysphoria (hysteroid* meaning a tendency to experience and display dramatic emotion; and *dysphoria* meaning severe unhappiness). The condition responded to antidepressants, he observed. Klein suggested that people with hysteroid dysphoria might have some sort of underlying chemical deficiency causing their depressions, which a love affair would temporarily reverse by squirts of euphoriant chemicals.

Why did Jean's love affairs keep going sour? First, the men she found exciting and chose as lovers were dashing and unpredictable.

The same novelty-seeking qualities that appealed to Jean, however, caused these men to tire quickly of her once they'd made their conquest. Jean found men of a steadier disposition to be boring; she tended to avoid them. Second, Jean's desperate need for her boyfriend to keep her "up" made her very dependent. Initially the men might find the intensity of her focus on them flattering or sexy, but it soon became a drag and they'd strike out for freedom.

Treatment with antidepressant medications helped stabilize Jean's moods, so that she became able to choose her boyfriends more wisely. Once in a relationship, she could strike a more independent posture, stating what she wanted to do or what was acceptable to her without constantly feeling a sinking dread that he would leave. Not only did Jean feel better about herself, but she was also treated with more respect by her boyfriends. Psychotherapy also helped Jean see that she was repeating a pattern of her mother's and that she did not need to behave like her mother to hold a man.

In another form of love addiction, the person spends large amounts of time just mooning around, fantasizing about the object of his affections—who may not even know she is the focus of his interest. Psychologist Dorothy Tennov has written about this type of fantasy addiction in her book *Love and Limerence*, which is based on interviews with hundreds of people who have suffered in this way.[85] Although happy reveries about a loved one are part of normal romance, people with this problem typically daydream far more and with much less real hope of living out their dreams. At the extreme end of this spectrum, one of Tennov's subjects engaged in a fifty-year unrequited love affair lived largely in his own mind.

Often these obsessions are oriented around people who are not romantically available in ways that are satisfying, and the person suffering from the obsession may undergo waves of elation or sorrow depending on what the object of his desire is doing. Even a pleasant greeting by the loved one can be cause for celebration; a frown will engender fears of rejection. The mood of the moonstruck admirer can rise or fall on a single gesture. Needless to say, such obsessional states of mind are unfulfilling and painful, as they are not rooted in a reciprocal relationship.

In my experience, romantic obsessions are more common among women, and sexual compulsions—the third major type of love addiction—among men. Those who suffer from compulsive sexuality may be driven to engage in sex with numbers of partners that seem extraordinary to ordinary people, a behavior made easier by the Internet. Often when hookups occur, there is minimal emotional investment, merely contact of a purely sexual nature. According to sex-addiction researcher Patrick Carnes, 8 percent of men and 3 percent of women suffer from sex addiction—a total of 15 million men and women.[86]

Many compulsive sex addicts report that after a while the sex becomes less and less fulfilling. As with drugs, it takes more and more sex to satisfy. Then, just like drug addicts whose fix has worn off, the sex addicts have a feeling of emptiness when they say goodbye to their latest contact. It is a never-ending quest for sexual pleasure or comfort, which, as with drugs, becomes harder and harder to attain. They feel they are wasting their lives, which have been taken over by their search for sexual gratification. Although they know full well that their condition can expose both them and their partners to venereal disease, acquired immune deficiency syndrome (AIDS), public humiliation, and the destruction of their families and careers, they persist in their behaviors.

At this time there is no formal category for sex addiction in the diagnostic manual used by psychiatrists to classify diseases. Many professionals are ignorant about the problem of sex addiction and some, including experts in drug addiction, have questioned whether sex addiction really exists. This is surprising to me. Anybody who listens carefully to the stories of sex addicts will be struck by the similarity between their predicament and those of drug addicts and alcoholics. They depend upon regular sex to regulate their mood, and they develop physical and psychological symptoms of withdrawal if deprived of sex. They feel out of control of their sexual behavior, despite knowing its potential for trouble. They often have to "hit bottom" before they can acknowledge the magnitude of their problem and do something about it.[87] Finally, the condition appears to respond to some of the same approaches that are helpful in treating other addictions.

A high percentage of sex addicts were sexually abused as children,[88] and in general, young men and women whose parents were inconsistent in their love are more addicted to love or more afraid of it than those who come from more secure backgrounds.[89]

In my clinical experience, both love and sex addicts can be helped by a variety of twelve-step programs that are patterned after the one used by Alcoholics Anonymous. Joining a twelve-step group, they are able to meet with other addicts, learn from their experiences, and talk about the aspects of their lives that they find shameful. Together, they experience the relief of not being judged. In addition, they can learn specific ways to change their patterns of obsessive and compulsive behavior. In this way many a sex or love addict has been able to regain control and a sense of dignity. Free from the wasted hours devoted to fantasy or compulsive behavior, sex and love addicts are able to rebuild their lives, including the kind of healthy love relationships that formerly seemed out of reach.

In addition to twelve-step programs, these individuals can benefit from both medications and psychotherapy. Antidepressants, in particular those that boost brain-serotonin levels, help reduce the power of the sexual cravings and enhance the sex addict's capacity to exercise restraint. Psychotherapy may help addicts connect their present behavior to their past experience: Once they see their lives as a coherent whole, people with sex and love addictions are better able to stop acting out their painful and repetitive patterns of behavior. Even more important, many then discover more fulfilling ways of expressing and experiencing love.

Monogamy: Monopoly or Monotony?

Anthropologists find that most human societies permit a man to take more than one wife, yet despite their promiscuous fantasies, few choose to do so.[90] A single partner is also the overwhelming pattern among women. For better or for worse, depending on your perspective, most people choose to marry or live with only one partner at a time.

Why? There are two ways in which monogamy furthers the interests of an individual's genes. First, ethologists reason that if a male invests a great deal of time and energy in raising offspring, he wants to be sure that it is his own. As far as his genes are concerned, there is no point furthering the success of some other male's offspring! In humans, of course, other factors must be at work, considering how many people, at least in the United States, are willing to jump through endless bureaucratic hoops to adopt a baby. Yet in the wild, the drive to further the interests of one's own genes is undeniable. Displays of jealousy are common in monogamous species as the male guards access to the female of his choice.[91] The second reason for monogamy is the work involved in raising a child to independent adulthood. The more caretakers the young ones have, the more of them are likely to survive.

Humans may not be all that different from other animals in their reasons for monogamy. Still, humans have additional reasons to stay together. Companionship, a common history, and economic considerations all factor in, and it is easier to face old age with a steady companion. In the wisdom of Ecclesiastes, "Two is better than one; because they have good reward for their labor," and more bleakly, "Woe to him that is alone when he falleth; for he hath not another to help him up."[92]

Underlying some of these practicalities is what researchers call the *mere exposure effect*, which I discussed briefly in chapter 2. According to that effect, across a wide range of experiments, in both humans and other animals, researchers find that familiarity, far from breeding contempt, actually breeds comfort.[93] For example, people asked to look at Chinese ideograms and say which they like best prefer the ones they've seen before. What's more, the familiar can be made even more appealing by pairing it with something positive such as a smiling face. And that holds even if the smile is presented too fast to register consciously. Indeed, much of the mere exposure effect probably operates at an unconscious level. This powerful effect may explain why we tend to befriend, hire, and marry people who are familiar in looks, lifestyle, or values. The "mere" comfort and familiarity of a well-known partner may be a strong factor in monogamy. At the level of the brain, repeated exposure presumably results in the creation of a neuronal network, with the familiar image or experience causing the set of linked neurons to fire together. Something about the firing of a familiar—as opposed to a novel—neuronal network tends to generate positive feelings.

Perhaps the most striking scientific work on monogamy has been performed on voles. Thomas Insel and colleagues have taken brilliant advantage of the fact that two very similar-looking species of voles have utterly different patterns of pairing off. Prairie voles, found in the Midwest, live in multigenerational burrows.[94] The males and females mate monogamously for life and live together in one burrow. Both parents care for the young, and they spend most of their time together. The males are intensely aggressive and readily fight off intruders.

In sharp contrast are the montane voles that dwell in the Rocky Mountains, where the males and females live in their own separate burrows. A pair will mate briefly, then the female will go on to deliver the young in her own burrow. For a short spell after the birth the mother will show some maternal behavior, but after that the youngsters must fend for themselves. It is very tempting to humanize these little creatures—the respectable Midwestern voles and the lonesome cowboys and cowgirls of the Rocky Mountains—but I am assured such comparisons have no scientific validity.

Insel's team has teased apart the biological underpinnings for these mating behaviors. To begin with, they would allow mating, separate the pair for a week, then let the female choose whether to be in a cage with the male with whom she had mated, with a different male, or on her own. They found that female prairie voles tend to choose the familiar male, whereas female montane voles will prefer to be in a cage of their own. In this way, the researchers determined that in the wild, mating is central to pair bonding in prairie voles: no sex, no bonding.

Next, by injecting hormones into the prairie voles' brains, the team teased out a hormonal basis for the bonding that occurs after sex: oxytocin and vasopressin in female and male prairie voles respectively are both necessary and sufficient for monogamy to develop.[95] In both sexes, these hormones appear to work via the neurotransmitter dopamine.[96] But injecting the montane voles had no such effect. The key difference between the lifestyle of the voles turns out to be the distribution of brain receptors for oxytocin and vasopressin. In the prairie vole, but not in the montane vole, the oxytocin and vasopressin receptors are located mostly in the reward pathways.

Recently Insel and colleagues discovered that prairie voles have an extra bit of DNA in the gene that controls the vasopressin receptors, one that the montane voles lack.[97] Does this extra string of DNA promote monogamy? To answer this question, the team managed to insert the DNA string into mice, which are normally promiscuous, and sure enough, the transgenic mice showed signs of pair bonding.

And in people? There's a variable area (meaning some people have it and others do not) in the human vasopressin gene, and its location bears a certain resemblance to the extra string of DNA in the prairie vole genes. It is only a matter of time before some researcher explores whether faithful and unfaithful spouses tend to differ with respect to this gene. So far, the only human condition that has been linked to a variation in this part of the gene is autism, which is intriguing, since autistic children have severe problems in developing relationships with others.

It is wondrous to consider that oxytocin and vasopressin have been conserved as important molecules for the expression of sex and attachment over millions of years of evolution and that they date back to an ancestor that humans share with voles: The same molecules that influence pair bonding in voles are responsible for sexual pleasure in humans. It seems likely for human couples, too, that sexual pleasure and intimacy have much to do with holding the pair together. Yet stable monogamous relationships do not necessarily depend on an active sex life. Over my years of seeing patients, I have been surprised to find how many couples stay happily together for years even in the absence of sex with each other or with anyone else. Even for these couples, however, oxytocin and vasopressin may play a role in maintaining their bond, as these molecules are also important in nonsexual forms of attachment.

There are many other molecules we know to be important in mediating affiliation, and probably many more to be discovered. As Insel points out, of the approximately 30,000 genes in the human genome, about 50 to 60 percent are expressed in the brain. So far, we know what only a small percentage of them do.

In addition, monogamy is not "merely" molecular by a long shot. John Gottman, professor of psychology at Washington University, can observe a couple of newlyweds and within three minutes predict with 96-percent accuracy whether they will stay together or get divorced—not by measuring their brain vasopressin receptors, but simply by observing their style of arguing. According to Gottman, whether a husband and a wife will feel satisfied with the sex, romance, and passion in their relationship depends by 70 percent on the quality of their friendship.[98]

Gottman has found several specific behaviors that predict a failing marriage. Couples who are destined for divorce start out an argument in anger, criticize, show contempt for each other, and act defensively. When one tries to make peace, the other refuses. Quite often one (usually the woman) will overwhelm the other, who withdraws emotionally. When their bodily responses are measured during the argument, both husband and wife show signs of fight-or-flight reaction, such as increased heart rate and sweating. Over months and years of arguing like this, couples amass so many bad memories that one or both of them just give up. To some extent, the couples may be recapitulating all-too-familiar relationships from their families of origin.

Clearly some individuals will be better off to leave a bad partnership and seek happiness elsewhere. For unhappy couples who wish to turn things around, however, Gottman and others have many excellent suggestions.[99] First and foremost is to understand your own emotional world and that of your partner. Thereafter, specific techniques can improve the couple's quality of friendship and connection, which gives romance a fighting chance.

In sum, monogamy is a preferred way of living for most people in the world. The ability to succeed in this regard may depend both on our genes and our will to make it work.

The Love Between Mother and Child

Fred, a businessman in his mid-fifties, has been married five times. He describes his life as one long search for love. A handsome, gregarious man with an extremely likable personality, Fred has never had trouble attracting women. Holding on to them was harder, in part because he was unable to remain faithful. However happy his home life, Fred felt a constant need for approval and love from other women— store clerks, receptionists, flight attendants, any attractive stranger who crossed his field of vision. As he puts it, "I confused sex for love." As an adult, Fred developed a variety of psychiatric and physical problems, including depression, anxiety, stomach ulcers, and drug and alcohol abuse.

After many years of therapy and soul-searching, Fred is able to trace his frenetic quest for love to his early childhood, when he suffered a kind of one-two punch. His mother left his father for another man when he was two years old. A year later, when she came back to claim him, his father left the family and moved to another city. Fred has no memory of the months that followed his father's departure. His sister, however, recalls him sitting in a corner, mute, sucking his thumb and rocking to and fro for hours.

Being loved in early childhood is so critical that, at the extreme, a total lack of love can be fatal. In a bizarre thirteenth-century experiment, Frederick II, king of Southern Italy, had a group of children raised without being spoken to in any way because he wanted to see what language they would "speak naturally." The children all died.[100]

In the early decades of the last century, several clinicians began to document the devastation caused by lack of love. One early pioneer, pediatrician Harry Bakwin, documented the experience of infants in hospitals where they were not touched in the interests of hygiene.[101] When Bakwin took over at the pediatric ward at Bellevue in 1931, he removed signs admonishing everyone to wash their hands and substituted signs instructing nurses to pick up the babies. Paradoxically, the infection rate among the infants decreased.

Others pointed out the psychological crippling caused by raising children in foster care and orphanages. The effects included a lasting inability to form attachments, deceitfulness, lack of empathy, and a pattern of superficial and promiscuous affection with no apparent depth of feeling.[102] These neglected children were portrayed most woefully in the widely viewed film *Grief*, produced by psychoanalyst René Spitz, who pointed out the high mortality rate of children in these institutions.[103]

At around the same time, British psychoanalyst John Bowlby first chronicled in depth the stages of attachment and loss that infants experience in relation to their mothers or mother surrogates. Drawing on scientific work in animals, he linked the experiences of humans and other animals. He saw the development of attachment between mother and child in evolutionary terms and recognized the critically important survival value of the bond between parent and child.[104]

In the later decades of the last century, Johns Hopkins psychologist Mary Ainsworth developed a groundbreaking model in which to study the mother-child attachment. She called it "the strange situation": a pleasant, toy-filled room. Mother and infant were brought into the room, where the infant was allowed to play for a while. Then, the mother left the infant briefly, before returning and reuniting. Ainsworth was able to divide the responses of one-year-old infants into three groups: the "secure" group, the "insecure-avoidant" group, and the "insecure-ambivalent/preoccupied" group.[105]

A typical secure infant will happily play with the toys while Mom is there, will show signs of missing her when she leaves the room, and will cry when left all alone. Then Mom returns. Mary Main, a former student of Ainsworth and now professor of psychology at Berkeley, describes the reunion between the mother and the "secure" infant as follows:

> When mother appears in the doorway, he creeps to her and pulls himself up on her legs. Picked up, he clings actively, and sinks into her body. . . . The observer has witnessed what appears to be a miniature drama with a happy ending.[106]

In contrast, an insecure-avoidant child shows no distress at Mom's departure and continues to play with the toys in the room. When she returns, there's no warm, fuzzy reunion. The child shows none of the responses seen in the secure child. Instead, the child avoids contact, sometimes even stiffening and turning away. A child from the insecure-ambivalent/preoccupied group shows the behaviors after which the group is named. The child does not explore the toys, as the other children do, showing either lack of interest or a fretful, clingy preoccupation with the mother. These children show great distress when Mom leaves.

One of Ainsworth's discoveries was the relationship between each infant's behavior in the "strange situation" and the records she had kept of the mother-child interactions in the year leading up to the study. As Main describes it:

> The mothers of the secure infants had been "sensitive to the signals and communications" of their infants, during the first year of life—responding promptly to crying, holding the baby tenderly and carefully, and providing tactful, cooperative guidance or distraction in circumstances in which maternal and infant desires conflicted.

Ainsworth also tracked some physical reactions. She found that although the way the avoidant infants continued to play looked as though life was easy for them, their bodies told a different story. Their heart rates during separation were higher. In the home, these insecure-avoidant children expressed extreme distress in response to even minor separations, and they seemed angry at their mothers.[107] As for their mothers, several of them said they disliked being touched. Ainsworth concluded that they had rejected their babies' attempts to bond and attach. Observer reports showed the mothers actively rebuffing the infants.

The mothers of the third group, the infants who appeared ambivalent or preoccupied, were found to be insensitive to the infants' signals and in their treatment of their children. Although most showed some warmth at times and considered themselves highly invested in being good mothers, the experienced observer was able to detect a lack of mothering skills. A high percentage were inept at handling their babies, showing a lack of tenderness and care. It was as if these infants got enough love so as to still have hope but not enough to feel secure.

There are various ways to interpret Ainsworth's studies. Possibly, a child's innate traits might influence parenting ability. I have myself observed babies who stiffened into boards when anybody, even a parent, tried to pick them up, no matter how tenderly. On the other hand, the patterns of a child's attachment and separation responses can clearly be influenced by the parents' emotional competence. An emotionally competent mother or father will be able to empathize with the baby, recognize the cues that signal the baby's needs and respond appropriately. In almost every case, the reward will be an emotionally competent baby. Parents who lack emotional competence will be less able to synchronize their responses to their baby's needs, and the result will be a child who has no gut sense of the world as an emotionally reliable and responsive place.

In general, secure children are able to soothe themselves when distressed, for example by a brief separation from the mother; insecure children are not, and their bodies will show signs of alarm, such as increased heart rate or stress hormones.[108] The former will settle down rapidly after a stress is over; the latter will not. If a style of interaction continues throughout childhood, it is easy to envisage how a secure child will turn into a secure adult, whereas an insecure child will not. As Wordsworth put it, "The child is father of the man."

Fred, the man who was married five times, was in a constant state of anxiety and overarousal, probably due to the early abandonment by both his mother and his father. He spent much of his adult life trying to soothe himself with brief unsatisfactory relationships, compulsive sexual behavior, drugs, and alcohol. After years of therapy and participation in twelve-step programs, however, Fred was able to connect his adult distress with his early childhood traumas and to shift his patterns of responses. Whereas his early abandonments had made him feel unlovable, he now learned to believe at a gut level that others could care about him for who he was, not just for what he could provide them.

Therapy worked for Fred, providing him not only with insight, but with an emotional experience that corrected some of the damage done in childhood. As part of the process, new synapses presumably sprouted in his brain that now conduct his responses to life challenges along more adaptive pathways. Fred has been married to his present wife for many years and says that the better he understands his problems, the better a husband he becomes.

He ruefully points out that the cure was painful. Although when he first went into therapy, he thought what he needed was immediate relief of suffering, he found out that what he really needed was to understand himself, based on his past losses and traumas, and then rebuild his view both of himself and of his world. This required making slow, painful, and difficult changes in his maladaptive behavior. Fred's frenetic search for women can be understood, to some extent, by considering animal models in which maternally deprived infants seek out surrogates for the nurturance they missed at a critical period in their lives.

Substitute Moms—The Monkey Model

While observations about the importance of attachment—and the right type of attachment—were being made in humans, studies were also conducted in animals. These underscored the critical importance of early experience in the development of an adult capacity to love.

In the1950s psychologist Harry Harlow at the University of Wisconsin initiated studies to explore the effects of separation in infant rhesus monkeys.[109] These studies are classics in the field as they have provided us with important insights. They have also provoked controversy, given the suffering endured by the infant monkeys separated from their mothers. It is important to realize, however, that before Harlow's work, scientists were unaware of the devastating effects of maternal deprivation. After his initial studies, Harlow became a leader in promoting more humane treatment of monkeys housed in laboratory settings.

Harlow showed that infant monkeys separated from their mothers for two weeks became extremely distressed, ran about in a disoriented way, climbed, screeched, and cried.[110] They played less with other infants and showed more aggression than they had before the separation. When their mothers returned, there was a touching reunion between infant and mother, who cradled and embraced the infant to a greater degree than before.

While the mother was gone, Harlow found that the infant monkeys would gravitate to an inanimate mother surrogate. In one experiment to test which aspects of the mother were most important to development, Harlow presented the lonely babies with a choice of two surrogates—a wire mesh "mother," which had a teat from which the infant could suckle; and a softer, terry-cloth-covered surrogate with no source of nutrition.

Surprisingly, the babies preferred the terry-cloth dummy, only jumping over to the wire-mesh "mother" when they were hungry. This experiment established the importance of touch—and not just milk—to infant primates. The babies also preferred a terry-cloth "mother" that was suspended an inch off the floor—and therefore able to swing—to one that was stationary.[111] In field studies, maternally deprived monkeys were found to seek out surrogates, even adult male monkeys, wherever they could find them.[112]

In later life, Harlow reported in a paper titled (with misplaced humor) "Lust, Latency and Love: Simian Secrets to Successful Sex" that maternally deprived monkeys are severely handicapped sexually. Sex comes easily to most adolescent monkeys, but not to these. Harlow illustrates the point by showing a socially deprived male monkey trying to mount a female, at first from the front and later from the side. In a similar fashion, a socially deprived female monkey sat on the floor while a male attempted to mount her.[113]

Later studies in monkeys who had experienced early social deprivation found long-term changes in brain areas known to regulate emotions and in neurotransmitter systems, such as the dopamine pathways, known to regulate pleasure.[114] It is not surprising, therefore, that people or animals who are maternally deprived (such as Fred) later experience problems in modulating their love relationships and other behaviors involving pleasure.

Harlow's work showed us that total maternal deprivation has devastating effects on the development of primates. Once that was understood, researchers backed off from such studies because of the hardship experienced by the experimental animals. In addition, they realized that total deprivation is rare in nature in animals that survive into adulthood. Instead, infants more typically experience lesser degrees of maternal deprivation. More recently, researchers have shifted their focus to understanding the effects of real-world stress on the mother-infant bond.

Leonard Rosenblum, one of Harlow's former students and now the director of primate research at the State University of New York at Brooklyn, and colleagues examined the effects of different foraging conditions on the mother-infant bond and infant development in bonnet macaque monkeys.[115] In one group, foraging was made easy; in a second group, more difficult; and in a third group, unpredictable.

Both the adult and the infant monkeys behaved quite differently in the different foraging conditions. The research team found that when foraging was easy, the adults seemed relaxed. There was little jockeying for position in the social hierarchy and much mutual grooming (a sure sign of affiliation or friendship among primates). The unpredictable condition was the most stressful, with the adult monkeys showing levels of aggression that the researchers had not seen in thirty years of studying this species. Like people, the animals had difficulty adjusting to unpredictability. As the fourteen weeks of the study went by, the stress levels seemed to mount and the monkeys' behavior became more and more hierarchical.

As you might expect, the mother-infant relationships and the behavior of the infants themselves also varied from group to group. Rosenblum's team found that while the secure infants of the predictable conditions readily explored and played out of sight of their mothers, those in the variable condition were clingiest, perhaps because their mothers would often break contact with them. In fact, over the months of the experiment, these stressed infants actually regressed, spending less and less time away from their mothers. They also showed low levels of play and exploration and were the most traumatized when separated from their mothers. By contrast, the infant monkeys in the other two conditions spent progressively more time playing and exploring away from their mothers. The researchers concluded that the variable conditions were conducive to insecure attachment.

These monkey studies by Rosenblum and colleagues shed light on Mary Ainsworth's infant-separation studies. The difficulties that some human infants have in being separated from their mothers may result from maternal stress. When mothers are stressed, they are unable to give their babies the quality of attention the little ones need to grow up feeling secure and confident enough to venture and explore the world. In addition, without the security of early love, the growing infant's physical development may also suffer, as revealed by recent studies in rats.

Love, Health and Survival

One day a serendipitous event occurred in the Columbia University laboratory of neuroscientist Myron Hofer. A mother rat managed to escape from her cage, leaving her infants behind. Hofer found that the rat pups had slowed heart rates and wondered why.[116] That question led Hofer and colleagues to perform an inspired series of experiments, investigating which elements of the mother's presence were necessary to maintain her infants in stable physical condition.[117]

Hofer went on to discover that when infant rats were separated from their mother, many physical functions became disturbed. Moreover, each disturbance resulted from a loss of a different aspect of the mother's presence. Amazingly, a specific function could be restored selectively by adding back a specific element of the mother's presence.

For example, by providing nutrients to the stomachs of separated pups, the researchers could normalize their heart rates. By providing different amounts of heat, they could produce pups with different

levels of reactivity, ranging from despairing to hyperactive. These influences on the rats did not have an all-or-none quality. They were
graded, with different levels of intervention producing different results.

What all this means is that in the course of evolution (and under
favorable circumstances) mothers have evolved so that they can provide whatever their babies need, through the mother-child attachment. Because of this bond, a healthy baby mammal grows into a
healthy adult, able to find food, defend itself, live a good life within
the community, mate, and pass on genes to the next generation. The
mother's loving presence literally regulates the infant's physiological
and psychological functions by helping the nervous system develop
along advantageous lines.

As Mary Ainsworth's studies showed, not all human mothers are
equally nurturing. Does the same apply to rats, and if so, does it
make a difference to the way the infant rat develops? The answer to
both of these questions is yes, as neuroscientist Michael Meaney from
McGill University in Montreal and many of his colleagues have
shown in recent years.[118] These researchers have classified mothers
into those that show high levels of nurturance (for a rat, that means a
great deal of licking and grooming of her pups and arching her back
to nurse them for longer durations) and those mothers that showed
less.

The researchers found that those rats raised by more nurturing
mothers showed lower stress levels throughout their lives. When
these animals were restrained (a stressful experience for a rat), they
released lower levels of stress hormones. They ventured out to explore
novel environments more readily and were less easily startled.
Meaney's group has actually been able to tease out the biochemical
pathways responsible for these effects. For example, they found that
the infants of nurturing mothers have lower levels of the receptors for
the stress hormone CRH and higher levels of the receptors for the
soothing neurotransmitter GABA in parts of the amygdala, which
might account for their reduced stress responses.

Meaney's group also investigated whether female infants nursed by
highly nurturing mothers go on to become highly nurturing mothers
themselves. This turns out to be the case, not because of their genes
but as a direct result of their early experience. The researchers reached

this conclusion after a series of ingenious studies in which they cross-fostered the infants of low-nurturing mothers to high-nurturing mothers and vice versa. When they grew up, the female rats showed maternal styles similar to those of their foster mothers rather than their biological mothers. Researchers have made similar observations in rhesus monkeys and humans: The quality of the bond between mother and child influences the kind of mother that the child will become.

We have seen that stress and negative emotions can have major impacts on long-term health. Stress is bad for the heart, blood vessels, and immune functioning. Anger and depression, if they continue over time, can kill people. If the bond between parent and child has long-term effects on the body, we would expect to see them play out in terms of health consequences over the duration of a person's life. What evidence do we have for this? Here are some examples of studies that suggest such long-term consequences:

- A close relationship with one's mother may halve the chances of serious illness in later life, according to a follow-up study of 126 middle-aged Harvard alumni who were questioned in the 1950s about their relationships with their parents.[119] Those who thirty-five years earlier had felt they had close relationships with their mothers were half as likely to have developed serious medical illnesses (45 percent), as compared with those who had not felt close (91 percent). Warm relationships with fathers also seemed to be a significant protector, though less so. Those who as undergraduate students had rated their relationship with their parents as cold and detached had a fourfold greater risk of chronic disease, not only of depression and alcoholism, but also of heart disease and type II diabetes.

- Over a period of five decades, the quality of the relationship between father and son was the single best predictor of which men would develop cancer, according to a follow-up study of men surveyed while they were medical students at Johns Hopkins.[120]

These and other studies, which are reviewed in Dean Ornish's book *Love and Survival,* bear testimony to the importance of love not only for our emotional development, but for our physical health as well.[121]

Research on humans and other animals shows that a mother's behavior toward her infant profoundly shapes the child's physical and emotional responses, not only in the child's early years, but throughout life. The best mothering provides all the necessary elements to a child. Even subtle deficits or irregularities in mothering may result in lasting insecurities or developmental aberrations in the adult offspring. On the positive side, even subtle mitigations can help. One important factor that may compensate for maternal deficits is the involvement of the father and others who show the child love at various points along the way.

Although it might seem sloppiness on the part of the English language for the word "love" to describe experiences as different as romantic passion and the bond that exists between mother and child, the same neurotransmitters and hormones mediate both states. To be a good mother, for example, a mammal requires oxytocin, the same hormone that is secreted after orgasm in humans.[122] Dopamine and endorphins, neurotransmitters involved in sexual pleasure, also appear to be important mediators of maternal behavior.[123] It makes sense then that young mothers often act as though they are in love with their babies—they are.

On the baby's part as well, natural opiates and oxytocin are known to be in play.[124] The baby is also in love, secreting endorphins and bonding. In time, as an adult, the same hormones will once again produce joy and a deep sense of coming home, as the cycle creates another generation.

The Many Shapes of Love

Phyllis, a professional in her mid-thirties, had a history of many romantic relationships, all of them troubled. Her friends gossiped about the fact that she never seemed to learn. Con men, drug addicts, deadbeats, abusers—all seemed to make a beeline for Phyllis. "I'm a magnet for turds," she would say wryly. She was the type of woman for whom numerous self-help books have been written, all of which she read and none of which succeeded in changing her behavior. She was a woman who loved too much, a smart woman who made foolish choices, and she knew it. Why, then, did Phyllis continue to bring this suffering on herself?

Although we can never say with certainty how someone came to be the way she is, the roots of the personality lie in childhood. In this regard, Freud was right. And now, in the light of research in parent-child bonding, we begin to see the specifics that shape the ways we greet and offer love.

In Phyllis's case, her mother was an alcoholic and unavailable to her much of the time. For much of her childhood her father was the dominant figure, driving her to school, checking her homework, and making sure that she followed the rules. He was a motor mechanic with limited emotional skills. Whenever Phyllis was hurt or upset, he would become angry, shout at her, and tell her she was stupid. In therapy it became clear that the men she picked resembled her father—competent in certain ways but emotionally limited and verbally abusive.

The "mere exposure" effect, which influences our preferences and actions as adults, has an even more powerful effect when the exposure occurs earlier in life. A vignette from one of Harlow's papers illustrates this point and helps us understand this tendency to reenact childhood relationships with nurturing figures. The first baby monkey who received a surrogate mother was born a month earlier than expected, so the researchers did not have time to paint a face on the surrogate's head, which was therefore just a blank piece of wood. The baby monkey had contact with the blank-faced surrogate for six months before being placed with two other surrogates, both of which had painted faces. Harlow notes:

> To our surprise the animal would compulsively rotate both faces 180 degrees so that it viewed only a round smooth face and never the painted, ornamented face. Furthermore, it would do this as long as the patience of the experimenter in reorienting the faces persisted. The monkey showed no sign of fear or anxiety, but it showed unlimited persistence.[125]

So it seems that the face we grow up to love is the one we saw in childhood. No doubt the same applies to other traits in our parents: the "mere exposure effect" at work once again. Our knowledge of neuroscience suggests that neural networks must be established in the early years, connecting early experiences with the circuits involved in the feelings of love. Phyllis pursued her unsuitable suitors with the same tenacity as the monkey, turning the surrogate's face around so that it looked familiar. But how can we understand pursuing relationships that actually hurt us? Surely simple learning theory dictates that we would become discouraged and pursue other avenues?

For a mammalian infant, the bond of love between mother and child is a matter of survival. For that reason, over the course of evolution, mammals have been hard-wired to stay connected to Mom. Whatever is required to keep our lifeline, we will do, just like other mammals, chicks, and ducklings. Once again, research on animals can help us see how powerful this effect can be. In Harlow's early studies, the female monkeys raised in isolation went on to become highly abusive toward their firstborn infants,[126] one of which died as a consequence,[127] while another had to be rescued. In spite of their abuse, the infants persisted in trying to nurse from their mothers and stay close to them. In an experiment by Rosenblum and Harlow, surrogate mothers were designed to emit nasty blasts of cold air. Unlike most aversive stimuli, however, the blasts did not deter the infants, who clung to the surrogate mother all the more strongly.[128]

As a psychiatrist, I have seen many people like Phyllis, who seek out and stay in abusive love relationships. If these are the only type of relationship the person knows, it may be less frightening to persevere with them than to risk loneliness and lack of love.

It may be that when a parent is erratic—sometimes loving, sometimes punitive—the infant grows up to be an adult in whose brain the experiences of love and punishment have been so intertwined that it is hard to experience the one without the other. Clinicians refer to such attachments as trauma bonds, which the adult survivor of early abuse tends to replicate in adult relationships. Presumably the neural networks connected to the experience of love overlap with those that register pain or degradation in such a way that it is hard for the adult to seek out—and experience—love without incorporating elements of physical or emotional pain in the process.

Adults who have somehow learned to confuse love with trauma also grow up with a damaged sense of themselves. One of the most common of these harmful ideas is the belief that one does not deserve to be loved, respected, and treated well. Instead, a person may take for granted that a precondition for being loved is being misused. It would follow from this assumption that if she (it is often a woman) is not willing to put up with, or even seek out, the abuse, she will have to forgo being loved.

And what happened to Phyllis? When I first saw her, her mother had died, but her father was still alive. I encouraged her to deal with her father around those issues to which he was best equipped to respond—mostly her car. Her old jalopy kept breaking down and her father was pleased to help her fix it. As long as all she asked from him was concrete assistance, as opposed to emotional support, he came through for her. In fact, he seemed delighted to be able to help. One day when she came to pick up the old car, he told her that he was sick and tired of the darn thing and had bought her a shining new one instead.

Phyllis spent several years in therapy and, over the course of time, was able to shift her patterns of response and behavior. She learned to tune in to her limbic news and, as soon as a prospective suitor did things that upset her, to register the fact and do something about it. Either she would try to resolve the issue or would choose not to see him any further. Gradually, she developed more self-respect and recognized that she deserved a relationship with a man who would treat her kindly. Phyllis credits her growing affection for kinder men both to her improved relationship with her father and to her relationship with me, her therapist. Through therapy, she was able to learn that not all men are abusive and that it felt good not to be abused any longer. She went on to marry a kind man with whom she was living when last I heard from her.

While some people like Phyllis are lucky to be able to turn their love lives around, sadly, not everyone succeeds. Although early animal studies such as Harlow's show that love-deprived animals can learn to love again, more research is needed to help those who are unhappy in love learn new ways of loving. Our scientific understanding of love and its maladies lags behind our knowledge of other emotions such as anxiety and depression. Yet as Harlow and others have shown, love and lust can be studied just like any other emotion. Our growing understanding of these vital emotions is an integral part of the Emotional Revolution.

Chapter 11

Sadness and Depression

He who learns must suffer. And even in our sleep pain that
cannot forget falls drop by drop upon the heart, and in our
own despair, against our will, comes wisdom to us
by the awful grace of God.
—Aeschylus, *Agamemnon*, 177[1]

The Gift of Sadness

I KNEW a woman once who loved a man with all her heart. Hours each day she spent musing about her love for him, remembering his features, his endearing qualities, and the ecstatic times they had spent together. Gradually she became aware that he was cheating on her. When she questioned him, he denied it with all the indignation of a man falsely accused, and she wanted to believe him. Yet she became increasingly unable to ignore the blocks of his time for which she could not account, his hours on the Internet, and a growing sense that he was drifting away. Her preoccupations shifted to ruminations about his waywardness, and the compulsive energy once spent in expressing ardor she now funneled into unearthing his lies. She succeeded, and on the advice of many friends, almost against her will, she broke up with him.

What followed was the pain of loss and utter desolation. In a landscape bereft of all color and joy, she would lie awake at night, lingering painfully over the fact that her happy times were now irretrievably lost. It was in those dawn hours that my friend would whisper the words of Aeschylus quoted above as "pain that cannot forget" fell drop by drop upon her heart. And in the end, as the great dramatist promised, wisdom came in the form of new insights, along with the slow healing of her broken heart.

Why would she want someone who was so indifferent to her feelings? she was now able to ask herself, not merely as an intellectual question, but with a sense of conviction. She deserved more! Was she not better off without such an unreliable source of comfort? What kind of love had it really been, given how badly she had been treated? These important questions were crucial for her recovery—not just from the loss itself, but from feeling doomed either to accept shoddy treatment or go unloved.

In my friend's case, sadness turned out to be an invaluable ally. Not only did it help her face her loss, but it served also as an indelible reminder that never again would she give her heart to an untrustworthy guardian. Her next relationship was with a loving and faithful man, and when I last spoke with her, they were happy together. She credited her earlier relationship—especially its painful aspects—with her newfound contentment. Just as a physical pain can safeguard us from subsequent physical harm, so can psychic pain prevent us from falling into situations that are unhealthy for us emotionally.

One critical function of sadness is that it informs us of loss. This information is not just intellectual and cognitive, but limbic as well. We must feel the loss to process it properly. When our emotions are in proper working order, the degree of grief and shock informs us of the significance of the loss. The capacity to understand the significance of the loss and to integrate it into our lives can be crucial to our survival. When a woman loses her husband of forty years, for example, she needs to come to terms with her new reality. She now has to fend for herself without his emotional, physical, and financial support. Her grief rapidly helps her understand her new reality and deal with it. Sadness has evolved to play that role over millions of years of evolution.

Loss has been studied in animals, such as chicks, rats, and monkeys, as well as in humans. It appears that all animals show comparable responses. John Bowlby, a pioneer in this field, chronicled the stages through which a chick moves if its mother is taken away.[2] At first, the chick makes cheeping noises, a stage Bowlby designated as "protest." Then it becomes very quiet, a stage Bowlby called "despair." And finally it shows evidence of attachment to another mother hen.

These stages obviously have survival value. Initially the separated chick has the best chance to find its lost mother if it makes as much noise as possible—a high-risk, high-yield strategy. It succeeds if the mother is nearby, but risks death if she is out of earshot.

After a certain amount of time in the wild, chances would be good that the mother has been killed or is too far away to hear, in which case cheeping is more likely to attract a predator. At that stage the chick's best bet is silence—a low-risk, low-yield strategy. Finally, if another mother hen should happen by, letting itself be adopted offers the best chance of survival into adulthood.

Distress calls like a chick's cheeping can be seen in many species. Infant sea otters bobbing up and down in the surf issue distinctive cries that help their mother find them when she emerges from the ocean's depths, where she has been hunting for fish.[3] When separated from their mothers, rat pups utter high-pitched cries, rhesus monkeys give out a "hoo-hoo" sound, and human infants cry. In general, distress cries develop when the young animal is first able to move independently and is thus at risk of getting lost. Separation distress in human infants, for example, first appears when the child crawls well and is on the verge of walking.

In all mammals, an infant's cry of distress will prompt the mother to return. Certainly in humans, and probably in other animals, the mother is moved by a resonant distress, and both mother and child feel a corresponding satisfaction or pleasure as reunion occurs. In later life, in the same way, sadness elicits love and support from those who care about us.

Loss and reunion are major themes in drama and literature, which invite us to relive this primal joy of reunion. Boy meets girl, boy loses girl, boy is reunited with girl is an essential story line of most love stories. As Shakespeare put it, "Journeys end in lovers meeting." Being lost and then found again is a variation on the theme. In *The Wizard of Oz*, Dorothy finds her way back to Kansas, proclaiming, "There's no place like home." The best-selling Harry Potter series may find part of its enormous popularity in the central theme of a magical orphan, given into cruel foster care with his aunt, finally finding a curious but welcome home in a school for witches and wizards.

Loss and sadness need not be about a person. Loss of power, money, social standing, or a long-sought goal may all cause sadness and, sometimes, reduced self-esteem. Afterward, the painful memory may spur us on to greater efforts or to choose another path. For some, fear of loss can act as an incentive. I see this in couples who are motivated to work hard to stay together in part because they imagine how sad they will feel separated.

Because humans are able to think symbolically, we are also capable of symbolic losses, which can hurt just as much as other types of loss. Recall the case of the admiral who committed suicide because he was discovered to be wearing a badge to which he was not entitled. The loss of the badge itself was unimportant—his lapels were covered with well-earned brass. The real loss was the respect of those whose opinions he prized. Likewise, losing faith in God can be devastating.

In short, sadness following loss provides vital information. It tells us that our world has changed. The depth of the sorrow tells us how important the loss was, and the pain pushes us forward to seek another source of comfort or resources, the better to survive in a difficult world.

Cheering Up

In many ways it was an unremarkable morning in downtown Johannesburg many years ago. I was in my early teens and a gloomy mood settled in like dark clouds spoiling a fine day. The reasons for my low spirits were as unclear to me then as they are now. On an impulse I bought an apple and a copy of *Mad Magazine*, then caught the bus bound for my home in the suburbs. As the bus meandered along its familiar route, I started to eat the apple and read the magazine, and before long I felt much better. I cannot say why. Maybe it was the bursts of sweet and sour sensations that flowed over my tongue as I munched on the juicy apple, maybe the magazine's irreverent cartoons or the lush suburban gardens I could see from the upper deck of the bus. For whatever reason, by the time I arrived home, I was in fine spirits, not the least because I had discovered something new: that I could actually alter my mood by simply acting in a certain way. Here was power!

It turns out that all of us do things to cheer ourselves up, and researchers have inventoried the various strategies that people use. Robert Thayer, professor of psychology at California State University in Long Beach, and colleagues interviewed 102 men and women of different ages about what they do to feel better. Their answers are listed below.[4]

- Call, talk to, or be with someone (54 percent).
- Control thoughts, for example, think positively, concentrate on something else, don't let things bother me, give myself a "pep talk" (51 percent).
- Listen to music (47 percent).
- Avoid the thing or person causing the bad mood (47 percent).
- Try to be alone (47 percent).
- Evaluate or analyze the situation to determine the cause of the bad mood (47 percent).
- Try to put feelings in perspective (44 percent).
- Change location, for example, go for a drive, go outside (44 percent).
- Rest, take a nap, close eyes, sleep (42 percent).
- Exercise, including taking a walk (37 percent).
- Engage in pleasant or fun activities (35 percent).
- Use humor, for example, laugh, make light of situation (34 percent).
- Eat something (34 percent).
- Tend to chores, for example, housework, schoolwork, gardening (31 percent).
- Engage in emotional activity, for example, cry, scream (29 percent).
- Go shopping (25 percent).
- Take shower or bath or splash water on face (25 percent).
- Read or write (24 percent).
- Engage in stress-management activities, for example, get organized, plan ahead, make lists (22 percent).
- Use relaxation techniques, for example, deep breathing,

> stretching and bending, muscle relaxation, massage,
> visualization (21 percent).
> • Drink alcohol (15 percent).
> • Drink coffee or other caffeinated beverage (12 percent).
> • Have sex (9 percent).
> • Smoke cigarettes (8 percent).
> • Use drugs (other than alcohol, cigarettes, and coffee)
>   (5 percent).

The researchers then went on to determine which techniques were most effective for altering a bad mood. The most successful strategies were *active ways of managing moods*, including relaxation, stress management, changing thought patterns, and exercising. Thayer concludes that exercise is overall the best strategy for reversing a low mood, and an extensive body of literature supports it.

The following emerges from dozens of research studies:

• Moderate exercise, for example walking briskly for 30 minutes a day five days a week, can improve mood even in people who are not clinically depressed.[5]

• Exercise can enhance feelings of well-being even without demonstrable increases in cardiovascular fitness.[6]

• The mood-enhancing benefits of a time-limited exercise program endure long after the program is completed. In a twelve-week study of aerobic exercise, for example, improvements could be detected as long as one year after the formal program had been discontinued.[7]

In Thayer's studies, the next most effective strategies involved pleasurable activities and distractions, such as hobbies and humor. Next came solitude and avoiding the trigger person or thing; calling or talking to someone; and doing something passive such as watching television, eating, or resting.

The least successful behaviors were geared to reducing tension here and now, such as drinking alcohol, taking drugs, or having sex.

The sexes differed. Thayer and colleagues found that men were more likely to distract themselves with pleasant activities or to use drugs, sex, or alcohol to control their moods. Women were more likely to seek support from others or to express their feelings openly. Women also tended toward passive distractors, such as watching television, drinking coffee, eating, and resting.

Some mood modifiers, such as eating sugary foods and drinking alcohol, produce short-lived results—and have a rebound effect in which one feels worse. In contrast, regular exercise, rest, stress management, and relaxation lead to a greater sense of well-being over a longer period of time.

Mourning and Melancholia

It is important to distinguish between the pain of sadness, which can be useful, and the agony of depression, which has no use and can be dangerous (because the suffering can be so intense that suicide may seem like a relief). In his classic essay *Mourning and Melancholia*, Freud distinguishes between these states: the first normal and time-limited, the second pathological and of indefinite duration. In normal grieving, Freud observes, the mourner is preoccupied by memories of what has been lost. Bereft of the loved one, the mourner's world feels empty. The melancholic, in contrast, experiences an internal sense of emptiness, a feeling that something inside of profound importance is missing.[8]

The more recent scientific quest to distinguish between normal sadness and depression reaches similar conclusions. Normal sadness, like mourning, informs us that something bad has happened in the outside world, whereas depression tells us that there is a problem with the inner workings of the mind. Thanks to the developments of modern medicine and other antidepressant treatments, today such internal glitches can usually be corrected or at least alleviated, thereby relieving one of the severest forms of suffering known to man.

The modern bible of psychiatric illnesses, the *Diagnostic and Statistical Manual of Mental Disorders*, volume IV (DSM-IV), sets out criteria that delineate the various profiles of clinical depression (see Appendix A). These include major depression, bipolar depression (in which affected people also suffer from mania); and chronic, low-grade, fluctuating depression, also known as dysthymia. People who meet the criteria for these conditions would do well to seek treatment. In general, clinicians use the term "clinical depression" to describe a state in which physical and other psychological symptoms accompany mood changes. The symptoms include increased or decreased sleep, increased or decreased appetite, weight gain or loss, decreased sexual interest, decreased energy, and difficulty concentrating.

Paradoxically, just as it is possible to be sad without being depressed, so is it possible to be depressed without being sad. Although many depressives do experience severe sadness, others feel only a pervasive loss of pleasure. Such emotional numbness, together with the physical symptoms of depression, is enough to establish a clinical diagnosis.

In many cases, the symptoms go untreated at a terrible cost to the person, the family, and society at large. Consider the following facts:

- Each year approximately 19 million adults in the United States suffer a major depression.[9]

- Only one-third of depressed patients seek help for their depression. Of these, less than half receive adequate treatment. In other words, fewer than one in six depressed patients gets proper care.[10]

- Worldwide, mood disorders rank among the top ten causes of disability.[11] Depression by itself poses a greater burden worldwide than do ischemic heart disease, cerebrovascular disease, or tuberculosis.[12] According to a recent World Health Organization study, unipolar depression promises to be the leading cause of ill-health in this century.[13]

- For reasons that are unclear, depression is becoming more common in the United States, striking people at younger ages than in earlier generations.[14]

- In the United States alone, the financial cost of depression has been estimated at approximately $43 billion per year, almost 4 percent of U.S. health expenditures in 2000.[15]

- Depression and manic-depression are the most common causes of suicide. A person with one of these disorders is fifteen to twenty times more likely to commit suicide than a member of the general population.[16]

- Suicide is the second most common cause of death worldwide for women between the ages of 15 and 44, and the fourth most common cause of death for men in the same age group.[17]

- Prolonged depression causes many physical problems, including cardiac disease and osteoporosis.

Depression: The Nature of the Beast

If there is one word that comes up time and again in the published accounts of depressed people, almost always written after they have emerged from the murky depths of disease, it is "indescribable." There is something about this state that words cannot capture, I think because languages are built around normal experience, and clinical depression feels anything but normal. William Styron, one of the many famous people afflicted by this condition, has called *depression* "a wimp of a word."[18]

In their best efforts to convey the experience, depressed people most often use the words "darkness" and "heaviness"—an unnatural, menacing darkness, an indescribable heaviness; it can feel as though one's very body has turned into stone. Many writers use the image of a beast to convey the sense that an alien has glommed on to them, tormenting their nights and sucking the joy out of their days. Winston Churchill referred to his depression as his "black dog," a grim image that conveys a dark, menacing, unwelcome presence. Some of my depressed patients speak of having a monkey on their back, while others compare depression to a thief that robs them of joy, hope, and comfort.

Each person's depression is unique because the illness is superimposed on each unique personality and is colored by that person's life circumstances. Nevertheless, it is useful to look at the traits that depressed people share.

Roughly speaking, depressed people can fall into two categories. In the first, sleep is ravaged by fits of fretful waking, leaving the individual exhausted during the day, yet agitated and physically restless.

Food becomes unpalatable (patients often say everything tastes like cardboard), and people lose interest in eating, resulting in weight loss. This type of depression has been called *melancholia*, after the Greek word for "black bile," which the ancients thought was overabundant in this condition. Melancholia carries a high risk of suicide, and people with this form of depression are often hospitalized.

In contrast to melancholia is *atypical depression*, in which the body takes the opposite tack. In atypical depression there is an apparently insatiable need for sleep. Given the chance, those severely afflicted will sleep for twelve hours a night and still want to nap the next day. While their capacity for pleasure is not entirely absent, it is constrained, so that the only pleasures tend to be eating, sleeping, and lying down. They gravitate toward sweet and starchy foods, which they find comforting and consume in great volumes. I recall one patient who typically ate twelve donuts before noon. Such a vast appetite, coupled with the tendency to lie around, results in weight gain, often ten to twenty pounds or more. Their ballooning weight is a further source of distress and lowered self-esteem for depressed persons.

People with atypical depression are at lower risk for suicide than those with melancholia, probably because they are less activated. To commit suicide requires energy and the ability to focus. For that reason, depressed people may be at greater risk of suicide as they start to recover and their energy returns.

Despite these differences, the two forms of depression share many features. Patients often feel anxious and fearful of all manner of things of a kind and to a degree that may seem ridiculous to outsiders. They may be racked by guilt over minor and inconsequential matters, or may torment themselves about crimes and misdemeanors they never committed. I remember one elderly depressed woman who could not be consoled for having stolen a hatpin from a box on her mother's dresser many decades before.

All manner of aches and pains may surface that diligent examination finds to have no clear physical basis. But in the mind of the sufferer, these portend a terrible undiagnosed illness such as cancer or some other devastation. At times the prospect of grave illness fills the mind with dread, while at other times it may provide cold comfort because death would at least mean escape from misery.

Both melancholic and atypical depressives may feel a profound sadness, which may be constant and unremitting or variable, worsening at a particular time of day. The sad feelings may be aggravated by triggers in the world outside. My patients often know that they are becoming depressed again, for example, when they break into tears at the sight of a dead squirrel or the television image of starving children from some faraway land. While these triggers are inherently sad, few of us respond with such a profound and personal grief. Sometimes the depressed person may be overwhelmed by a sadness with no clear cause or point of focus, yet so powerful she feels compelled to cast about for a reason. As one of my patients put it, "A depressed person can always find some reason for being depressed."

In all types of depression there is a loss of pleasure. Friends and loved ones no longer elicit the cheerful spirits of earlier days. The depressed person often sees her loss and isolation as one more failure, berating herself for indifference toward those who have been so good to her. Sexual interest, of course, is long gone by that point.

The impact of depression on productivity and creativity is devastating, with highly skilled people rendered unable to do anything but menial tasks. The writer's words dry up. The lawyer loses her ability to apprehend her client's case, let alone present it well. The doctor can barely tune in to what his patient is saying, so distracting are the inner voices that remind him a thousand times a day that he is inadequate. The mother may just lie on the sofa, unable to run after her children and ensure their safety, far less communicate with them or prepare meals or get them to school on time. At every turn the depressed person leaves others unhappy, mystified, and questioning, "What the devil is the matter with him?" Small wonder, then, that this disorder can be ruinous, for the longer the depression persists, the more the person's social and economic worlds unravel. Unremitting depression, I am happy to say, is quite rare.

The course of a depression may provide clues to its treatment. Depressions that alternate with manias (states of high energy and either euphoria or irritability) are known as bipolar depressions. One value of making this diagnosis is that the manic episodes present special problems. I will deal with mania in detail later, but I want to emphasize here that it is a potentially dangerous state of high energy and mood, and that it can be triggered in susceptible people by antidepressant medications. When there is a danger of mania developing, it is important to use medications to prevent it along with antidepressants.

The chronic, low-grade depression known as dysthymia exacts its toll not because of its severity (it's quite mild), but because it corrodes the quality of life and constrains accomplishments over many years. Many people with the condition have no idea they are ill. To them it seems quite normal to feel like Eeyore; they always have. Because of the cumulative effect, however, dysthymia should be treated. Friends and family of these people need to know it responds well to antidepressant medications. If you can get your dysthymic friend help, he will thank you later.

In a different type of mood disorder known as *brief recurrent depression*, short-lived but very severe plunges in mood are interspersed with periods of normal well-being. I once asked one of my patients with this condition, an engineer, how his moods had been on average. "That is the wrong way to ask the question," he responded wryly. "You can drown in a river that is only six inches deep *on average* if there are precipices in the riverbed." He was referring to the deep, dark places into which he was liable to fall suddenly, and from which he could see no escape even though they lasted just a few days. To date, treatment trials for this type of disorder have been disappointing.

Many people endure several months of depression each year during the fall and winter. We call this condition *seasonal affective disorder* (SAD). It is a variety of atypical depression that often responds well to facing a bright, artificial light each day, as well as to conventional antidepressants. In an opposite seasonal pattern, known as *reverse-SAD*, or *summer-SAD*, patients become depressed during the heat of the summer and feel better in the winter.

Depression comes in many shapes and sizes—and some people suffer from a mixture of several different kinds—but you can see already that when it comes to depression, we need to know the nature of the beast to treat it properly. Often an empathic primary physician can treat depression successfully. If not, seek out a specialist in mood disorders. Every year, we learn a little more about depression and its treatment.

Is Depression an Adaptation?

In distinguishing sadness from depression, I suggested that sadness communicates to both us and others that something is amiss in our world, while depression reflects an internal problem that needs correction. The first emotion is adaptive; the second maladaptive. Although such a distinction has the advantage of simplicity, some might regard it as too simplistic. Given the serious, sometimes crippling symptoms of depression, you might think that anyone would consider it to be a maladaptive emotional state. Yet in a provocative new essay, University of Michigan researcher Randolph Nesse raises the question as to whether depression might instead be an adaptation.[19]

Nesse opens with a quote from no less an authority on adaptation than Charles Darwin, who observed:

> Pain or suffering of any kind, if long continued, causes depression and lessens the power of action; yet it is well adapted to make a creature guard itself against any great or sudden evil.[20]

Nesse examines the symptoms of depression and attempts to explain them as adaptive responses to the challenges of life. Just as the chick separated from its mother goes into a phase of despair and a resulting listless quiet may save its life, so it may be that other animals in other situations benefit from the same state, called *conservation withdrawal*. The term emphasizes the value of conserving energy when spending it would be not only useless, but even dangerous, for example by attracting a predator. Another example of conservation withdrawal is seen in arctic reindeer, which become unnaturally tame during the winter. These animals simply stand on the icy ground, immobile. They don't even flee when approached.[21] Over the course of evolution, the energy conserved by this state, known as *arctic resignation*, has presumably had more value than vigilant alertness—for, after all, few predators can survive that harsh northern winter.

Atypical depression, which involves inactivity, oversleeping, overeating, and weight gain, certainly does resemble conservation withdrawal. I and others have hypothesized that patients with SAD might have had an advantage during the Ice Ages, for example, because of their apparent ability to conserve energy and store body fat over the winter. Today, however, food is available year round, and what we prize are slenderness and sharp wits year round. The deficits of conservation withdrawal clearly outweigh any long-gone benefits.

What possible advantage might accrue from melancholia, the type of depression characterized by insomnia, anorexia, and weight loss? The overall picture in melancholia is one of hyperarousal and increased vigilance, an overactivity of certain brain centers (such as the amygdala), and chronically high circulating cortisol levels. Melancholics live in a state of extreme stress, which hardly seems adaptive.

It could have been, however, according to Nesse. Imagine, for example, a chimpanzee deposed from his high standing in the colony. He is under a very different set of stresses from the orphaned chick. Not only does he have to process his loss of social standing, but he must be on constant alert against further assaults by the new alpha male. In that case, a hyperaroused stress-response axis might be life-saving.[22] In the same way, there must have been many points in human history when twenty-four-hour alertness was critical to survival.

Nesse points out that as situations change, many of the symptoms of depression could be adaptive. Pessimism and lack of drive, for example, could both be excellent policies in a world in which active efforts are frankly dangerous. By inhibiting action, they could prevent one from making a serious blunder.

Helplessness, too, could be adaptive. Helplessness is a feeling that develops when bad things keep happening no matter what you do. This feeling, also common during depression, might be adaptive in situations where any effort is doomed to failure. Take a flooding river: The creature that finds a high point and stays there does better than the brave one who opts to swim. Once again, conserving energy can help one survive.

Adaptation to repeated punishment is the basis of a commonly used animal model of depression—learned helplessness. This model, developed by researcher Martin Seligman, professor of psychology at the University of Pennsylvania, involves exposing rats to foot shocks that they cannot escape.[23] Ultimately, even when a way to escape opens, the rats ignore it. They collapse in a state of helplessness much like the capitulation seen in depression. Another animal model of depression that involves having a rat swim around in a beaker of water until it gives up likewise taps into the mechanics of surrender. According to Nesse, "Just as anxiety inhibits dangerous actions, depression inhibits futile efforts."

All these are interesting theoretical reasons for why a tendency to get depressed might be preserved in our gene pool. On the other hand, in actual cases of clinical depression, the symptoms are mostly blatantly maladaptive. At some point in my patient's history, it might have served him well to be passive—for example, in a family in which active initiatives were punished. But now, as an adult, his depression is maladaptive, by definition interfering with many aspects of his life. He is inactive when action is desirable or necessary. He feels helpless and despairing when there is much that he could do. It is the essence of cognitive therapy to tap into his bleak perceptions and habitual responses, helping him find hope by testing them against reality.

Another clearly maladaptive aspect of depression is difficulty in thinking, a prominent part of the interior landscape of some depressed people. In severe depression all brain functions seem to slow down, and it may be impossible to think clearly. The mind, once a well-oiled machine, now creaks at every turn. Those who could once race through complex and creative thinking now struggle to process the ordinary details of everyday life, such as paying bills on time. Trivial decisions, such as what clothes to wear, become impossible to make. There is a sluggish stasis of all brain functions. It is no wonder that in ancient times, melancholia was seen as a sludgy superabundance of black bile.

Just as the psychological aspects of depression are maladaptive, so are its physical features. The overactivation of the stress-response system, which manifests as insomnia, loss of appetite, and emaciation, yields no advantage. On the contrary, over time it grinds away at the mind and body, to the person's enormous detriment. Likewise, there is no evidence that the depressed person who sleeps for many hours gains any renewal or relief. On the contrary, torpor appears to be nothing but a nuisance. It prevents the sufferer from functioning normally for months at a stretch, damaging both relationships and professional functioning.

Of course, it is possible to turn any type of adversity to advantage in some way. Having suffered depression, one may become more sensitive to the suffering of others. Like Dante returning from the Inferno to inform others of his hellish journey, those who have emerged from depression to tell their tales have enlightened us and expanded our understanding of this unique form of suffering. Styron, in his heart-rending and detailed memoir, quotes Dante's famous lines:

> In the middle of the journey of our life
> I found myself in a dark wood,
> For I had lost the right path.

These remain an evocative description of the experience of depression. In the middle of life, the depressed person finds himself lost in a dark wood. The only consolation is that paths do exist. There is a way back into the light.

In considering how best to deal with sadness, it is necessary to bear in mind that healthy sadness informs us that some important aspect of our world is amiss and should be heeded, and depression informs us that something is wrong inside ourselves and needs to be corrected.

Assessing the Severity of Depression: Why It Matters

Depressions differ not only in their form and individual features, but also in their severity. The spectrum ranges from mild and tolerable to agonizing and incapacitating. As with other illnesses, it may be reasonable in mild forms of depression to attempt to treat oneself, and to seek out professional help only if you see no clear response over time. In cases of moderate and severe depression, however, it is unwise to attempt self-treatment and a professional should be consulted without delay. A guide to determine where you or someone you know falls on the depressive spectrum is provided in Appendix B.

Who Becomes Depressed?

My father was a man of mercurial temperament, with moods that ranged from expansive and ebullient to taciturn, irritable, and anxious. He came by it honestly as many in his family suffered from depressions far worse. Looking back, I can trace the depressive genes through his mother's side of the family, where I saw chronic discontent and major depressions. My own mother, by contrast, has never to my knowledge suffered a day's depression in her life. She instinctively pushes unpleasant thoughts from her mind and, in the words of the old song, accentuates the positive and eliminates the negative. A simple inspection of my own family made it clear to me, early on, that some people are vulnerable to depression while others are not.

By now, genetic propensity to depression is beyond question. Study after study has shown that depression runs in families, and complex statistical models can parse out genetic from environmental influences. A huge amount of effort, money, and brain power has been allocated to this line of investigation. However, we are still unclear as to which genes in which multiple configurations are responsible for making a person vulnerable to depression, nor can we predict how genes and environment interact to result in a full-blown depressive episode.

Environment is also important in the development of some depressions. Consider, for example, identical twins of whom only one develops depression. Since they carry identical genes, clearly something other than DNA is at work. Often the first onset of depression follows a severe life event, such as the death of a loved one. Thereafter, however, specific sad events are not required to trigger an episode. Psychiatrists speak of that first, critical event as kindling a depressive syndrome that may later flare up again with or without a cause. In women 80 percent of first episodes follow a severe life event.[24] But by the time the third depression occurs, no such relationship is seen.[25] Several studies suggest that an important loss in childhood makes a person susceptible to depressions later in life, though nobody knows how.[26]

Women seem about twice as likely to become depressed as men for reasons that remain unclear.[27] Another unexplained mystery is the recent observation that depression in the United States appears to be rising, with the onset coming at younger and younger ages. Again, a host of reasons have been advanced to explain this—the use of drugs, the stresses of modern life, dietary changes, the breakdown of traditional social support systems. Clearly we need answers. This is a major public health issue, given the vast toll the illness takes on millions of lives, as well as its impact on the economy.

The Ghost in the Machine: What Goes Wrong in Depression

In the quest to know what goes wrong in depression, we have many clues, but no good explanation. I might compare the modern depression researcher to a mechanic who is presented with many but not all the parts of a car. The mechanic has some sense of how the parts fit, but without the missing pieces, the car won't go. So it is with the research into depression.

By comparing depressed people with healthy controls, scientists have isolated abnormalities in genes, neurotransmitter functioning, hormone profiles, and brain images—but we can't yet make the car go. We know enough to help many people, but far from as much as we'd like. New knowledge is accumulating rapidly, however. Between that and the decoding of the human genome, it is a fair bet that within twenty-five years, we will understand depression as clearly and completely as we currently do, say, heart attacks. If you already know as much as you care to about brain chemistry, thumb ahead to chapter 12, where I discuss treatments. The rest of this chapter will examine what we do know about the biological underpinnings of depression—the pieces of the car.

One important problem in putting together the pieces is that depression is probably not a single disease, but several diseases. By calling them all "depression" we may be doing something akin to lumping pneumonia together with asthma as "troubled breathing." Sorting the various depressions into categories with more meaning will be a huge step forward. For the moment, however, let's look at depression as seen in the various systems it disturbs.

Neurotransmitters are central to depressions of many sorts, a fact that was suggested decades ago by the serendipitous discovery that drugs that deplete the brain of certain neurotransmitters can induce depression, whereas drugs that boost these same neurotransmitters can relieve depression.[28] Two key neurotransmitters are serotonin and norepinephrine, with a third, dopamine, a frequent player. As you might recall, neurotransmitters are the messenger boys of the nervous system. They are the chemicals released by the transmitting neuron at the synapse, the point where one neuron meets another. They zip across and stimulate receptors on the receiving neuron, and are then taken back up into the transmitting neuron to be broken down for spare parts and reuse.

Some antidepressants inhibit the reuptake of neurotransmitters into the transmitting neuron, thereby prolonging their action in the synapse—or so theory holds. These drugs include: Prozac (fluoxetine) Zoloft (sertraline), and Celexa (citalopram), all selective serotonin reuptake inhibitors, or SSRIs; Wellbutrin (bupropion), a selective norepinephrine and dopamine reuptake inhibitor; and venlafaxine (Effexor), which enhances the functioning of both serotonin and norepinephrine. The herb St. John's wort acts on all three systems. All of these antidepressants exert their effects "presynapically"—that is, between the transmitting neurons and the receiving neurons.

Once the receiving neuron has been stimulated, however, the message still has a way to travel, through a series of different events that I am lumping together here as "postsynaptic"—that is, they happen in the receiving neuron. At times, for reasons not fully understood, the treatment will succeed initially, but then stop working, perhaps because the postsynaptic neuron stops passing along the signals. Happily, when presynaptic approaches run out of steam, drugs that speed up the postsynaptic response can help. These include lithium carbonate, antiseizure medications such as valproic acid (Depakote), and hormones such as thryoxine. These substances often boost the effects of other antidepressants and stabilize mood swings.[29]

Although genetic approaches to understanding depression are just barely being formulated, we do have a few tantalizing clues. Not surprisingly, they involve serotonin. Best understood is the serotonin transporter gene, which tells the cell how to manufacture the protein reuptake site on the transmitting neuron. Once serotonin has done its job in the synapse, the transporter grabs it and takes it back up into the transmitting neuron. It turns out that the regulatory part of this gene exists in two forms, a long and a short variant. The short variant is less efficient than the long one and has already been implicated in depression and anxiety.[30] This gene will probably turn out to be only one in an array of genes that make people vulnerable to depression.

Stress response system overactivity has long been associated with depression.[31] Responding to signals from higher brain regions, the hypothalamus, that crucial regulatory center, secretes an excess of CRH. The excessive CRH, in turn, tells the pituitary gland to release excessive corticotrophin, which circulates through the bloodstream and stimulates the adrenal glands to oversecrete cortisol. In a very efficient manner, these elevated cortisol levels would normally turn off the hypothalamus and pituitary. But in major depressions, this self-regulatory loop does not work, so this major hormonal stress response system grinds away unsleepingly, overstimulating and damaging both the body and the brain.

A similarly overstressed picture is seen in measurements of the stress-responsive sympathetic nervous system, which is also overactive in depressed people. Conversely, the parasympathetic nervous system, which is responsible for relaxing the body, is underactive. These two key portions of the nervous system should be like dancing partners, each powering up or down as needed to keep the body in just the right balance between activity and relaxation. Perhaps a shift in this balance (too much stress response, too little relaxation response, or both) may be responsible for some of the ill-health associated with depression.[32]

New imaging studies are closing in on several brain areas that are abnormal in major depression.[33] As one might expect, we find abnormalities in the limbic system, including parts of the cerebral cortex known to process emotional information. Some of these areas show blood-flow changes only during depression, probably reflecting a transient abnormality associated with depression.

In other areas of the brain, however, abnormal blood flow persists even after patients recover. This implies that some people who develop depression have an underlying brain abnormality. Does the system work well enough until life gets too stressful in some particular way? That may explain why sometimes one identical twin—but not the other—becomes depressed. It will be some time before we can answer questions like this, but as brain imaging develops, we may even be able to watch a depression in the making. Then we will know precisely when to intervene.

Dying of a Broken Heart

Dying of a broken heart, a romantic notion, is a staple of pulp fiction. Rejected by a sweetheart, the hero or heroine literally dies of grief. Curiously, recent scientific studies show this may be exactly right. In fact, the impact of depression on cardiac functioning has become a hot new area of research.

Clinical depression is seen in almost half of the people who recently suffered a heart attack, which doctors have long thought was unfortunate but understandable.[34] After all, these people have just gone through a life-threatening medical emergency. So, because cardiac problems could cause depression, it has been difficult to sort out whether the opposite is also true. The results of recent longitudinal studies, however, have definitively answered this question. *Depression is a major risk factor for coronary artery disease.*

In one very large U.S. study almost 3,000 people over the age of 45 were followed for an average of twelve years. After controlling for all the other factors, those who reported a depressed mood at the beginning of the study had a 50 percent higher chance of dying from cardiac problems. And the depressed people who *also* expressed an extreme sense of hopelessness at the start of the study were twice as likely to die of heart attacks as the happy ones.[35] Other studies show similar results.

In people who have already suffered heart attacks, those who were depressed at the time were almost sixfold more likely to die within six months.[36] We also see this effect over a very long period of time. For example, in one study of 1,250 patients hospitalized for diagnostic coronary angiography, those who were diagnosed as moderately to severely depressed had a 69 percent greater chance of dying from cardiac disease over the ensuing nineteen years.[37]

Trevor Orchard and colleagues at the University of Pittsburgh studied the development of coronary artery disease (CAD) in over 600 adults with Type I diabetes (the kind in which the body is unable to produce insulin).[38] Surprisingly, over the next six years, depression at baseline was an important predictor of CAD—even better than blood glucose levels, the measure doctors use to assess how well these patients are doing.

Why is there more CAD in depressed people? Researchers are still puzzling over this, with no shortage of theoretical possibilities. The imbalance between the sympathetic and parasympathetic nervous systems, those functions that should be dancing together but don't in depression, may contribute to the sudden abnormalities in cardiac rhythm. In addition, many depressed patients suffer abnormal functioning of their platelets, the tiny blood elements responsible for clotting. If the platelets become too sticky, they can clog the coronary arteries. Or higher levels of cortisol may damage the delicate lining of the arteries in a number of ways. All these factors and more may be at work at once.

High circulating levels of cortisol may also cause other forms of disease and disability. For example, David Michelson and colleagues at the National Institute of Mental Health have found losses in bone density of up to 14 percent in patients with depression.[39] Once bone density is lost, it is hard to regain, and osteoporosis, or fragile bones, may result.

Excess cortisol also shrivels the delicate tendrils of the neurons in the hippocampus, that part of the brain responsible for recording memories. Yvette Sheline, professor of psychiatry at Washington University in St. Louis, and colleagues, using magnetic resonance imaging, found that the hippocampus was smaller and memory function worse in twenty-four women with recurrent unipolar depression as compared with an equal number of healthy women.[40] Similar results turned up in another study of middle-aged patients with chronic, treatment-resistant depression.

If depression is treated, do the medical complications lessen? Two large studies are currently under way to find out whether antidepressants can mitigate the cardiac complications of depression. As for memory problems with depression, we know that memory improves when the depression remits. In some cases, however, loss of memory may be irreversible.

One thing that is supremely clear, however, is that the medical complications of depression are just more of the many good reasons to treat this condition promptly and completely.

Bottom-Line Findings in the Biological Studies of Depression

Although we still have much to learn about the science of depression, most researchers and clinicians would agree on these important bottom-line facts:

- Much evidence suggests that the transmission of serotonin and norepinephrine are abnormal in depressed people. The drugs that enhance these neurotransmitter systems are effective antidepressants.

- Some genetic variants are associated with depression, but to date these discoveries are only tantalizing clues, not answers.

- Environmental and genetic influences interact in producing depression in ways that have yet to become clear.

- Researchers are beginning to zero in on some of the brain regions that are abnormal in depression.

- The stress response systems are chronically overactive in some depressed patients and may cause serious medical and neurological consequences.

- Depression should be rapidly diagnosed and treated, both out of compassion and to minimize the likelihood of suicide or medical complications. The majority of depressed people do not receive adequate treatment.

- Depression in people with cardiac problems should not be dismissed as a by-product. Depression increases cardiac mortality, so it is particularly important to diagnose and treat it promptly.

Chapter 12

Healing Depression

L ET me say first that doctors can now help almost everyone who suffers from depression. It may take a while to work out just the right treatment, because everyone is different, but there is hope. So this is a chapter about hope. In this chapter, I will sort out contentious questions such as: Is Prozac a miracle or a scourge?[1] Can a pill replace a therapeutic relationship, or is psychotherapy alone a reasonable alternative to medications? What can the depressed person do on her own? When is it essential to involve a doctor? And what can we learn from the latest research about treating this devastating disorder? If you or someone you love suffers from depression, these are questions of pressing importance.

Involving a Doctor

Depression can wreck a life, or even end it, and anybody who is more than mildly depressed should certainly consult a doctor. You should not assume, however, that the average doctor or even psychiatrist will be abreast of the latest developments, because the field is moving very fast. In obtaining optimal treatment for depression (to paraphrase the slogan of a popular discount-clothing store), an educated consumer is the best customer.

It can take tact to bring new information to your physician's attention without making him or her defensive. A good physician, however, appreciates learning new things from patients. I know I always do. To both doctor and patient, what matters in the end is a good result.

The information in this chapter is not intended to be a substitute for a physician's care. Those with only very mild depressive symptoms may choose to try some of these approaches on their own—but even then, if no significant improvement is seen within a month, I suggest you consult a physician. If you decide to add one of these approaches to your ongoing treatment, you should keep your physician fully informed.

As in all self-help, it is also important to remember that if you change your whole regimen at once, even if the result is good, you won't know why, so you won't be able to do it again. It pays to act like a scientist: Add, subtract, or modify only one item at a time, and stay current with your log of symptoms.

You can never go wrong consulting a doctor, however. In fact, following are five good reasons for involving a doctor:

1. *Severe depression is a medical emergency.* A person suffering from severe depression needs to get to a doctor without delay. This applies in particular to anybody who has thoughts of death, dying, or suicide.

2. *Other conditions can masquerade as depression, notably an under-functioning thyroid gland.* This condition can be diagnosed by a routine blood test, so be sure to ask your doctor to have your thyroid function tested. Thyroid hormone supplements can be amazingly effective, not only in correcting a thyroid deficiency, but also as a supplement to other treatments for depression.

   Other conditions may also mimic depression. A neighbor of mine twice developed symptoms that certainly looked like depression. Both times he was weak, listless, had difficulty concentrating on his work, and lost his zest for life. On the first occasion he turned out to have sleep apnea, a condition marked by cessation of breathing for periods while sleeping. This problem was banished by a machine that pushes air into the lungs during respiratory lapses. On the second occasion, his symptoms came from a tumor on his adrenal gland, for which he needed surgery.

The moral of the story: Be sure to have a proper medical work-up before the diagnosis of depression is made.

3. *Depression can coexist with another condition, physical or psychological.* For example, a patient of mine who initially appeared to be depressed turned out to have attention deficit disorder. Although he was very intelligent, his brain chemistry made it hard for him to focus and get his work done in a timely fashion, which made him depressed. Once the attentional problem was treated, his depression cleared up.

4. *It is often difficult to be the best judge and manager of your own moods.* A neutral expert can be invaluable, and not only because of his expertise. Assessment requires an outside objective view, which is why even psychiatrists do not generally treat themselves.

5. *Depression is a lonely state.* A good doctor can be a source of comfort and support as well as a provider of expert assistance.

6. *Remember, not all doctors are equally skillful at treating depression.* If your depression yields easily to the first or second attempt at treatment, as many do, then you will probably do fine with most doctors. If your problem proves less tractable, you might consider consulting someone who specializes in depression.

The Placebo Effect

One of the best-established facts about treating depression is that a high percentage of patients (about 40 percent in most studies) recover fully in response to a placebo, such as a sugar pill.[2] In my own experience of running placebo-controlled studies, I have often been amazed to find out which of the patients received the active drugs as opposed to the placebos. Some people responded so well that I would have sworn they had taken the active medications. Only a careful check of the data convinced me otherwise. Incidentally, people suffering from conditions besides depression also show high rates of placebo response, which is why double-blind studies are the standard for all treatment trials.

A placebo response can sometimes be just as impressive as the response to an active treatment.

Placebos work by triggering the amazing capacity of the mind and body to heal themselves, which can be enormously useful to anyone suffering from depression. After all, if something makes you feel better, do you really care whether it is working by a placebo effect or some other way? I wouldn't think so, which is why my first advice to all my patients is to use the placebo effect to maximum advantage.

The best placebos are those that a person believes will be helpful. This is well known, so as you read through the various treatment options that follow, consider which make the most sense to you, which you intuitively sense will be most helpful. Those are the ones that will likely have a powerful placebo effect for you. All the treatments that I discuss are supported by scientific studies indicating that they work by more than the placebo effect. Nevertheless, all can have a placebo effect as well. Use it.

Placebos are less likely to work for people with chronic depression that has already been extensively treated.

By embracing treatments that seem plausible and appealing to you, you are likely to benefit from the placebo effect. Let this effect work for you. Take advantage of the brain's amazing capacity to heal itself.

Antidepressants: The Good, the Bad, and the Ugly

Why is it, you may ask, that some have written about antidepressants as miracle cures while others portray them as a scourge? In part, the authors have different ideologies. But the split also reflects a sad truth: Response varies widely from person to person. For many people, these drugs have indeed been transforming, eradicating their depression with no side effects. Others have been less fortunate. In some unlucky souls, a whole series of antidepressants has failed to work. Others suffer unacceptable side effects even at very low dosages. The response to antidepressants, like life itself, is inherently unfair.

In fact, if one looks only at the research, antidepressants may look disappointing. In a recent meta-analysis of single-medication treatment trials, the magnitude of the treatment effect (known as the effect size), though greater than that for placebos, was not all that impressive.[3]

Research indicates that antidepressants prescribed outside of studies have better results, however. I believe this is because in a study, all the patients are treated according to a fixed protocol, and whether a certain patient responds or not, the researchers have to stick with the plan. Otherwise, they will not know what the results mean. But in clinical practice, it is possible to customize the treatment for each patient. We can switch drugs or doses or combine antidepressants as needed, guided largely by the patient's observations. It can take quite a period of collaborative tinkering to find the regimen that is best for a given patient, but we usually get there.

Here is another fact about antidepressants that might at first glance look discouraging: Antidepressants have been in use for fifty years, but there is no good evidence that the newly developed antidepressants are any more effective than the older ones—at least on average, when given to groups of depressed individuals. But again, things go better in practice because for any given individual, one antidepressant will usually work much better than another. Also, the new drugs do have one striking advantage: They have fewer side effects than most of the old ones. So in reality, as the list of drugs grows, so does the percentage of patients who recover.

Just as with antidepressant effects, side effects can vary greatly from person to person. Basic facts about both types of effects in the more widely used antidepressants can be found in Table 12.1.[4]

Someday, when we understand the biology of depression in detail, we will be able to pick the right drug for a particular depression right off the bat. In the meanwhile, we have to work by trial and error. Because we do know how different antidepressants work, however, we are already able to make educated guesses as to which family of drugs to try and in what sequence.

In systematically trying one antidepressant after another, I often feel like a curator of a museum with a huge bunch of keys in my line),

Table 12.1 Brief Overview of Antidepressants
(SE = serotonin; NE = norepinephrine; DA = dopamine
+ = slight; ++ = moderate; +++ = marked)

Name (Brand/Generic)	Neurotransmitters Affected	Potential Advantages	Potential Disadvantages
Tricyclic Antidepressants:			
Tofranil (imipramine)	SE ++ NE ++	Highly effective and good for anxiety as well as depression. Their sleepy side effects can be an advantage for those with insominia.	More side effects than modern antidepressants. Include dry mouth, constipation, blurred vision, fatigue, and weight gain.
Anafranil (chlorimipramine)	SE +++ NE +		
Elavil (amitriptyline)	SE ++ NE ++		
Norpramin (desipramine)	NE +++ SE +		
Pamelor/Aventyl (nortriptyline)	SE ++ NE ++		
Selective serotonin reuptake inhibitors (SSRIs):			
Prozac (fluoxetine)	SE +++	All are effective. Good for anxiety as well as depression.	Side effects include reduced sexual functioning, lethargy and weight gain.
Zoloft (sertraline)			
Paxil (paroxetine)			
Celexa (citalopram)			
Luvox (fluvoxamine)			
Effexor (Venlafaxine)	SE ++ NE ++	Effective. Good for anxiety as well as depression. May be	Can cause activation, sedation, and increased

Name (Brand/Generic)	Neurotransmitters Affected	Potential Advantages	Potential Disadvantages
		less likely to cause sexual side effects and weight gain.	blood pressure.
Wellbutrin *(bupropion)*	DA +++ NE ++	Effective. Good for people with sluggish depressions. Less likely to cause sexual dysfunction and weight gain.	Less effective for anxiety. May predispose to seizures, especially in vulnerable people.
Serzone *(nefadozone)*	SE ++ NE ++	Effective. Less likely to induce sexual side effects.	sedation, dry mouth, dizziness, and rarely, severe liver damage.
Remeron *(mirtazapine)*	SE ++ NE ++	Effective. Good for anxiety as well as depression. Highly sedating—good for insomnia. Fewer sexual side effects.	Most disturbing side effects include sedation and weight gain, both of which can be marked.
Drugs that affect receptors or the transmission of signals in the receiving neuron: Lithium carbonate		Can be highly effective, even in people who have no history of mania.	Toxic in overdosage. Can cause thyroid and, rarely, kidney problems. Blood levels need to be monitored.

Name (Brand/Generic)	Neurotransmitters Affected	Potential Advantages	Potential Disadvantages
Depakote (valproic acid)		Highly effective mood stabilizer.	In rare cases can cause liver, pancreas, and bone marrow problems.
Neurotin (gabapentin)		Effective mood stabilizer. Goes rapidly in and out of the body.	Needs to be taken several times per day.
Lamotrigine (lamictal)		Effective mood stabilizer; may be useful in refractory depression.	Can be sedating. Can cause very serious skin rash in some cases.
Topamax (topiramate)		Good mood stabilizer. Associated with weight loss.	Can cause sedation, slowing of thought processes, and rarely, eye problems.

hand, trying each key one by one, till finally the tumblers turn in the lock. Even in the most unyielding of depressions, it is often possible to find just the right medication—or combination of medications—to help turn things around without producing unacceptable side effects.

Most depressions respond to the first or second treatment we try.[5] But if relief does not happen for you, persevere. The prize is almost always worth the battle.

Nondrug Treatments of Depression

Recently I was visited by two very pleasant representatives of a major pharmaceutical company, people of the sort who visit doctors daily to advertise the latest good news about their products. After they showed me a few studies using their drug, in this case Zoloft (sertra line), I asked whether they were familiar with a recent study that found that exercise was as good as Zoloft in treating older depressed patients. They had never heard of it. I gave them copies and sent them on their way, but I would be very surprised if they ever mentioned it on their rounds.

Calls of this kind occur in doctors' offices by the thousands every day, and that is just the tip of the iceberg. With depression costing $43 billion per year in the United States alone, it is *big business*, and the scope of the sales push would be hard for a nonmedical person to appreciate. As well as lavish lunches, sales calls, and an endless flow of free samples—what you would expect in any business—pharmaceutical companies also sponsor symposia at vacation meccas such as San Francisco, the better to disseminate news about their products.

Doctors genuinely need the information, but the overall result is to skew their thinking. It is in the corporate interest of the pharmaceutical companies to exaggerate the benefits and minimize the shortcomings of their products—and especially to keep quiet about any treatment strategies that might interfere with sales.

Recently I was invited to participate in a symposium on alternative treatments for depression, which was to be held at a major psychiatric meeting. As the time drew near, however, the organizer called apologetically to cancel the symposium, for lack of funding. That came as no surprise. After all, why should a pharmaceutical company pay for a symposium to trumpet the benefits of exercise, psychotherapy, herbs, and other alternative treatments? It might be bad for business.

Here's the scoop: While antidepressant medications are invaluable, they often fail to reverse the symptoms fully, and they may cause unacceptable side effects (see Table 12.1). Even though I specialize in the medical management of depression and use antidepressants regularly in my practice, I have become increasingly aware of their limitations—and increasingly excited about nonpharmacological approaches. I have used many of these alternative approaches with excellent results.

For some people with depression, especially if the case is mild, non-drug treatments do the job. For others, these alternative approaches can supplement antidepressants, and they often make the difference between partial and complete recovery. Since medications are widely advertised and are essentially the province of the treating physician, I will focus here on alternative approaches to healing depression.

Psychotherapy for Depression

For depression, the most widely studied and successful form of psychotherapy is cognitive-behavioral therapy, a treatment that seeks to modify the patterns of thought and behavior.

Aaron Beck developed CBT after observing that most depressed patients make unwarranted assumptions about their lives, which Beck has called *automatic negative thoughts* (ANTs).[6] In CBT, the therapist encourages the patient to challenge these assumptions, like a scientist challenging a hypothesis. The different types of ANTs include "fortune-telling," "mind reading," and "black-or-white thinking." The therapist points out how the patient's ANTs are causing depression and suggests alternative, more positive thoughts. Once the patient has mastered the categories, she is given homework, that involves detecting and correcting ANTs as they arise during the course of the day.

"Fortune telling" represents unwarranted assumptions about the future. For example, a depressed person might do poorly in a job interview, then conclude, "I will never amount to anything." The therapist will help the patient ask, "What evidence is there that I won't amount to anything? Why should one mess-up guarantee future mess-ups?" Asking these questions helps a depressed person recognize that projecting a single failure into one's entire future is not warranted. It serves only to enhance feelings of depression and low self-esteem.

Instead, the therapist helps the patient formulate a more hopeful response. The person might be encouraged, for example, to say to herself, "Nobody succeeds every time. Even if I did not succeed this time, that does not mean I cannot succeed in future. Perhaps there is something I can learn from this experience." As you can imagine, this kind of self-message is more likely to produce resiliency, less likely to feed depression.

"Mind reading" occurs when a depressed person thinks he can tell what another person is thinking—nothing good, usually. For example, a young patient of mine once observed an unusual expression around my mouth and concluded this meant I did not like her. In fact, she had caught me swallowing a midafternoon snack. The cognitive therapist helps patients formulate alternative explanations for the behaviors they observe in others, explanations that will not compound their own depressed feelings.

Another patient of mine interpreted a moderately good work evaluation as a complete failure. Clearly, when it came to her own performance, she could not recognize shades of gray. I pointed out her black-or-white thinking pattern, and in time she learned to appreciate that success and failure come in different degrees, for her as for everyone else.

In the behavioral part of CBT, the therapist looks at the patient's behaviors and helps him evaluate their consequences. The patient is encouraged to ask which behaviors enhance his life and which detract from it. Once again, the patient is given homework, designed to help him review his particular patterns.

In seeking a suitable therapist for the treatment of depression, it is best to find one skilled in the practices of CBT.[7] Also check "Further Reading" on page 421 for self-help resources.

What the Research Shows

By now, dozens of well-controlled studies of CBT for depression have appeared in the professional literature. Here are some of their major conclusions:

- Compared to treatments consisting of simple support and counseling, research consistently shows that CBT is superior in alleviating depression.

- CBT can help severe depressions as well as mild ones. One review of four studies comparing CBT and antidepressants in severely depressed people found that the two treatments worked equally well.[8]

- CBT can help even patients with long-term depression, especially if given in conjunction with antidepressants. In a study recently published in the *New England Journal of Medicine*, for example, researchers at twelve academic medical centers compared three forms of treatment—the antidepressant Serzone, a form of CBT, and a combination of Serzone and CBT—in a total of 519 chronically depressed patients.[9] As in other comparative studies, the drugs kicked in quicker. But after twelve weeks, the response rates for the patients who completed the study were roughly equivalent (55 percent and 52 percent respectively). For patients who received both Serzone and CBT, the response rate jumped to 85 percent. This study confirms what clinicians have long maintained: Depressed patients tend to do best with *both* medications and therapy.[10]

In two of the groups, the medication-only group and the CBT-only group, about one in four of the participants dropped out, for reasons that highlight the very different drawbacks of each treatment: the psychotherapy dropouts did not wish to invest the time and effort required, while the medication dropouts were troubled by side effects.

- One common problem in treating depression is that many patients tend to relapse, while others get only partial relief. In a recent study, CBT significantly reduced relapse rates when compared to ordinary clinical care (from 47 percent to 29 percent) over a sixty-eight-week interval.[11]

The bottom line on CBT for depression is that CBT can be as good as medication even for chronic and severe depression. In fact, the most effective treatment regimen for depression is often a combination of antidepressants and CBT.

CBT involves more time and work than antidepressants and the benefits occur more slowly, but it has essentially no side effects. And it has staying power—it can reduce the relapse rates.

Ten Strategies for Healing Your Own Depression

Regardless of whether you are under a physician's or a therapist's care, here are ten strategies based on research findings and clinical experience that can help you combat depression.

Strategy 1: Become a Good Judge of Your Own Mood

Just as you weigh yourself when you begin a diet, then track your weight as you progress, so you should track your mood. You need to know your starting point, and you need to track the way your mood shifts. Many people fluctuate in quite predictable patterns across the day, week, month, or season, or in reaction to events.

Recognizing such patterns can help you work out how to improve your mood, as well as evaluate the results. I have used a very simple daily mood log with my patients for many years. A sample page appears in Appendix C. The log takes no more than two minutes each day to complete. If you suffer from depression, I suggest that you keep this mood and sleep log for a week or two before trying any of the suggested strategies. That way you will know whether the strategies really make a difference.

Strategy 2: Exercise in Moderation

Larry was a successful entrepreneur who came to me with acute depression. A highly driven individual, he mentioned in passing that one of his few passions was his regular competitive tennis game. But a month before, he had sprained his right elbow and had to stop playing tennis—and that was when his depression had kicked in.

Over the years I have noticed that many athletic people become depressed if something keeps them from their usual workout. So I suggested that Larry try some other form of exercise till he could play tennis again. He began walking briskly for a few miles each day, and his depression lifted within two weeks, with no need for either medication or therapy.

Although not all cases are that dramatic, researchers in the field agree that exercise can be a great antidepressant. So impressive are the data that in Belgium "psychomotor therapy" to treat depression and anxiety is already offered through the national health system.[12]

Here are some of the main research findings:

- Four prospective population studies indicate that those who become or remain fit are less likely to suffer from clinical depression.[13]

- Once anxiety and depression have developed, controlled studies indicate that exercise can reverse them.[14]

- Cardiovascular conditioning is probably not essential. In at least one study, weight training (which is nonaerobic) worked as well as aerobic exercise.[15]

- In at least one study, exercise appeared as effective as psychotherapy and also enhanced the benefits of psychotherapy.[16]

- The gains from a time-limited exercise program may last a year or more. In one study, depressed women who participated in an eight-week program of either aerobic exercise or weight training sustained their therapeutic benefits for more than a year after their formal exercise sessions ended.[17]

- In one impressive recent study of 156 depressed patients aged 50 years or older, a sixteen-week exercise program helped as much as the well-respected drug Zoloft. Exercise plus Zoloft were no better than either treatment by itself.[18]

Exercise, with or without antidepressants, is a powerful treatment for depression and anxiety. Regular exercise also appears to prevent depression.

Winston Churchill once said that he got enough exercise serving as a pallbearer at the funerals of friends who had exercised all their lives, a comment that captures the lack of enthusiasm a depressed person feels when exercise is suggested. What I frequently hear people say is, "If I had enough motivation to exercise, I wouldn't be needing your help in the first place." If exercise is to succeed, it has to be manageable and, better still, palatable. Here are some useful exercise tips, based on my experience with many depressed patients:

- Choose a form of exercise you like.
- Remember that even rather modest amounts of exercise, such as 30 minutes of brisk walking four or five times a week, can make a difference.
- If 30 minutes sounds like a lot to you, do 20, or 10, or 5 and work up. Don't do so much at the start that you hate it.
- Exercise in a setting that you find appealing. For some this might be the outdoors, for others a gym.

- Work out with a friend. This combines the benefits of exercise with those of companionship.
- Vary the exercise to make it more interesting. Remember, nonaerobic exercise, such as lifting weights or doing push-ups, can help as much as aerobic exercise.
- Do something enjoyable, such as listening to music or watching videotapes, while working out.
- If motivation is a problem and you can afford it, hire a trainer. This is a solution that I adopted for myself long ago and have never regretted.
- Schedule time in your day for exercise. Don't expect that you will be able to "just fit it in." Research shows that people who exercise first thing in the morning are more likely to stay with it.
- If your depression becomes worse in the winter or in response to not getting enough light, exercise in bright light—either outdoors or in front of a special light fixture. (For discussion of SAD, see page 347.)
- Give yourself a psychological reward, a pat on the back, each time you exercise. Say to yourself something like, "I have just done one of the most powerful things I can do to improve my mood and energy level. That proves I am not helpless, and I know that an investment of time and energy will repay itself many times over."

Strategy 3: Take Control of Your Life as Best You Can

One insight to be gleaned from Seligman's ideas about learned helplessness is that it is very depressing to be in a situation where you keep getting punished and cannot escape. Yet life can often feel that way. A punitive boss or an angry spouse can make you feel like a rat in Dr. Seligman's cage, getting shocked no matter what you do. However, you may have ways of escape that a caged animal does not, so analyze the situation with that in mind. Just knowing that a way out exists can ameliorate depression. Even if you then choose to stay in the marriage or the job, you have taken control. You are not being foot-shocked, but have made a choice. And you will then be in a better frame of mind to negotiate.

One important caveat: It is unwise to make major life decisions while in the grip of a depression because being depressed makes life look bleaker than it is. Your assessments are probably off. In general, it is best to recover from your depression before deciding to change your job or marital status. However, some jobs and marriages are, in fact, so unpleasant that feeling better depends on getting out. In those situations, perhaps, you really are being foot-shocked.

In deciding which case pertains to you, the wise counsel of a trusted friend or therapist can be invaluable.

Strategy 4: Tackle Stress

During a recent stroll through a quiet seaside village, a curious feeling of peacefulness came over me. It was early evening. All the shops were shut and the streets were empty of traffic. A few people strolled about, but most of the denizens of this quaint town were either at home or enjoying an early dinner in the few restaurants that were still open. I experienced a level of serenity quite unfamiliar to me in this secluded hamlet.

The experience came as a bit of a shock. Living in a metropolitan area, I had almost forgotten that life need not hustle and bustle long after the traditional workday is over. It makes me wonder whether the stress of modern life may be one reason why depression is affecting people in larger numbers and at younger ages. Most of us are working harder than ever, and our work encroaches upon times that were once reserved for rest—vacations and the night. Nowadays shops are open till late, stocks can be traded after hours, and cell phones ring in the most secluded places. Yet over the course of evolution, for millions of years, the night was reserved for rest. I suspect that our new way of living stresses our minds and bodies beyond their normal limits, with depression as one result.

Although we may feel like helpless victims, there are really many ways we can alleviate the stresses and strains of modern life, and the depressed person is well advised to do so. William Styron describes how his very severe depression was cured without any specific antidepressant treatment, but simply by entering a hospital where he was removed from the stresses of daily life. Even as I write these words, I hear in memory the voices of my many depressed patients who greeted the suggestion to slow down with a groan of frustration. "I can't afford to slow down," they say. (They are often working long hours to compensate for their depressed lack of focus.) I tell them they can't afford *not* to slow down.

Shakespeare noted, "When sorrows come, they come not as single spies but in battalions." One of the problems with depression is that the depressed person can be sluggish, forgetful, irritable, and generally hard to be with, which creates new sorrows, specifically trouble at work or home. These troubles in turn aggravate the depression and a vicious cycle develops.

This spiral downward needs to be somehow turned around, and that's where reducing stress comes in. It is essential to treat the depression directly. But it may also help to enlist family members and (carefully selected) colleagues or supervisors in the overall plan to lower stress.

Happily, this is easier to do than may at first appear. All it takes is a little creative thinking. For example, let's take the work site: For a person who struggles to get up in the morning, permission to work from ten to six instead of nine to five can make all the difference. Maybe he comes in at nine only for staff meetings. Or a low spell might be a good time to use a few vacation days, perhaps to create several three-day weekends. Or perhaps some projects can be postponed or delegated. Given leeway, the patient will feel better immediately in many instances, and work more effectively as well. For employer and patient alike, reducing stress is a win-win strategy.

Nevertheless, my patients often resist the idea, especially when the boss is already on their case or their family is already mad. Then they are surprised, relieved, and touched when critics turn into allies, as often happens. Often depression symptoms look like laziness, rudeness, or indifference to the needs of others, and managers may be delighted to learn, that it's not a personnel problem, but a medical problem *that is being addressed*—an important point to emphasize. By discussing the situation, one can usually negotiate something that meets the needs of all.

Strategy 5: Seek Out Social Supports

It is important for a depressed person—and indeed for all people—to know that others care. Just like primates, we are tribal animals. We will not thrive without mutual bonds of friendship and love.

This is another plausible reason why depression is becoming more prevalent, the breakdown of social networks. In times past, people grew up and spent most of their lives in one community, surrounded by family and friends from childhood. Nowadays, we must move about (once every few years for many in the United States), and many suffer divorces. More Americans than ever are living alone. Their closest family members may be a thousand miles away, and their only local friends may be people they've known a year or so—acquaintances, really.

We pay a high price for our privacy and mobility. Researchers have found that in animal models of depression, social supports can mitigate the effects of stress on the development of depressive-type symptoms. In one model, researchers cage a submissive rat with a dominant rat. The dominant rat will attack the more passive animal until the latter cowers in submission—a condition that resembles depression. If the submissive rat is then put in a cage alone, it will continue to huddle in a submissive posture. But if the rat is put back with its littermates, it will return to normal.[19]

So it is with humans—the comfort of family and good friends can be wonderful antidotes to depression. For those without these benefits, a surprising amount of help can be found in support and recovery groups. Some groups are geared specifically toward depression, while others focus on addictions. There is a great deal of wisdom to be found in the rooms where such groups meet. Even some of my more sophisticated and therapy-weary patients have been surprised at how much help they get from group meetings.

Strategy 6: Try Herbs, Nutrients, and Supplements

Stay me with apples; comfort me with flagons
For I am sick of love
—Song of Songs[20]

The idea that we can modify the way we feel by means of plants and herbal extracts is as old as the written word itself. In Homer's *Odyssey*, we are told that the beautiful Helen slipped the drug "heart's ease" into the wine of the wandering heroes. This drug was so powerful that it made them forget all their pain.

In the last few years, interest has revived in traditional herbal treatments for depression. While not all these nostrums are backed by

substantial scientific research, some are. Depression is linked to a surprising range of nutrients, even among people who appear well fed.

In this section I will describe those herbs, dietary supplements,
and nutrients that hold the most promise for raising wilted spirits
and alleviating depression.

ST. JOHN'S WORT (Hypericum Perforatum)
Used as a medication for at least 2,000 years, this flowering herb was
allegedly prescribed for the Emperor Nero. It came to public atten-
tion in the United States only in the mid-1990s, after the prestigious
British Medical Journal published a meta-analysis by German researcher
K. Linde and colleagues.[21]

In that study and others since, many researchers agree that the herb
is clearly superior to placebo in mild to moderate depression[22] (55-
percent versus a 22-percent response rate), and about as effective as
tricyclic antidepressants,[23] but with fewer side effects. It also appears
that St. John's wort may work for severely depressed (even hospitalized) patients, while two small studies found its results roughly
equivalent to those of Prozac.[24]

A large multicenter trial sponsored by the National Institute
of Mental Health is now under way to compare the herb with
Zoloft.

An important caveat about St. John's wort: A few recent reports
have shown that St. John's wort can interfere with a person's other
medications by boosting the liver's ability to break down drugs. The
medications affected include some used for cardiac problems, high
blood pressure, seizures, and HIV infection, as well as birth control
pills and and hormone replacements.[25]

*If you are considering taking St. John's wort and are on any other med-
ications, do not start without consulting your doctor. If you are already on
St. John's wort, be sure to tell your doctor about it before starting any new
medication.*

St. John's wort appears to work by inhibiting the reuptake of serotonin, norepinephrine, and dopamine into the presynaptic neuron.[26]
Conventional antidepressants also work that way, but none tested so
far can influence all three of these important neurotransmitters. The
herb's unique biochemical properties may explain why some of my

depressed patients who have not responded to any other antidepressant have succeeded brilliantly with St. John's wort.

The usual dose of St. John's wort for mild to moderate depression has been one 300-milligram tablet three times per day, though twice-a-day dosing may be just as good and more convenient. If necessary, doses of up to 1,800 mg per day can be used—but do not start there. I start most patients with 300 mg once a day for a few days, then twice a day, then three times a day. I keep the dose at that level for a few weeks, then look for evidence of response or side effects before deciding whether a further increase is warranted.

An important note about St. John's wort: Not all brands are equally good. Since herbal remedies are not produced under the same regulations and scrutiny as prescription medications, quality varies. The *Los Angeles Times* survey of ten brands of St. John's wort found they contained from 50 to 150 percent of the amount of extract that the package advertising claimed.[27] Clearly, that makes it hard to know what you are taking. The brand being used in the NIMH study is Kira, produced by a German company. Because of its excellent track record, I recommend Kira to my patients, though other quality brands such as Ze117 brands may work just as well.

As with other antidepressants, effects are seldom seen until the herb has been taken at full dosage for at least two weeks. If you feel no difference after a month at full dosage, the trial can be considered unsuccessful. Those interested in learning more about this herb are referred to my book on the topic, *St. John's Wort: The Herbal Way to Feeling Good* (HarperCollins, 1998).

OMEGA-3 FATTY ACIDS

While only one controlled study has been published on the use of fish oil extracts as an antidepressant (and that was in bipolar disorder), there is other evidence of their value, reviewed by Joseph Hibbeln, senior researcher at the National Institute of Alcoholism and Alcohol Abuse.[28] The fish oil components thought to be the most active against depression are the unsaturated omega-3 fatty acids docosahexaenoic acid (DHA) and eicosapenatenoic acid (EPA).

Hibbeln and colleagues compared the prevalence of depression with the amount of seafood consumed per year in nine different countries. They found that the more seafood the population ate, the lower was the prevalence of depression. Two subsequent studies concur. Hibbeln's team then went on to examine the prevalence of depression following childbirth (postpartum depression) in twenty-two countries, and looked at those numbers against the numbers for both seafood consumption and the concentration of DHA in the mother's milk.[29] Once again they found strong associations, with higher levels of DHA and seafood consumption being related to lower levels of depression. In addition, in the one treatment study published to date, fish oil extracts decreased the likelihood of both manic and depressive relapse in bipolar patients.[30]

The crucial tests as to whether fish oil extract will reverse depression in unipolar depressives (those who suffer from depression but not from mania) still need to be done. But in my own clinical experience and that of colleagues, fish oil does appear to have a significant, though subtle, effect as an antidepressant and mood stabilizer. As a booster for conventional treatments, it is well worth trying, especially since it is safe and confers other health benefits as well. For example, in 1999, an article in *The Lancet* reported that in over 11,000 recent heart attack survivors, the omega-3 fatty acids lowered the risk of both subsequent heart attacks and stroke.[31] After having a heart attack, people who eat as few as two fish meals a month cut their risk of fatal arrhythmias in half. Fish oils also help to build strong, dense bone.[32]

In making a case for using fish oil to treat depression, Hibbeln points out that DHA constitutes a full 30 percent of the brain's wet weight. Nerve cell membranes consist largely of unsaturated fatty acids, the concentration of which determines how well the membranes work. Since these membranes contain the all-important receptors, fatty acid deficiency may well shut down some receptors. The cardiac benefits of fish oil make sense because the fatty acids help conduct electrical signals in the heart as well as in the brain. In fact, fish oil may explain the link between depression and heart problems—both can be aggravated by insufficient omega-3 fatty acids in the diet.

Until we have studies, however, we have no scientific way to determine how much fish oil extract might be needed to relieve depression. Andrew Stoll, the assistant professor of psychiatry at Harvard University who led the bipolar fish oil study, estimates that for general health purposes, 1 to 2 grams of fatty acids (EPA plus DHA) is probably sufficient, whereas for treating depression, doses between 2 and 5 grams may be necessary.

Most people tolerate fish oil well, with the most common side effects being queasiness and a fishy aftertaste. These side effects can be minimized by purchasing brands that contain higher concentrations of EPA and DHA, requiring fewer capsules to be consumed. Ideally, the capsules should be spread out over the day and taken with meals.

According to pharmacologist Jerry Cott, there is a theoretical possibility that higher dosages of fish oils, meaning more than 3 grams per day, may increase a set of undesirable bodily reactions known as oxidation, or the production of free radicals. Cott strongly recommends that people who take high doses of fish oil also take antioxidants, specifically vitamin C (2 grams per day) and natural vitamin E (800–1,200 milligrams per day). These powerful antioxidants should be quite sufficient to counteract any increased oxidation, and will also prevent the fish oil supplements from being broken down in the body before they can do their good work.

Warning: If you are taking an anticlotting medication, such as Warfarin, consult with your doctor before starting fish oil extracts or vitamin E, both of which may interfere with clotting.

Even though mothers used to give their children cod-liver oil as a standard dietary supplement years ago, beware of using it as a fish oil supplement. Cod liver oil contains large amounts of vitamin D, which can be harmful if taken in excess.

SAMe (S-adenosyl-L-methionine)

There has been considerable media buzz about this chemical, which is produced naturally in the brain and takes part in essential chemical reactions. Its theoretical connection to what we know about the biochemistry of depression is tenuous. Studies on its benefits in depression took place, for the most part, in the late 1980s and early 1990s, and the data on its use in tablet form rest on just a few dozen depressed patients.[33] Nevertheless, SAMe did appear to reduce the depression scores in these few individuals, which provides some scientific basis if you want to give it a try.

The dosage used in most reported studies was 1,600 milligrams per day, which could prove expensive. Enthusiasts suggest that 400 milligrams per day may be sufficient. In my own limited clinical experience and that of colleagues, this supplement has been disappointing. SAMe appears to be free of side effects and interactions with other substances, which can be construed either as good news or as further evidence that it is no more than an expensive placebo.

L-TRYPTOPHAN, 5-HTP, AND CARBOHYDRATES

It may seem strange to cluster these three substances together—the one a naturally occurring amino acid, the second a nutritional supplement, and the third a part of every normal diet. Yet these three substances have one important thing in common—they all boost serotonin production in the brain. If depression results from deficient brain serotonin transmission, producing more might have an antidepressant effect.

L-tryptophan is the amino-acid building block that the brain uses to make serotonin. It is so central to the process that in its absence from the diet, fresh supplies of this important neurotransmitter cannot be made. 5-HTP is a chemical intermediary between L-tryptophan and serotonin. Both substances can be absorbed in capsule form, traveling via the bloodstream into the brain, which would theoretically enhance brain serotonin synthesis.

Even though carbohydrates, such as fruits, sweets, and starches, do not contain L-tryptophan in meaningful amounts, eating foods rich in this basic food element makes the pancreas secrete insulin. That, in turn, results in more L-tryptophan entering the brain and boosts serotonin synthesis. And this is why sluggishly depressed patients crave carbohydrates. For the moment, though alas only for the moment, sweets and starches do in fact make them feel better.

Research using L-tryptophan and 5-HTP to treat depression is, for the most part, twenty to thirty years old. L-tryptophan caused a major public health scare toward the end of the last century when it caused the death of several people in the United States, fatalities that were traced to an impurity in a batch of the product.

L-tryptophan has now been declared safe, but its history remains a cautionary tale to anyone under the misimpression that goods bought in a health food store are always free of risk.

I would say that L-tryptophan and 5-HTP might be useful supplements for people who fail to respond to conventional antidepressants alone. But there is no good reason to use them instead of conventional therapeutics. The evidence just is not there.

As for carbohydrates, for depressed people they are not a treatment but a trap, which is a shame. These people have already lost so much capacity for pleasure that to give up the one comfort many have counted on can feel like a major deprivation. I hate having to tell my patients to hold back on sweets and starches. Yet that is exactly what, in my experience, those depressives who tend to binge on these goodies need to do.

According to Bonnie Spring, professor of psychology at the University of Illinois, Chicago, carbohydrate-rich meals tend to make normal individuals sleepy.[34] But in a study that she and I conducted at the National Institute of Mental Health, depressed patients with SAD showed the opposite effect.[35] After three huge cookies for lunch, they solved puzzles with more energy and focus, not less.

This mood lift is extremely short-lived, however, and is followed by a rebound. As insulin enters the bloodstream, blood sugar drops sharply, and lethargy and somnolence return, worse this time because of the sharpness of the drop.

In summary, although nutritional methods of boosting brain serotonin sound good in theory, they have little value in practice.

B VITAMINS
The deficiency of certain B vitamins is associated with depressive symptoms, such as weakness, lethargy, and lack of interest in things. The most important B vitamins are folic acid, thiamine, vitamin B12, and pyridoxine, though all the B vitamins may be important in treating depression in ways that might surprise even a psychiatrist.

Folic Acid. A lack of folic acid is perhaps the most common and serious vitamin deficiency in the United States.[36] It has been estimated that three out of four American women obtain less than the recommended daily dosage. Many elders, children, and young adults also get too little of this critical vitamin, which is found in green vegetables. (You can remember that because "folic" comes from the same root as "foliage.") In one study, between 15 and 38 percent of depressed adults had blood levels of folic acid that were either low or almost low.[37] In a study of forty-four depressed patients, the researchers noted that even low-normal levels of folic acid predicted longer episodes of depression.[38]

And that's not all. Several studies link folic acid deficiency not only to depression, but also to a person's ability to respond fully to anti-depressant medications. Researchers Maurizio Fava and colleagues at Harvard University found that depressed people with lower blood levels of folic acid responded less well to Prozac.[39] This finding is consistent with that of another study in which the addition of folic acid enhanced the response to antidepressant medications.[40]

Researchers have speculated that folic acid may help depression by raising brain serotonin and brain SAMe levels.[41]

Depressed patients who do not respond readily to antidepressants should consider supplementing their diet with folic acid.

Thiamine (Vitamin B1). Of all the B vitamins, thiamine deficiency has been most consistently associated with low mood, in studies that go back half a century. The link is as true now as ever. For example, re-searcher David Benton and colleagues at the University of Wales in Swansea found a relationship between thiamine status and mood in healthy young British women. After taking a multivitamin supple-ment containing thiamine for four months, the women reported that their mood improved. Eight other vitamins showed no such effect.[42] Surprisingly, even though the women were young and healthy, the re-searchers found that one in five had a marginal or deficient thiamine status.

A study of more than 1,000 young German men found that almost one-quarter of them showed poor thiamine status, which was associ-ated with introversion, inactivity, fatigue, decreased self-confidence, and generally low mood.[43] Thiamine supplements for two months in a double-blind treatment trial made the men more sociable and sen-sitive. Similar results were found among young British women.

In fact, thiamine improves mood even in people who are not thi-amine deficient as usually defined. Benton points to no less than four double-blind placebo-controlled studies that say so.

All people with problems of mood, energy, and feelings of well-being should consider supplementing their diet with 50 milligrams of thiamine per day.

Vitamin B12. This vitamin is also deficient far more often than you would imagine in our affluent society. The average American woman over the age of 50 obtains less than half (43 to 48 percent) of the recommended amounts of B12 in her diet.[44] The corresponding values for men of the same age are 62 to 75 percent.

People with pernicious anemia or bowel diseases have trouble absorbing vitamin B12 from their diet and should get B12 shots every two to four weeks. For others, supplementing B12 in the diet is sufficient.

Pyridoxine (Vitamin B6). Pyridoxine appears to mitigate the mood problems that affect some women before the menstrual period. A recent state-of-the-art review supports up to 100 milligrams per day as likely to benefit premenstrual symptoms and premenstrual depression.[45]

DHEA

Dehydroepiandrosterone (DHEA) is a popular nutritional supplement widely advertised as promoting vigor and positive mood. Does it? After years of vague reports, we finally have some controlled studies.

DHEA is a natural hormone, synthesized and released into the bloodstream by the adrenal glands. As well as being converted into other hormones, namely testosterone and estrogen, DHEA has important biological effects of its own, including effects on mood.

Several uncontrolled treatment trials show that DHEA has antidepressant effects, and some population studies link low circulating DHEA levels with depression and anxiety, and high DHEA levels with greater enjoyment of life.[46] In a more rigorous study, Owen Wolkowitz, professor of psychiatry at the University of California in San Francisco, and colleagues recently compared DHEA to a placebo in a six-week study of patients with major depression. They found that five out of the eleven patients showed a marked improvement on the hormone, as compared with none on placebo.[47]

In another small but well-done study, Miki Bloch and fellow researchers at the National Institute of Mental Health studied the effects of DHEA in men and women over the age of 45 with a mild form of depression that began in later life.[48] They gave all the subjects either DHEA or a placebo for six weeks, then nothing for a short period, then the alternate treatment. Of the fifteen patients who persisted through this stop-and-go regimen, all showed a robust improvement in mood after taking the DHEA as compared with taking the placebo.

I would be jumping up and down for joy except that the side effects of DHEA include oily skin and acne, nervousness and overstimulation, and (less commonly) unwanted facial hair and deepening of the voice in women.[49] Also, since DHEA converts into estrogen and testosterone, it may possibly accelerate the growth of hormone-sensitive cancers, such as those of the prostate and breast. Given these medical considerations, it would be wise to consult a doctor before starting this supplement even though it is available over the counter.

The recommended dosage of DHEA is 30 to 90 milligrams per day.

TRACE MINERALS

Trace minerals are present in the body in tiny (trace) amounts and a few may specifically help with depression. This is what the research shows:

- The addition of chromium picolinate (200 to 400 micrograms per day) improved depressive symptoms in five dysthymic patients, all of whom had shown inadequate responses to conventional antidepressant medications.[50]

- Selenium in tiny amounts may contribute to normal mood regulation. In a study conducted by the U.S. Department of Agriculture, healthy young men were fed diets that were either high or low in selenium (220 micrograms or 33 micrograms per day respectively). Those on the high-selenium diet described themselves as more clear-headed, elated, agreeable, composed, confident, and energetic than did their selenium-deprived counterparts.[51]

- Zinc levels tend to be low in patients with treatment-resistant depressions, for whom small supplements (25 milligrams per day) are certainly worth a try.[52]

Rather than juggling all the various vitamins and trace minerals that might help relieve your depression, take an all-in-one tablet or combination pack. I suggest also that you photocopy Table 12.2,[53] which lists the vitamins and trace minerals that may affect depression,

**Table 12.2 Dietary Supplements
That May Be Helpful in Depression**

Supplement	Recommended Daily Dosage
Omega-3 fatty acids (EPA plus DHA) At higher levels of EPA and DHA be sure to add:	2–5 g
Vitamin C	2 g
Vitamin E (natural)	800–1,200 IU
Folic acid	1,600 mcg
Thiamine (Vitamin B1)	50 mg
Vitamin B12	500 mcg
Chromium picolinate	200 mcg
Selenium	200 mcg
Zinc	20 mg

and their recommended dosages. Study the labels at the drugstore till you find a good bet. I regularly recommend a comprehensive mix of vitamins and minerals to my patients, and take one myself.

Strategy 7: Attend to Your Sleep

Several decades ago, a depressed woman in Germany, struggling perhaps to get drowsy enough to fall asleep, spent the night riding around on her bicycle. To the amazement of all, she felt better in the morning.

That story is the first report of what has by now been observed many thousands of times—that sleep deprivation has a marked antidepressant effect in many depressed people. Unfortunately, after a night of recovery sleep, the patient generally relapses completely.

How to prevent that relapse has preoccupied depression researchers for years, and we have made some gains. One strategy currently used in Europe is sleep deprivation three nights a week. According to Siegfried Kasper, professor of psychiatry at the University of Vienna, patients get sustained benefits, feel consistently better, and the treatments can be stopped once the response has stabilized.

Sleep deprivation in the second half of the night, for example from 1:00 A.M. onward, can work as well as total sleep deprivation, yet cuts down on daytime fatigue. Still, if a person is going to wake up at one o'clock in the morning, he needs to go to bed in the early evening— or he will walk around exhausted all day.

Another approach combines sleep deprivation with another type of sleep manipulation called phase advancement of sleep. This technique, developed several decades ago by Thomas Wehr at the National Institute of Mental Health, involves moving back the patients' go-to-sleep and wake-up times earlier into the night.[54] Wehr and colleagues succeeded in reversing depressive symptoms by asking depressed patients to go to sleep at 7:00 P.M. and wake up at 1:00 A.M. The major problem is that most people prefer to sleep and wake at conventional times, to have a normal life. For a depressed person, whose social life is already troubled, missing out on the evening is generally too high a price to pay.

Recently, researcher Mathias Berger and colleagues in Germany have cleverly combined sleep deprivation and phase advancement in such as way as to make the treatment both effective and practical.[55] In controlled studies, the researchers deprived patients of sleep for a single night, next asked them to sleep much earlier than normal (from 5:00 P.M. to midnight), and then gradually moved their sleep onset time later, by thirty minutes each day, until the patients were going to sleep at their usual times. In one study of forty seriously depressed people, 70 percent improved following sleep deprivation. A full three-quarters of these patients stayed depression-free after undergoing a phase advancement of sleep, compared with only 40 percent who received a control treatment.

Sleep manipulation can be used in conjunction with medication, since they work synergistically: Both the drug and nondrug treatments are enhanced.

In general, depressed patients do best when they sleep and wake at regular times, and I advise my patients to do so when possible. This advice applies particularly to those depressives who may develop mania or a milder version, known as hypomania. In such people, staying up very late at night, and especially "pulling all-nighters," can fuel their mood instability and make it harder to control with medications.

Strategy #8. Alter Your Environmental Light

A good many people feel low moods during the months of the year when the days are short and dark, a type of depression in which I have specialized for many years. Based on my studies at the National Institute of Mental Health, I estimate that some 6 percent of the U.S. adult population suffer from seasonal affective disorder, a type of depression characterized by overeating, oversleeping, and craving sweets and starches. But the hallmark, the way we can tell this type of depression from the others, is how strongly it responds to environmental light. When people with SAD visit the tropics in the winter, they experience a profound improvement in mood. "It was an overnight cure," patients often say. But then their mood flips back just as quickly when they return. An additional 14 percent of the people in the United States are estimated to suffer from a milder version of SAD known as the winter blues.

In the last few decades, my colleagues and I at the NIMH and elsewhere in the world have worked out a number of ways to treat these winter depressions using bright environmental light:

- Go for outdoor walks on bright winter days, preferably in the morning.

- Bring more lamps into the home and use brighter lightbulbs.

- Trim any hedges around the windows, paint your walls light colors, and use pale carpeting.

- Obtain special light boxes that give off a large amount of bright light safely.[56] Sit in front of your box each day for as long as you need. The requirements vary from person to person, but the usual range is thirty minutes to two hours. The recommended distance is a few feet from the box. It is neither necessary nor desirable to stare at the light, as long as you sit facing it with your eyes open. Some light fixtures are attached to a stand that facilitates enjoying light therapy while working out.

- Get more light into your eyes even before you wake up in the morning. This effect can be achieved either by putting your bedside lamp on a timer set to turn on the lamp about an hour be-

fore you normally wake or by means of a special "dawn sim-
ulator." This latter device plugs into your bedside lamp and
turns the light on gradually in the predawn hours. In controlled
studies, these devices have been shown to help people feel less
groggy on a dreary winter's morning, as well as more energetic
and less depressed all day long.

Other verified treatments include trips to sunny places and devices
that emit negative ions into the room. And of course, all the strategies
that help regular depressions can also be applied to winter depressions. For more information on these topics, the interested reader is
referred to my book *Winter Blues: Seasonal Affective Disorder: What It Is
and How to Overcome It* (Guilford Press, 1998).

Strategy #9: Avoid Alcohol and Beware of Drugs

Over the years I have become extremely impressed with the detrimental effects of alcohol—of even a few glasses of wine or a few
beers—on people with mood disorders. It is difficult to persuade depressed people of the importance of avoiding alcohol for several reasons:

- The immediate effects may be exhilarating or relaxing, which
  can be very welcome to someone who is depressed and anxious.
  The depressive rebound is less obvious. It often occurs only over
  the next two or three days, and is difficult to connect to a small
  amount of alcohol consumed two nights before. This is an instance where a mood log can help illuminate how behavior triggers moods.

- The amounts of alcohol involved may fall well within the
  socially acceptable limits. What the depressed person needs to
  realize is that individuals with mood disorders often have
  heightened sensitivities to alcohol and other drugs that depress
  the nervous system.

- Depressed people often feel socially awkward, so the idea of giving up a drug that eases their social anxiety can be a frightening
  prospect indeed. For a person who does give up this solace, it is

important to find other ways to alleviate social anxiety, for example, by going to a party or business gathering with a friend.

- The many people who use alcoholic beverages to help fall asleep at night should be aware that within a few hours of their falling asleep, the alcohol wears off and they are likely to wake up in the wee hours of the morning. Since waking in the middle of the night is a common symptom of depression, alcohol confuses the clinical picture and aggravates any sleep difficulties that may already be present.

Despite all these reasons that depressed people give for continuing to drink, I have successfully encouraged several of my patients to avoid all alcohol, and invariably they are pleased with the outcome.

All observations made in relation to alcohol apply equally to other "recreational" drugs, including marijuana.

Some prescription drugs have also been associated with depressed mood. These include cholesterol-lowering drugs; Accutane, which is used to combat acne; and the antimalarial drug Lariam. If you are depressed and on prescription medications, it is a good idea to ask your doctor or pharmacist whether your medications may be contributing to your mood problems.

Strategy #10. Try Sensory Stimulation and Acupuncture

Many nonpharmacological ways of reversing depression involve stimulating the senses or manipulating some aspect of bodily function. To some degree, William James was right in suggesting that the way we experience the world through our senses has a profound effect on the way we feel.

Among the sensory nerves that influence our mood are those that pass directly through the skull and into the brain. These are known as the cranial nerves (see page 51). Exposure to light stimulates one pair of these nerves, the optic nerves. Another pair, the olfactory nerves, transmit sensations of smell to the brain. The fragrance of lemons lifts the mood of depressed patients with SAD, albeit to a small degree,[57] and a similar odor causes rats to persevere longer in the "forced swim test" model of depression.[58] It might, therefore, be helpful for depressed people to surround themselves with their favorite fragrances—especially if lemon is one of them.

The Chinese art of acupuncture, well known as a method for relieving pain, now turns out to be useful for depression as well. Classical acupuncture stimulates certain points on the body, some adjacent to major nerve pathways, with thin metallic needles. More recently, electrical currents have been added to "juice" the needles, which many believe makes the treatments more effective.[59] Electrical acupuncture can also be administered with polymer pads instead of needles, placed over traditional treatment points. These points can be located by machine, because they have a different electrical resistance than the surrounding skin.

Three Western-style studies published in the past few years all point to acupuncture as an effective treatment for depression. In one German study of 43 patients with minor depression, 10 sessions of needle acupuncture produced a 61 percent response rate, while only 21 percent of the controls responded—about what you would expect from a placebo.[60] This study shows how important it is to persist, as no difference between the groups could be detected after only 5 needle treatments.

In a second German study, researchers added acupuncture to an antidepressant in 22 patients with major depression, and compared the outcome with that of 24 patients on medication only.[61] Another 24 depressed patients on medications were given a placebo form of acupuncture in which the needles were placed at sites not predicted to be effective for depression. The patients who received medication plus either form of acupuncture did significantly better than those on the medication alone. The results of this study are less clear cut, but could be interpreted as another success for acupuncture, with even "placebo" acupuncture being effective.

Finally, in two studies from Beijing, six weeks of electro-acupuncture proved as effective as amitriptyline (Elavil), a standard antidepressant medication.[62] In the first of these studies, which was relatively small (29 depressed patients) and included a combination (electro-acupuncture plus amitriptyline) group, all the treatments were equally effective. In the second, far larger study (241 inpatient depressives), acupuncture and the amitriptyline were equally helpful at reversing depressive symptoms, with acupuncture producing far fewer side effects. This is a remarkable finding, not only because the patients were extremely depressed at the outset, but because very substantial improvements were noted.

The time is ripe to consider acupuncture very seriously as an alternative treatment for depression. For those out there who are suffering from depression, especially if it has not yielded to conventional approaches or if medication side effects have been intolerable, I would not wait for the results of U.S. studies. I would find a licensed acupuncturist and explore the possibility of this Eastern approach. It is important to persevere as the benefits appear to be cumulative. An acupuncturist I know says that acupuncture works by turning on the body's self-healing power—a very safe and gentle process, and one completely congenial with Western treatments.

Estrogen for Perimenopausal Depression

Hannah was a high school teacher who had never suffered from depression until her early fifties. Then menopause hit—or rather perimenopause, by which I mean that twilight zone between having periods and not having periods. Since she had been a teenager, she could depend on her periods arriving regularly and lasting for three days. Now they were unpredictable, skipping a month or two and then, when they arrived, lasting up to a week or more. In addition, she began to have unpleasant hot flashes. She consulted her gynecologist, who suggested that she hold off on starting hormone replacement therapy because her blood tests indicated that her hormones were not yet at menopausal levels.

At around that time Hannah began to feel less energetic. Teaching classes, always a source of pleasure, now became an unpleasant chore. Even more distressing, Hannah had outbursts of crying. These came on unexpectedly and often at inconvenient moments. For example, she would be standing in the supermarket, wondering what to make for dinner, when tears would start streaming down her face. At her urging, her gynecologist agreed to start her on an estrogen patch—and lo, within three weeks Hannah felt like her old self again.

According to Dr. Peter Schmidt, a researcher in the Behavioral

Endocrinology Branch at the National Institute of Mental Health, perimenopausal patients such as Hannah often respond to estrogen. Although estrogen was suggested for treating depression over a hundred years ago, its antidepressant powers in perimenopausal depression were definitively established only in the past year.

In a placebo-controlled study, Schmidt and colleagues administered an estrogen skin patch (Estraderm, 0.05 mg per day) to thirty-four women with perimenopausal depression.[63] Of these, a whopping 80 percent had a full or partial remission, as compared to 22 percent on placebo patches. These results have since been replicated. Interestingly, improvement in hot flashes, an expected consequence of estrogen replacement, bore no relationship to the antidepressant effects. Estrogen appears to relieve perimenopausal depression quite apart from its effect on hot flashes.

"Gynecologists are tending to use estrogen earlier in their premenopausal patients," says Schmidt, "in order to minimize the bone loss that tends to occur early on. In women with moderate levels of depression," he adds, "estrogen replacement is a real treatment option." This offers a kind of two-fer: treat the depression and prevent bone loss.

Women who become depressed while undergoing perimenopausal changes should consult their gynecologists about the use of estrogen replacement therapy.

When it comes to depression that sets in after menopause, postmenopausal depression, evidence suggests that estrogen replacement is far less helpful. For women in whom estrogen replacement is risky—for example, those with a family history of breast cancer—another option exists. According to Schmidt, phytoestrogens, which are found in soy products, stimulate the estrogen receptors primarily in the brain, less so in the other parts of the body. They can, therefore, reverse perimenopausal depression without influencing the other estrogen-sensitive tissues to the same degree.

Phytoestrogens are found in the fatty parts of soybeans, and women can obtain large amounts of these valuable chemicals by eating roasted soy nuts. The only drawback is that soy nuts are high in calories. On the other hand, soy products such as tofu and soy milk are low in fat, but therefore also have low levels of the phytoestrogens. Happily, extracts of phytoestrogens are now on the market, offering high levels of these chemicals without the fat. Schmidt suggests that women with perimenopausal depression may benefit from one to two tablets (equivalent to about 50 to 100 milligrams of phyto-estrogens per day).

Electrical and Magnetic Solutions—Not to Be Tried at Home

Electroconvulsive therapy (ECT) is one of the oldest effective treatments for severe depression and is still used when other treatments fail. Giving the brain electric shocks through the scalp can reverse serious depressions that do not respond to other treatments. In one review of nine seriously depressed, medication-resistant patients treated at the National Institute of Mental Health, eight experienced a sustained response following a course of ECT.[64] Researchers still don't understand how giving shocks to the scalp can change the pattern of neural transmission and reboot, as it were, the depressed brain. Many people are frightened by the idea of ECT, imagining something like Jack Nicholson's ordeal in the movie *One Flew Over the Cuckoo's Nest.* I'm happy to say that modern anesthetics have made the treatment both safer and less frightening than it used to be. Unfortunately, it still does have side effects, of which memory loss is often the most disturbing. However, memory of the events around the time of the ECT treatment are generally all that is lost, and research has found no evidence that later memories are recorded any less well. The memory loss can be minimized by administering the electric shocks to the right side of the scalp rather than to both sides. Recent research has shown that if the voltage is high enough, such unilateral ECT can be as effective as bilateral ECT.

If I myself had a severe and intractable depression, I would consent to the treatment. Depression itself hinders memory—and it can be a living hell. At a certain point, one has little to lose. At the same time, wouldn't it be nice if there were some other way to trigger the reboot? Researchers are working on that.

One alternative approach, so new that it is still experimental, also applies the therapy directly to the scalp, but the stimulus is magnetic, not electric.[65] During this treatment, known as repetitive transcranial magnetic stimulation (rTMS), the patient remains fully conscious. So far, it appears that rTMS may be modestly effective. Patients complain of headaches, however, as a result of the painful stimulation of the scalp muscles. Researchers hope that this novel form of therapy might be a milder approach to intractable depression, but right now the jury is still out.

The very latest approach involves stimulating yet another cranial nerve, the vagus nerve. In this approach, an electrode is installed under the skin on the left side of the neck, close to where the vagus nerve travels up toward the various centers in the brain. An electrical generator is installed under the skin in the chest and stimulates the electrode at a specific frequency. In an open (uncontrolled) trial of thirty treatment-resistant depressed outpatients, about 45 percent experienced significant relief.[66] Controlled studies are currently in the works.

Vagus nerve stimulation, originally a treatment for seizures, was tried for depression after some seizure patients found it improved their mood. The connection between mood and seizure disorders is worth noting. ECT induces seizures and improves mood, and some of the newer antidepressants first found their way into the formulary as antiseizure medications.

From my long years of treating many patients with depression, I have a single take-home message for those out there who are battling depression: *Never give up.* There are so many treatment strategies, with new ones coming along all the time. If the last one didn't work, the next one may. In my early years as a psychiatrist, I would sometimes think to myself, "This person will never get better." I have learned differently now. Time and time again I have seen the grimmest depressions turned around by using different strategies and by steadfast perseverance on the part of both the doctor and the patient.

Chapter 13

Happiness and Euphoria

I believe that the very purpose of our life is to seek happiness.
—The Dalai Lama[1]

*This is wonderful to be here. Wonderful! I feel like now really
to dive into this ocean of generosity. . . . It's a hailstorm of
kindness. . . . Really I would like to thank everybody who did
the movie . . . and I would like to thank my parents in their
very little village in Italy. They gave me the biggest gift of
poverty. It all goes back to love. They gave me their lives to
show that, despite everything, life is beautiful.*

*This is a terrible mistake because I used up all my English . . .
my body is in tumult because it is a colossal moment of joy. . . .
I would like to be Jupiter and kidnap everybody and lie down
in the firmament making love to everybody . . . . this is a
mountain of snow, so delicate, the suavity and the
kindness, it is something I cannot forget.*
—Actor Roberto Benigni, on receiving two Academy Awards[2]

FROM the Dalai Lama to an actor receiving an Academy Award,
people agree that happiness is vitally important, something to
pursue, nurture, and enjoy. Aristotle referred to happiness as
summum bonum, the supreme good. As with all emotions, however,
happiness, in excess, can cause trouble. As comedian Danny Kaye put
it on receiving an Academy Award, he was so happy that if he got any
happier, they would have to take him to a hospital. Manic euphoria
may, in fact, require such a drastic intervention. Under ordinary

circumstances, however, happiness has important survival value as it encourages us to explore and broaden our universe.[3]

The first century of studies on the emotions dealt mainly with negative feelings, such as depression and anxiety, with fourteen papers on negative emotions published for every one on positive emotions.[4] Although research into positive emotions continues to lag, there are encouraging signs that this trend is changing. Publications in the field of positive emotions increased fourfold during the 1980s.[5] The journal *American Psychologist* published an edition devoted specifically to "positive psychology" in January 2000, thereby starting the millennium off on an upbeat note.[6] A major conference was recently convened specifically to discuss the positive emotions,[7] and an excellent monograph on the topic was published in 1999.[8]

Subjective Well-Being

One way to find out how happy people are is simply to ask them. The resulting measure, *subjective well-being* (SWB), has been surveyed in the United States since 1957 and, more recently, in other countries as well.[9] As a result, we know a great deal about how happy people say they are.

Measurements of SWB correspond quite well to how happy people seem to be as judged by their friends and family members. Using questionnaires such as those shown in Figures 13.1 and 13.2, researchers have collected data from over a million people worldwide to answer questions such as: Is happiness stable over time? How happy are people in general? What are the most important factors associated with the levels of subjective well-being?[10]

The overall scores of well-being have been found to be quite stable in studies conducted over periods ranging from six months to six years.[11] Although there is some consistency in the level of happiness that most people report over time, for some people, happiness levels fluctuate considerably.

Survey Form

Below are five statements that you may agree or disagree with. Using the 1–7 scale below, indicate your agreement with each item by placing the appropriate number on the line preceding that item. Please be open and honest in your responding.

7 Strongly agree

6 Agree

5 Slightly agree

4 Neither agree nor disagree

3 Slightly disagree

2 Disagree

1 Strongly disagree

_____ In most ways my life is close to my ideal.

_____ The conditions of my life are excellent.

_____ I am satisfied with my life.

_____ So far I have gotten the important things I want in life.

_____ If I could live my life over, I would change almost nothing.

Add up the 5 subtotals to obtain your overall score for subjective well-being.

35–31   Extremely satisfied

26–30   Satisfied

21–25   Slightly satisfied

20   Neutral

15–19   Slightly dissatisfied

10–14   Dissatisfied

5–9   Extremely dissatisfied

Figure 13.1 Measuring Happiness[12]

Quiz question: After you have noted which of the faces applies most closely to you, see if you can estimate what percentage of the general U.S. population picks each of the above faces. For the answer, see Figure 13.3.

*Figure 13.2 Which of these faces represents
the way you feel about your life as a whole?*

How Happy Are We?

Would you say that most people in our country are more happy or unhappy? The answer: They are surprisingly happy. Playwrights and novelists throughout the ages have portrayed the human condition as tragic, and no less an expert than Freud observed that after neurosis has been cured, what remains is ordinary human misery. Modern surveys suggest that many people underestimate other people's level of happiness. For example, in one survey of Minnesotans, more than two-thirds of the respondents rated their capacity for happiness as falling within the upper 35 percent of people of their age and gender.[13]

In a sample of Detroit residents, two-thirds of all people rated themselves at the upper two levels of happiness, 93 percent of people rated themselves as more happy than unhappy, and only 3 percent of people rated themselves on the unhappy side of the scale.[14]

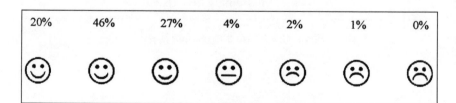

Figure 13.3 The answer to the quiz questions.

Another study conducted on about 1,000 American adults in 1998 asked, "Who of the following people do you think is the happiest?" The people were asked to choose from among Oprah Winfrey, Bill Gates, the Pope, Chelsea Clinton, and "yourself." Almost half of the responders (49 percent) chose themselves as the happiest, with Oprah Winfrey (23 percent), the Pope (12 percent), Bill Gates (12 percent), and Chelsea Clinton (3 percent) lagging far behind.[15]

As you might expect, some people, such as recently imprisoned inmates and students living in politically repressive regimes, are far less happy than free citizens living in the United States. Absent such circumstances, however, most people in developed countries tend toward being far happier than one might predict.

Who Is the Happiest of Us All?

Given that most people tend to be happy, who is the happiest? Where happiness is concerned, is it a man's world? Is race important? Do we become less happy as we age? What about beauty, intelligence, and education? How important are all of these factors in determining happiness? The answer, quite simply, is much less than we would expect.

Even though women are twice as likely as men to develop depression, a meta-analysis of 146 studies found almost no difference in the levels of subjective well-being of women and men.[16] One possible explanation for this paradox is that women may experience more powerful positive and negative emotions, and these opposite experiences may cancel each other out when averages are calculated. Two studies supporting this theory found that women were more likely than men to report extreme levels of happiness and SWB.[17]

Poets have long lamented the sorrows of aging. Gerard Manley Hopkins wrote of "age and age's evils, winding sheets, tombs and worms and tumbling to decay," while William Butler Yeats asked plaintively, "O who could have foretold that the heart grows old?" In a youth-oriented culture such as ours, many simply assume that aging is associated with unhappiness. Not so, according to data from almost 170,000 people from sixteen nations, surveyed between 1980 and 1986. The percentage of people declaring that they were satisfied with life remained steady at about 80 percent for each decade from 15 to over 65 years of age.[18]

While African-Americans do report slightly lower levels of happiness than Caucasians, they also seem slightly less vulnerable to depression.[19] Even though discrimination continues to be a problem for many of them, most succeed in maintaining their good spirits by focusing on their areas of excellence, comparing themselves within their group, and attributing their problems to factors over which they have no control, such as prejudice.[20]

Other factors that contribute less to reported levels of happiness than one might expect are attractiveness, intelligence, education, and objective levels of health.[21] Although education does bear a small relationship to SWB, this effect is due entirely to the improved income and social status that go along with it.[22]

The relationship between health and happiness is a curious one. When people are asked to rate the importance of various aspects of their lives, they rate good health right at the top of the list; yet objective levels of health, such as doctors' visits and hospitalization, correlate rather poorly with levels of happiness.[23] We can explain this paradox to some extent by the stronger relationship between happiness and *subjectively perceived* levels of health.[24] In other words, even though unhappy people might be as healthy as happy ones, they may regard themselves as less so.

In response to physical setbacks, the worst declines in levels of happiness are short-lived. In one widely cited study of individuals with spinal cord injuries, the researchers found them to be "not nearly as unhappy as might be expected."[25] On the other hand, these people do report lower SWB levels (1 point less than the controls on a 6-point scale) even some time after their injuries. In another study, quadriplegics and paraplegics were found to have adapted to their condition within two months of their spinal cord injuries.[26] Although these unfortunate individuals are understandably sad and afraid a week after the injury, by the eighth week, they report mostly positive emotions.

In summary, gender, race, age, attractiveness, education, social status, and health contribute less than one might expect to subjective reports of happiness. But what about that crucial element that so many of us crave? What about money?

Can Happiness Be Bought?

If you consider the millions of people who tune in their television sets every week to find out who will be America's next millionaire or who gazed at the women willing to marry a stranger simply because he was allegedly a millionaire, you might reasonably conclude that the key to happiness is simple—money, and lots of it. Become a millionaire. People buy books about the millionaire next door, analyze the mind of a millionaire, and collectively spend hundreds of millions of dollars for lottery tickets to try to become a millionaire.

Surveys of Americans find high hopes for wealth. When asked how satisfied they are with thirteen aspects of their lives, such as friends, housing, and schooling, Americans express the least satisfaction with the amount of money they have to live on.[27] When asked what would improve the quality of their lives, the most frequent response to a University of Michigan national survey was "more money."[28] In a 1990 Gallup poll, four out of five people earning more than $75,000 per year reported that they wanted to be rich.[29] Most people believe that more money will make them happier.[30]

In contrast to the promises that accompany wealth, television game shows, and images of ecstatic people receiving huge checks from sweepstakes, we are also raised with cautionary tales. In *The Great Gatsby*, the hero travels the world to find his fortune and comes back home to impress Daisy, the woman he loved and lost. He lives in a mansion, throws great parties, and even manages to recapture Daisy's love with his glittering possessions. Yet he meets a tragic end, and only three people show up at his funeral. Likewise, in *A Christmas Carol*, the wealthy Scrooge is miserly and miserable until four ghosts shock him into realizing the materialistic error of his ways.

So, whom should we believe, the game show hosts or the great novelists? How much does science tell us about whether happiness can be had at a price? Quite a bit, it turns out. Studies find that lottery winners are significantly happier only briefly after winning the lottery.[31] Indeed, winning the lottery can even sow unhappiness. In one British study, for example, 70 percent of lottery winners gave up their jobs, thereby losing the satisfaction and companionship of the workplace. Their lives were disrupted by friends and relatives requesting loans.[32] Contrary to popular belief, winning the lottery is not a sure path to happiness.

Studies comparing levels of happiness and income for the U.S. population as a whole reach similar conclusions. From the mid 1950s to the late 1990s, the after-tax, inflation-adjusted income of the average American more than doubled, from $8,000 to $20,000 per year. We are able to afford many more conveniences than we were a half-century ago. Yet overall levels of happiness have not shown a corresponding increase.[33] In fact, the proportion of the population reporting themselves as "very happy" has actually declined from 35 percent to 33 percent. As David Myers, professor of psychology at Hope University and author of *The Pursuit of Happiness*, points out, "We are twice as rich and no happier."

Even multimillionaires are not on average much happier than ordinary Americans, according to one survey of 49 out of the 100 wealthiest Americans listed in *Forbes* magazine.[34] Most of those surveyed agreed that money could increase or decrease levels of happiness depending on how it is used. And like Ebenezer Scrooge, some of these fabulously rich people were downright miserable.

How can one explain the disconnect between the promise of happiness that accompanies dreams of wealth and the disappointing reality? As we acquire new things, we shift our expectations so that what seemed like a fortune to us before now seems not quite enough. As one famous millionaire put it, "How much money is enough? Just a little bit more." Observing how greater wealth generates higher expectations, researchers refer to the "hedonic treadmill" theory, which compares the pursuit of happiness to a person on a treadmill, who has to keep working just to stay in the same place.[35]

There is evidence that materialistic goals are on the rise in this country and that they may actually be contributing to the declining levels of happiness. According to a survey of over 200,000 students entering college in the last three decades of the twentieth century, the proportion of those who considered it "very important or essential" that they become "very well off" rose from 39 percent to 74 percent. In fact, in the latter years of the study this goal was ranked highest in importance. Over the same period of time, the importance of developing a meaningful philosophy of life declined in an almost mirror image fashion from about 70 percent to about 40 percent.[36] Clearly materialism is on the rise among our young people. According to researcher Ed Diener, professor of psychology at the University of Illinois in Champaign, college students who say they value money more than love are less happy than those who respond to the contrary.

Although wealth does not produce happiness in developed countries, in the slums of Calcutta, where small amounts of money can make the difference between a full belly and starvation, those with money are significantly happier than those without.[37] Studies from various countries find the higher the country's per capita income, the greater the average level of SWB.

The Happiness Set Point

Happiness depends, as Nature shows,
less on exterior things than most suppose.
—William Cowper[38]

One of my favorite *New Yorker* cartoons has a grumpy-looking rich man, standing in the garden in front of his mansion, confiding to a friend that he could cry when he thinks of the years he wasted accumulating money only to learn that his cheerful disposition is genetic. The cartoon was inspired by recent research showing that life events have only small, transient effects on well-being. One illustration of this principle cropped up in a study of mood conducted by psychologist Randy Larsen. One of the people in Larsen's study who was receiving chemotherapy treatments for cancer learned that his cancer was in remission. As you might expect, his mood took a marked upturn, but within two days it returned to his baseline level.[39]

In one longitudinal study, researchers found that most life events influenced mood for no longer than three months.[40] According to one estimate, all the measurable external circumstances of a person's life added together account for only about 15 percent of SWB.[41]

Observations such as these have led to the Set Point Theory of happiness, which holds that people have a baseline level of happiness to which they tend to return regardless of what happens in their lives.

The idea of a set point for happiness is discouraging as it suggests that we're stuck at a certain level of happiness and there is nothing we can do to become happier. I disagree with this view, as does happiness expert Ed Diener. "There may be a set point for weight," Diener notes, "but if you surround yourself with sweet things, common sense dictates that you are going to gain weight." In a similar vein, recent research suggests that you can train yourself to be happier, regardless of your happiness set point.

Arguing against the idea of a rigidly determined set point for happiness is the observation that people do not adapt rapidly to some types of unfortunate life circumstances. Widows, for example, report a decline in happiness for an average of two to three years after the death of their spouses.[42] Likewise, long-term unemployment can cause a long-term decline in happiness. People with post-traumatic stress disorder clearly show that some events leave indelible imprints on people that prevent them from enjoying their lives. But for most people, the impact of events on their level of happiness is relatively transient. How can that be? To answer this question, researchers have looked to the genetics of happiness.

The Genetics of Happiness: The "Joy Juice Quotient"

Different people seem to have different levels of what happiness researchers have referred to as "joy juice." Some people, such as Mother Teresa, seem always to be smiling, upbeat, and energetic despite living in poverty. Others, such as Woody Allen, to judge by his public persona, seem always to be kvetching and whining despite fame, fortune, and the attention of beautiful women. It is hard to escape the conclusion that there must be something genetic behind the levels of joy juice that these people—and all people—experience in their daily lives.

The strongest evidence of a genetic basis for happiness comes from twin studies. Using data from the Minnesota Twin Registry, researchers David Lykken and Auke Tellegen compared the patterns of subjective well-being (SWB) in identical and fraternal twins who were reared together with those of twins who were adopted and reared separately. They found a 0.5 correlation between the same individuals tested at age 20 and at age 30. Of the portion of SWB that remained stable over that decade, the researchers attributed 80 percent to genetic factors.[43] Based on this study and other analyses, researchers have estimated that approximately 40 to 55 percent of SWB can be explained by genes.

Data such as those of Lykken and Tellegen might easily discourage people who are short in the joy juice department. Taking their own findings to an extreme conclusion, the researchers suggested, "It may be that trying to be happier is as futile as trying to be taller, and therefore counterproductive."

In my opinion, this is a very misleading statement. First, it is important to recognize that in the study, the trait of happiness was not all that stable over the decade between measurements. If you measure a person's height at age 20 and again at age 30, you would not find a correlation of 0.5 (as was the case for happiness in the study), but more like a correlation of 1.0. In other words, our height over a decade would remain much steadier than our level of happiness. There were major changes in the study subjects' levels of happiness between the ages 20 and 30, that must have been caused by something other than their genes.

In addition, other twin studies have not shown genetics to play as great a role in determining happiness as that of Lykken and Tellegen. Of particular interest are the results of two studies in older people, a Danish twin study and one conducted in older adults. In both of these studies, the tendency for happiness to be inherited was considerably lower than in the Minnesota twin studies.[44]

How can we explain these differences among the studies? First, it is likely that where the twins' environments were very similar, they may have accounted less for the differences between the individuals. The twins from Minnesota, even those reared apart, might have shared generally more similar environments than the subjects in the other studies. Second, environmental influences may play an increasingly important role over the course of a person's lifespan, accounting for their greater influence in the study of older subjects.

In twin studies, researchers have developed models for parsing out the influences exerted by the genetic factors and the environmental factors, which may be shared by siblings or unique to the individuals. Using such models, Lykken and Tellegen found that those environmental influences that siblings share account for a very low proportion of happiness. What could *not* be explained by genetics—a full 60 percent of happiness—could be attributed only to the unique experiences that occur in the lives of individuals. Other genetic researchers have reached similar conclusions.

Genetic factors aside, it is the unique experiences to which we are exposed and what we make of those experiences that determine our overall level of happiness.

The Year of Trading Dangerously: The Relationship Between Pleasure and Happiness

Martin, the chief operating officer of a wholesale poultry business, had done well for himself. Respected by his coworkers, he had amassed a few hundred thousand dollars and owned several properties. To anyone who might have asked him at the time, he would have replied that he was happy. But that was to change when he discovered the existence of online stock trading.

Deciding that he deserved to give himself a treat and spice up his life a little, Martin put aside $25,000 in an account to begin his new career as a trader, for which he had no training. But other people without training seemed to be making tons of money on the stock market. "Am I not entitled to the same opportunity to get rich quickly?" Martin asked.

His first few trades were successful and soon he had doubled his money. His days became thrilling as he congratulated himself on each clever trade he made and imagined a future of wealth and easy living. "Why should I bust my tail standing around in a stinky chicken house when I can make money by sitting in front of my computer screen and trading?" he wondered. He put all of his money into his trading account, rigged up two computer monitors, and began to trade during work, which he now viewed mostly as a distraction from his greatest source of pleasure.

Sadly these halcyon days were not to last. By now Martin was trading on margin, investing money that he did not have in the hopes of amplifying his gains. A few bad trades triggered his broker to place a margin call and he had to sell stock to cover his losses. He began to panic. Had he lost his touch? Desperate to recapture his past victories, he shifted rapidly from stock to stock, unable to wait out the ordinary vicissitudes of the market. His neglect of his job and contemptuous attitude caused him to be fired. Out of work, down to his last $10,000, and on the brink of suicide, he sought out a therapist.

After years of therapy and attending Debtors Anonymous meetings, Martin has now rebuilt his life. Employed once again, he is slowly pulling himself out of debt and is able to provide for his family again. He has stopped all trading in stocks, and although he misses the thrill of the game, he is grateful each day for life's simple pleasures—time with his wife and children, the reward of a job well done, and the quiet pleasures of playing golf and hanging out with friends. He quotes T. S. Eliot's famous words that the end of exploring is to arrive back at the beginning and know it for the first time.

I tell this story to illustrate the difference between pleasure and happiness. Pleasure is a transient experience associated with a specific reward. Happiness is a more enduring state related to an overall assessment of one's life. Happy people experience pleasure in their everyday lives. Pleasures, on the other hand, do not lead to happiness if they are inconsistent with, or adverse to, a person's larger goals. In Martin's case, these larger goals were being engaged in a meaningful occupation and enjoying a stable marriage and family life. His attempt to accomplish this through his online trading activities was poorly conceived and, in the end, disastrous.

Subjective well-being, though easy to study in humans, cannot be determined in animals. One might even question whether the concept of happiness is applicable to animals since it implies a level of conscious reflection. On the other hand, we can certainly tell when an animal is experiencing pleasure, as any owner of a dog or cat will readily confirm. For this reason, what we know about positive emotions in animals refers primarily to displays of pleasure or responses to rewards, rather than happiness.

A Cook's Tour of the Pleasure Centers

We can now see, thanks to imaging techniques, which parts of the brain light up when we experience pleasure. Cocaine addicts who are asked to fantasize about smoking crack show increased activity in the *nucleus accumbens*, a structure buried beneath the cerebral cortex and part of the limbic system. (For a picture, see page 44.)[45] The nucleus accumbens, an extension of the amygdala, is a sort of central pleasure processor, reinforcing actions that reduce fear and increase pleasure.[46] In other words, it translates emotions into action.

A second brain center of importance for happiness is the *left prefrontal cortex* (PFC), which becomes active in anticipation of pleasure. (For a discussion of the PFC, see chapter 3.) It tends to move you toward your goal. Happier people tend to have greater left over right PFC dominance than less happy people.

Even in infants, neuroscientist Richard Davidson has found that contented infants have greater left PFC activity than fussy, unhappy infants. It may be possible to increase left PFC dominance. In fact, the person with by far the greatest left-sided dominance that Davidson has studied so far is a Buddhist monk who spent many years practicing the art of meditation.

A third pleasure center, known as the reward or self-stimulation system and situated in the lateral part of the hypothalamus, has been a source of fascination to researchers ever since it was described by James Olds and Peter Milner almost half a century ago.[47] Rats will press a lever 3,000 times an hour to give themselves short bursts of electrical stimulation to this brain region.

If a rat is stimulated electrically in this area and food is available, it will eat voraciously. If given access to a willing partner, it will copulate with gusto.[48] And if you teach it to give itself brief bursts of stimulation (say by pressing a lever), it will ignore both sex and food and turn its attention entirely toward doing whatever is necessary to get more stimulation.

One curious thing is that animals do not appear to become bored or tired of stimulating this center, but neither does the exercise appear to satisfy them the way most pleasurable activities do. Normally, after animals eat, they become full; after they have sex, they are satisfied, at least for a while. They then abstain from these activities until they have had a chance to recover. Not so with the self-stimulation of this reward system. Given the chance, a rat will go on pushing the lever that stimulates this area all day and all night.[49] These observations led researchers to conclude that the self-stimulation center is not responsible for the integrated experience of pleasure. Instead, it looks like a seeking center, involved more in pursuing pleasure than in registering satisfaction.[50]

The last brain center we will consider, somewhat controversial as a mediator of pleasure, is the amygdala, which is responsible mostly for unpleasant emotions such as fear and rage. Yet Johns Hopkins neuroscientist Michaela Gallagher and colleagues have recently found that monkeys with damage to the amydgala are unable to learn the reward values of certain cues, such as apples or raisins.[51] Other research also finds increases in amygdala firing in monkeys when they take sips of something tasty such as fruit juice.[52]

Although I refer to all of these regions as "pleasure centers," they are better understood as part of circuits or neural networks involved in the experience of pleasure.[53] Modern neuroscientists recognize that such "centers" are intricately connected with other parts of the brain, all of which are necessary for experiencing any emotion.

The Pleasure Centers at Work at a Restaurant

To get a picture of how the major pleasure centers work together, imagine a trip to a favorite restaurant. Some friends are visiting from out of town and you have told them about Antoine's, your favorite French restaurant. When you call ahead of time to make reservations, your left prefrontal cortex already imagines the delicious canapés, succulent entrées, and foamy dessert soufflés that are the specialties of the house. Your PFC signals wildly to your nucleus accumbens, which remembers the pleasures associated with your earlier trips to Antoine's, and your mouth waters.

On the evening in question, you and your friends set off for the country inn. The sun is setting and the path leading toward the thatched croft house is flanked by mushroom lights. As you approach the front door, the fragrant smells of Antoine's cooking waft into your nostrils, sending signals to your brain that set your prefrontal cortex and your nucleus accumbens atwitter. Your lateral hypothalamus wheels into gear, putting you in search mode. Where is your table, where is your waiter, where is the menu that spells out the familiar delights? The pleasure centers consult avidly like businessmen eager to clinch a deal.

To stave off your hunger, the waiter passes around a tray of canapés while he takes the order for drinks. Your nucleus accumbens works furiously, evaluating your metabolic status (you are so hungry you could eat a horse), and your caloric and nutrient needs (four courses at least). Your PFC is deluged with information about your blood sugar, your fat stores, your protein needs, and your body temperature, all of which help determine your order. Your lateral hypothalamus keeps firing, seeking more pleasurable stimuli. Your hippocampus reminds you which waiter had the tray of canapés. Your cortex directs you to look around and wonder, "Where on earth has he gone with the snacks?"

He returns with a glass of grape juice (you are the designated driver), the sight of which sends signals to your amygdala, and as the sweet nectar glides over your tongue, the signals keep coming. The cells in your PFC, recognizing the familiar taste of grape juice, fire off approvingly to your nucleus accumbens.[54] Now, had the waiter given you prune juice, different cells in your PFC would have fired instead. Your cortex would then relay this information to your nucleus accumbens, which would weigh how much pleasure it got from prune juice versus grape juice, and signal back to your cortex, which would decide whether the prune juice was okay or should be sent back to the bar.

When the food finally arrives, all the major pleasure centers set about enjoying it. The left PFC anticipates each mouthful and directs you to mix the different foods on your plate in just the right proportions. The lateral hypothalamus, in active search mode, urges you on to complete course after course. The nucleus accumbens stays online, assessing your pleasure and telling you how to enhance it. "Waiter, more gravy, please! Also, another basket of rolls, the ones with the raisins!" All these instructions are engineered by your cortex, which is updated constantly by your nucleus accumbens as to how good it all is.

And so the cycle continues, each pleasurable stimulus reinforcing the next through activation of these interconnected centers. Hors d'oeuvres whet your appetite for salad, which paves the way for the main course, which urges you to conclude with dessert and coffee. Slowly, you become full and satisfied. Your PFC now goes offline, its job done for the present. When you leave the restaurant, the fragrant aromas and the sight of the dessert cart, which captivated your attention so entirely when you entered the restaurant, have by now lost their appeal.

In the quest for pleasure, there are two fundamental phases, pursuit and enjoyment. First we hunt or gather, then we eat and feel satisfied. If you think of anything you have ever wanted or pursued, and obtained or achieved, you will easily relate to these two fundamental phases. Although we are still in the early stages of understanding the neural basis for pleasure, this area of research promises better strategies for helping people lead happier lives.

Curious Facts About Pleasure

Before considering the chemistry of pleasure, here are a few curious facts that science has revealed about this most delightful of emotions. First, pleasure can be unconsciously experienced. Second, some pleasures are hardwired into our nervous systems. Finally, researchers can separate pleasurable memories and anticipation from the current experience of pleasure. Let us consider each of these curious facts in turn.

Unconscious Pleasure

As I mentioned in chapter 2, we may be unconscious of our emotions, including pleasure, yet our emotions may nevertheless drive our actions. As we discussed earlier, studies of cocaine addicts revealed that the subjects pressed a lever to give themselves hits of a very dilute cocaine solution more often than a control saline solution, even though they were not consciously aware that the dilute solution included any cocaine.

Core Pleasure

Certain pleasures are so hardwired biologically that they are universally experienced from the earliest age. If you put sugar water in the mouth of a three-week-old infant, the baby's lips will widen and his cheeks and brow will relax, which any empathic parent will recognize as signs of blissful serenity.[55] Put salty water in the mouth of that same infant, though, and you will see a very different picture—puckered lips and wrinkled cheeks and brow, which are unmistakable evidence of disgust. Laboratory rats respond similarly. As Kent Berridge, professor of psychology at the University of Michigan in Ann Arbor, puts it: "Sweet tastes elicit a hedonic pattern of reactions such as tongue protrusions—sort of a pattern of licking of the lips—paw licking and related movements. Bitter tastes elicit an aversive pattern of different expressions such as gapes, headshakes and frantic wiping of the mouth."[56]

Pleasure Past, Present, and Future

Let's say that there is something you enjoy—ice cream, for example. You have memories of enjoying it in the past. When you go to buy ice cream, you anticipate the pleasure of eating it. And when you actually eat it, you enjoy it in the present. All those elements combine in your mind into one category—the pleasure of eating ice cream. But researchers have been able to separate these experiences. Although this may seem like merely an academic exercise, it turns out that teasing these aspects of pleasure apart—past, present, and future—is useful.

If you had a taste of the same ice cream each day for a week, how much do you predict you would enjoy it by week's end, as compared with day one? Investigating this question, Daniel Kahnemann, professor of psychology at Princeton, and colleagues found that although the study subjects correctly predicted that they would like the ice cream less after a week than they did initially, they overestimated by a large margin how much their enjoyment would drop off.[57] Apparently even the same flavor of ice cream stays delicious over time to a greater degree than you would imagine.

In a similar study, this research group gave people a spoonful of somewhat unpleasant yogurt, then asked how much they would like to eat a full helping of it the following morning and at the end of a week during which they had eaten it every day. Again, their predictions were wrong. They underestimated how unpleasant they would find their first full helping of yogurt as judged by the taste of a single spoonful. More surprisingly, they overestimated how unpleasant the yogurt would be after a week of eating it every day.[58] Apparently they acquired more of a taste for the unpleasant yogurt than they would have predicted.

These findings are in line with "the mere exposure effect," according to which familiarity is comforting. *Over time, pleasant things do not become as boring as you might think, while unpleasant things become more tolerable.*

The distinction between wanting (pleasure anticipated) and liking (pleasure experienced) has been extended into animal studies, where scientists are unraveling the different neurochemical bases for these separate experiences.

The Chemistry of Pleasure

Pleasure signals, like all nerve signals, involve neurotransmitters. We have already encountered the most important chemicals that mediate pleasure: dopamine, a mainstay of the pleasure system; norepinephrine, responsible for alertness and arousal; serotonin, involved in calming and soothing; and endorphins, which abolish pain and give us warm, fuzzy feelings. We have already considered serotonin and norepinephrine in chapters 11 and 12. Now let's turn our attention to two vitally important joy juices: dopamine and the endorphins.

Dopamine: A Chemical Worth Working For

In the realm of the pleasure neurotransmitters, dopamine is king. Rats and monkeys are willing to push levers time and again for a little squirt of this precious chemical; drug addicts will kill or die for it. The nucleus accumbens, that major pleasure center, is rich with neurons packed with dopamine and ready, under the right circumstances, to release their sweet messages.

In monkeys, individual dopamine cells will respond to a reward, such as an apple or raisin, says neuroscientist Wolfram Schultz from the University of Fribourg in Switzerland. After Schultz has trained a monkey, the animal's dopamine neurons will fire even when it just sees the reward, in anticipation of eating it. The amount of firing depends on the nature of the reward—more for a fresh raisin than a dry one, more for a fresh apple than a fresh raisin, and so on. Schultz finds neurons that register the reward value of different objects.

The brain allocates a greater number of neuronal responses for *predicting* a reward than for actually obtaining it, no doubt because of the evolutionary importance of anticipating rewards.[59] Anticipatory brain systems help us locate and obtain sources of pleasure, such as food or sex, that enhance our chance of surviving and passing on our genes. For example, foreplay releases more dopamine than the orgasm itself.[60] That may be why we talk more about pursuing happiness than enjoying it. From an evolutionary point of view, pursuit may be more important than enjoyment.

An unpredicted reward will generate a more powerful signal in the dopamine neurons than will a predicted one, which may explain why unexpected pleasures are often the most enjoyable. If a reward is expected but not forthcoming, a dopamine cell gives off an electrical signal in a direction opposite to what occurs following a reward. In other words, you can measure disappointment at the very level of the cell itself. The discrepancy between what you predict and what you experience is the basis for learning, as an animal (or human) adjusts expectations so that they are more in line with what the world has to offer.

One strategy for finding happiness is to have low or, at least, reasonable expectations. Then the world will be full of unexpected pleasures. Unrealistically high expectations, on the other hand, are a formula for repeated disappointments.

DOPAMINE AND ADDICTION
Jerri first tried crack at one of the fashionable clubs in Washington, D.C., where the disk jockey spins hard rock into the early hours of the morning under flashing strobe lights and a cloud of smoke. It seemed like a chic thing, that first time, but she was unprepared for the intensity of the experience—a flood of pleasure such as she had never experienced before, nor has she since.

Jerri divides her life into two—before and after that first hit of crack. From that time on, it seemed like all her waking hours were directed toward recapturing that first great high. She came closest to it when the night was young. "There is nothing like the first high of the evening," she says. "I have often spent the rest of the night chasing it, trying to find it, but never quite getting there again."

The first crack pipe was offered to Jerri without charge, but later she discovered that pushers do business by hooking people on drugs that they will then be willing to pay for, no matter what it takes to get the money. And Jerri did. She used up all her savings, sold her possessions, and had to move back in with her parents. Her most shameful experience was the night she let a man have sex with her in exchange for a few rocks of crack. "That was my low point," she said. "The next morning I realized I had to do something about it or I would die. Thank God I didn't get AIDS."

Jerry went into a detoxification program and has since attended Narcotics Anonymous. She has been off cocaine for several years now, but still craves it from time to time. "I expect I always will," she says. Sometimes she has "using dreams," in which she imagines she is smoking crack again, and wakes up in a cold sweat with her heart pounding. But after she reorients herself, she feels grateful that she is still clean and sober. She avoids the people, places, and things that trigger these cravings. Researchers have found permanent brain changes after chronic cocaine use, which may explain the enduring cravings, which outlast the acute phase of drug withdrawal.[61]

Slowly Jerri has put her life back together again and is determined never to confuse the intense transient pleasure of manipulating her dopamine system with the happiness that comes from a life of spiritual fulfillment, steady relationships, pride of accomplishment, and ordinary pleasures.

Many drugs of abuse work through the dopamine system. These drugs, such as cocaine, "speed" (methamphetamine), and "angel dust" (phencyclidine) cause rats to run around in their cages pressing levers just for the sound of it.[62] Too much of any of these drugs will make the animals manic and distrustful of other rats.

An endogenous excess of dopamine in humans is believed to be responsible for many of the symptoms of mania, a condition that can start slowly, but rapidly zoom out of control. In the early stages, a manic person typically feels exuberant.[63] Everything seems fun and funny. Words and situations strike him as interesting or peculiar. He sees the world in a new way. One manic person marveled for the first time at the beauty and straightness of the white lines painted down the middle of the road, though he had driven that same road thousands of times. Another commented on the vividness of ordinary flowers, which seemed to glow like neon lights.

At this point, the manic person is playful, finding rhymes and puns in everyday conversation and interesting new meanings to things. One wealthy manic patient of mine invented a new game with his servants. They had to guess certain things or answer certain questions to score points that qualified them for prizes. The manic needs less sleep and has boundless energy. Life is a delight. One manic I treated sang out, "I'm happy, happy, H-A-P-P-Y," and the huge smile on her face left no doubt that she was.

Happy manics, like euphoric cocaine addicts, are hard to treat because they don't want to give up their exuberance, and often object to the very idea of it. Indeed, more than one of my manic patients has suggested that I was the one who needed treatment. "Look at you all," one young lady commented to a group of doctors, of which I was one, sitting around in white coats with concerned looks on our faces. "You are a bunch of dead ducks! And you say I'm the one who needs treatment."

Mania can be a time of intense creativity. But in a manic state there is too little organization to capitalize on the brainstorms. One of my manic patients, an accountant's clerk, insisted that he would soon be a millionaire as a result of his latest discovery—a novel bikini that would surely set a new fashion in beachwear. When his mania passed over, he realized that there was nothing special about the design. It only seemed that way in his manic state.

Like drug addicts, manics can be very skillful at manipulating people so as to maintain their state of euphoria. But like a cocaine-induced euphoria, mania cannot be sustained indefinitely. It either escalates out of control or shifts into a crashing depression. Sometimes it does both.

When mania escalates, it is no longer fun. Things begin to move too quickly. Sleep becomes impossible and energy reaches frenetic heights. Instead of euphoria, the person now experiences irritability and a painful state that can feel like depression. It is now no longer possible to interact reasonably with other people, who are perceived as obstacles and irritants and often treated as such. Everybody else seems to be moving too slowly, and angry outbursts are common.

As the mania escalates further, the person becomes even more out of contact with reality. One young manic man I treated, believing himself to be invincible, walked down the midline of a busy highway with cars whizzing by on either side until the police finally stopped him. In another episode, he picked up a hitchhiker in the middle of the night and drove him to one of the most dangerous areas of the city. Once the hitchhiker had reached his destination, he ordered my patient to strip naked; stole his car, his clothes, and all his possessions; and left him naked to fend for himself in a strange and dangerous neighborhood on a cold winter night.

Manic delusions and hallucinations are often grandiose. One manic I encountered insisted that like Superman, she had X-ray vision. Others, believing themselves to be fabulously wealthy, may spend their entire life savings. A manic may believe he is some major political or religious figure. In Jerusalem the police are quite familiar with people who walk into the streets wrapped up in sheets, behaving as though they were biblical figures. The psychosis of advanced mania can also take on a paranoid flavor. A person might believe that the CIA is out to get him or that people are plotting to harm him because he is so important or knows too much. Fortunately many drugs are now available for treating and preventing mania.

Once the mania subsides, it may give way to depression—and often the higher the mania, the lower the depression. It is as though all the spare dopamine reserves have been used up, leaving the person depleted of dopamine. As one researcher put it, "a brain without dopamine is like a boat without a sail."[64]

A lack of dopamine for any reason may lead to depression in both humans and animals, who become sluggish and apathetic. People with Parkinson's disease, a condition in which the dopamine cells are destroyed, often become depressed. The drug bupropion (Wellbutrin or Xyban) boosts dopamine transmission, which may be one reason why it is an effective antidepressant. The same drug can also help people quit smoking cigarettes. (Nicotine also works via the dopamine system.)

Endorphins: Warm Fuzzy Chemicals With a Backlash

There is strong scientific support for the role of the opiates in experiencing pleasure.[65] Endorphins are important for feelings of love and attachment, and even for the grooming behavior between monkeys. They are the chemicals that give the warm, fuzzy feelings that go along with cuddling and comforting touch.

Anyone who enjoys sweets will know the comfort associated with eating cake or candy. It turns out that sweet foods cause opiates to be released into the brain.[66] Sweet syrups are a traditional way of comforting babies in distress, and now scientists have shown that putting sugar water into the mouths of babies makes them less sensitive to pain and less inclined to cry.[67]

Opiates are also important for sexual pleasure. If a rat is allowed to copulate, he will subsequently choose the place where he has had sex over another place, presumably in the hope of getting lucky again. But if, after copulation, the rat is given an opiate blocker, the site of his former romantic encounter will lose all its charm.[68] He will not choose the site over another, suggesting that the pleasure of anticipating sex apparently depends on opiate stimulation.

The easy pleasures associated with the opiate system make the opiate drugs major candidates for abuse. Odysseus in his travels encountered the island of the lotus-eaters. Once his men had eaten from the lotus, they had no wish to do anything but remain there in a dream-like state and continue to eat the flower. They lost all will to find their native land again. Perhaps Homer was inspired by observations that those who partake of the opium poppy are drawn into a state of blissful indifference to the outside world and lose all motivation. Even long-held ambitions that were once vigorously pursued feel meaningless under the power of the poppy. For this reason, the opiate drugs are among the most widely abused and strongly controlled substances throughout the developed world.

There is some evidence that in response to drinking alcohol, alcoholics may release endorphins (endogenous opiates) into the brain to a greater extent than nonalcoholics. This may explain why some people are more susceptible than others to alcohol addiction. One medical strategy for treating alcoholism, the use of a drug that blocks the effects of the endorphins, has met with some success.

The endorphins may play a role in another condition familiar to psychiatrists but less well known to the general public—self-mutilation. Sharon, a young woman, was repeatedly seen in the emergency room for cutting her arms and legs with a razor blade. The cuts always took the same pattern: fine, superficial, parallel to one another, and on the upper part of the limbs. Careful questioning revealed that Sharon was neither trying to commit suicide nor looking for attention. Why then did she keep cutting herself?

Sharon had a long and sad history of abuse and neglect by her family. In fact, she was suffering from post-traumatic stress disorder, triggered by situations that reminded her of her abusive stepmother. At these times she would feel an overwhelming sense of panic and terror, along with the conviction that if she did not do something to get rid of this feeling, she would die.

Somewhere in the course of her life, Sharon had discovered that cutting herself would bring numbness and take away all her painful feelings. "It was like a runner's high," she said. She began to experiment with how to achieve this effect most readily and found that a series of shallow cuts with razor blades kept specifically for this purpose worked best. She was very ashamed of her behavior and cut herself only on the upper parts of her limbs so that they would be covered by her shorts or her shirtsleeves and others would not think of her as a "psycho."

After considerable therapy Sharon is now well and has learned to soothe herself in less destructive ways when she feels anxious or upset. Regular exercise has helped stabilize her mood swings. At one point in her treatment, the use of an opiate blocker helped her to stop cutting herself. By blocking the relief associated with the release of endorphins after cutting, Sharon was able to break the self-destructive cycle to which she had become addicted.

Prolactin: The Hormone of Serenity

So far we have considered the chemistry of exhilaration (mediated by dopamine) and bliss (mediated by opiates), but what about serenity? Serenity, a state of lucid and pleasurable calmness, can follow meditation. Recent research suggests that serenity may be induced by the hormone prolactin, which, as its name implies, is responsible for stimulating the breast tissue to produce milk in nursing mothers. No wonder mothers appear so serene when they breast-feed their infants. Prolactin is secreted by the pituitary gland in men as well as in women and has functions that extend beyond the production of milk. One of these functions may be the induction of a state of quiet tranquillity.

Studies of Transcendental Meditators have found that during meditation, prolactin levels rise in the blood.[69] Researcher Thomas Wehr at the National Institute of Mental Health has conducted studies during which he has had people lie down in a quiet darkened room for fourteen hours each night, conditions similar to those under which we evolved during the millions of years before the discovery of artificial light. Under these conditions, the subjects reported a state of pleasant relaxation coupled with a crystal-clear consciousness. While they felt this way, the pituitary released prolactin into the bloodstream.[70]

In separate experiments the researchers told subjects who were lying in the dark that a nurse might come in and draw a blood sample. The anxiety caused by the expectation that someone might enter the room at any moment was sufficient to shut off the prolactin secretion. Wehr has suggested that this form of quiet restfulness, a condition that our ancestors enjoyed for hours each day, might have certain restorative effects. According to him, the use of artificial light, which has extended the active part of the day, may be depriving us of the benefits of serenity that our ancestors enjoyed while lying restfully in the natural night.

One reason rest, relaxation, and meditation exercises may be beneficial is that they foster the production of prolactin, which may have restorative effects on the mind and body.

Suggestion: Besides resting in a darkened room and meditating, a simple way to give yourself a shot of prolactin is to take a warm, relaxing bath. Research shows that heat causes prolactin to be released into the bloodstream.

The Pursuit of Happiness

As the Declaration of Independence states, Americans should have the right to "life, liberty, and the pursuit of happiness." It is certainly high time for psychologists and other students of emotions to follow this far-sighted vision and broaden the scope of their efforts beyond the relief of suffering to the enhancement of well-being.

There are moments in psychotherapy that stand out in one's mind. One such moment occurred in a session with a family I was seeing. John, a laborer, had lost his foot in an accident about a year before. He was working again but at the minimum wage and had been unable to afford a prosthesis to replace the missing limb. He had divorced his first wife, who had serious difficulties with drugs and alcohol, leaving his two sons, both under ten years of age, with her. He had remarried a steadier woman and, after his ex-wife had been found guilty of abusing the two boys, had taken his sons in to live with him and his new wife.

John's second wife was kind to the boys and organized the home so that they could begin to function like a healthy family. She was educated about the aftermath of trauma and was patient with the boys, understanding their mistrust and rudeness to be part of their problem. The family developed routines that comforted them and during one particular session we reviewed their activities of the previous week.

When it was the younger boy's turn to talk, he discussed how much he had enjoyed giving to the poor. Realizing how poor they themselves were, I asked what sort of things they gave. "Whatever we don't need," he said, "clothes, books, toys," and his face broke into a huge grin, revealing the gaps left behind by the milk teeth he had lost and not yet replaced. "We love giving to the poor," the older boy chimed in. The whole family was now smiling—and I had learned an important lesson. There is nobody who is so poor that he does not have something to give, and that giving can lead to happiness.

The Four Traits of Happy People

Although happiness is determined to some extent by factors that are beyond our control, such as genetics, to some degree each of us must find our own happiness. What can research teach us about how to do so?

One way to answer this question is to examine the differences between happy and unhappy people. Happy people have certain traits and habits, and pursue certain activities. Would it help an unhappy person to emulate the behavior of a happy one? In a series of studies, researcher James Laird from Clark University in Worcester, Massachusetts, found that asking students to assume facial expressions associated with subtle smiling or frowning made them happier or angrier.[71] In another study, the group found that people think cartoons are funnier when they smile broadly with their cheeks raised while reading them than when they frown.[72] Likewise, college students asked to walk around with long strides, holding their heads up, felt happier than those asked to walk in small shuffling steps with their eyes downcast.[73]

Facial expressions tend to be contagious. A happy smile readily elicits smiles in others, while a frown is more likely to elicit frowns or expressions of concern. Even neutral expressions can raise eyebrows, as researcher Ed Diener discovered while exploring whether faking happiness could result in genuine happiness. In Diener's study, one group of people was instructed to act in a happy way, while a control group was instructed to act neutrally. But Diener had to discontinue the study prematurely because friends and relatives of the controls became worried that they were becoming depressed. As Diener puts it, "apparently it is not acceptable to behave neutrally in the United States."

Research findings suggest that we can become happier by studying happy people and emulating them. But what are the traits and habits of happy people?

Trait 1. *Happy people like themselves.* They believe themselves to be more ethical, more intelligent, better able to get along with others, and healthier than the average person.[74]

As a psychiatrist, I hear a lot about self-esteem. Many of the parents I see keep telling their children how wonderful they are in an effort to improve their self-esteem. It seems to me, though, that self-esteem works best when it is earned. I encourage parents to help their children undertake activities of which they can legitimately feel proud, whether that be schoolwork, sports, or community service. In a culture such as ours that places such a high premium on performance, I like to see parents emphasizing elements of kindness, understanding, and good deeds as part of the reward system with which they raise their children. Children should learn to temper their feelings of self-esteem with gratitude for what they have. Pouring praise upon children who do nothing to deserve it is a formula for raising monsters of entitlement.

For adults who lack self-esteem, it is not too late to acquire some. First it is important to be sure that you are not suffering from clinical depression, a condition that corrodes self-esteem and other sources of pleasure, and can be readily treated (see chapter 12). Besides reversing depression, there are many things you can do to enhance your self-esteem. Everybody has some skill or talent. When I was a boy, I remember one elderly woman who baked a certain kind of ginger cookie for which she was famous in the community. She would bake tins of these moist cookies and give them out as gifts. Everybody raved about them. Once I was introduced to her but failed to recognize her. "Don't you remember me?" she said. "I'm Minnie, the one who makes the ginger cookies." Of course I did—and praised the cookies extravagantly, for which I was rewarded with a smile of pure delight.

Simply repeating to yourself those qualities that make you feel proud can enhance your self-esteem. Studies show that feigning increased levels of self-esteem can actually lead to more positive feelings of self.

As in the story of the poor family who gave their castoffs to those who needed them, you can enhance your self-esteem by counting your blessings and giving to those who are less fortunate.

Trait 2. *Happy people feel in control of their lives.* People who feel as though they have little control over their lives, such as the residents of nursing homes or citizens of repressive regimes, have lower levels of subjective well-being than those who are free. Health and well-being improve in nursing homes where residents are given greater say in their daily activities.

If you find yourself in a situation where you have little control, analyze your circumstances and determine what you can and cannot change. Then work on accepting the former and changing the latter.

Trait 3. *Happy people are optimistic.* As you might expect, happy people are generally more optimistic than unhappy ones. Although pessimists are more accurate in appraising their situation and predicting the future, optimists are more likely to succeed. It may, therefore, be more important to be optimistic than to be right.

Optimists are at an advantage in situations that call for innovation, expansion, and growth. When their backs are to the wall, optimists fare best. Among the most memorable words of the twentieth century are the war speeches of Winston Churchill, who helped maintain the morale of a beleaguered island nation against all odds. "We shall fight them on the beaches," he declared before the House of Commons in the early years of the Second World War. "We shall never surrender." Pessimists, on the other hand, may fare best when more caution is warranted and when the cost of everything has to be tallied up. Churchill was voted out of office shortly after the war.

Can optimism be learned? Although the scientific jury is still out on this question, psychologist Martin Seligman claims in his book *Learned Optimism* that it can be.[75] Using the mnemonic ABC, Seligman says that an Adverse event leads to a pessimistic Belief, which has a negative Consequence for the individual. He then suggests Disputing this belief and Energizing oneself to shift into an optimistic mode. While such cognitive strategies can reverse depression, it remains to be seen whether they can enhance happiness. But they are certainly worth a try.

Trait 4. *Happy people are extraverted.* Extraverts are generally happier than introverts, not just when they are around others, but even when they are alone. They have more positive expectations than introverts. Even when alone, an extravert might say to himself, "I can always call a friend and get together; I'm sure he'll be happy to hear from me." By contrast, an introvert might say, "I don't think I should call him. He's probably busy and doesn't want to be interrupted." One way for an introverted person to get around this problem is to find people who really would be happy to hear from him—and then to make the effort to be in touch. Even introverts can enjoy and derive benefit from the company of friendly people.

The Seven Habits of Happy People

Happy people tend to adopt certain patterns of behavior, or habits, as listed below. Emulating some of these habits may lift your spirits, too.

Habit 1: Having Close Relationships With Other People

Happy people have more friends, allies, and confidants than unhappy ones.[76] Not only do friends enrich one's life and enhance happiness, but many studies have shown that having friends improves health, for example by lowering blood pressure and boosting immune functioning.

Of course, to have friends one needs to be a friend. Happy people make good friends. Since they feel good about themselves, they are able to rejoice in their friends' successes. They are willing to share their optimistic worldview with others, are more likely to be generous and available, and are less likely to be self-absorbed in a way that might make people want to avoid them. Just as depression is contagious, so is happiness.

Habit 2: Being Married

Married people, on the average, are happier than those who are separated, divorced, or living alone, and are in better physical and mental health. People who live with someone are, on average, a little less happy than married folk, but happier than those who live alone.[77] Three out of four married people say that their spouse is their best friend and four out of five say that they would marry the same person again.[78] Of course, not all marriages are happy and some people are better off out of a bad marriage.

Research suggests that marriage does a little more for the happiness of women than for men, but helps the physical and mental health of men more than women.[79]

Habit 3: Participating in an Organized Religion

As a doctor, I have seen many people lose their loved ones—to disease, accidents or suicide. These are always wrenching experiences, but somehow those people with the strongest faith in God seem to weather best the horrors life can bring. Studies support these observations. For example, recently widowed women who worship regularly report more joy in their lives than those who do not.[80] People of faith tend to do better in difficult life circumstances including having to take care of children with special needs,[81] going through divorce, or being unemployed or seriously ill.[82] Even outside of such dire circumstances, however, religion can provide a sense of meaning and richness to life and be a path to happiness.[83]

Jenny, a woman of about 50, was reasonably content with her life. She had a loving husband, a satisfying career, two grown children who caused her no trouble, and enough money for the present and the likely future. Nevertheless, she felt a certain emptiness, a lack of meaning and an indescribable desire for something more. One day a flier arrived in Jenny's mailbox informing her that a new place of worship was opening up nearby. Although she had been raised in a religious family, Jenny had barely participated in her religion for years. She decided to check out the new congregation.

The people she met there were warm and friendly, and didn't pressure her to participate in any religious activities. Gradually, however, she started wanting to learn more and more about the religion and applying it to her daily life. Her religion gave her life structure and introduced her to a whole new circle of friends. She was encouraged to do good deeds, which were rewarding. Jenny experienced a reawakening of a spiritual longing that she had not enjoyed since childhood, and satisfaction in rediscovering religion. She felt happier and more fulfilled than she had in years. Jenny's story is consistent with the literature, which finds a clear connection between religious participation and happiness.

Researchers attempting to understand this connection offer several explanations. The major religions prescribe a healthy way of life, encouraging their members to rest and refrain from harmful habits and activities. Religion offers automatic membership in a supportive community. Most important, perhaps, religion provides the believer with an explanation for his or her place and significance in a mystifying and daunting cosmos.

Habit 4: Pursuing the Right Goals in the Right Way

As we have seen, the pursuit of any goal has two phases, a pre- and a post-goal attainment phase. Both phases can be pleasurable. One problem with our society, according to researcher Richard Davidson, is that many of us have not struck a good balance between these two phases. We work hard to achieve our goals, then barely take the time to enjoy them before setting new goals. In this way we can become slaves to the "hedonic treadmill" and miss out on a key part of the experience of happiness—that it should be enjoyed and not just pursued.

There is much pleasure to be had, however, in the pursuit of goals if these goals are meaningful, if they are neither too easy nor too difficult. Goals that are too easy will be boring; those that are too difficult overwhelming. Happy people set goals that are challenging but manageable.

The process of being completely and blissfully wrapped up in the pursuit of a meaningful goal has been called "flow" by writer and researcher Mihaly Csikszentmihalyi.[84] During periods of flow, when a person is engaged in a task, time seems to stop and an ecstatic sense of focus takes over in which nothing other than the task and its accomplishment seems to have any meaning. The nature of the enterprise is not confined to any particular field, and Csikszentmihalyi gives diverse examples of flow, such as musicians composing a new piece of music and a mother and daughter baking cookies.[85] Flow is more likely to occur when people are actively engaged in a task or activity than when they are passively absorbing their surroundings.

As a researcher for many years at the National Institute of Mental Health, I observed firsthand the enormous impact of work satisfaction on happiness. It is in our work that most of our experiences of "flow" occur. In my own case, the initial discovery that some people become regularly depressed in the winter and that their symptoms can be reversed by exposure to bright light was one of the most joyful experiences of my life. Trying to unlock nature's secrets was an all-consuming passion for both me and my fellow scientists.

Work is most satisfying when we are able to choose what we want to do and believe that it has some intrinsic value. We are also more likely to be happy with our work if we have the resources necessary for getting it done and management that values and facilitates the work.

At the NIMH it was easy to detect how researchers were being treated by the management in power at any particular time. When their work was promoted and fostered, the researchers would stride jauntily up and down the halls with smiles on their faces. In less favorable times, however, the scientists would slouch around dejected, and in some cases, their health would suffer. I recall one prominent researcher who fell afoul of the administration and suffered a heart attack shortly after a harsh review of his program. Clearly one key to happiness is finding work that is congruent with your goals and offers a supportive work environment for attaining them.

Goals do not have to be work related to be pleasurable, however. Leisure-time activities can also be a great source of pleasure. Satisfaction with one's life is related to satisfaction with leisure-time activities.[86] One follow-up study of about 1,500 high school students over a twenty-four-year period found that leisure time in adolescence was associated with happiness in adult life.[87] Observations such as these should give pause to those parents who pressure and schedule their children to such an extent as to squeeze all leisure out of their lives. This strategy, intended to result in success, may actually be a recipe for unhappy workaholism or rebellion in later life.

All sorts of leisure-time activities may lead to greater happiness. Sports and exercise can be very satisfying for several reasons. They involve not only challenging goals and the company of teammates, but also physiological benefits, such as the release of endorphins.[88] Experiments in which young unemployed people received training in sports and access to facilities had very positive results.

In one study, volunteers reported that their work made them very happy.[89] When asked which benefits of the work they regarded as very important, the most frequent responses were: "I really enjoy it" (72 percent); "it's the satisfaction of seeing the results" (67 percent); "I meet people and make friends through it" (48 percent); and "it gives me a sense of personal achievement" (47 percent).[90] Their work also made them feel more skillful, gave them a sense of achievement, and made them feel less selfish and self-absorbed.

Habit 5: Having Values

Living a life without values is a bit like going on a car trip without a road map. People who have a clear sense of the values that guide their lives tend to be happier. In the pursuit of happiness, it appears that not all values are equal. Researchers have found that those who rate financial success as more important than self-acceptance, community feeling and relationships are less happy.[91] Having values is what gives meaning to goals, but no man is an island and goals are most likely to result in happiness when they are valued by the culture or subculture to which the man belongs.[92]

Habit 6: Not Keeping Up With the Joneses

Have you ever gone to a movie that you really wanted to see only to find that the line was already around the block? You joined the line but were discouraged by all the people ahead of you. After ten minutes you looked behind you and realized that dozens of people had arrived after you, and since they had tickets, they were obviously going to get into the movie house. Also, they would probably end up in the front rows, leaving you with a better seat. Suddenly you felt quite cheerful and once again looked forward to the movie.

What you were doing in the movie line was making two comparisons, first with the people in front of you (an upward comparison), then with the people behind you (a downward comparison). These two comparisons had opposite effects on your mood. In response to the common question, "How is your wife?" comedian Henny Young-man's famous one-liner was, "Compared to who?" Behind the joke was a nugget of wisdom. If you compare yourself and what you have to people you perceive as being better off, you set yourself up for misery. Looking to those who have less is a better route to happiness.

Although the populations of developed countries have become more affluent over the past five decades, they have not become any happier, probably because of ever-rising expectations and increasingly ambitious goals. Media commercials are designed to play into our tendency to make upward comparisons. We see television images of blissful people enjoying material delights, which urge us to take that same road to bliss. The wheels of capitalism are driven by upward comparisons. But as researchers David Myers and Ed Diener put it, "Satisfaction is less a matter of getting what you want than wanting what you have."

The impoverished family I mentioned who rejoiced in giving to the poor illustrates this point. Each week they did several things that lead to happiness—giving to charity, joining together around a goal that was meaningful to all of them, thinking of people who were less well off than they were (making a downward comparison), and taking a moment to count their blessings and reflect on the pleasures of the week. When actor Roberto Benigni thanked his family for their gift of love and of poverty, he was expressing his gratitude to them for instilling in him the values that helped him realize that life is beautiful.

Habit 7: Enjoying Daily Pleasures

Although the impact of pleasure is transient, many pleasurable days woven together can provide the fabric for a happy life. As Benjamin Franklin observed, "Happiness is produced not so much by great pieces of good fortune that seldom happen as by little advantages that occur every day." Remember how the people in the ice cream experiment enjoyed the same flavor ice cream every day over the course of a week to a greater degree than they predicted? Happy people ensure that their days contain at least some pleasurable activities along with the necessary tasks and chores that routinely confront us all.

Becoming Happier

Can we learn to become happier? According to researcher Richard Davidson, "the answer is a resounding 'yes,'" and other happiness experts, from psychologists to the Dalai Lama, agree. According to Davidson, "Researchers have not yet given the idea of training ourselves to become happier a chance. We don't yet know the limits or constraints on the plasticity of the happiness system."

Davidson compares learning how to be happy with acquiring skills in other areas. I heartily agree. He sees the path to happiness as the acquisition of specific skills or habits and the regular practice of these habits, setting realistic goals, and allowing sufficient intervals of time to enjoy one's accomplishments before proceeding to the next goal.

There is much wisdom in the old and well-known Chinese proverb, "Give someone a fish, you give him a meal. Teach him to fish and you feed him for life." Life's pleasures are like fish, enjoyed and then forgotten. But learning how to be happy is like learning to fish: you learn how to fill your plate each day with good feelings. Some research-based suggestions for leading a happy life are listed below.

Ten Keys to a Happier Life

1. *Fake it till you make it.* Ask yourself, "How would an optimist see this situation? What would a more extraverted person do?" These lines of thinking will help direct you to actions that you might not usually consider, but that can make you feel better. Smile, hold your head high, and walk with brisk strides. Looking happier will make you feel happier and others will respond to you in kind.

2. *Think of what you do well.* Everybody is good at something. By playing to your strengths, you will help others become aware of them as well.

3. *Devote more time to friendships.* Work to make new ones, rekindle old ones, and nurture those you already have.

4. *Set goals that are both important to you and realistic.* These goals should be neither too easy nor too difficult. As you move to-

ward your goals, let yourself get immersed in the process, so that you can experience the exhilaration of "flow."

5. *Enjoy your accomplishments.* Allow yourself time to enjoy the satisfaction of accomplishment once you attain a goal before moving on to the next project.

6. *Find work that you value in a place where you are valued.* Friendly colleagues and appreciative management can go a long way to making your workday enjoyable and rewarding. It also helps if you yourself value the work you do.

7. *Check the tendency to think continually about what you don't have* (as advertised on television, for example). Instead, count your blessings and consider those who have less than you do.

8. *Find something that brings you pleasure and practice it.* This can be meditation, fly fishing, or volunteer work.

9. *Enjoy the small pleasures of everyday life.* Remind yourself of these pleasures while you are enjoying them to amplify your appreciation of the good things life brings. Happiness can easily bypass our consciousness. What a shame to let it slip by!

10. *Take care of both your physical health and your spiritual well-being.* Get sufficient rest and exercise. Consider becoming more involved in a religious or spiritual community.

PART THREE

CHANGE

Chapter 14

Pathways to Change

*Nature has placed mankind under the governance of two
sovereign masters, pain and pleasure. It is for them alone
to point out what we ought to do, as well as to determine
what we shall do.*

—Jeremy Bentham[1]

A s we have seen, when feelings work properly, they provide us
with important information—limbic news. When they are out
of whack, they cause needless suffering. In earlier chapters, I
outlined some specific measures that can help you reverse painful
feelings and enhance pleasurable ones. In this chapter, I address
some general principles that can help you change the way you feel.

The development of medications to treat depression, anxiety, and
other painful emotional states has given help and hope to millions.
Despite their limitations, such as side effects and a lack of effectiveness for some people, their value is unquestionable. Since they are
the subjects of entire books, however, I will not address them here.
Rather, I will focus on other things people can do to lead happier
lives.

Traditionally, people wanting to change their emotional landscape
have entered psychotherapy. One question that everyone wants to
know about psychotherapy is, "Does it work?" Many different types
of therapy are available and the consumer can be forgiven for being
confused as to which is best and who should dispense it. Emotional
change also occurs outside therapy. Without attempting to be com-

prehensive, I will share some effective pathways to change, based on my clinical and personal experience.

In the past there has been a tendency to think of strategies for change in terms of the "brain" or the "mind," as exemplified, respectively, by antidepressants or psychotherapy. The more we learn about the workings of the emotional brain, the more these two concepts blur. When we soothe or stimulate our minds, we change our brains. When we do things that affect brain functioning, we affect our state of mind too.

Does Psychotherapy Work?

In recent decades, researchers have refined this question by doing double-blind controlled studies that ask which specific therapies are effective for which specific emotional disorders. The great strength of these studies is their scientific form: They control for the placebo effect and other variables. For example, only patients meeting certain diagnostic criteria can enter the studies. The treatment techniques are clearly spelled out, then implemented in a standardized way for a fixed period of time. So, at the end of such a study, one can say with reasonable confidence that, for example, cognitive therapy helps people with depression, while behavior therapy helps people with phobias. And I believe both statements are true.

The problem is that the "psychotherapy" in these studies bears only a rough resemblance to the therapy in the real world. In real life, patients seldom fit into clear-cut diagnostic categories, and sometimes they have more than one illness. Whether they find their way to the "right" form of therapy is mostly a matter of luck. And anyway, because we're now talking about real life, the approach may need to change as the patient progresses. Often people seek help less for a specific psychiatric condition than for unhappiness with their family life, work, or sexuality—highly individual matters. All in all, I can't imagine any way to design a psychotherapy study that would control for all the important variables in a person's life.

What can be said, then, about the effectiveness of psychotherapy as it is really practiced? In my own experience, as a practitioner and recipient of psychotherapy, I am convinced that it works when the right type of therapy is given to a patient by a competent professional. I came to this conclusion despite having begun my psychiatric residency as a hard-nosed skeptic. As a young man, all excited about the science of the mind, I became convinced of the value of therapy only after I had been exposed to supervision by consummate clinicians. To my surprise, when I implemented their suggestions, my patients actually got better.

In the years since then, I have seen therapy produce some astonishing turnarounds. Personal anecdotes aside, what can be said about the effectiveness of psychotherapy in the real world? The most useful answers I have found come from the popular magazine *Consumer Reports*. In 1995, *Consumer Reports* surveyed its thousands of readers about their experiences with mental health services.[2] A total of 4,100 responders reported that they had consulted a professional for problems related to mental health, and their responses were written up and discussed in a 1995 article in *American Psychologist* by Martin Seligman, professor of psychiatry at the University of Pennsylvania.[3] Here are some highlights from the survey:

- Most of the respondents improved a great deal. Approximately 90 percent of the 1,212 people who had reported feeling "very poor" or "fairly poor" when they began treatment said that they felt significantly better at the time of the survey.

- Long-term therapy (lasting for more than two years) worked much better than short-term therapy (lasting for less than six months).

  This finding is consistent with the impressions of many therapists. Robert Glick, chief of the Columbia Psychoanalytic Clinic, told me that many patients come to him and his colleagues after they have already received short-term therapy with only partial success. Short-term therapies may be most helpful for young people with short-term difficulties, but lifelong problematic patterns of behavior generally take more time to heal.

- There were no differences in outcome between those who received psychotherapy in combination with medications and those who received psychotherapy alone. This is consistent with the results of some controlled studies, though others show greater benefits when the treatments are combined.

- All the mental health professionals (psychiatrists, psychologists, and social workers) did equally well, and all emerged as more helpful than marriage counselors. Family doctors were as helpful as the mental health professionals in the short term (less than six months) but less so over long periods. These differences are of special interest because they suggest that specific training is important, especially for patients with complicated problems.

- In the present era of managed care and stingy reimbursement for mental health coverage, it is interesting that individuals whose duration of care or choice of therapist was limited by insurance fared significantly less well.

- No specific form of therapy did better than any other for any particular emotional problem.

Getting the Most Out of Psychotherapy

The following eight tips are based on the *Consumer Reports* study:

1. Actively shop around to find a therapist who feels right for you. If you were in the market for a house, you would seldom buy the first one you saw. The same principle should apply when you invest in a psychotherapist.

2. Therapy will work better if you are going because you think you need it, rather than if you are going simply at the urging of someone else.

3. When interviewing a potential therapist, feel free to ask questions about his or her qualifications and experience, as well as about the cost and recommended frequency of the sessions.

4. During therapy, be as open as possible. The therapist will not be able to help you optimally if you conceal information.

5. Feel free to ask questions about your diagnosis or any terms the therapist uses that are unclear to you.

6. Do your homework between sessions. In other words, try to actively implement the lessons you learn from therapy in your daily life.

7. Cancel as few sessions as possible.

8. During your therapy sessions, feel free to discuss your feelings about your therapy and the therapist, including any negative feelings. This last point is especially important because many of us were trained to be polite, especially to those who are trying to help. You should nevertheless make the effort to be candid. It is an important part of your treatment.

Nine Pathways to Change

In the real world, therapy combines many different elements culled from different disciplines. Here are some general principles, based on my clinical and personal experience, and the latest scientific developments.

Pathway 1: The Fox Versus the Porcupine

There is an old saying that the fox has many tricks, whereas the porcupine has one big trick. In the world of emotions, you are better off as a fox than a porcupine. For example, the husband who always withdraws from his wife when he is angry is severely handicapped. This porcupine has a limited repertoire of emotional responses. He will benefit by learning new skills to communicate dissatisfaction.

The fox is curious. He sniffs around and asks questions. He doesn't let himself become trapped in a corner, but finds ways around obstacles. According to psychoanalyst Robert Glick, the best predictors of response to psychotherapy are foxlike traits: curiosity, candor, and the capacity for self-reflection. I agree. Whenever I evaluate a patient for treatment, I always observe how he or she handles new information.

A sense of openness and flexibility, coupled with a willingness to be proactive, usually signals an easier treatment course and a better outcome.

Sometimes combining different strategies enhances outcome. For example, a recent multicenter study of depression showed that combining an antidepressant with psychotherapy produced excellent results—significantly better than either treatment alone. On the other hand, different strategies can interfere with one another. For example, in treating panic disorder, those patients who received both medications and cognitive-behavior therapy (CBT) were more likely to relapse after treatment was discontinued than those who received cognitive therapy alone.

When it comes to adopting different paradigms for change, more is often better but sometimes less is more.

Pathway 2: Change Versus Acceptance

In the pursuit of pleasure and avoidance of pain, animals must constantly evaluate their circumstances, and they depend upon their emotions to help them do it. Consider a squirrel in pursuit of some delicate morsel that lies at the feet of potential danger—you or me, eating lunch in the park. Hunger drives the squirrel forward; fear holds it back. Depending on its hunger, its past experience with humans, and other squirrelly imponderables, the animal decides. It either approaches or avoids the tidbit.

This same type of dilemma faces humans and other animals every day—in the face of an obstacle, should we be active? Should we attempt to change the environment? Or should we be passive? Is this something we must accept? It is easy to imagine how, in the course of evolution, the ability to decide correctly whether to act or accept could make the difference between life and death. This fundamental dilemma, which requires both the primitive emotional brain and the more recently evolved neocortex, is nowhere more eloquently expressed than in the Serenity Prayer, attributed to theologian Reinhold Niebuhr:

> God, grant me the serenity
> To accept the things I cannot change

> The courage to change the things I can
> And the wisdom to know the difference.[4]

The more I think about this prayer, the more profound it seems. Often I have encountered patients (or friends, for that matter) who are preoccupied with issues over which they have no control, while they ignore important but tractable problems. The Serenity Prayer can be used as a sort of mantra to help us focus on investing our energies where we can expect a payoff.

There are many situations over which we have no control, such as being in prison, having a terminal illness, and being an addict. In such cases, we must accept—by which I do *not* mean gritting your teeth and angrily enduring. Acceptance, rather, is a form of letting go. It implies release: You allow yourself to relinquish responsibility for changing the unchangeable.

Once you accept, something curious happens. An internal shift occurs. The prisoner can now focus on life in prison and how to make the most of it. The cancer patient can make his last days as good as possible. And the addict can develop parts of her life that do not involve her drug (or addictive behavior) of choice. Perhaps that is why it has become a tradition for meetings of Alcoholics Anonymous and other twelve-step groups to end with the Serenity Prayer.

Pathway 3: Focus Versus Distraction

In the movie *Life Is Beautiful*, a father helps his son deal with the terror of being in a Nazi concentration camp by pretending that the experience is part of a game. Although the movie is allegorical, some concentration camp prisoners did indeed divert themselves from their suffering. They would actively pursue some goal—form a chorus, devise a chess set, or help the others. One such prisoner who survived the camps was the Viennese neurologist Viktor Frankl. In the closing years of the last century, which corresponded to the last years of his life, I was fortunate enough to meet him.

Then in his early nineties, Frankl had taught a course at the University of Vienna with a friend of mine, Siegfried Kasper, chairman of psychiatry at Vienna. One autumn afternoon, I accompanied

Kasper and his wife, Anita, to meet the great man in his small suburban home. Frankl was of short stature but upright bearing, with clear blue eyes that looked out at the world intelligently, though they had lost much of their sight. His greeting was friendly, his English excellent, and his mind as lucid as any I have ever encountered.

He discussed his harrowing experiences in Auschwitz factually, without sentimentality. It was clear that he had come to terms with the horrors long ago—both his own internment and the death of his wife and mother at the hands of the Nazis. When he was recovering from the physical depredations of the camp, he met a young nurse whom he subsequently married. She was there that afternoon, an elderly woman now, and joined in our discussion.

Frankl told us that his experiences in the camps had taught him the value of focusing on the positive things in life, on the present and the future rather than on the past. In his widely influential book *Man's Search for Meaning*, Frankl describes how the life of the mind and the use of art, imagery, music, and humor can enable a person to survive and find meaning even in the direst circumstances.[5]

During our meeting Frankl told a story about the philosopher Immanuel Kant. Kant had a beloved servant, Lumpe, who was caught stealing and had to be dismissed. To get over his sorrow, Kant wrote a memorandum to himself that he kept on his desk at all times. It said, "Lumpe must be forgotten." Frankl smiled as he thought about the foolishness of the great philosopher. His point was, "Don't dwell on things that make you unhappy when there is nothing you can do about them."

Instead, Frankl recommended that a person stimulate his mind by focusing on those things that will infuse his life with pleasure and significance. In this regard, Frankl differed with Freud, with whom he had corresponded as a young man many years before. By focusing on a source of sorrow, as Freud had encouraged his patients to do, Frankl suggested that you might compound your unhappiness.

In my clinical and personal experience, both focus and distraction have their place in the quest for happiness. For example, one area in which distraction can help a lot is in the management of addictions. Elmer is a case in point. He has been addicted to multiple substances and behaviors over the years. "Sex, drugs, rock and roll. You name it, I've been addicted to it," Elmer says. Now clean and sober, thanks to detoxification programs, therapy, and several twelve-step programs, Elmer has learned ways to stave off a relapse. Among these, he has learned the value of distraction.

"When the cravings come over me, I tell myself, 'They will pass,'" Elmer says. "In the meanwhile, I must distract myself. I call one of my program buddies, or if I can't reach anyone, I get busy with whatever I'm doing. Sometimes I pray for help. Next thing I know, the craving has passed."

Currently there is no scientific evidence to support the value of systematically distracting oneself from a problem. Clinical observations of its value, however, suggest that research into this approach would be highly worthwhile.

In contrast, good research has been conducted on the value of focusing on a source of anguish or concern in a systematic way. The best and cleanest illustration of this principle appears in the many written self-disclosure studies by James Pennebaker and colleagues who have adapted his technique. (For more information on Pennebaker's technique, see pages 201–205). Research has found written self-disclosure to be of value for groups as disparate as fired engineers, concentration camp survivors, and patients with chronic medical illnesses. Many studies of psychotherapy, which essentially involves focusing on problems rather than distracting oneself from them, also substantiate the value of the examined life. As a psychiatrist, I find that it is usually a challenge to help people focus on the source of their problems as there is a natural tendency to push unpleasant matters to the side.

In practice, it is probably best to shift between distraction and focus depending on the situation, using judgment as to how and when to shift strategies. Once again, the way of the fox is best.

Pathway 4: Plumbing the Depths Versus Exploring the Surface

Should we delve deep into the unconscious, as Freud recommended? Or would our time be better spent examining those thoughts and feelings that are readily accessible? Modern therapists are divided over where it is best to put one's energies.

Science has demonstrated the existence of unconscious emotions capable of driving our actions. (For a discussion of this, see chapter 2.) But does it pay to go after them? "There is always more going on than meets the eye," psychoanalyst Robert Glick told me, underscoring the importance of the unconscious in the work of modern analysts. We now know, based on neuroscientific research, that memories may be explicit (readily retrievable, such as facts or figures) or implicit (unconsciously encoded in ways that cannot readily or voluntarily be retrieved). Implicit memories emerge through our actions (such as driving a car or hitting a ball with a golf club) or when cued by certain triggers (a fragrance that your old lover always used to wear). Emotional memories are implicit.

Freud discovered that, in therapy, people tend to replay elements of earlier relationships in dealing with the therapist. According to Glick, this so-called transference of feelings "is more alive than ever as a human experience that can be helpful in the treatment process. We carry around with us complex modes of relating to others, a lens through which we greet the world." By returning to the therapist's office again and again, Glick suggests, the patient "makes shifts in implicit memory that can make a tremendous difference in the way he perceives the world and chooses to lead his life.

"Say you have as a patient a woman who mistrusts men because of her experiences with men in the past, such as a sadistic or overly seductive father. If you can help her feel differently in this particular way so that she is able to develop a satisfactory relationship, get married, and have a family, then you have changed the direction of her life."

A successful relationship with a therapist might counteract the damage caused by traumatic relationships experienced in the past—a so-called corrective emotional experience. In Harlow's studies, some of the social and emotional damage suffered by monkeys reared in isolation could be alleviated by putting them together with surrogate parents. In other words, Harlow provided the monkeys with a corrective emotional experience, and to some degree, it worked.

More recently, Stephen Suomi, a former student of Harlow's and now at the National Institute of Health, studied genetically highly reactive infant rhesus monkeys which were cross-fostered to live with different types of mothers for the first six months of their life.[6] Whereas those infants cross-fostered to highly nurturant mothers showed precocious development, those infants reared by control mothers showed developmental deficits—an example of how corrective emotional experiences can overcome genetic influences.

In the future, I expect new imaging techniques will reveal changes in the emotional brain resulting from therapy.

In sharp contrast to the Freudian approach is the work of Aaron Beck, professor of psychiatry at the University of Pennsylvania. Frustrated at the imprecision of psychoanalytic teaching, Beck questioned the value of digging around in a patient's unconscious, suggesting instead that the patient's problems might be quite evident in his conscious thought processes. "There is more to the surface than meets the eye," Beck is fond of saying.[7] Depressed people, for example, think poorly of themselves in ways that are often at variance with the facts. Beck speculated that these inaccurate thoughts might actually make a person more depressed, and if those thoughts can be tackled logically, his mood might improve.

To their credit, Beck and his followers have tested their treatment strategies scientifically and, in study after study, have shown that altering thoughts can alter feelings. Such scientific success has made cognitive therapy one of the most rapidly growing forms of therapy in the United States. Cognitive therapists have shown that the neocortex, where ideas are generated, if properly trained, can powerfully influence the emotional parts of the brain. In a recent meta-analysis of 325 cognitive therapy studies, researchers Andrew Butler and Judith Beck found that cognitive therapy can benefit numerous conditions, including depression, generalized anxiety disorder, panic disorder, and social phobia. Cognitive therapy is also helpful for marital distress, anger problems, and chronic pain.[8]

As for therapies that plumb the unconscious, there are no scientific studies that match the rigor of the cognitive therapy trials. Yet, as a practicing psychiatrist, I have to acknowledge the value of such approaches in my work and in the work of many of my colleagues. If a patient becomes angry with me and I have done nothing to merit it, I will direct her attention to her relationship with her father or mother. I use "transference" all the time. If she brings me a dream, I will try to understand it along with her. If you avoid the unconscious, you miss a lot of important information. On the other hand, nowadays, doing therapy without using any elements of cognitive therapy is like driving a car without a fully functioning steering wheel.

Once again, remember the fox and be ready to shift strategies. Examine your dreams, gut feelings, and odd associations, but be sure to heed the information that is under your nose. There is always something going on under the surface, but there is also more to the surface than meets the eye.

Pathway 5: Self-Help Versus Establishment Help

One of the most dramatic developments in mental health has been the growth of the self-help movement. Self-help groups empower individuals who participate in them and create a healing community. Such a community, which often contrasts sharply with the dysfunctional families from which its members arise, affords a corrective emotional experience in a group setting.

The prototype of self-help groups is Alcoholics Anonymous (AA), founded in the early decades of the last century by Bill Wilson, a Wall Street businessman and a serious alcoholic.

Wilson wrote eloquently about his harrowing experiences with alcohol, his numerous well-intentioned efforts to stop drinking, and his repeated dangerous and mortifying relapses.[9] After many years of unsuccessful efforts to conquer his addiction, he found help from an unlikely source—a visit by an old friend and former drunk who had discovered through religion a pathway to sobriety and a better life. Wilson admitted himself to a detoxification program of the type he had previously undergone without lasting success, but this time he came to a critical fork in the road. He described the pivotal decision that he made while in the hospital recovering from delirium tremens:

> There I humbly offered myself to God, as I then understood Him, to do with me as He would. I placed myself unreservedly under His care and direction. I admitted for the first time that of myself I was nothing; that without Him I was lost. I ruthlessly faced my sins and became willing to have my new-found Friend take them, root and branch.

For Wilson this was a paradigm shift. Instead of attempting to conquer his alcoholism and change the course of his life by force of his own will, he surrendered control of his life to an entity outside of himself, his conception of God. An acknowledgement of powerlessness over an addiction is regarded as the first step toward recovery in programs such as AA.

At a later time, when Wilson was alone, almost broke and struggling to hold on to his newfound sobriety, he sought out Dr. Bob Smith, a man described as "a talented surgeon and hopeless drunk." They talked for many days and Smith, after having succumbed to one more tremendous drinking binge, decided to try Wilson's new program. When it proved successful, the two went on to found Alcoholics Anonymous, which has become a hugely popular form of self-help therapy for alcoholics.

Patterned after AA are programs for drug addicts, overeaters, compulsive gamblers, perennial debtors, and sex addicts.

Although there is little scientific evidence for the effectiveness of twelve-step programs, the percentage of respondents in the *Consumer Reports* survey who reported improvement from attending AA was higher than the percentage who reported improvement using other treatments. Although this result is not scientific, the finding is consistent with my experience and that of colleagues that for some forms of emotional problems, such as addiction, self-help groups patterned after AA are potent ways to effect change even when other forms of treatment have been unsuccessful.

Given the appropriate emphasis on anonymity, twelve-step groups have generally shied clear of the mainstream medical establishment and have not been subjected to much research. This is unfortunate. Physicians, therapists, and scientists have a great deal to learn from twelve-step programs. Addicts, in turn, could benefit from professionals with a better understanding and expertise in addiction and the new research ventures that such contacts might stimulate.

How can untrained people help one another sometimes more effectively than trained professionals? How and under what circumstances does it help to "turn over" one's will to a "Higher Power"? What are the active elements in these hugely popular programs? These are just a few of the questions that I hope researchers in this new century will find some way to study.

Pathway 6: New Ways to Treat Trauma

The recent rediscovery of the long-term consequences of trauma has spawned a series of novel treatment approaches. Some have been investigated scientifically; others have not. While innovative treatment approaches offer new hope, evaluate them with caution and common sense. Here are some approaches that seem most promising to me.

EYE MOVEMENT DESENSITIZATION AND REPROCESSING (EMDR)

Developed by California psychologist Francine Shapiro, EMDR has been extensively studied and used for treating the victims of trauma.[10] A recent panel of experts agreed that EMDR is an effective treatment. I have personally been impressed by its effects. One young woman I treated who suffered from nightmares and flashbacks as a result of having been raped several years earlier felt a tremendous sense of relief after a few sessions of EMDR. Her nightmares vanished and she reported feeling as though "some cosmic housekeeper had swept the debris of the rape out of my mind, leaving it clean and fresh again."

When dealing with a single traumatic event, one or two sessions of EMDR may be sufficient to resolve matters. In people who have been abused seriously or repeatedly over time, many more sessions may be necessary.

EMDR is one of several novel treatments that involve input from the body designed to influence internal emotional states. More recently the technique has been expanded to include other forms of stimuli presented in a way that alternately stimulates the left and right sides of the brain, such as tones presented alternately to the left and right ears or buzzing sensations presented alternately to the left and right hands. For more information about EMDR, see chapter 8.

FLASHING COLORED LIGHTS

A different form of visual stimulation coupled with psychotherapy called Emotional Transformation Therapy has been developed by Texas psychotherapist Stephen Vasquez. This treatment involves flashing lights of different colors at different frequencies to patients as they talk about their problems. Vasquez claims that the different colors and frequencies have specific benefits for different types of problems. Although several hundred practitioners in the United States and Europe are now using Vasquez's method, it has not as yet been scientifically tested.

BODY THERAPIES

Since many emotional memories are registered and stored in the body, treatments that combine bodily input with psychological methods seem particularly promising for survivors of trauma. One such form of treatment called Hakomi Integrated Somatics combines psychotherapy with various bodily interactions between therapist and patient. Pat Ogden, director of a center for this form of therapy in Boulder Colorado, uses videotapes to show how touch can be used to promote healing.

The interventions may range from a hand on the shoulder—a comforting show of support—to an invitation to the patient to push the therapist's hands away. Many abuse victims are later unable to set proper boundaries with people. A secretary, for example, might allow her boss to paw her without complaining. A sophomore may be unable to tell her date she doesn't want to sleep with him. And although less common, men may have the same kind of problems. By allowing the patient to push against his hands, the therapist not only gives her permission to set her own boundaries, but allows her *the actual physical experience* of doing so. The idea is simple: Since feelings of powerlessness are partly physical, empowering the body is an important way to learn to set boundaries. Indeed, some abuse victims try to do this by resorting to violence or aggression. Ogden's method teaches you to set boundaries without being violent.

I used one of Ogden's techniques in treating a young man who had been molested many years before. He had few memories of the molestation, but kept holding his arms up against his chest when talking about it. He and I speculated that while being molested, his arms might have been pinned up against his body, compounding his feelings of helplessness. I encouraged him to splay his arms outward against the resistance of my own arms held upright. Much stronger than I, he easily pushed my arms apart, an action that gave him a feeling of amazing exuberance. "Can I do that again?" he asked. And so we repeated the movement several times. He then realized that he often splayed his arms out like that when in an exuberant mood.

Like many novel forms of therapy, body treatments, though promising, have not been studied scientifically. Despite their promise, whether you are a patient or a therapist, I recommend that you proceed very carefully with any technique that involves physical contact. Such contact can easily be misconstrued, and sadly, there are documented cases where therapists have abused their positions of authority to touch patients inappropriately.

TRAINING ORDINARY PEOPLE TO TREAT TRAUMA
Considering the widespread need for human healing, the cost of therapy, and the limited number of available therapists, one potentially useful approach would be to train people in the community to treat specific types of emotional difficulties under proper professional supervision. Researcher and psychologist Edna Foa has successfully implemented such a plan with rape victims, who were treated by trained members of their community supervised by professionals. Surprisingly, the community members proved to be as effective as trained professionals in helping the rape victims.[11]

Although this is an exciting finding, there are limitations to how much can be expected of a person with limited training. As the *Consumer Reports* study showed, in longer-term treatment, qualified professionals outperformed family doctors, suggesting the importance of expertise, especially for complicated problems.

Pathway 7: Healing One Another

Humans have natural talents for healing one another. When a small child hurts his hand, a mother will "kiss it better." When an older child performs poorly on an exam or at a sporting event, his parent might give him an encouraging pat on the shoulder and say a few kind words to communicate that things will be okay. We talk and listen to each other and make sympathetic noises. This is all part of the mind healing that goes on—or should go on—between people on a regular basis.

Even animals exhibit such actions in their daily lives. For example, researcher Frans de Waal, director of the Links Program at Emory

University, has taken pictures of chimpanzees engaged in reconciliation rituals, illustrating that other primates also have the capacity to reach out to one another with a healing gesture.[12]

The health benefits of friends and other social contacts have now been scientifically validated. Being connected to others socially, or participating in religious activities, is good for both your physical and your emotional health.

Pathway 8: Changing Your World

During my first winter in the United States, I didn't know what hit me. I had arrived the previous summer from South Africa to start my psychiatric residency. For the first months I flourished, had never felt better. Then came the end of daylight savings time and the short, dark, dreary days of winter in New York City. I became sluggish, found it hard to focus on my work, and developed other symptoms of what I later recognized to be seasonal affective disorder. Inspired by work with animals, which showed the effects of light on seasonal rhythms, my colleagues and I at the National Institute of Mental Health developed light therapy for this condition. For the last 20 years I have used light therapy and so have hundreds of thousands of others.

The paradigm shift: Sometimes you need to change your environment, not yourself.

Many people can benefit from this basic principle. Summer depressives can benefit from keeping the air-conditioning down low. Environmental chemicals, such as office pollutants (toner, correction fluid, pesticides, and cleaning fluids, to name just a few), can cause headaches, depression, and memory difficulties. I have helped a few of my chemically sensitive patients by recommending that they live and work in well-ventilated places. Allergic people should do whatever they can to get rid of allergens in their environment, rather than relying exclusively on sedating antihistamines.

And it is not only the physical environment that can be toxic. People can be toxic too. People who put you down can make you feel bad about yourself. People who tempt or enable you can help provoke a relapse of an addiction. Envious people can be dangerous, as Shakespeare's Caesar recognized when he observed, "Yond' Cassius has a lean and hungry look. . . . Let me have men about me that are fat." Often we have to deal with such people, but where possible, it is best simply to avoid them.

Our emotions equip us to recognize dangers and avoid them. Foul-smelling food elicits disgust. Poisons taste bitter. Untrustworthy faces trigger the amygdala to signal an alarm. This is our limbic news. We need to listen to it—and act. And one important option is to remove ourselves from the toxic influence.

This strategy might seem obvious, but you would be surprised how often people ignore their limbic news and pay the price. First, a toxic influence may be hard to identify. For centuries, most people who suffered from SAD (and their doctors) were unaware that it was due to darkness. If you feel bad, sad, or mad and can't explain it, ask yourself, "Has anything changed in my environment? A new medication or dietary supplement? A new office? A new colleague?" Sometimes you have to consciously ask yourself to find the cause and deal with it. Second, you might recognize the danger but ignore it, overriding your limbic news. Pride, denial, or stubbornness may get in your way. That is what happened to Caesar on the Ides of March. His wife and a soothsayer both warned him not to venture out that day. But he was Caesar, above such warnings, and we all know what happened to him.

Pathway 9: Emotional Learning, or Lessons from Neuroscience

From his very earliest description of the neuron, Spanish scientist and far-sighted researcher Ramon y Cajal hypothesized that experiences shape the brain by causing neurons to link together in specific patterns.[13] Later, the psychologist Donald Hebb suggested that when neurons fire in conjunction with each other, they develop anatomical connections, which has turned out to be the case.[14] As mentioned earlier, a well-known saying among neuroscientists is that "cells that fire together wire together." Psychotherapy is believed to work by causing this type of rewiring to occur. Perhaps better ways to promote brain rewiring can be discovered by examining developments in the fields of neurology and neuroscience. Following are some examples.

MOBILIZING PARALYZED ARMS AND PARALYZED MINDS

Consider a stroke patient who has lost the use of his right arm as a result of a blood clot in the brain that caused the neurons responsible for moving his right arm to die. His natural tendency would be to use his left arm whenever possible. According to Edward Taub, a researcher at the University of Alabama at Birmingham, this is a big mistake, an example of what he calls "learned nonuse." The person learns not to use the affected arm and, in doing so, may make the disability permanent. Taub and colleagues are trying a different approach, inactivating the good arm while training the stroke victim to use the paralyzed arm.[15]

In a study of thirteen stroke victims in Alabama and at the Freidrich Schiller University in Jena, Germany, researchers prevented stroke patients from using their good arms either by putting them in slings or covering their hands with mitts. At the same time they trained the stroke patients in the use of their affected arms for six hours a day for about two weeks. Amazingly, the patients showed considerable improvement in the functioning of their affected arms, and when their brains were restudied by means of imaging techniques, the area responsible for control of the right arm had almost doubled in size. Even the patients whose arms had been paralyzed for years showed substantial gains, which tended to persist over time. A multicenter study is currently under way to see whether Taub's encouraging preliminary results can be replicated.

The potential application of Taub's findings to the emotional aspects of brain functioning is clear. Emotional difficulties may result from gross or subtle injury, such as early abuse or neglect, to the emotional areas of the brain. Just as trauma to the motor part of the brain can lead to paralysis, trauma to the emotional part of the brain may lead to disruption of the neural circuits responsible for emotional responses. The result: maladaptive ways of thinking, feeling, and behaving. It might be possible to help people with emotional handicaps in the same way as stroke victims, with rigorous training that prevents the old form of behavior and encourages the new form.

To some extent this is already happening. We urge phobics to face their fears; pessimists to consider alternative, more optimistic ways of thinking; and chronically angry people to develop better ways of expressing their feelings. But in dealing with emotional problems, we rarely undertake the type of rigorous, systematic training that Taub used with his stroke patients. One exception is the behavioral treatment of obsessive-compulsive disorder.

Specially trained behavioral therapists spend hours with OCD patients, reviewing the minute details of their obsessions and compulsions. They then instruct these patients not to practice their compulsive behaviors. Take the example of Henry, a young man who is a compulsive hand washer. Henry's continuing to wash his hands compulsively is analogous to a stroke victim continuing to use only his good arm. Just as the latter will not learn to use his bad arm, so Henry will not learn better ways of dealing with his anxiety.

Instead, Henry should be encouraged to endure his anxiety without washing his hands. If he does, his anxiety will decrease and somehow he will be able to get on with productive activities. In the process, Henry is growing new neural networks in the emotional areas of his brain. Indeed, imaging studies of OCD patients have shown normalizing brain changes following behavior therapy.

Behavior therapy for OCD patients also resembles Taub's training of stroke patients in that the sessions typically go on for hours, far longer than the standard fifty-minute psychotherapy session. This may be an important element for achieving change. When Taub and colleagues treated their stroke patients less intensively, they did not find the same dramatic improvements that occurred with the more rigorous program.

One of my patients recently complained that he has the habit of talking in a loud voice and often uses sarcasm. This upsets his wife and others in his life. I suggested he try to change his manner of talking. "I've spoken like that all my life," he replied. " There's no way that I can change." I told him about Taub's work with the stroke patients. If someone can learn to use a paralyzed arm, why should it be impossible for this man to learn to talk more softly and kindly? To my patient's credit, this is exactly what he did—and he enjoyed a welcome improvement in his home life.

Once you realize that something is possible and that all it requires is will and practice, who knows what you can accomplish? It is intriguing to consider the possibility that we can heal emotional difficulties with the same type of treatments that work for other brain problems. The steps for applying Dr. Taub's research to your own emotional problems are simple:

1. Recognize an emotional problem. Accept it, but decide to change it.
2. Deliberately stop the maladaptive behavior, thoughts, or feelings. (This is analogous to putting your good arm in a sling.)
3. Adopt an alternative pattern that didn't seem possible before (such as talking softly or mobilizing your paralyzed arm).
4. Practice the alternative pattern as much as you can on a regular basis.

Interestingly, a traditional Japanese form of psychotherapy called Morita Therapy, which is about a hundred years old, contains elements that are very similar to the steps mentioned above.[16]

TREATING EMOTIONAL DYSLEXIA

Another source of inspiration from the annals of neurology is research into language functioning. A novel treatment for language disorders in children, for example, may prove to be a model for how we might treat emotional difficulties. Researcher Paula Tallal, professor of neuroscience at Rutgers University, observed that children with language disorders have a fundamental difficulty in discriminating sounds that are slightly different, such as "ba" and "da." They need about ten times as long as normal children to discriminate between these different sounds. Tallal hypothesized that this fundamental sound-processing problem might be responsible for the complex language difficulties seen in these children.[17]

Tallal was aware of work by researcher Michael Merzenich that showed that even in adult animals, brain circuitry is highly plastic, meaning that it can be reshaped according to the animal's experiences. Merzenich and colleagues showed that they could train monkeys to identify sounds more and more quickly and that, in doing so, the cerebral cortexes of these monkeys expanded and became reorganized.[18] Tallal teamed up with Merzenich to determine whether they could apply similar principles to retrain children with language difficulties and presumably, in the process, reshape the language areas of their brains.[19]

They developed computer games that challenged children to discriminate between similar sounds presented to them at varying intervals. The games were fun, rewarding the children for getting the answer right as in regular video games. The researchers designed the games so that the children, who have repeatedly experienced failure in their regular lives, would succeed about 80 percent of the time. As the children improved in their performance, the computer presented the sounds to them at intervals that were closer and closer together.

So far the approach has been extremely successful in over 4,000 children. After training, the children are able to process sounds far more quickly, in some cases approaching the speed of children with normal language functioning. More impressive, though, the improvement extends to general language skills. In one study, after the children had worked on the computer program for forty minutes per day, five days a week, for four to eight weeks, 90 percent made as much progress as typically occurs after one-and-a-half to two years of standard teaching.

Maybe we should consider applying the methods of Tallal and Merzenich to people with emotional difficulties. People who are out of touch with their feelings, unempathic, or emotionally unsuccessful in other ways may actually have fundamental information processing problems in the parts of the brain that handle emotions.

Consider someone who is unable to distinguish between a friendly and a hostile expression, tone, or gesture as readily as his more emotionally adept counterparts. When you make a joke, he responds with a blank stare because he is slow to figure out whether you are laughing at him or trying to make him laugh. By the time he does, you are already on to something else. You leave the conversation with a strange feeling that "the guy really didn't get it." Imagine how such an interaction, replayed time and again in a person's life, might isolate him and interfere with both his success and his well-being.

What Tallal and colleagues have shown is that complex behavioral problems such as language difficulties may actually result from an elementary problem with information processing. Perhaps the same is true for people who are unable to muster appropriate emotional responses. Maybe retraining these people in emotional perceptual skills may be more efficient than conventional psychotherapy.

Such retraining could involve the same type of computer games used with the dyslexic children, except in this case, people with emotional difficulties might be asked to discriminate between friendly and hostile faces, tones of voice, and gestures. Or perhaps the problem lies not at the level of discrimination but in the degree to which the individual becomes upset by an angry face or a hostile voice. There again, people could learn to modulate their responses to upsetting triggers using a computer game. Each time they succeeded, they could be rewarded, just like the dyslexic children, and the training could then be increased in difficulty until the desired level of emotional competency is reached.

The language retraining of Tallal, like all successful attempts to change patterns of behavior, emphasizes active participation on the part of the subject and repeated practice. Good psychotherapy involves the same principles. Psychotherapists might learn a great deal from the techniques of Tallal. Although psychotherapists already attempt to alter brain circuitry, computer-based strategies could make their work much more efficient.

LEARNING NEW SKILLS

A recent study of language function shows that it is never too late to learn new skills. It has been accepted as fact that if a person doesn't learn to distinguish certain sounds by the age of 10, he never will. The difficulty in distinguishing L from R for Japanese people is a case in point. There is no distinction between these two consonants in the Japanese language. Therefore, no matter how hard they try, if they have learned no language other than Japanese by the age of 10, they cannot distinguish between "light" and "right"—until now, that is.

Using a computerized presentation, researcher Jay McClelland, codirector of the Center for the Neural Basis of Cognition in Pittsburgh, studied thirty-four native Japanese speakers for three 20-minute sessions under one of two conditions. In the control condition, the subjects heard pairs of words such as "road" and "load," and "right" and "light," spoken in a normal fashion, and had to say whether they were L words or R words.[20]

In the experimental condition, the subjects heard these words presented in a way that was exaggerated by the computer, so that each sound's specific frequency was accentuated. As the subjects became better at discriminating between L and R words, the computer program modified the words to sound more like regular language. The control group showed no improvement in the ability to discriminate between the letters, but after one hour of training, all the experimental subjects were able to distinguish "right" from "light." The researchers speculate that the training resulted in the development of separate brain circuits for hearing the letters "L" and "R."

This simple experiment teaches us two important lessons. First, our old assumptions about what we can and cannot change may be incorrect. Apparently, you can teach an old dog new tricks. Second, if we develop new ways of altering brain circuits by exposing people to highly specific forms of experience, we may be more successful in producing brain changes than we are with conventional approaches.

Many emotional problems that appear to be hard-wired or irreversible may actually prove to be amenable to change if we can develop new ways of approaching them. We should look to animal studies, as Tallal did for her language-impaired children, and paradigms that have worked in other fields. Computer games may prove to be highly useful in bringing about such change, but the type of input will need to be carefully tailored to the particular problem. For example, the "L versus R" program would be useless for an English-speaking person who is already able to discriminate between the consonants.

There are many ways in which human beings can be distinguished from other animals. We have been variously described as "the naked ape,"[21] "the third chimpanzee,"[22] "a work of art," and "little lower than the angels." To this partial list of epithets I would add yet another, "the self-healing ape." For we have at our disposal the will and capacity to look into ourselves and each other and figure out better than any other creature on earth how to help ourselves and others seek pleasure and avoid pain.

We can use the amazing reasoning power of our expanded neocortex to plumb the depths of our emotional brain and develop strategies for changing it. At last, thousands of scientists and clinicians are doing just that in a systematic and coordinated way. With the regularity of the newspaper landing on your front doorstep, we are coming up with novel answers to old problems. That is what the Emotional Revolution is all about and I, for one, am delighted that it has arrived.

Conclusion

As this book goes off to press, my son begins his training as a psychiatrist, some twenty-five years after I did. I wonder what Brave New World he will encounter in his efforts to help his patients, and what techniques will be available to him that were unthinkable when I began.

Samuel Goldwyn said that any man who goes to a psychiatrist should have his head examined. During these next few decades that may just happen. After relating your problems to your psychiatrist, she or he will ask you to put your head in a scanner. Watching while you talk, you will see how your amygdala guns into action when you discuss your obnoxious boss. Your right prefrontal lobe will glow with rage and despair, while the corresponding part on the left wilts, pale and lusterless.

Over the next three or four meetings, your psychiatrist or therapist might stimulate you electrically at various trigger points, might flash lights, massage you, or help you reprogram your responses with a series of musical tones. On rescanning your brain, you and your doctor will be happy to see that the amygdala has settled down and your left prefrontal lobe has come into its own, reassuring you that everything is manageable and life is not so bad after all.

Or perhaps new and ever more wonderful drugs will make such complicated interventions a waste of time. Newly developed molecules will zero in with laserlike precision to fix whatever chemical problem exists, so surgical in their accuracy as to cause no side effects. My son and I will laugh at the old drugs—Prozac and Zoloft. We will shake our heads ruefully at the days when we had to use drugs so imprecise in their actions that they caused messy side effects.

Or I can imagine your doctor reviewing your genetic map with you, explaining why you are so chronically anxious. "Do you see that sequence over there?" she might say. "That guanine molecule ought to be a cytosine. No wonder you're a nervous wreck." Then she will show you the little jar of viruses into which a corrective strip of DNA has been inserted. These infectious agents, long the bane of humankind, will be harnessed to serve as efficient messengers for genetic splicing. One shot of the minuscule wrigglers might do the job and give you, as humorist Garrison Keillor might say, the strength to do what needs to be done. Or maybe, instead, you will receive an injection of stem cells into specific sites in your brain to repair the damage from traumas in your distant past.

For infants whose mothers are unable to care for them properly, there will be mother surrogates undreamed of in the days of Harlow. These warm, soft robots will rock infants with endless patience, feed them milk from lifelike breasts, burp them, change their diapers, dandle them, and sing them lullabies until they doze off into blissful sleep.

Tests of emotional intelligence will be developed to a fine art. How in tune are you with your own feelings? How empathic are you with the emotions of others? Are you able to bring your emotions into line with your life goals? If not, you can be sure that there will be techniques of ever-increasing sophistication and effectiveness to help you do so.

Whatever technology brings, our emotions themselves will always be with us—even the unpleasant ones. They are an essential part of our programming and we will need them in the future as much as we ever have. They are part of our evolutionary heritage and will continue to play an important role in passing on our genes.

Part of the fun of gazing into the future is that it is never really predictable—and sometimes surprises bring more delight than do accurate predictions. Regardless of what happens in the field of emotions, of one thing I am sure. In the next ten to twenty years, we will see amazing advances in our ability to relieve emotional suffering. The Emotional Revolution is under way, and I plan to take a ringside seat and watch it unfold along, perhaps, with those of you who have been good enough to keep me company right to this very last word.

Further Reading

IN RESEARCHING *The Emotional Revolution*, I found many books both interesting and informative. For those who wish to find out more about the emotions in general or some specific aspect of the emotions, here are the books that I found most informative, most enjoyable, or both.

GENERAL

Carper, Jean. *Your Miracle Brain*. HarperCollins, 2000. A readable, comprehensive, and up-to-date review of the beneficial effects of nutrients on brain function.

Damasio, Antonio. *Descartes' Error*. Putnam, 1994. This groundbreaking popular book combines original research with a new theory of emotions that challenges the age-old assumptions about the preeminence of reason over emotion in making decisions.

Darwin, Charles. *The Expression of the Emotions in Man and Animal*. Oxford University Press, 1998. This classic work is introduced by Paul Ekman, a noted expert in the field of emotions. Ekman has annotated the book in such a way as to make it current and even more interesting than it was in its original form.

Hamer, Dean, and Peter Copeland. *Living with Our Genes: Why They Matter More Than You Think*. Anchor Books, 1999. A fascinating review of the genetic underpinnings of behavior by an expert on the genetics of behavior.

LeDoux, Joseph. *The Emotional Brain*. Touchstone Books, 1998. An excellent introduction to the science of emotion by a leading expert on the emotional brain. Thoroughly recommended.

Panksepp, Jaak. *Affective Neuroscience: The Foundation of Human and Animal Emotions*. Oxford University Press, 1998. Although somewhat technical for the general reader, this masterful review is an excellent resource for anyone wanting to dig deeper into the science of the emotions. For a professional book, it is surprisingly entertaining and, in parts, moving.

MEMORY

Schacter, Daniel, L. *Searching for Memory*. Basic Books, 1996. A highly readable, informative, and authoritative book by a leading memory researcher.

Squire, Larry R., and Eric R. Kandel. *Memory: From Mind to Molecules*. Scientific American Library, 1999. An entertaining and informative guide (with enjoyable illustrations) by two experts in the field.

EMOTIONAL INTELLIGENCE

Goleman, Daniel. *Emotional Intelligence: Why It Can Matter More than IQ*. Bantam, 1995. The best-selling book that brought the concept of emotional intelligence to the general public. An important and entertaining primer on the topic.

Pennebaker, James W. *Opening Up: The Healing Power of Expressing Emotions*. Guilford Press, 1997. In this book, an innovative researcher makes his important and very useful research available to the general public.

Thayer, Robert E. *The Origin of Everyday Moods: Managing Energy, Tension and Stress*. Oxford University Press, 1997. A useful guide to mood management for everyone—not just those suffering from depression—by a leading researcher in the field.

FEELINGS THAT KILL OR CURE

Rabin, Bruce. *Stress, Immune Function and Health*. Wiley-Liss, 1999. Although somewhat technical for the general public, this authoritative book is packed with information that underscores the important connections between emotional health and the immune system.

Sapolsky, Robert M. *Why Zebras Don't Get Ulcers: An Updated Guide to Stress, Stress-Related Diseases, and Coping*. W.H. Freeman & Co., 1998. A highly entertaining guide to the dangerous effects of stress, written by an authority on stress.

FEAR AND ANXIETY

Davidson, Jonathan R. T., and Kathryn M. Connor. *Herbs for the Mind: What Science Tells Us About Nature's Remedies for Depression, Stress, Memory Loss and Insomnia.* Guilford Press, 2000. A useful handbook on herbal remedies for anxiety and other ailments.

De Becker, Gavin. *The Gift of Fear.* Dell, 1998. A fascinating book on the importance of listening to your fear; and what to do when you feel it. Gripping reading and sound advice from an expert at dealing with menacing and violent people.

Herman, Judith. *Trauma and Recovery.* Basic Books, 1997. The classic guide by the Harvard psychiatrist and pioneer in the areas of trauma and recovery. Highly recommended.

Ross, Jerilyn. *Triumph over Fear: A Book of Help and Hope for People with Anxiety, Panic Attacks and Phobias.* Bantam, 1995. A very helpful guide by someone who has looked at the broad spectrum of anxiety from both sides—as a patient and a consummate clinician.

Shapiro, Francine. *Eye Movement Desensitization and Reprocessing: Basic Principles, Protocols and Procedures.* Guilford Press, 1995. Although written more for the interested professional than the general reader, this is the definitive guide to EMDR, the most innovative technique for treating trauma, written by the woman who discovered it.

A series of self-help guides for various anxiety disorders is available from *TherapyWorks,* a division of *The Psychological Corporation.* They are expensive, considering how slender they are, but are written by experts in the field and in such a way as to be directly useful to people suffering from these conditions. Examples include *Mastery of Obsessive Compulsive Disorder* by Edna B. Foa and Michael J. Kozak; *Mastery of Your Anxiety and Worry* by Michelle G. Craske, David H. Barlow, and Tracy A. O'Leary; and *Mastery of Your Anxiety and Panic* by Craske and Barlow. These guides are not available in bookstores, but can be ordered from 1-800-228-0752 or off the web at www.psychcorp.com.

ANGER

Williams, Redford. *Anger Kills: 17 Strategies for Controlling the Hostility That Can Harm Your Health.* HarperPerennial, 1994. A very readable book about the physical dangers of anger and what you can do to prevent them, written by an authority on anger who has also grappled personally with the problem.

LOVE

Carnes, Patrick. *Don't Call It Love: Recovery from Sexual Addiction*. Bantam, 1992. A helpful guide to sex addiction and how to treat it.

Christensen, Andrew, and Neil Jacobson. *Reconcilable Differences*. Guilford Press, 1999. A useful book that showcases the authors' approach toward helping people accept differences in their partners, rather than trying to change them.

Etkoff, Nancy. *Survival of the Prettiest: The Science of Beauty*. Anchor Books, 1999. An entertaining and well-written review of this fascinating topic.

Fisher, Helen. *The Anatomy of Love: A Natural History of Mating, Marriage and Why We Stray*. Fawcett Books, 1995. An anthropologist's perspective on the values and limitations of monogamy makes compelling reading.

Gottman, John M., and Nan Silver. *The Seven Principles for Making Marriage Work: A Practical Guide from the Country's Foremost Relationship Expert*. Three Rivers Press, 1999. Data based advice on what does and does not help couples stay together.

Hendrix, Harville. *Getting the Love You Want: A Guide for Couples*. HarperPerennial, 1990. Some of my patients have found this book useful in working through their problems. It showcases the author's *Imago Therapy*, based on the idea that we unconsciously choose partners who express qualities of our parents, which can cause problems in relationships.

Karen, Robert. *Becoming Attached: First Relationships and How They Shape Our Capacity to Love*. Oxford University Press, 1998. Detailed and geared primarily to professionals, but very well written and comprehensive, this book could appeal to the general public as well.

Lewis, Thomas; Farni Amini; and Richard Lannon. *A General Theory of Love*. Random House, 2000. A concise and very readable guide to what science can tell us about love.

Liebowitz, Michael. *The Chemistry of Love*. Little, Brown and Company, 1983. Although out of print, this pioneering book still makes fascinating reading.

Ornish, Dean. *Love and Survival*. HarperCollins, 1999. A readable and comprehensive review of the field.

Tennov, Dorothy. *Love and Limerence: The Experience of Being in Love*. Scarborough House, 1999. A fascinating descriptive work about the thrills and agonies of infatuation.

DEPRESSION AND THE TREATMENT OF DEPRESSION

Burns, David. *Feeling Good: The New Mood Therapy*. Wholecare, 1999. A first-rate primer on how to use cognitive-behavior therapy to treat your own depression.

De Paulo, J. R. *How to Cope With Depression: A Complete Guide for You and Your Family*. Ballantine, 1996. A valuable resource for depressed people and their loved ones, written by a leading mood-disorders expert.

Hedaya, Robert, with Deborah Kotz. *The Antidepressant Survival Program: How to Beat the Side Effects and Enhance the Benefits of Your Medication*. Crown, 2000. An excellent guide to alternative treatments for depression.

Jamison, Kay Redfield. *Night Falls Fast: Understanding Suicide*. Knopf, 1999. A thorough, well-written, and often gripping review of this major public health problem.

Rosenthal, Norman. *St. John's Wort: The Herbal Way to Feeling Good*. HarperCollins, 1998. A guide to the use of this flowering herb in the treatment of depression.

Rosenthal, Norman. *Winter Blues: Seasonal Affective Disorder: What It Is and How to Overcome It*. Guilford Press, 1998. A book that describes how most people tend to experience changes in energy level, behavior, and creativity with the changing seasons; it provides guidelines for diagnosing and treating seasonal depression.

Solomon, Andrew. *The Noonday Demon: An Atlas of Depression*. Scribner, 2001. This National Book Award winner is a riveting first-person account of depression, and a comprehensive intellectual exploration of the topic.

Stoll, Andrew. *The Omega-3 Connection: The Groundbreaking Anti-depression Diet and Brain Program*. Simon & Schuster, 2001. Useful dietary advice by an expert on the subject.

Styron, William. *Darkness Visible: A Memoir of Madness*. Vintage Books, 1992. A moving personal account of depression and recovery by the prize-winning novelist.

HAPPINESS AND EUPHORIA

Csikszentmihalyi, Mihaly. *Flow: The Psychology of Optimal Experience*. HarperCollins, 1991. A justifiably popular book that outlines the concept of "flow"—the sense of being alive while actively engaged in meaningful activities.

Dalai Lama and Howard Cutler. *The Art of Happiness: A Handbook of Living*. Riverhead Books, 1998. A highly popular and intriguing guide to finding happiness in a non-Western way.

Jamison, Kay Redfield. *An Unquiet Mind*. Random House, 1997. A powerful and gripping memoir of manic-depression. This firsthand description of the stages of mania—beginning with exuberant fun and ending in madness—offers hope to those suffering from this painful illness.

Kahnemann, Daniel, Ed Diener, and Norbert Schwartz (editors). *Well-Being: The Foundations of Hedonic Psychology*. Russell Sage Foundation. 1999. An outstanding monograph containing chapters by leading researchers in the fields of happiness and positive psychology.

Myers, David. *The Pursuit of Happiness: Discovering the Pathway to Fulfillment, Well-Being and Enduring Personal Joy*. Avon, 1993. A highly readable and enjoyable book by a leading expert in happiness research. Packed with good stuff.

Seligman, Martin. *Learned Optimism: How to Change Your Mind and Your Life*. Pocket Books, 1998. The researcher who developed the "learned helplessness" model of depression explores ways to improve one's attitude toward oneself, the world, and the future. Basically, a cognitive-behavioral approach—as yet untested, but worth a try.

PATHWAYS TO CHANGE

Carnes, Patrick. *A Gentle Path Through the Twelve Steps: The Classic Guide for All People in the Process of Recovery*. Compcare Publications. 1994. A helpful basic text for people seeking recovery from addictions; a good introduction to twelve-step programs.

Frankl, Victor. *Man's Search for Meaning*. Washington Square Press, 1998. American readers rate this profoundly important book by the late neurologist and Holocaust survivor as one of the most meaningful books they have ever read. From his concentration camp experience, Frankl shapes a philosophy and a therapy, illustrating how one can find meaning even in the direst of circumstances.

Seligman, Martin. *What You Can Change . . . and What You Can't: The Complete Guide to Successful Self-Improvement: Learning to Accept Who You Are*. Fawcett Books, 1995. A handy guide to what research shows about what therapy can do to reverse the different types of emotional disorders.

Websites

THE FOLLOWING associations have websites that will provide additional information, as well as links to even more websites. The telephone numbers of the organizations are also provided.

GENERAL

National Alliance for the Mentally Ill
800-950-6264
www.nami.org

FEAR AND ANXIETY

Anxiety Disorders Association of America
301-231-9350
www.adaa.org

The Ross Center for Anxiety and Related Disorders
202-363-1010
www.rosscenter.com

LOVE AND LUST

Sex and Love Addicts Anonymous
781-255-8825
www.slaafws.org

Sexaholics Anonymous
615-331-6230
www.sa.org

DEPRESSION

Depression and Related Affective Disorders Association
410-955-4647
www.med.jhv.edu/drada

National Depressive and Manic-Depressive Association
800-826-3632
www.ndmda.org

DSM = IV Criteria

DSM-IV Criteria for Major Depressive Disorder

A. Five (or more) of the following symptoms have been present for two solid weeks. This is different from your usual functioning. At least one of the symptoms must be either (1) depressed mood or (2) loss of interest or pleasure.

1. depressed mood most of the day, nearly every day, either experienced by yourself or observed by others
2. markedly diminished interest or pleasure in all, or almost all, activities, most of the day, nearly every day
3. significant weight loss when not dieting, or weight gain, or decrease or increase in appetite nearly every day
4. sleeping too much or too little nearly every day
5. being agitated or depressed to such a degree that others could notice it—not just internal feelings of restlessness or being slowed down
6. fatigue or loss of energy nearly every day
7. feelings of worthlessness or excessive or inappropriate guilt nearly every day—more than just feeling guilty because your depression doesn't enable you to function adequately
8. decreased ability to think or concentrate, or difficulty making decisions, nearly every day
9. recurrent thoughts of death (not just fear of dying), recurrent ideas of suicide or attempting or planning suicide

AND

B. These symptoms cause significant distress or impairment in your social, occupational, or other important areas of functioning.

AND

C. The symptoms are not directly due to the physical effects of medications, drugs, or alcohol, nor are the result of a medical condition, such as underactive thyroid functioning.

Now, many people who feel quite depressed do not exactly fit into the DSM-IV criteria for major depression. The diagnostic schema allows for those types of depression as well. These include briefer depressions that occur premenstrually (premenstrual dysphoric disorder), and recurrent depressions that can be very severe even though they may last for only a few days at a time (recurrent brief depressive disorder). The good news is that all of these depressions, as well as those that accompany medical conditions or may be associated with drugs and alcohol, may be helped by the same treatments that are helpful for major depression.

One diagnosis, which has its own code in DSM-IV, is *dysthymic disorder*, a milder form of depression that causes a great deal of misery because of its chronic nature. I have modified the DSM-IV criteria for dysthymic disorder and have listed them below.

DSM-IV Criteria for Dysthymic Disorder

A. Depressed mood for most of the day, for more days than not, either experienced by yourself or observed by others, for at least two years.

AND

B. Presence, while depressed, of two or more of the following:
   1. poor appetite or overeating
   2. insomnia or sleeping too much
   3. fatigue or low energy
   4. low self-esteem
   5. poor concentration or difficulty making decisions
   6. feelings of hopelessness

AND

C. During a two-year period you have never been without the symptoms in A or B for more than two months at a time.

AND

D. The symptoms are not due to the direct physical effects of medications, drugs, or alcohol or to a general medical condition, such as underactive thyroid functioning.

As you read through the criteria, it will become obvious that they are somewhat arbitrary. What if you were free of symptoms for two and a half months? Does that mean that you are not dysthymic or wouldn't benefit from treatment? Although systematic diagnostic schemas have been useful for standardizing diagnoses for research and other purposes, the seasoned clinician and the savvy patient should relaize that diagnosis is not a precise science and not get too hung up on whether someone exactly meets the criteria or not, before deciding on whether or how to treat. It is clear that when we are dealing with depression, in all its forms, we are dealing with a continuum, with happy, normal mood at the one end and serious depression at the other, and all sorts of gradations in between. The same treatments that help the severer forms of depression will generally also help the milder forms and vice versa. The most important determinants of whether or not you seek and receive treatment are, therefore, how bad you feel and whether you are willing to reach out for help.

A Guide to Evaluating Where You Fit on the Depressive Spectrum

Level of Depression	Symptoms	Effects
Stressed out; down in the dumps; under the weather.	Fatigue; mild anxiety; lack of zest; less fun than usual.	Others may well not notice anything amiss; no effect on functioning.
Mild depression.	A few symptoms listed above, but none are severe.	Slightly diminished quality of life, productivity, or creativity; you notice this but others would probably not.
Moderate depression.	Meet the criteria for DSM-IV major depression, listed in Appendix A.	Significant impact on functioning in work or relationships; significant impact on physical functioning; it is, however, possible in many cases to function well in certain respects, making others unaware of how bad you are feeling; those close to you are likely to be aware that something is amiss.
Severe depression.	Meet the criteria for DSM-IV major depression listed in Appendix A; any suicidal ideas or intentions.	It is difficult to function adequately at work or in relationships; significant impact on physical functioning can be a threat to your relationship, your job, or if you are suicidal, to life itself; others are very likely to be aware that something is amiss and to be concerned about you.

Daily Mood Log

+5	Feel really great	+2	Quite happy	-1	Slightly down/low	-4	Extremely low
+4	Feel great	+1	Slightly happy	-2	Quite down/low	-5	The "pits"
+3	Very happy	0	Normal	-3	Very down/low		

NAME_____ MONTH RECORDED_____ YEAR_____

MOOD RATING (see page 330)	DAY OF MONTH	HOUR OF DAY (24-hour clock) MARK SLEEPING* HOURS																							DAY MON
		A.M.										P.M.														
		1	2	3	4	5	6	7	8	9	10	11	12	13	14	15	16	17	18	19	20	21	22		
	1																									1
	2																									2
	3																									3
	4																									4
	5																									5
	6																									6
	7																									7
	8																									8
	9																									9
	10																									10
	11																									11
	12																									12
	13																									13
	14																									14
	15																									15
	16																									16
	17																									17
	18																									18
	19																									19
	20																									20
	21																									21
	22																									22
	23																									23
	24																									24
	25																									25
	26																									26
	27																									27
	28																									28
	29																									29
	30																									30
	31																									31

* ● = sleeping   ◻ = lying in bed

	DRUGS AND DOSE					STRESSFUL AND EXICITING EVENTS (Indicate date with —)
	1	2	3	4		

DAY OF MONTH					DAY OF MONTH	
1					1	_____
2					2	_____
3					3	_____
4					4	_____
5					5	_____
body 6					6	_____
7					7	_____
weight 8					8	_____
9					9	_____
10					10	_____
11					11	_____
body 12					12	_____
13					13	_____
14					14	_____
weight 15					15	_____
16					16	_____
17					17	_____
18					18	_____
19					19	_____
body 20					20	_____
21					21	_____
weight 22					22	_____
23					23	_____
24					24	_____
25					25	_____
26					26	_____
body 27					27	_____
28					28	_____
weight 29					29	_____
30					30	_____
31					31	_____

Notes

Chapter 1. Welcome to the Emotional Revolution

1. E. R. Kandel, *American Journal of Psychiatry* 155:4 (1998): 457–469.
2. J. T. Cacioppo and W. L. Gardner, *Annual Review of Psychology* 50 (1999): 191–214.
3. T. S. Kuhn, *The Structure of Scientific Revolutions*, 2nd ed. (Chicago: University of Chicago Press, 1970).
4. Nobelfoersamlingen, Karolinska Institutet, Press Release, October 9, 2000. URL: www.nobel.se/medicine/laureates/2000/press. html
5. For information on animal emotions, see L. Tangley, "Animal Emotions," *U.S. News & World Report*, October 30, 2000, 129 (17): 48–52.

Chapter 2. The Intelligence of Emotions

1. B. Pascal, *Pensees*, No. 277, 1670. In the original, "Le coeur a ses raisons que la raison ne connait point."
2. M. Wollstonecraft, "Letters written during a short residence in Sweden, Norway and Denmark," (1796): Letter 19.
3. C. Darwin, *The Expression of the Emotions in Man and Animals*, 3rd ed. with Introduction, Afterword, and Commentaries by Paul Ekman. (New York: Oxford University Press, 1998), p. 43.
4. S. Mineka et al., *Journal of Abnormal Psychology* 93 (1984): 355–372.
5. J. E. LeDoux, *Scientific American* 270:6 (1994): 150–157.
6. Facts regarding Rosa Parks were taken from her book: Rosa Parks with Jim Haskins, *Rosa Parks: My Story* (New York: Dial Books, 1992).
7. D. Goleman, *Emotional Intelligence* (New York: Bantam Books, 1995).
8. Professor Robert Solomon, *Love and Vengeance, a Course on Human Emotion* (University of Texas: The Teaching Company, 1994).
9. Although in Western philosophy reason has been given precedence over feeling as most important to making decisions, some philosophers, such as David Hume (1711–1776), took the opposite view.

Hume said, "reason is, and ought only to be the slave of passions, and can never pretend to any other office than to serve and obey them." *A Treatise upon Human Nature*, Book 2, Part 3, 1739. For further discussion of this subject, see Antonio Damasio's book *Descartes' Error: Emotion, Reason and the Human Brain* (New York: Grosset/Putnam, 1994).

10. The story of Phineas Gage can be found in *Descartes' Error* cited above.

11. A. R. Damasio, *Phil. Trans. R. Soc. Lond. B.* 351:1413–1420, The Royal Society, 1996.

12. A. Bechara et al., *Cognition* 50 (1994): 7–15.

13. A. Bechara et al., *Cerebral Cortex* 6 (1996): 215–225.

14. H. Cleckley, *The Mask of Sanity* (St. Louis: Mosby, 1976).

15. American Psychiatric Association, *Diagnostic Statistical Manual of Mental Disorders*, Fourth Edition (Washington, D.C.: American Psychiatric Press, 1994).

16. S. W. Anderson et al., *Nature Neuroscience* 2: November 1999: 1032–1037.

17. R. Plushnick-Masti, "A Family's Shame: Sheinbein's Parents Describe Their Pain, Bafflement," *Washington Post*, November 5, 1999, p. B-1.

18. A. Raine et al., *Archives of General Psychiatry* 57:2 (2000): 119–127.

19. A. Camus, *The Stranger*, trans. Joseph Laredo. (New York: Knopf, 1987).

20. Janet Halperin, "Why Should Robots Have Emotions?" (lecture given at National Institute of Mental Health, July 10, 2000, in seminar on the Emotions).

21. R. B. Zajonc, *American Psychologist* 35:2 (1980): 151–175.

22. R. F. Bornstein and P. R. D'Agostino, *Journal of Personality and Social Psychology* 63:4 (October 1992): 545–552.

23. K. C. Berridge, "Pleasure, Pain, Desire and Dread: Hidden Core Processes of Emotion," in D. Kahneman et al. (eds.), *Well-Being: The Foundations of Hedonic Psychology* (pp. 525–557). (New York: Russell Sage Foundation, 1999), p. 530.

24. R. K. Kushwaha et al., *IEEE Trans. Biomed. Eng.* 39:2 (1992): 165–175.

25. P. J. Whalen et al., *Journal of Neuroscience* 18:1 (January 1, 1998): 411–418.

26. J. S. Morris et al., *Nature* 393:6684 (June 4, 1998): 467–470.

27. J. LeDoux, *The Emotional Brain: The Mysterious Underpinnings of Emotional Life* (New York: Simon & Schuster, 1998).

28. I. Fried et al., *Nature* 391:6668 (February 12, 1998): 650.

29. R. E. Nisbett and T. D. Wilson, *Psychological Review* 84 (1977): 231–259.

30. M. W. Fischman and R. W. Foltin, "Self-Administration of Cocaine by Humans: A Laboratory Perspective," in G. R. Bock and J. Whelan (eds.), *Cocaine: Scientific and Social Dimensions.* (pp. 165–180) (Chichester, England: Wiley, 1992).

Chapter 3. The Anatomy of Feeling

1. E. Dickinson, "There's a certain slant of light," No. 258 (c.1861), St. 1.
2. J. Keats, Poems, 1817. Sonnet: "On first looking into Chapman's Homer."
3. B. Russell, *The Autobiography of Bertrand Russell* (Boston: Little, Brown & Co., 1967).
4. J. E. LeDoux, *Scientific American* 270:6(1994):150–157.
5. W. James, "What is an emotion?" *Mind* 9 (1884): 188–205.
6. W. James, *Principles of Psychology* (New York: Dover, 1880/1950).
7. J. T. Cacioppo, personal communication, 2000. Antonio Damasio's recently formulated somatic marker hypothesis of emotions, which emphasizes the importance of the physical aspects of emotional responses in making decisions, has echoes of the original James-Lange hypothesis. See A.R. Damasio *Descartes' Error*, 1994, cited above, at pages 165–201; also A.R. Damasio *Phil. Trans. R. Soc. Lond. B* 351: 1413–1420,1996.
8. L. Squire and E. R. Kandel, *Memory: From Mind to Molecules* (New York: W.H. Freeman Company, 1998).
9. S. Blakeslee, "A Decade of Discovery Yields a Shock About the Brain," *New York Times,* January 4, 2000, p. D-1; also, G. Kempermann and F. H. Gage, "Neurogenesis in the adult hippocampus," Novartis Found Symposium, 231 (2000): 220–241; also P.S. Eriksson et al., *Nature Medicine* (November 1998): 1313–1317; also, G. Kempermann and F. H. Gage, *Nature Medicine* 4: 5(1998): 555–557.
10. E. Gould et al., *Science* 286 (October 15, 1999): 548–552.
11. For further description of the neuron and the synapse, see L. Squire and E. Kandel, *Memory: From Mind to Molecules,* cited above.
12. R. J. Davidson et al., *Science* 289: 5479 (July 28, 2000): 591–594.
13. J. E. LeDoux, *The Emotional Brain: The Mysterious Underpinning of Emotional Life* (New York: Simon & Schuster, 1998), pp. 138–141.
14. E. Goode, "Rats May Dream, It Seems, of Their Days at the Mazes," *New York Times,* Thursday, January 25, 2001.
15. E. G. Boring, *A History of Experimental Psychology* (New York: Appleton-Century-Crofts, 1950).
16. F. Plum and B. T. Volpe, "Neuroscience and Higher Brain Function: From Myth to Public Responsibility," in F. Plum (ed.), *Handbook of*

Physiology, Section 1: The Nervous System, vol. 5 (Bethesda, Md.: American Physiological Society, 1987).

17. J. Panksepp, *Affective Neuroscience: The Foundations of Human and Animal Emotions*. (New York: Oxford University Press, 1998), pp. 52–54.

18. See note 13, above.

19. J. H. Martin, *Neuroanatomy: Text and Atlas* (Stamford, CT: Appleton & Lange, 1989).

20. J. P. Lorberbaum et al., *Depression and Anxiety* 10 (1999):99–104.

21. P. D. MacLean, "The Triune Brain, Emotion and Scientific Bias," in F. O. Schmitt (ed.), *The Neurosciences: Second Study Program* (New York: Rockefeller University Press, 1970).

22. For descriptions of research on how animals are conditioned to fearful stimuli, read J. LeDoux, *Scientific American* 270:6 (1994): 50–57.

23. LeDoux made this comment in a presentation on his work to the National Institutes of Health in 1998.

24. A. R. Damasio et al., *Nature Neuroscience* 3:10 (2000):1049–1056.

25. K. Beeckmans and M. Michiels, *Acta Neurol. Belg.* 96 (1996): 35–42; also J. P. Flynn, in R. G. Grenell and S. G. Abau (eds.), *Biological Foundations of Psychiatry* (pp. 275–295). (New York: Ravens Press, 1976).

26. L. Squire and E. Kandel, *Memory: From Mind to Molecules* (New York: W. H. Freeman Company, 1998).

27. H. Terzian and G. D. Ore, *Neurology* 5 (1955): 373–380.

28. R. Joseph, *Neuropsychiatry, Neuropsychology and Clinical Neuroscience* 2nd ed. (Baltimore: Williams & Wilkins, 1996) 227–228, 588.

29. G. Stuzmann, *Journal of Neuroscience*, 18:22: (November 15, 1998): 9529–9538.

30. M. Fava and J.F. Rosenbaum, *Journal of Clinical Psychiatry*, 60, Suppl. 15 (1999): 21–24.

31. For further information about the hypothalamus and other anatomical structures in the limbic system, see chapter 5, "The Limbic System," pages 161–205 in R. Joseph, *Neuropsychiatry, Neuropsychology and Clinical Neuroscience*, 2nd ed. (Baltimore: Williams and Wilkins, 1996); also R. Joseph, *Psychoanalytic Review* 79:3 (fall 1992): 405–456.

32. R. R. Llinas and U. Ribary, "Temporal Conjunction in Thalamo-cortical Transactions," in H.H. Jasper et al. (eds.), *Consciousness: At the Frontiers of Neuroscience, Advances in Neurology* (vol. 77, pp. 95–103). (Philadelphia: Lippincott-Raven Publishers, 1998).

33. M. Davis and Y. Lee, *Cognition and Emotion* 12:3 (1998): 277–305.

34. These observations regarding the relationship between seizure ac-

tivity and manic depression are discussed in a review article: R. M. Post et al., *Neuropsychobiology* 38:3 (October 1998): 152–166.

35. M. H. Teicher, C. M. Andersen, S. L. Andersen, et el., Unpublished manuscript, "Neurobiological correlates of childhood maltreatment," 2000; also M. H. Teicher, *Cerebrum*, The DANA Forum on Brain Science 2:4 (fall 2000): 50.

36. "The Listening Project." URL: www.education.umd.edu/EDHD/faculty/porges/Hp/Hp.html

37. B. Woodward and S. Armstrong, *The Brethren: Inside the Supreme Court* (New York: Simon & Schuster, 1979).

38. G. Gainotti, *Cortex* 8 (1972): 41–55.

39. S. E. Starkstein et al., *Journal of Neuropsychiatry and Clinical Neuroscience* 3:3 (summer 1991): 276–285.

40. R. J. Davidson et al., *Current Opinion in Neurobiology*, 9 (1999): 228–234.

41. M. C. Zinser et al., *Journal of Abnormal Psychology* 108:2 (May 1999): 240–254.

42. R. J. Davidson et al., *Biological Psychiatry* 47 (2000): 85–95.

43. N. A. Fox et al., *Development and Psychopathology* 8 (1996): 89–102.

44. J. Kagan, *The Nature of the Child.* (New York: Basic Books, 1984).

45. J. Levy et al., *Brain and Cognition* 2 (1983): 404–419.

46. P. Shammi and D. T. Stuss, *Brain* 122 (Oxford University Press, 1999), pp. 657–666.

47. I. Fried et al., *Nature* 391:6668 (February 12, 1998): 650.

Chapter 4. Mixing Memory and Desire

1. E. Claparede, "Recognition and 'ME-NESS,'" in D. Rapaport (ed.), *Organization and Pathology of Thought* (pp. 58–75). (New York: Columbia University Press, 1911).

2. B. Milner et al., *Neuron*, 20 (March 1998): 445–468.

3. L. Squire and E. Kandel, *Memory: From Mind to Molecules* (New York: W. H. Freeman Company, 1998), 15.

4. D. Warrington and L. Weiskrantz, *Neuropsychologia* 20 (1973): 233–248.

5. D. Warrington and L. Weiskrantz, *Nature* 217 (1968): 972–974; also D. Warrington and L. Weiskrantz, *Neuropsychologia* 12 (1974): 419–428.

6. A. Bechara et al., *Science* 269 (August 25, 1995): 1115–1118.

7. J. E. LeDoux, *Annual Review of Psychology* 46 (1995): 209–235; also W. J. Jacobs and L. Nadel, *Psychological Review*, 925 (1985): 512–531.

8. For a discussion of fugues, see E. Slater and M. Roth, *Clinical*

Psychiatry, 3rd ed. (London: Bailliere, Tindall and Cassell Ltd., 1970).

9. D. L. Schacter, *Searching for Memory: The Brain, the Mind and the Past* (New York: Basic Books, 1996), p. 225.

10. R. Sapolsky, *Science* 273:749 (August 9, 1996): 749–750.

11. L. C. Terr, *Unchained Memories* (New York: Basic Books, 1994).

12. D. L. Schacter, *Searching for Memory*, cited above, p. 250.

13. C. Grumman, "Controversial Doctor Faces Loss of License," *Chicago Tribune*, August 13, 1998.

14. M. L. Bruck and S. J. Ceci, Amicus Brief for *The State of New Jersey v. Michaels*, presented by the Committee of Concerned Social Scientists, Psychology, *Public Policy and the Law* 1 (1995): 272–322.

15. Dr. Cheit's URL: www.brown.edu/Departments/Taubman_Center/Recovmem/Archive.html

16. D. L. Schacter, *Searching for Memory*, cited above, pp. 250–251.

17. S. Warmbit, "State Pushes Case Against Doctor," *Chicago Daily Herald* (Legal Affairs), September 29, 1998.

18. S. Roth and M. J. Friedman (eds.), *Childhood Trauma Remembered: A Report on the Current Scientific Knowledge Base and its Applications.* (International Society for Traumatic Stress Studies ("ISTSS"), 1993), 15.

19. S. L. McElroy and P. E. Keck Jr., *Psychiatric Annals* 25 (1995): 731–735.

20. S. Roth and M. J. Friedman (eds.), *Childhood Trauma Remembered,* cited above, p. 11.

21. C. A. Courtois, *Recollections of Sexual Abuse: Principles and Guidelines for Treatment* (New York: W.W. Norton, 1999).

22. I. E. Hyman et al., *Applied Cognitive Psychology* 9 (1995): 181–197.

23. D. L. Schacter, *Searching for Memory*, cited above, p. 110; also I. E. Hyman and J. Pentland, "Guided Imagery and the Creation of False Childhood Memories," *Journal of Memory and Language* 35 (1996): 101–117.

24. S. J. Ceci, "False Beliefs: Some Developmental and Clinical Considerations," (pp. 91–128) in D. L. Schacter et al., (eds.), *Memory Distortion: How Minds, Brains and Societies Reconstruct the Past* (Cambridge: Harvard University Press, 1995).

25. E. F. Loftus and H. G. Hoffman, *Journal of Experimental Psychology: General,* 118:1 (March 1989): 100–104.

26. M. A. Stadler et al., *Memory and Cognition* 27:3 (May 1999): 494–500.

27. D. L. Schacter et al., *Neuron* 17:2 (August 1996): 267–274.

28. B. Gonsalves and K. A. Paller, *Nature Neuroscience* 3:12 (2000): 1316–1321.

29. J. Briere and J. Conte, *Journal of Traumatic Stress* 6 (1993): 21–31.

30. D. L. Schacter, *Searching for Memory: The Brain, the Mind and the Past* (New York: Basic Books, 1996), pp. 255–261.

31. L. M. Williams, *Journal of Consulting and Clinical Psychology* 62 (1994): 1167–1176; also L. M. Williams and V. L. Banyard, "Perspective on Adult Memories of Childhood Sexual Abuse: A Research Review," in D. Spiegel (ed.), Section II, *American Psychiatric Review of Psychiatry* 16, chapter 9, pp. II–123 to II–151, 1997.

32. C. S. Widom and S. Morris, *Psychological Assessment* 9 (1997): 34–36.

33. Several corroborated cases are on record. See Ross Cheit's website: www.brown.edu/Departments/Taubman_Center/Recovmem/Archive.html ; also S. Duggal and L. A. Stroufe, *Journal of Traumatic Stress* 11:2 (April 1998): 301–321; also D. L. Bull, *American Journal of Psychotherapy* 53: 2 (Spring 1999): 221–224.

34. L. Cahill et al., *Nature* 371 (October 20, 1994): 702–704.

35. A. H. van Stegeren et al., *Psychopharmacology* (Berlin) 138:3–4 (August 1998): 305–310.

36. R. Yehuda, *Psychoneuroendocrinology* 21:2 (June 1998): 359–379.

37. L. Cahill, *Annals of the New York Academy of Sciences*, 821 (June 21, 1997): 238–246.

38. J. E. LeDoux, *The Emotional Brain: The Mysterious Underpinnings of Emotional Life* (New York: Simon & Schuster, 1998).

39. V. I. Reus et al., *American Journal of Psychiatry*, 136:7 (1979): 927–931.

40. D. L. Schacter, *Searching for Memory*, cited above, p. 62; also J. LeDoux, *The Emotional Brain*, cited above, p. 212.

41. L. Squire and E. Kandel, *Memory: From Mind to Molecules* (New York: W. H. Freeman Company, 1998), pp. 199–200; also T. Ebert et al., *Science* 220 (1995): 21–23.

42. A. Karni et al., *Proceedings of the National Academy of Science, USA* 95:3 (February 3, 1998): 861–868.

43. M. Merzenich et al., "Cortical Plasticity Underlying Perceptual, Motor and Cognitive Skill Development: Implications for Neurorehabilitaion," *Cold Spring Harbor Symposia on Quantitative Biology*, vol. LXI. (Cold Spring Harbor Laboratory Press, 1996).

44. M. Merzenich et al., *Science* 271 (1996): 77–81.

45. L. Squire and E. Kandel, *Memory*, cited above, pp. 144–145.

46. J. M. Schwartz et al., *Archives of General Psychiatry* 53:2 (1996): 109– 113.

47. B. McEwen and R. Sapolsky, *Current Opinion in Neurobiology* 5 (1995): 205–216.

48. K. Nader et al., *Nature* 406 (August 17, 2000): 722–726.

49. Ibid.

50. G. E. Schafe and J. E. LeDoux, *Journal of Neuroscience* 20: 18 (September 15, 2000): RC 96.
51. W. Shakespeare, *Macbeth* (1606), Act V, Scene 5, Line 9.

Chapter 5. Emotional Intelligence or Competence

1. P. Salovey et al., "The Positive Psychology of Emotional Intelligence," in C. R. Snyder and S. J. Lopez (eds.), *The Handbook of Positive Psychology*. (New York: Oxford University Press, 2000).
2. "What's Your EQ? The First Good Test . . ." *Time Magazine*, 2 October, 1995.
3. H. Gardner, *Frames of Mind* (New York: Basic Books, 1983).
4. P. Salovey and J. D. Mayer, *Imagination, Cognition and Personality* 9 (1990): 185–211.
5. In the cited source, the table was adapted from Mayer and Salovey (1997). The original table was © 1997 by Peter Salovey and David Sluyter.
6. J. D. Mayer et al., "Models of Emotional Intelligence," in R. J. Sternberg (ed.), *Handbook of Intelligence* (pp. 396–420). (Cambridge, UK: Cambridge University Press, 2000).
7. P. Salovey et al., "Current Directions in Emotional Intelligence Research," cited above; also D. Goleman, *Healthcare Forum Journal* (March/April 1998), 36–76.
8. P. Salovey et al., "The Positive Psychology of Emotional Intelligence," cited above.
9. D. R. Trinidad and C. A. Johnson, unpublished data (University of Southern California, 1999).
10. P. Gay (ed.), *The Freud Reader* (New York: W.W. Norton & Co., 1989), 78.
11. J. D. Mayer et al., "Models of Emotional Intelligence," in R. J. Sternberg (ed.), *Handbook of Intelligence* (pp. 396–420). (Cambridge, UK: Cambridge University Press, 2000).
12. D. O. Hebb, "Emotion in Man and Animal: An Analysis of the Intuitive Processes of Recognition," *Psychological Review* 53 (1946): 88–106.
13. V. J. Derlega et al., *Personality: Contemporary Theory and Research* (Chicago: Nelson Hall, 1999).
14. M. W. Fischman and R. W. Foltin, "Self-Administration of Cocaine by Humans: A Laboratory Perspective," in G.R. Bock and J. Whelan (eds.), *Cocaine: Scientific and Social Dimensions* (vol. 166, pp. 165–180). (Chichester, England: Wiley, 1992).
15. D. Watson et al., *Journal of Personality and Social Psychology* 54 (1998): 1020–1030.

16. C. E. Ainscough, *Journal of Psychosomatic Research* 34:1 (1990): 35–45.

17. D. Watson, Personal communication, 2000.

18. D. Watson and A. Tellegen, "Toward a Consensual Structure of Mood," *Psychological Bulletin* 98 (1985): 219–235.

19. M. S. George et al., *American Journal of Psychiatry* 152:3 (1995): 341–351; also A. R. Damasio et al., *Nature Neuroscience* 3:10 (2000): 1049–1056.

20. J. W. Pennebaker, *Psychological Science* 8 (1997): 162–166; also J. W. Pennebaker "Health Effects of the Expression (and Non-expression) of Emotions Through Writing," in A. Vingerho et al. (eds.), *The (Non) Expression of Emotions in Health and Disease* (Tilburg: Tilburg University Press, 1997).

21. J. W. Pennebaker, *Opening Up: The Healing Power of Expressing Emotions* (New York: Guilford Press, 1997).

22. J. Littrell, *Clinical Psychology Review* 18:1 (1998): 71–102.

23. C. Darwin, *The Expression of Emotions in Man and Animals* Definitive Edition, Introduction, Afterword and Commentaries by Paul Ekman. (Oxford: Oxford University Press, 1998).

24. L. A. Parr et al., *Journal of Comparative Psychology* 114:1 (March 2000): 47–60.

25. P. Ekman and R. J. Davidson (eds.), *The Nature of Emotion: Fundamental Questions* (New York: Cambridge University Press, 1994), 347–350.

26. M. S. Livingstone, "Is It Warm? Is It Real? Or Just Low Spatial Frequency?" *Science* 290: 549 (November 2000): 1299.

27. R. W. Levenson and A. M. Ruef, *Journal of Personality and Social Psychology* 63:2 (1992): 234–246.

28. P. D. MacLean, *Archives of General Psychiatry* 42 (1985): 405–417.

29. A. Sagi and M. L. Hoffman, *Developmental Psychology* 12 (1976): 175–176.

30. M. Dondi et al., *Developmental Psychology* 35:2 (March 1999): 418–426.

31. This and other points concerning empathy in children are beautifully described in a paper by C. Zahn-Waxler, "The Development of Empathy, Guilt, and Internalization of Distress: Implications for Gender Differences in Internalizing and Externalizing Problems," in R. Davidson (ed.), *Anxiety, Depression and Emotion. Wisconsin Symposium on Emotion*, vol. I (New York and Oxford, UK: Oxford Press, 2000).

32. C. Zahn-Waxler and J. Robinson, "Empathy and Guilt: Early Origins of Feelings of Responsibility," in K. Fischer and J. Tangney

(eds.), *Self-Conscious Emotions: Shame, Guilt, Embarrassment and Pride* (pp. 143–173). (New York: Guilford Press, 1995).

33. C. Zahn-Waxler, "The Development of Empathy, Guilt and Internalization of Distress: Implications for Gender Differences in Internalizing and Externalizing Problems," cited above.

34. A. Raine et al., *Journal of the American Academy of Child and Adolescent Psychiatry* 36:10 (1997): 1457–1464.

35. C. Zahn-Waxler et al., *Developmental Psychology* 26:1 (1990): 51–59.

36. N. Eisenberg et al., *Child Development* 62 (1991): 1393–1408.

37. J. E. Grusec and H. Lytton, *Social Development: History, Theory and Research* (New York: Springer-Verlag, 1988); also E. E. Macoby and J. A. Martin, "Socialization in the Context of the Family: Parent-Child Interaction," pp. 1–101 and M. Radke-Yarrow, C. Zahn-Waxler, and M. Chapman, "Children's Prosocial Dispositions and Behavior," pp. 469–545, both in P. H. Mussen (series ed.) and E.M. Hetherington (vol. ed.), *Handbook of Child Psychology*; vol. 4, *Socialization, Personality and Social Development* (4th ed.). New York: Wiley, 1983).

38. C. Zahn-Waxler and M. Radke-Yarrow, *Motivation and Emotion* 14: 2, (1990): 107–130.

39. R. W. Levenson and A. M. Ruef, *Journal of Personality and Social Psychology* 63: 2 (1992): 234–246.

40. P. Salovey et al., "Current Directions in Emotional Intelligence Research," in M. Lewis and J. M. Haviland-Jones (eds.), *Handbook of Emotions* (2nd ed., pp. 504–520). (New York: Guilford Press, 2000).

41. K. R. Jamison, *Touched with Fire: Manic-Depressive Illness and the Artistic Temperament* (New York: Free Press, Maxwell Macmillan/ Internat'l., 1993).

42. N. Snidman et al., *Psychophysiology* 32:3 (May 1995): 199–207.

43. E. P. Davis et al., *Developmental Psychobiology* 35:3 (November 1999): 188–196.

44. S. J. Suomi, "Attachment in Rhesus Monkeys," in J. Cassidy and P. R. Shaver (eds.), *Handbook of Attachment: Theory, Research, and Clinical Applications* (pp. 181–197). (New York: Guilford Press, 1999).

45. R. M. Sapolsky, *Why Zebras Don't Get Ulcers: An Updated Guide to Stress, Stress-Related Diseases, and Coping* (New York: W. H. Freeman & Company, 1999).

46. C. R. Cloninger, *Current Opinion in Neurobiology* 4 (1994): 266–273.

47. C. R. Cloninger and N. G. Margin, *Journal of Personality and Social Psychology* 66:4 (1994): 762–775.

48. C. R. Cloninger, *Current Opinion in Neurobiology* 4 (1994): 266–273, cited above.

49. B. Knutson et al., *American Journal of Psychiatry* 155:3 (1998): 373–379.

50. D. Watson et al., *Journal of Personality and Social Psychology* 63:6 (December 1992): 1011–1025.

51. D. Watson and L. M. Walker, *Journal of Personality and Social Psychology* 70: 3 (1996): 567–577.

52. D. Watson and L. A. Clark, *Journal of Personality* 60:2 (1992): 441–476.

53. J. D. Mayer and P. Salovey, "The Intelligence of Emotional Intelligence," *Intelligence* 17 (1993): 433–442.

54. P. Salovey et al., "Current Directions in Emotional Intelligence Research," in M. Lewis and J. M. Haviland-Jones (eds.), *Handbook of Emotions* (2nd ed., pp. 504–520). (New York: Guilford Press, 2000).

55. M. R. Barrick and M. K. Mount, *Personnel Psychology* 44 (1991): 1–26.

56. A. Mehrabian, "Beyond IQ: Broad-Based Measurement of Individual Success Potential or 'Emotional Intelligence,'" *Genetic, Social and General Psychology Monographs* 126 (2000): 133–239.

57. J. D. Mayer et al., "Models of Emotional Intelligence," in R. J. Sternberg (ed.), *Handbook of Intelligence* (pp. 396–420). (Cambridge, UK: Cambridge University Press, 2000).

58. W. D. Tenhouton et al., *Psychotherapy and Psychosomatics* 44 (1985): 113–121.

59. J. Cohen, "Social and Emotional Learning, Past and Present: A Psycho-Educational Dialogue," in J. Cohen (ed.), *Educating Minds and Hearts: Social Emotional Learning and the Passage into Adolescence* (pp. 2–23). (New York: Teachers College Press, 1999).

60. T. P. Shriver et al., "Why SEL Is the Better Way: The New Haven Social Development Program," in J. Cohen (ed.), *Educating Minds and Hearts: Social Emotional Learning and the Passage into Adolescence* (pp. 43–60). (New York: Teachers College Press, 1999); also J. L. Aber et al., *Teaching Conflict Resolution; An Effective School-Based Approach to Violence Prevention* (New York: National Center for Children in Poverty, Joseph L. Mailman School of Public Health, Columbia University, 1999).

61. C. Cherniss, *Model Program Summaries: A Technical Report Issued by the Consortium for Research on Emotional Intelligence in Organizations.* 1999. Available at the website www.eiconsortium.org.

62. N. S. Jacobson and A. Christensen, *Integrative Couple Therapy: Promoting Acceptance and Change* (New York: Norton, 1996).

Chapter 6. Emotions that Kill and Cure

1. *Holy Bible*, King James Version, Proverbs 17:22.
2. O. Wilde, *The Importance of Being Earnest*. (New York: Dover Publications, 1990; from First Edition, London: Leonard Smithers & Co., 1890).
3. G. Engel, *Annals of Internal Medicine* 74:5 (1971): 771–782.
4. *Homer: The Odyssey*. Robert Fales (translator). Introduction and Notes by Bernard Knox. (New York: Viking, 1996).
5. For further description of the stress response, see R. M. Sapolsky, *Why Zebras Don't Get Ulcers: An Updated Guide to Stress, Stress-Related Diseases, and Coping* (New York: W. H. Freeman & Company, 1998).
6. R. Ader and N. Cohen, *Psychosomatic Medicine* 37:4 (July-August 1975): 333–340.
7. J. W. Pennebaker, *Behavioral Research and Therapy* 31:6 (1993): 539–548.
8. J. K. Kiecolt-Glaser et al., *Psychosomatic Medicine* 53 (1991): 345–362; also J. K. Kiecolt-Glaser et al., *Lancet* 346 (1995): 1194–1196.
9. J. K. Kiecolt-Glaser et al., *Psychosomatic Medicine* 53, cited above.
10. J. K. Kiecolt-Glaser et al., *Psychosomatic Medicine* 46 (1984): 7–14.
11. W. T. Boyce et al., *Psychosomatic Medicine* 57 (1995): 411–422.
12. S. Cohen et al., *Journal of Personality and Social Psychology* 64 (1993): 131–140; also S. Cohen et al., *Journal of Personality and Social Psychology* 68 (1995): 159–169.
13. R. Glaser et al., *Brain, Behavior and Immunology* 13:3 (September 1999): 240–251; also R. Glaser et al., *Psychoneuroendrocinology* 19: 8 (1994): 765–772.
14. S. W. Cole et al., *Psychosomatic Medicine* 58:3 (1996): 219–231.
15. P. Salovey et al., *American Psychologist* 55:1 (2000): 110–121.
16. B. S. Siegel, *Love, Medicine and Miracles: Lessons Learned About Self-Healing from a Surgeon's Experience with Exceptional Patients* (New York: Harper & Row, 1986).
17. R. M. Sapolsky, *Why Zebras Don't Get Ulcers: An Updated Guide to Stress, Stress-Related Disorders and Coping* (New York: W. H. Freeman & Company, 1999), 151–154; also M. Markman, *Cleveland Clinical Journal of Medicine* 65: 2 (1998): 107–109.
18. D. Spiegel et al., *Lancet* 2 (October 14, 1989): 888–891.
19. A. J. Cunningham et al., *Psycho-Oncology* 7 (1998): 508–517.
20. D. P. Phillips et al., *Lancet* 342: 8880 (November 6, 1993): 1142–1145.

21. F. I. Fawzy et al., *Archives of General Psychiatry* 50 (September 1993): 681–689.
22. J. K. Kiecolt-Glaser et al., *Journal of Behavioral Medicine* 8 (1985): 311–320.
23. J. K. Kiecolt-Glaser et al., *Psychosomatic Medicine* 49 (1987): 523–525.
24. J. J. Gross and R. W. Levenson, *Journal of Abnormal Psychology* 106 (1997): 95–103.
25. N. A. Cummings and W. T. Follette, "Brief Psychotherapy and Medical Utilization," in H. Darken (ed.), *The Professional Psychologist Today* (San Francisco: Jossey-Bass, 1976); also K. Jones and T. Vischi, *Medical Care* 12 (Suppl. 2): 1–82: (December 1979).
26. E. J. Murray et al., *Journal of Social and Clinical Psychology* 8 (1989): 414–429; also J. W. Pennebaker et al., *Journal of Consulting and Clinical Psychology* 56 (1998): 239–245.
27. J. M. Smyth et al., *Journal of the American Medical Association* 281:14 (April 14, 1999): 1304–1309.
28. R. M. Sapolsky, *Why Zebras Don't Get Ulcers*, cited above, p. 267.
29. J. Weiss, *Scientific American* 226 (June 1972): 104–113.
30. J. Rodin, *Science* 233 (1986): 1271–1276.
31. C. Chapman and H. Hill, "Patient Controlled Analgesia in a Bone Marrow Transplant Setting," in K. Foley (ed.), *Advances in Pain Research and Therapy* vol. 16. (New York: Raven Press, 1990), 16.
32. W. Shakespeare (1554–1616), *Hamlet, Prince of Denmark*, Act II, Scene 2, line 232. (1564–1616. *The Oxford Shakespeare* 1914.
33. J. M. Weiss et al., *Journal of Comparative Physiology and Psychology* 90: 3 (March 1976): 252–259.
34. P. Deats and C. L. Fleischer, "Why Dogs Smile and Chimpanzees Cry," *The Discovery Channel*, 2000.
35. L. F. Berkman and S. L. Syme, *American Journal of Epidemiology* 109 (1979): 186–204; also J. S. House et al., *Science* 241 (1988): 540–545.
36. R. Williams and V. Williams, *Anger Kills: 17 Strategies for Controlling the Hostility That Can Harm Your Health* (New York: HarperCollins, 1993).
37. T. W. Kamarck et al., *Psychosomatic Medicine* 52:1 (January–February 1990): 42–58.
38. J. L. Anthony and W. H. O'Brien, *Behavioral Medicine* 25:2 (Summer 1999): 78–87.
39. S. Cohen et al., *Journal of the American Medical Association* 277:24 (June 25, 1997): 1940–1944.
40. R. Kraut et al., *American Psychologist* 53:9 (1998): 1017–1031.

41. R. Jevning et al., *Neuroscience and Biobehavior Review* 16:3 (fall 1992): 415–424. also R. Cooper et al., *Postgraduate Medical Journal* 61 (1985): 301–304.

42. W. F. Fry and C. Rader, *Journal of Biological Psychology*, 19 (1977): 39–50; also W. F. Fry, "Humor and the Human Cardiovascular System," in H. Mindess and J. Turek (eds.), *The Study of Humor.* (Los Angeles: Antioch University Press 1979); also W. F. Fry and M. Savin, "Mirthful Laughter and Blood Pressure," *Third International Conference on Humor*, Washington, DC, 1982; also L. S. Berk et al., *The American Journal of the Medical Sciences* 298:6 (December 1989): 390–396.

43. C. Mueller and E. Donnerstein, *Journal of Research in Personality* 11 (1977): 73–82; also L. S. Berk et al., *The American Journal of the Medical Sciences* 298:6 (1989): 390–396.

44. L. S. Berk et al., in *The American Journal of the Medical Sciences,* cited above; also L. S. Berk et al., *Clinical Research* 36 (1988): 435A; also L. S. Berk et al., *Clinical Research* 36 (1988); and L. S. Berk et al., *Clinical Research* 37 (1989): 115A.

45. M. G. Newman and A. A. Stone, *Annals of Behavioral Medicine* 18:2 (1996): 101–109.

46. M. F. Scheier and C. S. Carver, *Cognitive Therapy and Research* 16 (1992): 201–228; also M.F. Scheier et al., *Journal of Personality and Social Psychology* 57 (1989): 1024–1040.

47. P. Salovey et al., *American Psychologist* 55:1 (2000): 110–121.

48. L. M. Irving et al., *Journal of Personality* 66 (1998): 195–214.

49. B. Q. Hafen et al., *Mind/Body Health: The Effects of Attitudes, Emotions and Relationships* (Boston: Allyn & Bacon, 1996).

50. B. S. Rabin, *Stress, Immune Function, and Health: The Connection.* (New York: Wiley-Liss, Inc., 1999, at p. 289); also G.W. Comstock and K. B. Partridge, *Journal of Chronic Diseases* 25 (1972): 665–672.

51. J. D. Kark et al., *Israel Journal of Medical Sciences* 32 (1996): 185–194.

Chapter 7. What Doesn't Kill You Makes You Stronger

1. A. Öhman, "Fear and Anxiety as Emotional Phenomena: Clinical Phenomenology, Evolutionary Perspectives, and Information-Processing Mechanisms," in M. Lewis and J. M. Haviland (eds.), *Handbook of Emotions* (pp. 511–536). (New York: Guilford Press, 1993).
2. B. L. Fredrickson, *Review of General Psychology* 2 (1998): 300–319.
3. J. M. Gottman and N. Silver, *The Seven Principles for Making Marriage Work* (New York: Three Rivers Press, 1999).
4. J. A. Piliavin, *Transfusion* 30 (1990): 444–459.
5. M. D. Goldstein and M. J. Strube, *Personality and Social Psychology Bulletin* 20 (1994): 57–64.
6. M. S. George et al., *American Journal of Psychiatry* 152:3 (1995): 341–351; also A. R. Damascio et al., *Nature Neuroscience* 3:10 (2000): 1049–1056.
7. J. T. Cacioppo and W. L. Gardner, *Annual Review of Psychology* 50 (1999): 191–214.
8. Y. Klar and E. E. Giladi, *Journal of Personality and Social Psychology* 73 (1997): 885–901.
9. S. E. Taylor, *Positive Illusions: Creative Self-Deception and the Healthy Mind* (New York: Basic Books, 1992); also R. C. Colligan et al., *Journal of Clinical Psychology* 50:1 (1994): 71–95.
10. L. B. Alloy and L. Y. Abramson, *Journal of Experimental Psychology: General* 108 (1979): 441–485.
11. J. T. Cacioppo and W. L. Gardner, *Annual Review of Psychology*, (1999), cited above.
12. S. E. Taylor, *Psychological Bulletin* 110 (1991): 67–85.

Chapter 8. Fear and Anxiety

1. R. Kipling, "Song of the Little Hunter," The King Ankus, in *The Second Jungle Book* (Doubleday, 1895).
2. M. E. de Montaigne (1533–1592), *Essays*, Book 1 (1590). "To the Reader," #18.
3. J. E. LeDoux, *Scientific American* 270:6 (1994): 50–57.
4. D. G. Amaral et al., "Anatomical Organization of the Primate Amygdaloid Complex," in J. P. Aggleton (ed.), *The Amygdala: Neurobiological Aspects of Emotion, Memory and Mental Dysfunction* (pp. 1–66). (New York: Wiley-Liss, 1992).
5. M. Davis, *Biological Psychiatry* 44:12 (December 15, 1998): 1239–1247.
6. M. Davis, *Journal of Neuropsychiatry* 9:3 (summer 1997): 382–402.

7. M. Davis and D. I. Astrakhan, *Journal of Experimental Psychology and Animal Behavior Process* 4 (1978): 95–103.
8. R. W. Butler et al., *American Journal of Psychiatry* 147 (1990): 1308–1312.
9. W. A. Falls and M. Davis, "Behavioral and Physiological Analysis of Fear Inhibition: Extinction and Conditioned Inhibition," in M. J. Friedman, et al. *Neurobiological and Clinical Consequences of Stress: From Normal Adaptation to PTSD* (pp. 177–202). (Philadelphia: Lippincott-Raven Publishers, 1995).
10. C. Grillon et al., *Biological Psychiatry* 42 (1997): 453–460.
11. M. Davis, *Biological Psychiatry* 44:12 (December 15, 1998): 1239–1247.
12. Y. Lee and M. Davis, *The Journal of Neuroscience* 17:16 (August 15, 1997): 6434–6446.
13. A. Levin et al., "Pilot Kennedy Was Such a Conscientious Guy," *USA Today*, Gannett Co., Inc., July 22, 1999.
14. W. Sherman and K. McCoy, "Retracing Hours before Sad Fate Delays Plagued Kennedy and Bessettes," New York *Daily News*, July 22, 1999.
15. K. P. Lesch et al., *Science* 274:5292 (1996): 1527–1531.
16. J. Benjamin et al., *Nature Genetics* 12 (1996): 81–84.
17. D. Hamer and P. Copeland, *Living with Our Genes: Why They Matter More Than You Think* (New York: Doubleday, 1998).
18. C. Spielewoy et al., *Behavioral Pharmacology* 11:3–4 (June 2000): 279–290.
19. L. K. Heisler et al., *Proceedings of the National Academy of Science, USA* 95:25 (December 8, 1998): 1,5049–1,5054.
20. Anxiety Disorders Association of America News release, December 13, 1999. Website: www.adaa.org
21. P. H. Wender and D. F. Klein, *Mind, Mood and Medicine*. (New York: Farrar, Straus, Giroux, 1981).
22. J. Panksepp, "Modern Approaches to Understanding Fear: From Laboratory to Clinical Practice," in J. Panksepp (ed.), *Advances in Biological Psychiatry*, (vol. 2 pp. 207–228) (Greenwich, Conn.: JAI Press, 1996).
23. K. H. Bourden et al., "National Prevalence and Treatment of Mental and Addictive Disorders," in R. W. Manderscheid and M. S. Sonnenschein (eds.), *Mental Health: US.* (pp. 22–51), (Rockville, Md.: Center for Mental Health Services, 1994).
24. A. Bisaga et al., *American Journal of Psychiatry* 155:9 (1998): 1178–1183; also A. Malizia et al., *Archives of General Psychiatry* 55 (August 1998): 715–720.

25. P. E. Greenberg et al., *Journal of Clinical Psychiatry* 60:7 (1999): 427–435.
26. D. F. Klein, "Anxiety Reconceptualized," in D. F. Klein and J. Rabkin (eds.), *Anxiety: New Research and Changing Concepts* (pp. 235–264). (New York: Raven Press, 1981).
27. D. F. Klein, *Anxiety* 1:1 (1994): 1–7.
28. J. M. Kent et al., *American Journal of Psychiatry* 158:1 (2001): 58–167.
29. J. G. Johnson et al., *Journal of the American Medical Association* 284: 18 (November 8, 2000): 2348–2351.
30. W. A. Falls and M. Davis, "Behavioral and Physiological Analysis of Fear Inhibition: Extinction and Conditioned Inhibition," in M. J. Friedman, et al., *Neurobiological and Clinical Consequences of Stress: From Normal Adaptation to PTSD* (pp. 177–202). Philadelphia: Lippincott-Raven Publishers, 1995).
31. D. H. Barlow, *Journal of Clinical Psychiatry* 58 (Suppl. 2)(1997): 32–37; also D. H. Barlow et al., *Journal of the American Medical Association* 283:19 (May 17, 2000): 2573–2574.
32. W. A. Falls and M. Davis, 1995, cited above.
33. T. Nordenberg, *FDA Consumer* 33:6 (November–December 1999): 27–33.
34. R. G. Heimberg et al., *Archives of General Psychiatry* 55:12 (1998): 1133–1141.
35. F. R. Schneier et al., *American Journal of Psychiatry* 157:3 (2000): 457–459.
36. S. J. Perlmutter et al., *Lancet*, 354:9185 (October 2, 1999): 1153–1158.
37. L. R. Baxter, Jr. et al., *Archives of General Psychiatry* 49:9 (1992): 681–689.
38. S. J. Petruzello et al., *Sports Medicine* 11:3 (1991): 143–182.
39. J. Moses et al., *Journal of Psychosomatic Research* 33:1 (1989): 47–61.
40. K. E. K. Osei-Tutu and P. D. Campagna, *Medical Science Sports Exercise* 30 (Suppl. 5):(1998): s117.
41. For information on St. John's wort, see Norman E. Rosenthal's book *St. John's Wort: The Herbal Way to Feeling Good* (New York: HarperCollins Publishers, 1998).
42. L. H. Taylor and K. A. Kobak, *Journal of Clinical Psychiatry* 61:8 (2000): 575–578.
43. For more information on the medicinal uses of kava-kava, see V. Schulz et al., *Rational Phytotherapy: A Physician's Guide to Herbal Medicine.* (New York, Berlin and Munich: Springer-Verlag, 2000).
44. J. R. T. Davidson and K. M. Connor, *Herbs for the Mind: Depression,*

Stress, Memory Loss, and Insomnia (New York: The Guilford Press, 2000).

45. V. Schulz et al., *Rational Phytotherapy,* cited above.
46. J. R. T. Davidson and K. M. Connor, *Herbs for the Mind,* cited above.
47. J. Heller, *Catch-22: A Novel* (New York: Simon & Schuster, 1961).
48. American Psychiatric Association, *Diagnostic and Statistical Manual of Mental Disorders,* Fourth Edition. (Washington, DC: American Psychiatric Press, Inc., 1994).
49. B. A. van der Kolk, *Harvard Review of Psychiatry* 1:5 (1994): 253–265.
50. T. V. Gurvits et al., "Reduced Hippocampal Volume on Magnetic Resonance Imaging in Chronic Posttraumatic Stress Disorder," presented at the Annual International Society for Traumatic Stress Studies. Miami, Florida, 1995; also J. D. Bremner et al., *American Journal of Psychiatry* 152 (1995): 973–981; also M.B. Stein et al., "Neuroanatomical and Neuroendocrine Correlates in Adulthood of Severe Sexual Abuse in Childhood," presented at the 33rd Annual Meeting, American College of Neuropsychopharmacology, San Juan Puerto Rico, December 15, 1994.
51. T. V. Gurvits et al., *Biological Psychiatry* 40:11 (December 1, 1996): 1091–1099.
52. R. Yehuda et al., *American Journal of Psychiatry* 152:7 (1995): 982–986.
53. R. Yehuda et al., *Biological Psychiatry,* 40 (1996): 79–88.
54. R. Yehuda, *Psychoneuroendocrinology* 21:2 (June 1998): 359–379.
55. A. C. McFarlane et al., "The Acute Stress Response Following Motor Vehicle Accidents and Its Relation to PTSD," in R. Yehuda and A. C. McFarlane (eds.), *Psychobiology of PTSD* (pp. 437–439). (New York: New York Academy of Sciences, 1997).
56. S. L. Rauch et al., *CNS Spectrums* 3 (1998): 37–43.
57. M. Van Etten and S. Taylor, *Clinical Psychology and Psychotherapy* 5 (1998): 126–144.
58. S. P. Spera et al., *Academy of Management Journal* 37 (1994): 722–733.
59. N. Amir et al., *Journal of Traumatic Stress* 11:2 (1998): 385–392.
60. J. Pennebaker, *Opening Up: The Healing Power of Emotional Expression.* (New York: Guilford Press, 1997). Also see James Pennebaker's website: http://homepage.psy.utexas.edu/HomePage/Faculty/Pennebaker/Pennebaker.html
61. M. L. Van Etten and S. Taylor, *Clinical Psychology and Psychotherapy* 5 (1998): 126–144.
62. M. J. Lohr et al., *Behavior Therapy* 29 (1998): 123–156; also, R. J. McNally, *PTSD Research Quarterly* 10:1 (winter 1999): 1–3.
63. J. Shepherd et al., *Psychol Med* 30:4 (July 2000): 863–871.

64. E. B. Foa and E. A. Meadows, *Annual Review of Psychology* 48 (1997): 449–480.

65. E. B. Foa, "Cognitive Behavioral Treatment of PTSD," course presentation, Boston University School of Medicine Conference on "Psychological Trauma: Maturational Processes and Therapeutic Interventions," March 10–11, 2000.

66. M. L. Van Etten and S. Taylor, *Clinical Psychology and Psychotherapy* 5 (1998): 125–144

67. L. Cahill and J. L. McGaugh, *Proceedings of the Western Pharmacological Society* 39 (1996): 81–84.

68. M. B. Kirchner and R. Rand, "Gray Matters: Emotion and the Brain," WAMU Radio in association with the DANA Alliance for Brain Initiatives, 2001. For transcript, call 1-800-65-BRAIN.

Chapter 9. Anger and Rage

1. L. Carroll, *Alice in Wonderland*. (New York: Grosset & Dunlap, c. 1957).

2. A. Siegel and M. Brutus, "Neural Substrates of Aggression and Rage in the Cat," in A. N. Epstein and A. R. Morrison (eds.), *Progress in Psychobiology and Physiological Psychology* (pp. 135–233) (San Diego: Academic Press, 1990).

3. J. Panksepp, *Affective Neuroscience: The Foundations of Human and Animal Emotions* (New York: Oxford University Press, 1998), 189; also J. Campos et al., *Monographs, Social Research on Child Development* 59 (1994): 284–303.

4. W. A. Mason and S. P. Mendoza (eds.), *Primate Social Conflict.* (Albany, New York: State University of New York Press, 1993).

5. E. B. Ebbesen et al., *Journal of Experimental Social Psychology* 11 (1975): 192–204; also W. A. Lewis and A. M. Bucher, *Psychotherapy* 29:3 (1992): 385–392; also R. Warren and R. Kurlychek, *Corrective and Social Psychiatry and Journal of Behavior Technology, Methods and Therapy* 27 (1981): 135–139.

6. M. Fava and J. F. Rosenbaum, *Journal of Clinical Psychiatry* 60 (Suppl. 15) (1999): 21–24.

7. K. Rubenstein and The Associated Press, "Mike Tyson to Tell Panel about Zoloft Withdrawal at Hearing Wednesday," *Court TV Online*, February 5, 1999.

8. FOXNews.com National Front, "Tyson: Zoloft Keeps Me From 'Killing Y'All'," Friday, September 15, 2000.

9. R. Yehuda, *Journal of Clinical Psychiatry*, 17 (Monograph 2): (1999): 25–27.

10. M. H. Teicher, C. M. Andersen, S. L. Andersen, et al., Unpublished paper, *"Neurobiological correlates of childhood maltreatment,"* 2000.
11. J. B. Rosen et al., *Behavioral Neuroscience* 110 (1996): 43–50.
12. M. Fava and J. F. Rosenbaum, *Journal of Clinical Psychiatry* 60 (Suppl. 15): (1999): 21–24.
13. R. C. Tafrate, "Evaluation and Treatment Strategies for Adult Anger Disorders," in H. Kassinove (ed.), *Anger Disorders: Definition, Diagnosis and Treatment* (pp. 109–129). (Washington, D.C.: Taylor & Francis, 1995); also R. Beck and E. Fernandez, *Cognitive Therapy and Research* 22:1 (1998): 63–74.
14. J. Panksepp, *Affective Neuroscience: The Foundations of Human and Animal Emotions* (New York: Oxford University Press, 1998) p. 194.
15. J. Panskeep, *Affective Neuroscience,* cited above, pp. 196–198.
16. J. P. Flynn, "The Neural Basis of Aggression in Cats," in D. Glass (ed.), *Neurophysiology and Emotion* (pp. 40–59). (New York: Rockefeller University, 1967).
17. R. M. Sapolsky *Why Zebras Don't Get Ulcers: An Updated Guide to Stress, Stress-Related Disorders and Coping* (New York: W. H. Freeman & Company, 1999), p. 281.
18. J. Friedman and R. Rosenman, *Type A Behavior and Your Heart* (New York: Knopf, 1974).
19. R. Williams et al., *Psychosomatic Medicine* 42:6 (November 1980): 539–549.
20. J. Barefoot et al., *Psychosomatic Medicine* 45 (1983): 59–63.
21. J. Barefoot et al., *Psychosomatic Medicine* 51 (1989): 46–57.
22. R. H. Rosenman et al., *Journal of the American Medical Association* 233:8 (August 25, 1975): 872–877.
23. Review Panel on Coronary Prone Behavior and Coronary Heart Disease, "Coronary Heart Disease: A Critical Review," *Circulation* 65 (1978): 1199–1215.
24. D. S. Krantz and S. B. Manuck, *Psychological Bulletin* 21 (1984): 39–46; also T. W. Smith, *Health Psychology* 11:3 (1992): 139–150.
25. R. Williams and V. Williams, *Anger Kills: 17 Strategies for Controlling the Hostility That Can Harm Your Health* (New York: HarperCollins, 1993).
26. R. Ross and J. A. Glomset, *Science* 180:93 (June 29, 1973): 1332–1339.
27. E. C. Suarez et al., *Psychosomatic Medicine* 60 (1998): 78–88.
28. E. C. Suarez et al., *Annals of Behavioral Medicine* 20:2 (1998): 59–63.
29. E. C. Suarez and R. B. Williams, *Psychosomatic Medicine* 51 (1989): 404–418.
30. T. W. Smith, *Health Psychology* 11:3 (1992): 139–150.

31. J. C. Barefoot et al., *Psychosomatic Medicine* 49 (1987): 450–457.
32. J. Soles and G. S. Sanders, "Why Do Some Behavioral Styles Place People at Coronary Risk?" in A. W. Siegman and T. M. Dembroski (eds.), *In Search of Coronary-Prone Behavior: Beyond Type A* (pp. 1–20). (Hillsdale, N.J.: Lawrence Erlbaum Associates, Inc., 1989).
33. R. B. Shekelle et al., *Psychosomatic Medicine* 45 (1983): 109–114; also L. W. Scherwitz et al., "Cooke-Medley Hostility and Detrimental Health Behaviors in Young Adults: The CARDIA Study." Paper presented at the meeting of the Society of Behavioral Medicine, Washington DC, 1991.
34. M. Koskenvuo et al., *Psychosomatic Medicine*, 50 (1988): 330–340.
35. Ibid.
36. R. Williams and V. Williams, *Anger Kills*, cited above, pp. 57–58.
37. E. A. Lenerise, "The Development of Anger and Hostile Interactions," in M. Lewis and J. M. Haviland (eds.), *Handbook of Emotions*. (New York: Guilford Press, 1993); also K. A. Dodge and J. E. Lochman, *Journal of Consulting and Clinical Psychology* 62 (1994): 366–374.
38. B. Seay et al., *Journal of Abnormal Psychology*, 69 (1964): 345–354.
39. N. H. Kalin, "Primate Models and Aggression," *Journal of Clinical Psychiatry*, Monograph 17:2 (1999): 22–24.
40. S. J. Suomi, "A Biobehavioral Perspective on Developmental Psychopathology: Excessive Aggression and Serotonergic Dysfunction in Monkeys," in A. J. Sameroff et al. (eds.), *Handbook of Developmental Psychopathology* (pp. 237–256). (New York: Kluwer Academic/Plenum Publishers, 2000).
41. R. J. Nelson et al., *Nature* 378:6555 (November 23, 1995): 383–386; also L. J. Kriegsfeld et al., *Brain Research* 769:1 (September 19, 1997): 66–70.
42. J. M. Koolhaas et al., *Aggressive Behavior* 16 (1990): 223–229.
43. J. Panksepp, *Affective Neuroscience*, cited above, p. 199.
44. E. P. Monaghan and S. E. Glickman, "Hormones and Aggressive Behavior," in J. B. Becker et al. (eds.), *Behavioral Endocrinology* (pp. 261–285). (Boston: MIT Press, 1992).
45. R. Michael and D. Zumpe, *American Journal of Psychiatry* 140:7 (July 1983): 883–886.
46. J. Panksepp, *Affective Neuroscience*, cited above, p. 199.
47. A. Mazur and T. A. Lamb, *Hormones and Behavior* 14 (1980): 236–246; also W. R. Yates, *Archives of General Psychiatry* 57:2 (February 2000): 155–161; also A. Booth et al., *Journal of Health and Social Behavior* 40 (June 1999): 130–140.
48. A. Booth et al., *Hormones and Behavior* 23 (1989): 556–571.

49. P. F. Brain, "Pituitary-Gonadal Influences on Social Aggression." in B. B. Svare (ed.), *Hormones and Aggressive Behavior* (pp. 3–25). (New York: Plenum Press, 1983); also N. G. Simon et al., *Annals of the New York Academy of Science* 794 (1996): 8–17.

50. M. M. McCarthy et al., *Annals of the New York Academy of Science* 652 (1992): 70–82.

51. G. M. Lavergne, *A Sniper in the Tower* (New York: Bantam Books, 1997). The quotes pertaining to this murder come from original research documents that Gary Lavergne was kind enough to make available to me in 1999.

52. A. Raine et al., *Behavioral Science and Law* 16:3 (1998): 319–332.

53. A. Raine et al., *Archives of General Psychiatry* 57:2 (February 2000): 119–129.

54. Horace (Quintus Horatius Flaccus) 65–8 B.C., *Epistles Book I*, Number 2, line 62.

55. R. C. Tafrate, "Evaluation of Treatment Strategies for Adult Anger Disorders," in H. Kassinove (ed.), *Anger Disorders: Definition, Diagnosis, and Treatment* (pp. 109–129). (Washington, D.C.: Taylor & Francis, 1995).

56. J. L. Deffenbacher, "Cognitive-Behavioral Conceptualization and Treatment of Anger," *JCLP/In session: Psychotherapy in Practice* 55:3 (1999): 295–309.

57. T. Jefferson, *A Decalogue of Canons for Observation in Practical Life.* February 21, 1825.

58. S. Clemens, *Pudd'nhead Wilson.* (1894), chapter 19.

59. E. Brondolo et al., *Cognitive and Behavioral Practice*, 4 (1997): 75–98.

60. Ibid.

61. R. C. Tafrate, "Evaluation of Treatment Strategies for Adult Anger Disorders," 1995, cited above.

62. Ibid.

63. E. Brondolo, et al., cited above.

64. J. Wolpe, "The Experimental Foundations of Some New Psychotherapeutic Methods," in A. J. Bacherach (ed.), *Experimental Foundations of Clinical Psychology* (New York: Basic Books, 1962): 554.

65. R. C. Tafrate, 1995, cited above.

66. A. C. Swann, *Journal of Clinical Psychiatry* 60 (Suppl. 15): 1999): 25–28; also R. Yehuda, 1999, cited above.

67. M. Fava and J. Rosenbaum, 1999, cited above.

68. See all references cited in chapter 9, note 5.

69. B. J. Bushman et al., *Journal of Personality and Social Psychology* 76:3 (1999): 367–376.

70. K. Kaltiala-Heino et al., *British Medical Journal* 319 (1999): 348–351.

71. S. Scott, *British Medical Journal* 316 (1998): 202–206.

72. Ibid.

73. L. J. Schweinhart and D. P. Weikert, "A Summary of Significant Benefits: The High Scope Perry Preschool Study Through Age 27" (Ypsilanti, Mich.: High Scope, 1993).

74. D. G. Sukhodolsky and H. Kassinove, Unpublished manuscript, "Cognitive-Behavioral Therapy for Anger and Aggression in Youth: A Meta-Analysis Review," presentation to 105th Annual Convention of the American Psychological Association, Chicago, August 15–19, 1997.

75. S. Scott, *British Medical Journal* 316 (1998): 202–206; also E. L. Feindler, *Issues in Comprehensive Pediatric Nursing* 18 (1995): 233–260.

76. L. A. Seneca, ca. 4 B.C.–A.D. 65, *Stoic Philosophy of Seneca: Essays and Letters of Seneca/Translated and with an introduction by Moses Hadas.* (New York: Norton, 1958).

Chapter 10. Love and Lust

1. D. H. Lawrence, *Lady Chatterley's Lover* (New York: Grove Press, 1959). The descriptions of Lady Chatterley and Mellors are also taken directly from the book.

2. R. G. Heath, *Journal of Nervous and Mental Disorders* 154 (1972): 3–18.

3. M. R. Murphy et al., *Journal of Clinical Endocrinology and Metabolism* 65:4 (1987): 738–741.

4. C. S. Carter, *Neuroscience and Biobehavior Reviews* 16 (1992): 131–144.

5. C. A. Pederson et al., *New York Academy of Sciences, Special Issue,* vol. 652, 1992.

6. M. S. Carmichael et al., *Journal of Clinical Endocrinology and Metabolism* 64 (1987): 27–31.

7. P. Richard et al., *Physiological Review* 71 (1991): 331–370.

8. R. L. Moss and C. A. Dudley, "The Challenge of Studying the Behavioral Effects of Neuropeptides," in L. L. Iversen et al. (eds.), *Handbook of Psychopharmacology* (vol. 18, pp. 397–454). (New York: Plenum Press, 1984).

9. R. Arletti et al., *Annals of the New York Academy of Science* 652 (1992): 180–193.

10. G. F. Jirikowski et al., *Cell Tissue Research* 256:2 (1989): 411–417.

11. G. J. DeVries et al., *Annals of the New York Academy of Science* 652

(1992): 387–396. For a good discussion of the relationship between these hormones in male and female animals, see chapter XII of Jaak Panksepp's book, *Affective Neuroscience: The Foundations of Human and Animal Emotions* (New York: Oxford University Press, 1998).

12. A. Tuiten et al., *Archives of General Psychiatry* 57:2 (2000): 149–156.
13. G. Schatze et al., *Prostate* 44:3 (August 1, 2000): 219–224.
14. M. R. Melis and A. Argiolis, *Neuroscience and Biobehavior Reviews* 19 (1995): 19–38.
15. N. Edens and W. P. Newton, *Journal of Family Practice* 45:2 (August 1997): 101–102.
16. W. P. Oldenburger et al., *Hormones and Behavior* 26 (1992): 214–228.
17. C. F. Levinthal, *Messengers of Paradise: Opiates and the Brain* (New York: Doubleday, 1998); also J. Davis, *Endorphins: New Waves in Brain Chemistry* (Garden City, NY: Dial Press, 1984).
18. A. Agmo and R. Berenfeld, *Behavioral Neuroscience* 104 (1990): 177–182; also A. Agmo and M. Gomez, *Behavioral Neuroscience* 107 (1993): 812–818.
19. M. R. Murphy et al., *Journal of Endocrinology and Metabolism* 71:4 (1990): 1056–1063.
20. R. Seecoff and F. S. Tennant, Jr., *American Journal of Drug and Alcohol Abuse* 12:1–2 (1986): 79–87.
21. R. Joseph, *Neuropsychiatry, Neuropsychology and Clinical Neuroscience* 2nd ed. (Baltimore: Williams & Wilkins, 1996), 357.
22. P. Soubrie, *Behavior and Brain Science* 9 (1986): 319–364; also X. Zhuang et al., *Neuropsychopharmacology* 21:2S (1999): 52S–60S.
23. R. A. Figler et al., *General Comparative Endocrinology* 73 (1989): 223–232.
24. R. V. Short and E. Balaban (eds.), *The Difference Between the Sexes* (Cambridge, UK: Cambridge University Press, September 1994).
25. This and other points about male/female differences may all be found in B. A. Shaywitz et al., "Sex Differences in the Functional Organization of the Brain for Language," *Nature* 373 (1995): 607–609.
26. L. S. Allen et al., *Journal of Neuroscience* 9 (1989): 497–506.
27. Y. Oomura et al., *Brain Research* 266 (1983): 340–343.
28. R. C. Gur et al., *Science* 267 (1995): 528–531.
29. *U.S. News & World Report*, March 27, 2000.
30. E. S. Person, *By Force of Fantasy: How We Make Our Lives* (New York: Basic Books, 1995); also E. S. Person, *Dreams of Love and Fateful Encounters: The Power of Romantic Passion* (New York: Norton, 1988).

31. E. Gilbert, "She Spoke Volumes," *New York Times Magazine*, p. 21, January 7, 2001.
32. Romance Writers of America (RWA) compiled these statistics from the Book Industry Study Group and American Bookseller Association Reports, and from tallies in *Ingram's Catalogue* of all book releases (2000).
33. E. Hatfield and S. Sprecher, *Journal of Adolescence* 9 (1986): 383–410.
34. D. M. Buss, *Annals of the New York Academy of Science* 907 (April 2000): 39–49.
35. Ibid.
36. K. Grammar and R. Thornhill, *Journal of Comparative Psychology* 108 (1994): 233–242; also R. A. Johnstone, *Nature* 372:6502 (November 10, 1994): 172–175.
37. F. Galton, *Nature* 18 (1878): 97–100; also J. H. Langlois and L. A. Roggman, *Psychological Science* 1 (1990): 115–121.
38. D. I. Perrett et al., *Nature* 368 (1994): 239–242.
39. J. Fischman, "Why We Fall In Love," *U.S. News & World Report*, 128: 5 (February 7, 2000): 42–48.
40. N. L. Etcoff, *Survival of the Prettiest: The Science of Beauty* (New York: Doubleday, 1999): 78.
41. J. Mazur and C. Keating, *American Journal of Sociology* 90 (1984): 125–150.
42. U. Mueller and A. Mazur, *Social Forces* 74 (1996): 823–850.
43. N. L. Etcoff, *Survival of the Prettiest*, cited above.
44. R. Thornhill et al., *Animal Behavior* 50 (1995): 1601–1615.
45. W. C. Jordan and M. W. Bruford, *Heredity* 81 (Pt.2): (August 1998): 127–133.
46. C. Wedekind and S. Furi, *Proc R Soc Lond B Biol Sci* 264:1387 (October 22, 1997): 1471–1479.
47. D. I. Perrett et al., *Nature* 394 (1998): 884–886.
48. I. S. Penton-Voak et al., *Nature* 399:6738 (June 24, 1999): 741–742.
49. R. C. Pillard and J. M. Bailey, *Human Biology* 70:2 (April 1998): 347–365; also D. Hamer and P. Copeland, *Living With Our Genes: Why They Matter More Than You Think* (New York: Doubleday, 1999).
50. J. M. Bailey et al., *Journal of Personality and Social Psychology* 78:3 (2000): 524–536.
51. J. M. Bailey and R. C. Pillard, *Archives of General Psychiatry* 48 (1991): 1089–1096; also R. C. Pillard and J. D. Weinrich, *Archives of General Psychiatry* 43:8 (1986): 808–812.
52. G. Rice et al., *Science* 284:5414 (April 23, 1999): 665–667.

53. S. Hu et al., *Nature Genetics* 11:3 (November 1995): 248–256; also D. H. Hamer et al., *Science* 261: 5119 (July 16, 1993): 321–327.

54. S. Hu et al., *Nature Genetics* cited above.

55. J. D. Haynes, *Journal of Homosexuality* 28:1–2 (1995): 91–113; also T. R. McGuire, *Journal of Homosexuality* 28:1–2 (1995): 115–45.

56. J. C. Hall, *Science* 264 (1994): 1702–1714; also L. C. Ryner et al., *Cell* 87 (December 13, 1996): 1079–1089.

57. F. Berta et al., *Nature* 348 (1990): 448–450.

58. C. D. Toran-Allerand, "On the Genesis of Sexual Differentiation of the Central Nervous System: Morpho-Genetic Consequences of Steroidal Exposure and Possible Role of Alpha-Fetoprotein," in G. J. DeVries et al. (eds.), *Sex Differences in the Brain: Special Issue of Progress in Brain Research* 61 (1984): 63–98.

59. J. Imperato-McGinley et al., *New England Journal of Medicine* 300 (1979): 1233–1237.

60. I. L. Ward, *Psychoneuroendocrinology* 9 (1984): 3–11.

61. J. Panksepp, *Affective Neuroscience: The Foundations of Human and Animal Emotions* (New York: Oxford University Press, 1998), p. 237.

62. A. A. Ehrhardt et al., *Archives of Sexual Behavior* 14:1 (1985): 57– 77.

63. Ibid.; also H. F. Meyer-Bahlburg et al., *Psychosomatic Medicine* 47:6 (November–December 1985): 497–511.

64. T. J. Williams et al., *Nature* 404 (March 30, 2000): 455–456.

65. W. L. Jaffee et al., *Psychoneuroendocrinology* 5:1 (1980): 33–38; also J. Downey et al., *Hormones and Behavior* 21:3 (September 1987): 347–357.

66. R. C. Friedman and J. Downey, *Journal of Neuropsychiatry* 5:2 (spring 1993): 131–153.

67. M. Diamond and H. K. Sigmundson, *Archives of Pediatric and Adolescent Medicine* 151 (March 1997): 298–304.

68. D. Hamer and P. Copeland, *Living with Our Genes: Why They Matter More Than You Think* (New York: Doubleday, 1999): 167–169.

69. M. Duberman, *Cures: A Gay Man's Odyssey* (New York: Plume, 1991).

70. Plato, "Symposium," in J. D. Kaplan (ed.), *Dialogues of Plato: The Jowet Translations* (pp. 161–234). (New York: Pocket Books, 1950).

71. A. C. Grayling, "Love's Story," *The Guardian (London)*, 12 February, 2000.

72. J. A. Lee, *Psychology Today* (October 1974): 44–51.

73. W. Shakespeare (1564–1616), "Romeo and Juliet," Act I, Scene 5, line 46 (1597).

74. V. B. Dröscher, *They Love and Kill: Sex, Sympathy and Aggression in Courtship and Mating* (New York: E. P. Dutton & Co., 1976).

75. A. Bartels and S. Zeki, *Neuroreport* 11:17 (November 27, 2000): 3829–3834.
76. M. R. Liebowitz, *The Chemistry of Love* (Boston: Little, Brown & Co., 1983).
77. F. Karoum et al., *Journal of Neurochemistry* 33 (1979): 201–212.
78. S. M. Siviy et al., "Opiates and Palatability," in B. G. Hoebel and D. Novin (eds.), *The Neural Basis of Feeding and Reward* (pp. 517–524). (Brunswick, Maine: Haer Institute, 1982).
79. I. B. Adams et al., *Life Sciences* 56 (1995): 2041–2048.
80. D. Benton and R. T. Donohoe, *Public Health Nutrition* 2:3a (1999): 403–409.
81. M. R. Liebowitz, *The Chemistry of Love* (Boston: Little, Brown & Co., 1983).
82. J. Panksepp et al., *Neuroscience and Biobehavior Reviews* 4 (1980): 473–487; also J. Panksepp, "Brain Opioids: A Neurochemical Substrate for Narcotic and Social Dependence," in S. Cooper (ed.), *Progress in Theory in Psychopharmacology* (pp. 149–175). (London: Academic Press, 1981).
83. H. E. Fisher, *Anatomy of Love: A Natural History of Mating, Marriage and Why We Stray* (New York: Fawcett Columbine, 1992).
84. M. R. Liebowitz, *The Chemistry of Love*, cited above, 99.
85. D. Tennov, *Love and Limerance: The Experience of Being in Love* (Chelsea, Mich: Scarborough House, 1979).
86. Griffin-Shelley E. (ed). *Sex and Love Addiction, Treatment, and Recovery,* Praeger, 1991.
87. P. J. Carnes, *Don't Call It Love: Recovery from Sexual Addiction* (New York: Bantam Books, 1991).
88. P. J. Carnes, *Contrary to Love: Helping the Sexual Addict* (Minneapolis, Minn.: Comp Care, 1989): 125.
89. C. G. Hindy et al., *If This Is Love Why Do I Feel So Insecure?* (New York: Atlantic Monthly Press, 1989).
90. H. E. Fisher, *Anatomy of Love*, cited above.
91. J. T. Winslow et al., *Nature* 365 (October 7, 1993): 545–548.
92. *Holy Bible*, King James Version, Ecclesiastes 4, Verses 9–10.
93. J. Panksepp, *Affective Neuroscience*, cited above, 259–260.
94. T. R. Insel, *American Journal of Psychiatry* 154:6 (1997): 726–735; also A. O. Adams, "Why Do Voles Fall in Love?" *Emory Magazine* (spring 1999): 10–13.
95. T. R. Insel et al., "Oxytocin, Vasopressin, and the Neuroendocrine Basis of Pair Bond Formation," in H. H. Zingg et al. (eds.), *Vasopressin and Oxytocin* (New York: Plenum Press, 1998).
96. Z. Wang et al., *Behavioral Neuroscience* 113:3 (June 1999): 602–611.

97. T. R. Insel, Lecture to the 6th Annual Wisconsin Symposium on Emotion, "The Neurobiology of Positive Emotion," *HealthEmotions*, Research Institute, University of Wisconsin, April 13, 2000.

98. J. M. Gottman and N. Silver, *The Seven Principles for Making Marriage Work.* (New York: Three Rivers Press, 1999).

99. G. Hendricks and K. Hendricks, *Centering and the Art of Intimacy* (New York: Prentice-Hall, 1985).

100. T. Lewis et al., *A General Theory of Love* (New York: Random House, 2000): 68–69.

101. H. Bakwin, *American Journal of Diseases of Children* 63 (1942): 30–40.

102. M. D. S. Ainsworth, "The Effects of Maternal Deprivation: A Review of Findings and Controversy in the Context of Research Strategy," in *Deprivation of Maternal Care: A Reassessment of Its Effects,* Public Health Papers #14 (Geneva, Switzerland: World Health Organization, 1962).

103. R. Spitz, "Grief: A Peril in Infancy," [film]. (University Park, Pennsylvania: Penn State Audio Visual Services, 1947).

104. J. Bowlby, "The Making and Breaking of Affectional Bonds," The 50th Maudsley Lecture, *British Journal of Psychiatry* 130 (1977): 421–431; also J. Bowlby, *Attachment and Loss* (New York: Basic Books 1969).

105. M. D. S. Ainsworth, "A Sketch of a Career," in A. N. O'Connell and N. F. Russo (eds.), *Models of Achievement: Reflections of Eminent Women in Psychology* (pp. 200–219). (New York: Columbia University Press, 1983).

106. M. Main, "Recent Studies in Attachment: Overview, with Selected Implications for Clinical Work," in S. Goldberg et al. (eds.), *Attachment Theory: Social, Developmental and Clinical Perspectives* (pp. 407–474). (Hillsdale, N.J.: The Analytic Press, 1995).

107. This and other facts relating to the development and behavior of these children are covered in the book chapter by Mary Main cited in note 106 above.

108. D. D. Francis and M. Meaney, *Current Opinion in Neurobiology* 9 (1999): 128–134.

109. H. F. Harlow and M. Harlow, *American Scientist* 54:3 (1966): 244–272.

110. H. F. Harlow, "The Nature of Love," Address of the President, 66th Annual Convention of the American Psychological Association, Washington, DC, August 31, 1958, *American Psychologist* 13 (1958): 673–685.

111. H. F. Harlow and S. J. Suomi, *American Psychologist* 25:2 (1970): 161–168.

112. H. F. Harlow and M. Harlow, *American Scientist* 54:3 (1966): 244–272.

113. H. F. Harlow, "Lust, Latency and Love: Simian Secrets to Successful Sex," *The Journal of Sex Research* 11:2 (May 1975): 79–90.

114. L. J. Martin et al., *The Journal of Neuroscience* 11:11 (1991): 3344–3358.

115. L. A. Rosenblum and M. W. Andrews, *Acta Paediatr Suppl* 397 (1994): 57–63.

116. T. Lewis, F. Amini, And R. Lannon, *A General Theory of Love* (New York: Random House, 2000).

117. M. A. Hofer, *Child Development* 58 (1987): 633–647.

118. C. Caldji et al., *Proceedings of the National Academy of Science. USA,* 95 (April 1998): 5335–5340.

119. L. G. Russek and G. E. Schwartz, *Psychosomatic Medicine* 59:2 (1997): 144–149.

120. C. B. Thomas and K. R. Duszinski, *Johns Hopkins Medical Journal* 134 (1974): 251.

121. D. Ornish, *Love and Survival: The Scientific Basis for the Healing Power of Intimacy* (New York: HarperCollins, 1998). Ornish cites personal communication with M. Horsten et al.; also K. Orth-Gomer et al., *European Heart Journal* 19:11 (1998): 1648–1656.

122. J. Rosenblatt, "Hormone-Behavior Relations in the Regulation of Parental Behavior," in J. B. Becker et al. (eds.), *Behavioral Endocrinology* (pp. 219–259). (Cambridge, Mass.: MIT Press, 1992).

123. J. Panksepp et al., *Acta Paediatrica* 397 (Suppl): (1994): 40–46.

124. T. R. Insel, *American Journal of Psychiatry* 154:6 (1997): 726–735.

125. H. Harlow, *The American Psychologist* 13 (1958): 673–685.

126. H. F. Harlow and M. K. Harlow, *Scientific American* 207:5 (1962): 136–146.

127. L. A. Rosenblum and H. F. Harlow, *Psychological Reports* 12 (1963): 83–85.

128. Ibid.

Chapter 11. Sadness and Depression

1. E. Hamilton (translator), Aeschylus, *Agamemnon*, line 177.

2. J. Bowlby, *Attachment and Loss* (New York: Basic Books, 1969).

3. J. Panksepp, *Affective Neuroscience: The Foundations of Human and Animal Emotions* (New York: Oxford University Press, 1998).

4. R. E. Thayer, *The Origin of Everyday Moods: Managing Energy, Tension, and Stress* (New York: Oxford University Press, 1996).

5. K. R. Fox, *Public Health Nutrition* 2:3a (1999): 411–418.

6. E. J. Doyne et al., *Journal of Consulting and Clinical Psychology* 55 (1987): 748–754.
7. T. M. DiLorenzo et al., *Preventive Medicine* 28 (1999): 75–85.
8. S. Freud, "Mourning and Melancholia," (1917) in P. Gay (ed.), *The Freud Reader* (pp. 584–589). (New York: W. W. Norton & Co., 1989).
9. W. Katon and H. Schulberg, *General Hospital Psychiatry* 14 (1992): 237–247; also US DHHS, *Mental Health: A Report of the Surgeon General* (Rockville, Md.: US DHHS, Substance Abuse and Mental Health Services Administration, Center for Mental Health Services, NIH, NIMH, 1999).
10. National Mental Health Association, "Depression: What You Need to Know," 2000.
11. R. M. Nesse, *Archives of General Psychiatry* 57:1 (2000): 14–20.
12. C. J. Murray and A. D. Lopez, *The Lancet* 349:9063 (1997): 1436–1442.
13. C. J. Murray and A. D. Lopez, *Global Burden of Disease* (Boston: Harvard University Press, 1996).
14. M. M. Weissman and G. L. Klerman, *Annual Review of Public Health* 13 (1992): 319–339.
15. E. Lasley (ed.), "Depression and Other Mental Disorders," *The DANA Alliance for Brain Initiatives, Update 1998: Reshaping Expectations.* (Washington, DC: The DANA Press, 1998).
16. G. K. Brown et al., *Journal of Consulting Clinical Psychology* 68:3 (June 2000): 371–377.
17. World Health Organization, *Prevention of Suicide: Guidelines for the Formulation and Implementation of National Strategies* (Geneva, Switzerland: World Health Organization, 1996).
18. W. Styron, *Darkness Visible: A Memoir of Madness* (New York: Random House, 1990).
19. R. M. Nesse, *Archives of General Psychiatry* 2000, cited above.
20. R. M. Nesse and G. C. Williams, *Why We Get Sick: The New Science of Darwinian Medicine* (New York: Times Books, 1995).
21. A. S. Blix, "Arctic Resignation: Winter Dormancy Without Hypothermia," in A. Malan and B. Canguilhem, (eds.) *Living in the Cold* (vol. II, pp. 117–119). (Tromso, Norway: Colloque INSERM/ John Libbey Eurotext Ltd., 1989).
22. J. S. Price, *The Lancet* 2 (1967): 243–246; also F. B. deWaal, *Peacemaking Among Primates* (Cambridge, Mass.: Harvard University Press, 1989).
23. M. Seligman, *Helplessness: On Depression, Development and Death.* (San Francisco: W. H. Freeman, 1975).

24. G. W. Brown and T. Harris, *Social Origins of Depression* (New York: The Free Press, 1978); also G. W. Brown et al., *Psychological Medicine* 25 (1995): 7–21.

25. E. Frank et al., *Archives of General Psychiatry* 51 (1992): 519–524.

26. G. C. Mireault and L. A. Bond, *American Journal of Orthopsychiatry* 62 (1992): 517–524.

27. M. M. Weissman et al., "Affective Disorders," in L. N. Robins and D. A. Regier (eds.), *The Epidemiological Catchment Area Study* (pp. 53–80). (New York: Free Press, 1991).

28. R. M. Hirschfeld, *Journal of Clinical Psychiatry* 61 (Suppl. 6): (2000): 4–6.

29. R. M. Post et al., *Neuropsychobiology* 38:3 (October 1998): 152–166.

30. D. A. Collier et al., *Molecular Psychiatry* 1:6 (December 1996): 453–460; also A. Frisch et al., *Molecular Psychiatry* 4:4 (July 1999): 389–392.

31. C. B. Nemeroff et al., *Science* 226 (1984): 1342–1344.

32. D. L. Musselman et al., *Archives of General Psychiatry* 55 (July 1998): 580–592.

33. W. C. Drevets, *Biological Psychiatry* 48:8 (October 15, 2000): 813–829.

34. R. M. Carney et al., *Annals of Behavioral Medicine* 17 (1995): 142–149.

35. R. Anda et al., *Epidemiology* 4 (1993): 285–294.

36. J. C. Barefoot et al., *American Journal of Cardiology* 78 (1996): 613–617.

37. K. H. Ladwig et al., *The Lancet* 343:8888 (January 1, 1994): 20–23.

38. K. Y. Forrest et al., *Atherosclerosis* 148:11 (January 2000): 159–169.

39. D. Michelson and P. W. Gold, *Annals of the New York Academy of Science* 840 (May 1998): 717–722; also D. Michelson et al., *New England Journal of Medicine* 335:16 (October 17, 1996): 1176–1181.

40. Y. I. Sheline et al., *Journal of Neuroscience* 19:12 (June 15, 1999): 5034–5043.

Chapter 12. Healing Depression

1. P. D. Kramer, *Listening to Prozac* (New York: Viking, 1993); also P. R. Breggin and G. R. Breggin, *Talking Back to Prozac: What Doctors Won't Tell You About Today's Most Controversial Drug* (New York: St. Martin's Press, 1994); also J. Glenmullen, *Prozac Backlash: Overcoming the Dangers of Prozac, Zoloft, Paxil, and Other Anti-Depressants with Safe, Effective Alternatives* (New York: Simon & Schuster, 2000).

2. F. M. Quitkin, *American Journal of Psychiatry* 156:6 (1999): 829–836.

3. R. Joffee et al., *Canadian Journal of Psychiatry* 41 (1996): 613–616.
4. Table compiled from multiple sources.
5. R. Guscott and P. Grof, *American Journal of Psychiatry* 148 (1991): 695–704.
6. E. Goode, "Scientist at Work: Aaron T. Beck: Pragmatist Embodies His No-Nonsense Therapy," *New York Times*, 11 January 2000, p. 1-F, col. 1 (Science Times); also A. T. Beck et al, *Cognitive Therapy for Depression* (New York: Guilford Press, 1979).
7. D. D. Burns, *Feeling Good: The New Mood Therapy* (New York: Morrow, 1980).
8. R. J. DeRubeis et al., *American Journal of Psychiatry* 156:7 (1999): 1007–1013.
9. J. Scott, *New England Journal of Medicine*, 342:20 (May 18, 2000): 1518–1520.
10. M. B. Keller et al., *The New England Journal of Medicine* 342:20 (May 18, 2000): 1462–1470.
11. E. S. Paykel et al., *Archives of General Psychiatry* 56 (1999): 829–835.
12. K. R. Fox, *Public Health Nutrition* 2:3a (1999): 411–418, citing P. Van de Vliet et al., "Psychomotor Therapy for Depressive Psychiatric Patients: Effects on the Mood and Self," *Proceedings of the European Congress on Sport Psychology*, Part 2, 271–273, Prague, July 1999.
13. K. R. Fox, *Public Health Nutrition* 2:3a (1999): 411–418.
14. A. Byrne and D. G. Byrne, *Journal of Psychosomatic Research* 37:6 (1993): 565–574.
15. E. J. Doyne, et al., *Journal of Consulting and Clinical Psychology* 55 (1987): 748–754.
16. J. H. Griest, M. H. Klein, R. R. Eischens et al., *Comparative Psychology* 20:1 (1979): 41–54.
17. E. J. Doyne et al., *Behavioral Therapy* 14 (1983): 434–440.
18. J. A. Blumenthal et al., *Archives of Internal Medicine* 159:19 (October 25, 1999): 2349–2356.
19. M. A. W. Ruis et al., *Psychoneuroendocrinology* 24 (1999): 285–300.
20. *Holy Bible*, King James Version, Song of Solomon 2:5.
21. K. Linde et al., *British Medical Journal* 313:7052 (August 3, 1996): 253–258.
22. B. Gaster and J. Holroyd, *Archives of Internal Medicine* 160:2 (January 24, 2000): 152–156.
23. E. U. Vorbach et al., *Pharmacopsychiatry* 30 (Suppl. 2): (September 1997): 81–85.
24. E. Schrader, *International Clinical Psychopharmacology* 15:2 (March 2000): 61–68; also G. Harrer et al., *Arzneim-Forsch/Drug Res.* 49:1 (November 4, 1999): 289–296.

25. FDA, *Journal of the American Medical Association* 283:13 (April 5, 2000): 1679.
26. A. Singer et al., *The Journal of Pharmacology and Experimental Therapeutics* 290:3 (1999): 1363–1368.
27. T. Monmaney, "Remedy's U.S. Sales Zoom, but Quality Control Lags; St. John's Wort: Regulatory Vacuum Leaves Doubt About Potency, Effects of Herb Used for Depression," *Los Angeles Times*, 31 August 1998, Part A, page 1, Metro Desk.
28. J. R. Hibbeln, *The Lancet* 351 (April 18, 1998): 1213.
29. J. R. Hibbeln, "Seafood Consumption and the DHA Content of Mothers' Milk Predict Lower Prevalence Rates of Postpartum Depression: A Cross-National Ecological Analysis," Unpublished manuscript for submission to *Journal of the American Medical Association*, April 17, 2000.
30. A. L. Stoll et al., *Archives of General Psychiatry* 56:5 (1999): 407–412; also L. Marangell, www.mdoc.org/staff/marangell.html
31. "Dietary Supplementation with n-3 Polyunsaturated Fatty Acids and Vitamin E after Myocardial Infarction: Results of the GISSI-Prevenzione Trial." *The Lancet*, 354 (August 7, 1999): 447–455; also, M. Brown, "Do Vitamin E and Fish Oil Protect Against Ischaemic Heart Disease?" *The Lancet*, 354 (August 7, 1999): 441–442. (Commentary).
32. K. K. Makino et al., "Pathophysiological Mechanisms Linking Cardiovascular Morbidity and Major Depression: Aggravation by an Insufficiency of Omega-3 Fatty Acids," Unpublished manuscript for submission to *Biological Psychiatry*, April 25, 2000.
33. R. Brown et al., *Stop Depression Now—SAM-e* (New York: Putnam's, 1999).
34. B. J. Spring et al., *Nutrition Review* (Suppl.): (May 1986): 51–60.
35. N. E. Rosenthal et al., *Biological Psychiatry* 25:8 (April 15, 1989): 1029–1040.
36. J. Carper, *Your Miracle Brain* (New York: HarperCollins Publishers, 2000).
37. J. E. Alpert and M. Fava, *Nutrition Review* 55 (May 1997): 145–149.
38. A. J. Levitt and R. T. Joffe, *Biological Psychiatry* 25 (1989): 867–872.
39. M. Fava et al., *American Journal of Psychiatry* 154:3 (1997): 426–428.
40. P. S. A. Godfrey et al., *The Lancet* 336 (1990): 392–395.
41. S. N. Young and A. M. Ghadrian, *Progress in Neuropsychopharmacology and Biological Psychiatry* 13:6 (1989): 841–863.
42. D. Benton and R. T. Donahoe, *Public Health and Nutrition* 2:3a (September 1999): 403–409.

43. H. Heseker et al., "Psychiche Veranderungen als Fruhzeichen einer Suboptimalen Vitaminversorgung," *Emahrgrunge-Umschau* 37 (1990): 87–94.
44. J. Carper, *Your Miracle Brain* (New York: HarperCollins Publishers, 2000).
45. H. Doll et al., *J R Coll Gen Pract* 39: 326 (September 1989): 364–368; also K. M. Wyatt et al., *British Medical Journal* 318:7195 (May 22, 1999): 1375–1381.
46. O. M. Wolkowitz et al., *Psychiatric Annals* 30:2 (2000): 123–128.
47. O. M. Wolkowitz et al., *Annals of the New York Academy of Science* 774 (December 29, 1995): 337–339.
48. M. Bloch et al., *Biological Psychiatry* 45:12 (June 15, 1999): 1533–1541.
49. O. M. Wolkowitz et al., *American Journal of Psychiatry* 156:4 (1999): 646–649.
50. M. N. McLeod et al., *Journal of Clinical Psychiatry* 60:4 (1999): 237–240.
51. J. W. Finley and J. G. Penland, *Journal of Trace Elements in Experimental Medicine* 11 (1998): 11–27.
52. M. Maes et al., *Biological Psychiatry* 42 (1997): 349–358.
53. Table compiled from multiple sources.
54. T. Wehr et al., *Science* 206:4419 (November 9, 1979): 710–713.
55. D. Riemann et al., *European Archives of Psychiatry and Clinical Neuroscience* 249:5 (1999): 231–237.
56. For guidance in obtaining and using such devices, see N. E. Rosenthal, *Winter Blues: Seasonal Affective Disorder: What It Is and How to Overcome It* (New York: Guilford Publications, 1998); or Dr. Norman Rosenthal's website www.normanrosenthal.com
57. T. T. Postolache et al., *Journal of Affective Disorders* 56:1 (November 1999): 27–35.
58. T. Komori et al., *European Neuropsychopharmacology* 5:4 (December 1995): 477–480.
59. G. A. Ulett et al., *Biological Psychiatry* 44 (1998): 129–138.
60. H. Eich et al., "Akupunktur bei leichten bis mittelschweren depressiven Episoden und Angststoerungen," *Fortschr Neurol Psychiat* 68 (2000): 137–144.
61. J. Roeschke et al., *Journal of Affective Disorders* 57 (2000): 73–81.
62. H. Luo et al., *Psychiatry and Clinical Neurosciences* 52 (Suppl.) (1998): S338–S340.
63. P. J. Schmidt et al., *American Journal of Obstetrics and Gynecology* 183:2 (August 2000): 414–420.
64. S. M. Paul et al., *American Journal of Psychiatry* 138:4 (1981): 486–489.

65. M. S. George et al., *Archives of General Psychiatry* 56 (April 1999): 300–311.
66. A. J. Rush et al., *Biological Psychiatry* 47:4 (February 15, 2000): 276–286.

Chapter 13. Happiness and Euphoria

1. His holiness the Dalai Lama and H. C. Cutler, *The Art of Happiness: A Handbook for Living* (New York: Riverhead Books 1998).
2. The 71st Annual Academy Awards, Sunday, March 21, 2000.
3. B. L. Fredrickson, "Cultivating Positive Emotions to Optimize Health and Well-Being," *Prevention and Treatment* 3 (March 7, 2000): 1–28, Article 0001a; also http://journals.apa.org/prevention/volume3/ pre0030001a.html
4. D. G. Myers, *American Psychologist* 55:1 (2000): 56–67.
5. D. G. Myers and E. Diener, *Psychological Science* 6:1 (1995): 10–19.
6. *American Psychologist*, vol. 55, no. 1, January 2000.
7. The 6th Annual Wisconsin Symposium on Emotion, "The Neurobiology of Positive Emotion," Health/Emotions Research Institute, University of Wisconsin, April 13–14, 2000.
8. D. Kahneman et al., (eds.), *Well-Being: The Foundations of Hedonic Psychology* (New York: Russell Sage Foundation, 1999).
9. D. G. Myers and E. Diener, *American Psychologist* 6:1 (1995): 10–19.
10. E. Diener et al., *Psychological Bulletin* 125:2 (1999): 276–302.
11. E. Diener, *Social Indicators Research* 31 (1994): 103–157; also K. Magnus and E. Diener, "A Longitudinal Analysis of Personality, Life Events, and Subjective Well-Being," Paper presented at the 63rd Annual Meeting of the Midwestern Psychological Association, Chicago, May 1991.
12. W. Pavot and E. Diener, "Review of the Satisfaction with Life Scale," *Psychological Assessment* 5 (1993): 164–172.
13. D. Lykken, *Happiness* (New York: Golden Books, 1999).
14. D. G. Myers and E. Diener, *Scientific American* 274:5 (1996): 54–56.
15. A. L. Black and McCafferty, "The Age of Contentment," *USA Weekend*, July 3–5, 1998, pp. 4–6.
16. D. G. Myers and E. Diener, *Psychological Science*, 6:1 (1995): 10–19.
17. W. Wood et al., *Psychological Bulletin* 106 (1989): 249–264.
18. R. Inglehart, *Culture Shift in Advanced Industrial Society* (Princeton, N.J.: Princeton University Press, 1990).
19. E. Diener et al., *Social Indicators Research* 28 (1993): 195–223.
20. J. Crocker and B. Major, *Psychological Review* 96 (1989): 608–630.

21. M. Argyle, "Causes and Correlates of Happiness," in D. Kahneman et al. (eds.), *Well-Being: The Foundations of Hedonic Psychology* (pp. 353–373). (New York: Russell Sage Foundation 1999).
22. H. Cantril, *The Pattern of Human Concerns* (New Brunswick, N.J.: Rutgers University Press, 1965).
23. A. Campbell et al., *The Quality of American life* (New York: Russell Sage Foundation, 1976).
24. E. Diener et al., *Psychological Bulletin* 125:2 (1999): 276–302.
25. P. Brickman et al., *Journal of Personality and Social Psychology*, 36:8 (1978): 917–927.
26. R. L. Silver, "Coping With an Undesirable Life Event: A Study of Early Reactions to Physical Disability," Doctoral dissertation, Northwestern University, Evanston, Illinois, 1982.
27. Roper Organization, untitled survey, August/September 1984, *Public Opinion*, p. 25.
28. D. G. Myers, *American Psychologist* 55:1 (2000): 56–67.
29. G. G. Gallup, Jr. and R. Newport, "Americans Widely Disagree on What Constitutes Rich," *Gallup Poll Monthly*, July 1990, pp. 28–36.
30. D. G. Myers and E. Diener, *Psychological Science*, 6:1 (1995): 10–19.
31. P. Brickman et al., *Journal of Personality and Social Psychology* 36 (1976): 917–927.
32. S. Smith and P. Razzell, *The Pools Winners* (London: Caliban Books, 1975).
33. M. E. P. Seligman, "Explanatory Style: Predicting Depression, Achievement and Health," in M. D. Yapko (ed.), *Brief Therapy Approaches to Treating Anxiety and Depression* (New York: Brunner/ Mazel, 1989).
34. E. Diener et al., *Social Indicators* 16 (1985): 263–274.
35. P. Brickman and D. T. Campbell, "Hedonic Relativism and Planning the Good Society," in M. H. Appley (ed.), *Adaptation-Level Theory: A Symposium* (pp. 287–304) (New York: Academic Press, 1971).
36. D. G. Myers, *American Psychologist* 55:1 (2000): 56–67.
37. E. Diener and R. Biswas-Diener, Unpublished manuscript, "Will Money Increase Subjective Well-Being? A Literature Review and Guide to Needed Research," September 2, 2000.
38. W. Cowper, *Table Talk* (1782), line 246.
39. R. J. Larsen, *Journal of Personality and Social Psychology* 52 (1987): 1195–1204.
40. E. Suh et al., *Journal of Personality and Social Psychology* 70 (1996): 1091–1102.
41. M. Argyle, "Causes and Correlates of Happiness," 1999, cited above.

42. W. Stroebe and M. S. Stroebe, *Bereavement and Health* (Cambridge, UK: Cambridge University Press, 1987).
43. D. Lykken and A. Tellegen, *Psychological Science* 7:3 (May 1996): 186–189.
44. M. McGue and K. Christensen, *Journal of Abnormal Psychology* 106 (1997): 439–448; also M. Gatz et al., *Journal of Abnormal Psychology* 101 (1992): 701–708.
45. S. Grant et al., *Proceedings of the National Academy of Science* 93 (1996): 12,040–12,045.
46. B. G. Hoebel et al., "Neural Systems for Reinforcement and Inhibition of Behavior: Relevance to Eating, Addiction and Depression," in D. Kahneman et al. (eds.), *Well-Being: The Foundations of Hedonic Psychology* (pp. 558–572). (New York: Russell Sage Foundation, 1999).
47. J. M. Liebman and S. J. Cooper (eds.), *The Neuropsychopharmacological Basis of Reward* (Oxford, UK: Clarendon Press, 1989); also J. R. Stellar, *The Neurobiology of Motivation and Reward* (New York: Springer-Verlag, 1985).
48. B. G. Hoebel et al., 1999, cited above.
49. Ibid.
50. J. Panksepp, *Affective Neuroscience: The Foundations of Human and Animal Emotions* (New York: Oxford University Press, 1998), p. 151.
51. Wisconsin Symposium on Emotion, "The Neurobiology of Positive Emotion," *Health Emotions*, Research Institute, University of Wisconsin, April 13, 2000.
52. E. T. Rolls, *The Brain and Emotion* (Oxford, UK: Oxford University Press, 1999).
53. J. Panksepp, *Affective Neuroscience*, cited above, p. 147.
54. E. T. Rolls, "Central Taste Anatomy and Neurophysiology," in R. L. Doty (ed.), *Handbook of Olfaction and Gustation* (pp. 549–573), (New York: Marcel Dekker, 1995).
55. K. C. Berridge, *Neuroscience and Biobehavioral Reviews* 20:1 (1996): 1–25.
56. K. C. Berridge, "Pleasure, Pain, Desire, and Dread: Hidden Core Processes of Emotion," in D. Kahneman et al. (eds.), *Well-Being*, (pp. 525–557). (New York: Russell Sage Foundation, 1999).
57. D. Kahneman and J. Snell, *Journal of Behavioral Decision Making* 5 (1992): 187–200.
58. Ibid.
59. W. Schultz, "Reward Processing in Primate Basal Ganglia and Frontal Cortex," Lecture at the 6th Annual Wisconsin Symposium on Emotion at the HealthEmotions Research Institute, University of Wisconsin April 13, 2000.

60. G. Damsma et al., *Behavioral Neuroscience* 106:1 (1992): 181–191.
61. E. D. London et al., *Critical Review of Neurobiology* 13:3 (1999): 227–242.
62. G. D. Ellison and M. S. Eison, *Psychological Medicine* 13 (1983): 751–761.
63. G. A. Carlson and F. K. Goodwin, *Archives of General Psychiatry* 28:2 (1973): 221–228.
64. B. G. Hoebel, "Neural Systems for Reinforcement and Inhibition of Behavior: Relevance to Eating, Addiction, and Depression," in D. Kahneman et al. (eds.), *Well-Being*, cited above, p. 562.
65. J. Panksepp, *Affective Neuroscience*, cited above, p. 184.
66. J. Dum et al., *Pharmacology Biochemistry and Behavior* 18:3 (1983): 443–447.
67. J. Panksepp, *Affective Neuroscience*, cited above, p. 184.
68. A. M. Hughes et al., *Psychopharmacology* (Berlin) 102:2 (1990): 243–256.
69. R. Jevning et al., *Psychosomatic Medicine* 40 (1978): 329–333.
70. T. A. Wehr et al., *American Journal of Physiology* 265:4 Pt 2 (October 1993): R846–R847.
71. J. D. Laird, *Journal of Personality and Social Psychology* 29:4 (1974): 475–486.
72. J. D. Laird, *Journal of Personality and Social Psychology* 47 (1984): 909–917.
73. S. E. Snodgrass et al., "The Effects of Walking Behavior on Mood," Paper presented at the American Psychological Association Convention, Washington, DC, August 1986; also see D. G. Myers, *The Pursuit of Happiness: Discovering the Pathway to Fulfillment, Well-Being, and Enduring Personal Joy* (New York: Avon Books, 1992), 125.
74. D. G. Myers and E. Diener, *Psychological Science* 6:1 (1995): 10–19.
75. M. Seligman, *Learned Optimism* (New York: Knopf, 1991).
76. D. G. Myers, *American Psychologist*, 55:1 (2000): 56–67.
77. S. L. Knock, *Journal of Family Issues* 16 (1995): 53–76.
78. A. M. Greely, *Faithful Attraction* (New York: Tor Books, 1991).
79. M. Argyle, "Causes and Correlates of Happiness, " in D. Kahneman et al. (eds.), *Well-Being*, (pp. 353–373). (New York: Russell Sage Foundation, 1999).
80. C. D. Harvey et al., *Social Psychiatry* 22 (1987): 65–72.
81. W. N. Friedrich et al., *Health Care* 17 (1988): 40–44.
82. C. G. Ellison, *Journal of Health and Social Behavior* 32 (1991): 80–99; also D. N. McIntosh et al., *Journal of Personality and Social Psychology* 65 (1993): 812–821.
83. D. G. Myers, *American Psychologist* 55:1 (2000): 56–67.

84. M. Csikszentmihalyi, *Flow: The Psychology of Optimal Experience* (New York: HarperCollins, 1990).
85. M. Csikszentmihalyi, *American Psychologist* 54 (1999): 821–827.
86. R. Veenhoven and coworkers, *World Database of Happiness: Correlates of Happiness* (Rotterdam, The Netherlands: Erasmus University, 1994).
87. B. W. Headey et al., *Social Indicators Research* 17 (1985): 211–234.
88. M. Argyle, "Causes and Correlates of Happiness," in D. Kahneman et al. (eds.), *Well-Being* (pp. 353–373). (New York: Russell Sage Foundation, 1999).
89. M. Argyle, *The Social Psychology of Leisure* (London: Penguin, 1996).
90. P. Lynn and J. D. Smith, *Voluntary Action Research* (London: Volunteer Centre, 1991).
91. T. Kasser and R. M. Ryan, *Journal of Personality and Social Psychology* 65 (1993): 410–422.
92. N. Cantor and C. A. Sanderson, "Life Task Participation and Well-Being: The Importance of Taking Part in Daily Life," in D. Kahneman et al. (eds.), *Well-Being* (pp. 230–243). (New York: Russell Sage Foundation, 1999).

Chapter 14. Pathways to Change

1. J. Bentham, *Principles of Morals and Legislation* (New York: Hafner, 1948, originally published in 1789).
2. *Consumer Reports*, November 1995.
3. M. E. P. Seligman, "The Effectiveness of Psychotherapy: The Consumer Reports Study," *American Psychologist* 50:12 (1995): 965–974.
4. *The Serenity Prayer*, Reinhold Niebuhr, 1926.
5. V. Frankl, *Man's Search for Meaning* (New York: Washington Square Press, 1998).
6. S. J. Suomi, "Attachment in Rhesus Monkeys," in J. Cassidy and P. R. Shaver (eds.), *Handbook of Attachment: Theory, Research, and Clinical Applications* (pp. 181–197) (New York: Guilford Press, 1999).
7. E. Goode, "Pragmatist Embodies His No-Nonsense Therapy," *New York Times*, Tuesday, 11 January, 2000, D-1 ("Science Times").
8. A. C. Butler and J. S. Beck, *Journal of Norwegian Psychological Association* (in press), June 10, 2000.
9. F. Hartigan, *Bill W; A Biography of Alcoholics Anonymous Co-Founder Bill Wilson* (New York: St. Martin's Press, 2000); also The Big Book website: www.recovery.org/aa/bigbook/ww/index.html
10. F. Shapiro, *Eye Movement Desensitization and Reprocessing: Basic Principles, Protocols and Procedures* (New York: Guilford Press, 1995).

11. E. Foa, "Cognitive Behavioral Treatment of PTSD," course presentation, Boston University School of Medicine Conference on "Psychological Trauma: Maturational Processes and Therapeutic Interventions," March 10–11, 2000.

12. F. B. de Waal, *Science* 289:5479 (July 28, 2000): 586–590.

13. L. R. Squire (ed.), *Encyclopedia of Learning and Memory* (New York: Macmillan, 1992).

14. D. O. Hebb, *The Organization of Behavior* (New York: Wiley, 1949).

15. S. Blakeslee, "Study Offers Hope for Use of Limbs Disabled by Stroke," *New York Times*, 2 June 2000; also E. Taub, *Stroke* 31: 4 (2000): 986–989; also E. Taub et al., *Journal of Rehabilitation Research and Development* 36:3 (July 1999): 237–251.

16. Sussex Publishers, Inc., "Sayonara, Shyness; Therapy for Shyness in Japan," *Psychology Today* 25:3 (May 1992): 14.

17. P. Tallal et al., *Science* 271:5245 (January 1996): 81–84.

18. G. H Recanzone et al., *Journal of Neuroscience* 13:1 (1993): 87–103.

19. M. M. Merzenich et al., *Science* 271:5245 (January 1996): 77–81.

20. S. Blakeslee, "Old Brains Can Learn New Language Tricks," *New York Times on the Web*, National Science/Health, April 20, 1999.

21. D. Morris, *The Naked Ape: A Zoologist's Study of the Human Animal* (New York: McGraw-Hill, 1967).

22. J. Diamond, *The Third Chimpanzee: The Evolution and Future of the Human Animal* (New York: HarperCollins, 1992).

Index